THOMAS BECKET

'The Donatists glory in their persecution. But what could be more wretched and perverse than this open refusal to be confounded by the punishment for their wickedness – even more, their desire to be praised for it. For with extraordinary blindness they do not see, or with damnable audacity conceal their knowledge, that it is not the penalty which makes true martyrs, but the cause.'

ST AUGUSTINE,
Letter no. 89, Migne *PL*, xxxiii. 310

THOMAS BECKET

Frank Barlow

FELLOW OF THE BRITISH ACADEMY
EMERITUS PROFESSOR OF HISTORY IN THE
UNIVERSITY OF EXETER

University of California Press
BERKELEY AND LOS ANGELES

University of California Press
Berkeley and Los Angeles, California

First Paperback Printing 1990

Library of Congress Cataloging-in-Publication Data

Barlow, Frank.
    Thomas Becket.

    Bibliography: p.
    Includes index.
    1. Thomas, á Becket. Saint, 1118?–1170.
2. Statesmen—Great Britain—Biography.   3. Christian
saints—England—Biography.   4. Great Britain—History—
Henry II, 1154–1189.   I. Title
DA209.T4B27   1986   942.03′1′0924[B]   86-7072
ISBN 0-520-07175-1

Printed in the United States of America

3 4 5 6 7 8 9

The paper used in this publication meets the minimum
requirements of American National Standard for Information
Sciences—Permanence of Paper for Printed Library Materials,
ANSI Z39.48-1984. ∞

CONTENTS

ILLUSTRATIONS

Diagrams in the text

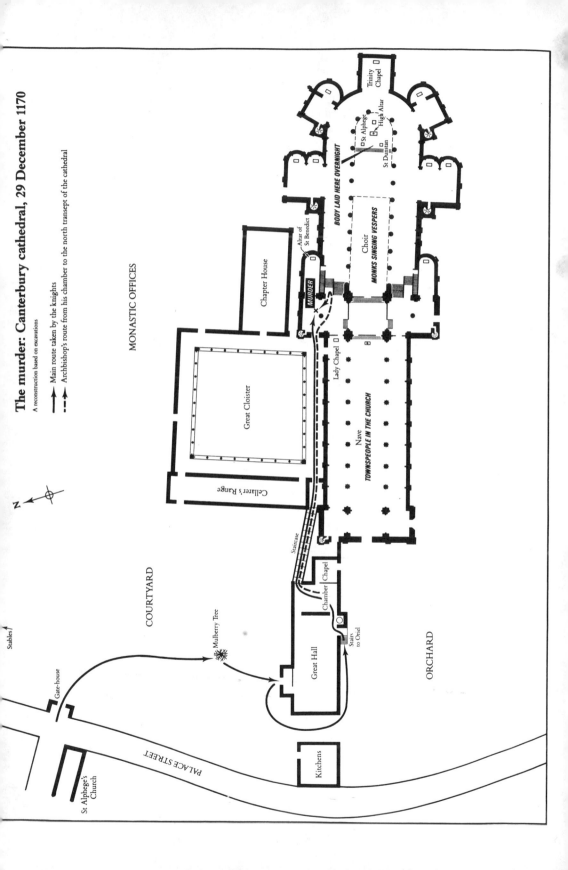

The murder: Canterbury cathedral, 29 December 1170

A reconstruction based on excavations

→ Main route taken by the knights
--→ Archbishop's route from his chamber to the north transept of the cathedral

N

MONASTIC OFFICES

Chapter House

Great Cloister

Cellarer's Range

Altar of St Benedict

MURDER

Choir
MONKS SINGING VESPERS

BODY LAID HERE OVERNIGHT

St Alphege
High Altar
St Dunstan

Trinity Chapel

Lady Chapel

Nave
TOWNSPEOPLE IN THE CHURCH

Staircase

Chamber | Chapel

Great Hall

Stairs to Oriel

Mulberry Tree

COURTYARD

Stables

Gate-house

St Alphege's Church

PALACE STREET

Kitchens

ORCHARD

PREFACE

In the early 1930s, in my postgraduate years at Oxford, I edited the letters of Arnulf, bishop of Lisieux, a colleague of Thomas Becket. Ever since, I have had the intention of returning to that scene. But only after fifty years of exploring other fields has it come to pass.

Although the second half of the twelfth century is comparatively well furnished with letter collections of a more intimate kind than before, historical accounts by a more worldly breed of chroniclers and saints lives that are relatively historical in tone, only some of the *dramatis personae* receive the kiss of life. On the whole it is the attendant figures, such as John of Salisbury and Herbert of Bosham, who come most alive. The principal actors, Thomas of Canterbury, King Henry II, Pope Alexander III, perhaps because they wear the uniform of their great offices, rebuff our vulgar curiosity. In this biography, therefore, I have concentrated upon the story. I have tried particularly to establish the facts and produce an account of Thomas's life as historically true as possible, that is to say, to present the events in their contemporary setting and trace an evolving story, avoiding hindsight to the best of my ability.

While the selection and presentation of facts must always depend to some extent on the views of the author, I consider that my own views in this case are fairly neutral. I am not a partisan of either royal or ecclesiastical power, of either Henry or Thomas. I admire both men. My main interest is in how and why everything happened, and therefore in the complexities of the story, the irregularities and nuances which have to be ignored in shorter studies. And if I have elucidated the story correctly, it is open to my readers, should they so wish, to reflect further or draw the moral. The passage from St Augustine printed at the beginning of this book, which furnished a text used by both royalists and supporters of the archbishop, is worth pondering.

It was, and remains, an extraordinary story. Here I will simply remark that in 1173, or thereabouts, two of Thomas's oldest friends and champions, John of Salisbury and Peter of Celle, were still regarding with amazement the unimaginable and inexplicable events in which they had played some part.

While writing this book I have received many kindnesses and services from friends, colleagues, librarians and archivists. I wish to thank especially David Bates, Christopher and Mary Cheney, Anne Duggan, Bob Higham, Christopher Holdsworth, Jim Holt, Derek Keene, Anne Oakley, Nicholas Orme, Timothy Reuter and Pamela Tudor-Craig. My thanks are also due to Juliet Gardiner, Linden Lawson and Simon Cobley of Weidenfeld and Nicolson. I trust that St Thomas too will not be ungrateful.

FRANK BARLOW
Kenton, Exeter
September 1985

Note to the paperback edition:
For this edition I have corrected those errors that have come to my notice. Christopher Brooke very kindly sent me a most useful detailed critique.

FRANK BARLOW
April 1987

INTRODUCTION

On the fifth day of Christmas 1170, the morrow of the festival of the Holy Innocents, that is to say, Tuesday, 29 December, Thomas, archbishop of Canterbury, primate of the whole of England and legate of the Holy See, was murdered in his cathedral church by four noble knights from the household of his lord and former patron and friend, King Henry II. He had just celebrated what was thought to be his fiftieth birthday. The horror which the killing inspired and the miraculous cures performed at his tomb transfigured the victim into one of the most popular saints in the late-medieval calendar and made Canterbury one of the greatest pilgrim shrines in the West. The modern Lourdes, although doubtless better organized, gives some idea of medieval Canterbury with its phials of water tinctured, if faintly, with the blood of the martyr, and its highly charged atmosphere, a combination of the pathetic hopes of the sick and the jollity of the holiday-makers.

Chaucer's *Canterbury Tales* kept the saint's memory green after the Reformation, and the drama has attracted distinguished modern playwrights. The saint's legend has, of course, changed with the times. Each age has reinterpreted the events in accordance with its own preoccupations. But one constant has been a conviction that not only were great principles involved but also great men; and no one has ever doubted the magnificent courage of the archbishop, even if it has also been occasionally the cause of some regret.

In the 1170s, however, popular enthusiasm for the new saint concealed a variety of views among those who had been more involved in the events. Some of his enemies thought that he had got what he deserved. Many sympathizers felt relief as well as sorrow when they heard the news. Thomas's had not been a model life; his notorious faults had given a handle to his enemies and been a trial to his friends; and the transformation of a supremely worldly man into a stiff-necked prelate, a trouble-maker, who in the end seemed almost to invite martyrdom, was for some hard to forgive, for many hard to understand. It was difficult to apportion responsibility

I

for the tragedy, since even the saint's greatest friends were not prepared, for a variety of reasons, to put the blame squarely and exclusively on the king. Herbert of Bosham, one of Thomas's most loyal and intemperate servants, in his *Liber Melorum* (Book of Melodies), which he appended to his history of the events, paid a great tribute to Henry, whose grandeur was spotted only by this unaccountable feud and disaster. Some observers doubted whether there was sufficient cause for martyrdom, many were aware that Thomas, even if he had not courted death, had done nothing to avoid it. Unlike John of Salisbury and William of Canterbury, he had not fled from persecution.[1]

But these hesitations were lost in a growing stream of popular enthusiasm for the martyr. The murder was so shocking and the case of such interest that at least ten men were inspired to write about it within a decade of the event, followed by two or three more, including Herbert of Bosham, in the 1180s. John of Salisbury described the martyrdom in a letter (*Ex insperato*) written immediately afterwards to a former colleague in Archbishop Theobald's court, John of Canterbury, then bishop of Poitiers and later archbishop of Lyons, a letter which became widely known and was familiar to most of the biographers. And he probably soon followed with a brief Life. Others who were in the cathedral on that calamitous day, such as Edward Grim, William of Canterbury, William fitzStephen and Benedict of Peterborough, were no doubt encouraged to write because of their participation. But it was, above all, their witness to the miracles, that erupted so dramatically, and the papal canonization of March 1173 which required them and others to compose Passions and Lives. This spate of almost instant hagiographical writing was unprecedented. And it was still running strongly at the Jubilee in 1220, when Archbishop Stephen Langton translated Thomas's relics into a new shrine and was presented with a copy of Roger of Crowland's version, completed in 1213, of Elias of Evesham's composite life of the saint, *Quadrilogus*, which he had fashioned in 1198–9. This literary corpus is also, in its use of documentary evidence and dominant historical tone, almost unique for the Middle Ages. But, because of the very nature of the genre, its coverage of Thomas's career is unbalanced.

Most of the biographers, men closely connected either with the convent of Christ Church or with Thomas as archbishop, who form what can be called the Canterbury group, not only concentrate upon the eight years after 1162, the term of his prelacy, but also pay particular attention to his quarrel with the king, culminating in the martyrdom. At the centre of popular interest was the *passio*. The posthumous miracles – unusually, there were no *ante-mortem* signs – were also of great interest to some of the memorialists. Thomas had passed from death unto life; and this heavenly life with Christ was more important than his previous existence in the vales of sorrow and misfortune. Only one writer, William fitzStephen, one of Thomas's clerks when royal chancellor who accompanied him to Canterbury, made a serious attempt to describe the first forty-two years of his subject's life. Moreover, none of the biographers paid much attention to Thomas as archdeacon of Canterbury, for everyone was familiar with the satirical question, 'Is it possible for an archdeacon to be saved?' The archbishop's exile is poorly treated. This insufficiency, however, is more than remedied by the large collections of correspondence, assembled as a complementary exercise, which, likewise ignoring the early years, are concerned almost exclusively with the exile and the quarrel in all its wordy ramifications.

Nevertheless, although the Canterbury group omitted most of the story which in their eyes did least credit to the saint, they were painfully aware of it and accepted that it was the inescapable background to what they wanted to dwell upon. Their story was meaningless without a knowledge of the other. It was Thomas's earlier career in the world which made his episcopacy particularly difficult, and it was only his change of character, his being 'born again', which turned him into a saint and martyr. The earliest biographers could assume that their readers would know the background well. They had no need to labour it.

The three writers who knew him best were his clerks, John of Salisbury, William fitzStephen and Herbert of Bosham. The first, possibly to spare himself pain, possibly because of embarrassment over his behaviour at the martyrdom, but possibly only because his *Vita* was merely an introduction to a projected collection of 'Becket correspondence', wrote a short, cool and careful account which from the start was considered inadequate. The second, a Londoner, although devoted to Thomas, sympathetic to his cause and staunch at the martyrdom, reverted to royal service, both in 1164 and 1171. An obvious outsider to the Canterbury set, he produced by far the best account of the externals of Thomas's career, straightforward, factual and anecdotally informative. It is significant that his work, indeed his very existence, is ignored by all writers from John of Salisbury to Herbert of Bosham, most of whom had known him well. The last, whose background was in some ways similar to fitzStephen's, was Thomas's inseparable companion, teacher and friend after 1162. The most intimate with the saint and the most involved in his aspirations, he wrote a Life which is complementary to fitzStephen's, garrulous, sometimes tedious, the searchings of a disappointed old man who found the recollection of these amazing events both puzzling and painful. By allowing his pen to record his wandering thoughts he was now and then uncomfortably indiscreet. Even his theological excursions can tail into a blundering revelation.

As the several biographers are frequently referred to in the following chapters, and their order of writing and inter-relationships are important for evaluating their evidence, their names and some of the most relevant information about them are listed here and illustrated opposite.

1. **John of Salisbury**, the famous scholar and author, a prolific letter writer, who served popes as well as Archbishops Theobald and Thomas as clerk. A candid friend of the last, in exile from 1164 to 1170 and, although not in the archbishop's company, much involved in his affairs, he rejoined him before the return to Canterbury in 1170, and took refuge behind the altars during the murder. He wrote his epistolary account of the death immediately after the event and his very brief Life probably shortly afterwards, although many historians have adhered to the inherently improbable theory that the latter was produced in 1173–6 and was almost entirely derivative. In 1176 he became bishop of Chartres and died in 1180. *BHL* 8178, 8180; *Mats.* ii. 301.

2. **Edward Grim**, a clerk and master, born at Cambridge, and probably the deprived rector of Saltwood, Kent,[3] who returned from Normandy in time to be present at the martyrdom, where he behaved heroically. He was dead by 1186. He wrote an ill-organized Life, based on personal knowledge and Canterbury information, but with often hazy detail, in 1171–2. It became one of the most influential. *BHL* 8182; *Mats.* ii. 353.

3. **Anonymous II**, sometimes known as 'of Lambeth' after the provenance of the only manuscript of the work, and clearly connected with the diocese of London.[4] An alleged but unlikely witness to the murder, who later became a monk at Christ Church, Canterbury, he wrote his Life in 1172–3. Traces of a prejudice against the archbishop, no doubt originating in London, appear in his work. *BHL* 8187–8; *Mats.* iv. 80.

4. **Benedict of Peterborough**, monk of Christ Church, prior in 1175 and abbot of Peterborough 1177–93; present in the church at the time of the martyrdom. The first custodian of the shrine, he made the most primitive, and eventually the most influential, collection of miracles. The Passion he wrote in 1173–4, to serve as an introduction to this, is known only from fragments embedded in *Quadrilogus*, a later compilation. *BHL* 8170–1; *Mats.* ii. 1.

5. **William of Canterbury**, monk of Christ Church and ordained deacon by Thomas in 1170; present at the martyrdom until blows were struck. In June 1172, as Benedict's colleague or successor at the shrine, he began to edit the existing records of miracles and add to them. His collection was presented by the convent to Henry II, at the king's request, probably

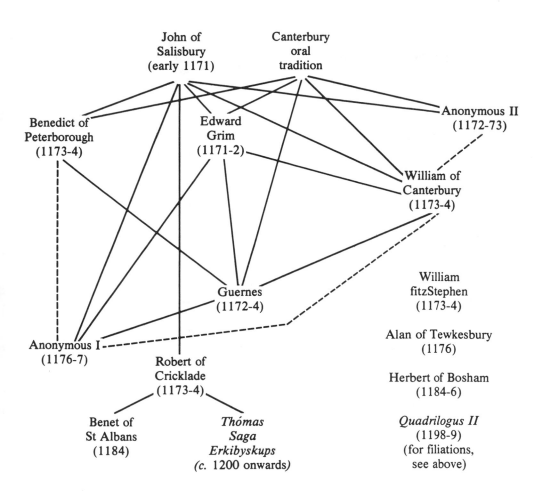

Key

—————— confirmed filiation

-------- suspected filiation

The main relationships between the early biographers

in the autumn of 1174 after the royal penance at the tomb. During the same period, most likely in 1173–4, William wrote a full-scale Life, which is particularly valuable for his account of the events of December 1170 in which he was closely involved. *BHL* 8184–5; *Mats.* i. 1.

These five writers, all, except the first two, Canterbury monks, were writing at roughly the same time and creating and transmitting the story which must have been told countless times to pilgrims at the shrine. It looks as though William of Canterbury, who may have read Anonymous II, reorganized and particularized Edward Grim's account; but all five works are both inter-related in some way and also in part independent contributions.

6. **William fitzStephen**, by his own account, Thomas's fellow citizen (of London), clerk and friend, drafter (*dictator*) in his chancery, his subdeacon when he celebrated in chapel and his reader of letters and documents when he sat on the bench, sometimes, when required, an advocate in his court.[5] As he tells us more than the others about Thomas as royal chancellor and made his peace with the king when his master went into exile, it is most likely that he had also been with Thomas in the royal chancery before 1162. He rejoined Thomas probably towards the end of 1170 and was one of the few actually at hand when the archbishop was killed. He may then have returned to the king, for a William fitzStephen was sheriff of Gloucester from 1171 to 1189 and an itinerant justice from 1175 to 1188, a second 'apostasy' which would help to explain the suppression of his name and role in Thomas's life by all the other early biographers. He wrote his *Vita* in 1173–4, independently of the others and with a quite different slant. For example, he drew on the Gilbert Foliot collection of letters instead of the Canterbury archives. *BHL* 8176–7; *Mats.* iii. 1.

7. **Guernes of Pont-Sainte-Maxence**, a vagrant clerk from that place in the Isle de France, on the River Oise, near Senlis, a *trouvère* who wrote two versions of the Life in French verse (*romans*). Only the second, finished by the end of 1174, after a stay at Canterbury and a visit to Thomas's sister Mary at Barking, is extant. Essentially a translation of Edward Grim, sometimes modified or amplified by reference to William of Canterbury and Benedict of Peterborough, and enriched by personal reflections and interesting detail, it is firmly in the Canterbury tradition. Ed. E. Walberg (Lund, 1922).

8. **Robert of Cricklade**, a master and canon of Cirencester, prior of St Frideswide, an Augustinian convent at Oxford, from 1141 to 1174, he wrote,

in 1173–4, probably because the saint cured his bad leg, a Life which has unfortunately disappeared, possibly because it was too favourable to the king. It was, however, one of the sources of Benet of St Albans and of the Icelandic Sagas, and its possible contents have been reconstructed by Margaret Orme, 'A reconstruction of Robert of Cricklade's Vita et Miracula S. Thomae Cantuariensis', *Analecta Bollandiana*, 84 (1966), 379–98. Among Robert's sources was John of Salisbury.[6]

9. **Anonymous I**, an unknown clerk who served Thomas in exile and was priested by him. He is sometimes identified as Roger, monk of Pontigny (and the editors of *Councils and Synods*, p. 843n., accept it as probable); but in his Life, composed in 1176–7, he wrote little of Thomas's stay there and drew on several of his Canterbury predecessors.[7] *BHL* 8183; *Mats.* iv. 1.

10. **Alan of Tewkesbury**, an English master who became a canon of Benevento before returning to Canterbury about 1174 and becoming prior in 1179. He was abbot of Tewkesbury from 1186 to 1202. His main work was his 'definitive edition' of the Becket correspondence (first edition, comprising 535 items, assembled in 1174–6), to which he prefaced John of Salisbury's *Vita*, supplemented by a contribution of his own (*Explanatio*), written in 1176.[8] He may have owed some information to Lombard of Piacenza, one of Thomas's *eruditi*, who became archbishop of Benevento in 1171. *BHL* 8179, 8181; *Mats.* ii. 299, 323.

11. **Lansdowne Anonymous (III)**, an anonymous writer, probably from the circle of Odo, prior of Canterbury, who gives an original account of some consequences of the murder up to October 1172, when the MS, B.L.Lansdowne 398, breaks off owing to damage. *BHL* 8201; *Mats.* iv. 158–85.

12. **Benet of St Albans**, monk of St Albans under Abbot Simon (1167–83), he wrote, about 1184, a Life in French verse based in part on Robert of Cricklade's lost work. Ed. F. Michel, *Chronique des ducs de Normandie* (Docs. inédits sur l'histoire de France, Paris, 1844), iii. 461–509, 619–25.

13. **Herbert of Bosham**, a pupil of Peter Lombard at Paris, a Hebraist, theologian and notable scholar; one of Thomas's clerks as chancellor (before 1157) and his confidential agent, teacher, counsellor and friend throughout his archiepiscopacy. His constant companion and the only biographer to give a firsthand account of the exile, to his undying regret he missed the martyrdom because Thomas had sent him on a mission to France. He wrote

his History well after most of the others in 1184–6 and sometimes echoes or indirectly answers them. Often he runs parallel to William fitzStephen. *BHL* 8190–1; *Mats.* iii. 155.

14. ***Quadrilogus II***, a conflation of the Lives by John of Salisbury, Benedict of Peterborough, William of Canterbury, Alan of Tewkesbury and Herbert of Bosham made in 1198–9 by Elias of Evesham at Crowland Abbey. The thirteenth-century expansion, *Quadrilogus I* (*BHL* 8200), contains also extracts from an interpolated version of Edward Grim, including the story of Thomas's Syrian mother, and from the Life by William fitzStephen. *Quadrilogus II* was one of the components of Roger of Crowland's Life and Letters of Thomas completed in 1213. *BHL* 8195; *Mats.* iv. 266.

15. ***Thómas Saga Erkibyskups***. Robert of Cricklade's *Vita* was translated into Icelandic *c.*1200, probably by the priest Berg Gunnsteinsson, and later Icelandic versions were expanded from other English Latin sources, including John of Salisbury's *Vita* and Benedict of Peterborough's *Miracula*, and the Norwegian translation of *Quadrilogus II*. The only extant complete version was made *c.*1320–50.[9] Ed. E. Magnússon (Rolls ser., 1875–83).

Some of the events of Thomas's life are also featured by the chroniclers of the period. The first half of Henry II's reign is surprisingly obscure. The only current recorder of the events is the annalist Robert of Torigni (de Monte), monk of Bec from 1128 to 1154 and then abbot of Mont St Michel until his death in 1186, who continued the *Gesta Normannorum Ducum*, begun by Dudo at the end of the tenth century. A strong supporter of his patron Henry II, he chose largely to ignore the 'Becket affair', but does supply some important dates.[10] Roger, parson of Howden (Hovedene) in Yorkshire, a protégé of Hugh of le Puiset, bishop of Durham, and a royal clerk, started keeping annals about 1169. He put his first version, misleadingly known as *Gesta Regis Henrici Secundi Benedicti Abbatis*, into its final form in 1192–3 and then absorbed it into his *Chronica*, which were written between that date and 1201–2, when he died.[11] Both versions provide some details of the archbishop's career unrecorded elsewhere.

Ralf of Diss (Diceto) in Norfolk, archdeacon of Middlesex in 1152 and dean of St Paul's in 1180, closely observed the English ecclesiastical scene, but, like Robert of Torigni, because of his admiration of the king refused to get much involved in the great quarrel in his *Abbreviationes Chronicorum* and *Ymagines Historiarum*, written in the 1180s and 1190s.[12] William, canon of Newburgh in North Yorkshire, who wrote his substantially derivative *Historia Rerum Anglicarum* at the very end of his life (1136–98), has always been highly regarded for his veracity, common sense and independence of mind.[13] Gervase of Canterbury, the only one of these chroniclers to give the archbishop considerable attention, entered Christ Church and was ordained by Thomas shortly after 1162 and was present at the martyr's burial. But he composed his account, as he tells us, after John of Salisbury, Benedict of Peterborough, William of Canterbury and Herbert of Bosham had made their contributions and Alan of Tewkesbury had collected the correspondence.[14]

CHAPTER ONE

THE LONDON MERCHANT'S SON:
BACKGROUND AND YOUTH, 1120–1143

In the afternoon of St Thomas the Apostle's day (21 December), perhaps in 1120, there was born to Matilda, wife of Gilbert Beket, a prosperous merchant and citizen of London, a son. The birthplace was probably the large house in the very centre of the city, on the north side of the West Market (Cheapside), in the block between Ironmonger Lane and Old Jewry, which remained in the family until about 1228. The child may have looked sickly, for he was baptized that same evening in the tiny parish church of St Mary Colechurch, which occupied an upper room in the next-door property on the Old Jewry corner. He was named after the saint. As Thomas does not seem to have been a family name, it indicates either Matilda's outstanding piety or the special need of heavenly aid. The infant's christening robe was carefully preserved by his parents, and then by Thomas himself, to go with him into his grave.[1]

If the year is correct – and 1120 has been used as the baseline throughout this book for the sake of simplicity – it was the first of the Tuesdays which were to be so fateful in his life. Accordingly, the child was born in the thirteenth year of the pontificate of the bishop of the city, Richard de Beaumais, also known as Rufus, an old soldier and sheriff from the Montgomery lands on the Welsh March, and in the twenty-first year of the reign of King Henry I, the youngest son of the Conqueror, who ruled from 1100 to 1135.

The king, who had been living in Normandy since April 1116, had embarked on 25 November 1120 for England. He was at the very height of his power and influence. He had almost absorbed Wales and was the overlord of Scotland. Duke of Normandy, he was also in control of Boulogne, Ponthieu, Brittany, Bellême and Maine. He had made friends and allied with the new count of Flanders. His sister's son was count of Blois and Chartres; his daughter was married to the German emperor and his son to the heiress of Anjou. In 1119 he had defeated in a pitched battle at Brémule his own overlord, Louis VI, king of France, and they had since been reconciled. But on the return journey from the port of Barfleur one of the fleet, the White Ship, laden with many of the most aristocratic young men in the king's household, including his heir William, foundered with the loss of almost every soul; and from that moment Henry's fortunes began to decline.

Thomas's parents were both of Norman birth and ancestry. One biographer (Anonymous I) believed that Gilbert came from Rouen. William fitzStephen, however, gives us to understand that Gilbert, like Archbishop Theobald of Canterbury, hailed from the vicinity of Thierville (Eure), 5 kilometres north of the abbey of Le Bec Hellouin in the valley of the Risle, and about 40 kilometres south-west of Rouen. The two men had once talked about their neighbours and kinsfolk. FitzStephen mentions that one of the two – it is not clear which – was the son of a knight. But the identity is not of the greatest importance. In the eleventh century the ordinary knight was still simply a cavalry soldier, a follower or vassal of some feudal lord, in status not much above the farmers, and lucky if he received from his lord a small estate, or fief, in return for faithful service in the military household. It matters little, therefore, whether Gilbert was the son of a soldier or of a free agricultural tenant. The remembered origins of the family were relatively humble.[2]

Gilbert would have been born about 1090 and his father about 1060, an exact contemporary of the second Norman king of England, Henry I's elder brother, William Rufus. It is just possible that Gilbert's father was himself called William.[3] If he indeed came from the neighbourhood of Thierville, he would, like the Theobalds, have been a tenant or vassal of the count of Brionne, a scion of the ducal family. Before the end of the eleventh century, however, the lordship of Brionne had passed to the Beaumont family, who in England held the earldoms of Leicester and Warwick. It does not appear that this aristocratic connection was useful to either Gilbert or Thomas. Robert, second earl of Leicester, until his death in 1168 one of Henry II's co-justiciars and a colleague of Thomas when chancellor, had the melancholy duty on 13 October 1164 at Northampton of declaring the royal court's verdict that the archbishop was guilty of perjury and treason, and so brought about Thomas's flight and exile. But, according to Herbert of Bosham, he had always loved Thomas and found the task repugnant.[4] Another nobleman connected with the valley of the Risle, Richer of Laigle, with his seat further south near the river's source, and with estates near Caudebec-en-Caux, Rugles and Conches, to the north and south of Thierville, was, however, as we shall see, a visitor to his humbler neighbour's house in London. As for Theobald, although he and Gilbert chatted about their old homes and kin, it seems unlikely, both from fitzStephen's words and other evidence, that they were related, except possibly in a distant way.

At some time Gilbert acquired the surname Beket, as it was almost invariably spelled at the time. It is a diminutive of the French *bec*, which ordinarily means 'beak', but in Normandy also 'beck' or 'brook'. Opinion is divided over which of these senses Gilbert's name carried. Nicknames based on physical characteristics were very common. Beket could be 'Beaky'; and Thomas is known to have had a prominent nose, doubtless an inherited feature. On the other hand, as the English surname Brook shows, the other explanation cannot be ruled out. Bec is a common place-name, usually in compounds, in the basin of the Seine – for example, Herluin's monastery of Le Bec in the valley of the Risle in the Brionne territory. There is a hamlet of Le Becquet north of the Seine between Lillebonne and Bolbec; and, closer to Thierville, south-west of Elbeuf, are hamlets called Le Becbéquet and Le Bec Thomas. No doubt there are, or were, many more.[5]

Whatever the original meaning of Beket, it was not an aristocratic type of surname. Nor was it necessarily hereditary. Although one of Gilbert's daughters, Agnes, was commonly known as Beket even after her marriage, there is no evidence that Gilbert's son ever employed the name; and when it was used of him, it was probably in derision, an allusion to his non–noble origins. After he had left his birthplace he was Thomas of London until he could qualify his name by his office – archdeacon, chancellor or archbishop. In this he was following one of his seniors in Archbishop Theobald's household, who witnessed his lord's charters as Roger of Pont-l'Evêque until he was promoted archdeacon. Since, however, the Londoner has become so generally known as Thomas Becket and the surname is helpful in distinguishing him from the 'Angelic Doctor', St Thomas Aquinas, it has been used in the title to this book and, of course, retained in phrases such as 'the Becket affair'. But much less tolerable is the 'à Becket' surname, which seems to have been a post-Reformation invention, and from which Thomas should be spared.

As Gilbert Beket left the Thierville area in order to become a trader, he may have been affected by the disputes and wars over the ownership of Brionne or simply a younger son who had to make his own way. He seems to have settled in Rouen for a time before moving on to London. Since he took up residence in a part of Cheapside associated, at least later, with mercers, he may have been in textiles. He had undoubtedly bettered himself materially and probably socially too. His wife was named in its Latin form Matilda, in French Mahaut, sometimes anglicized to Maud. It was the name of William the Conqueror's wife and of the queen who died just about the time of Thomas's birth. One biographer thought that she was called Roheise (*Roesia*), a name which certainly ran in the family, and that she came from Caen. If he was right about the place, well to the west of Thierville and Rouen, Gilbert had met her while on his travels. And if she was the daughter of a burgess of that important and thriving town which the Conqueror had turned almost into his ducal capital, Gilbert had married into money and a trade.

In London, by 1120, they had purchased, for an unknown sum, the fine property in Cheapside in an area which by 1200 was inhabited by families of mayoral and aldermanic rank. Their house was on the fief of the Marmion family, barons of middling status, to whom an annual quit-rent of 20s. was due. It had a street frontage of 40 feet, a depth of 165 feet and a rear width of 110 feet. A visionary dream which the mother had of the infant Thomas's ever-expanding coverlet involved a bedchamber, a hall (the main room) and a courtyard. It is known that around 1200 the neighbouring houses were substantial structures with stone walls, cellars, well-built latrines and gate houses. The property passed to Gilbert Beket's daughter Agnes, thence to her heir, Theobald of Helles, and finally to Theobald's son, Thomas. In 1227–8 he gave it to the hospital of St Thomas of Acre, which had been founded in the Holy Land during the First Crusade (1091–2), in order to provide it with an appropriate outpost in London.[6]

Owing to the reticence of the hagiographers and chroniclers, who were little interested in the martyr's relatively undistinguished social background, it is impossible to be sure how many children Gilbert and Matilda had. The fact that a daughter seems to have been their heir makes it likely that Thomas was the only, or only surviving son. There were at least three daughters, Agnes, Roheise and Mary. The first two married men whose names were not remembered and had children. Mary (and this may not be her baptismal name) became a nun and in 1173 was appointed by the king abbess at nearby Barking in Essex. The greatest mystery is the exact identity of Agnes's heir, Theobald of Helles or Hulles. He described himself as the nephew of St Thomas, and Agnes as the saint's sister. He must have been the son of one of Gilbert's daughters and, most likely, despite the evasions, the son of Agnes. If not, he probably represents an unrecorded daughter.

Theobald took his name from what was later Hills-Court, an estate in Kent between Sandwich and Ash and a member of the great archiepiscopal manor of Wingham. He is described as a knight; the family arms were sable, a bend, argent, which were carved on the roof of the cloisters at Canterbury; and his estates in Kent, Essex, Middlesex and London presumably combined the Helles and Beket inheritances. He had a brother, Robert Agodeshalf (For God's sake), who had a son Roger.[7]

Gilbert and Matilda's son spent most of his first twenty-five years, that is to say half his life, in or around London. In that world he had a privileged position. He belonged to the urban aristocracy, the landowning, capitalist,

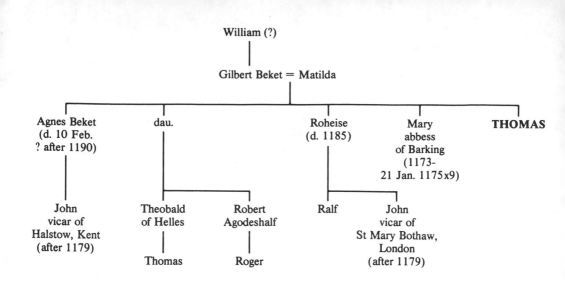

William (?)
|
Gilbert Beket = Matilda
|
Agnes Beket   dau.   Roheise   Mary   **THOMAS**
(d. 10 Feb.   (d. 1185)   abbess
? after 1190)   of Barking
(1173-
21 Jan. 1175x9)

John   Theobald   Robert   Ralf   John
vicar of   of Helles   Agodeshalf   vicar of
Halstow, Kent   St Mary Bothaw,
(after 1179)   London

Thomas   Roger   (after 1179)

(other grandchildren of Gilbert Beket: Gilbert, Geoffrey)

Thomas's family

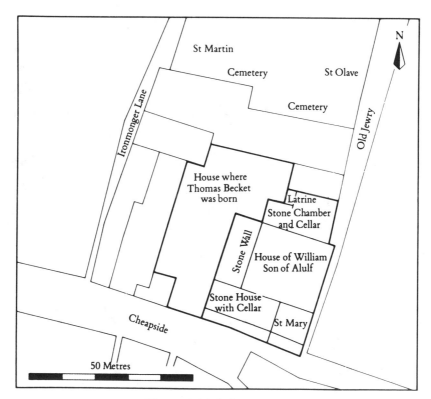

Thomas's birthplace

14

merchant class, members of a guild, increasingly involved in the government of the city and with pretensions to be ranked with the king's barons. The citizens had hunting rights in the forests and chases outside the city and sometimes had an interest in country properties. The Saturday horse fairs at Smithfield were one of the marvels of the city. But the bourgeoisie had its own distinctive urban culture, of which, as we can see from William fitzStephen's glowing description of London life at this time, it was inordinately proud. William wrote that Gilbert Beket was not engaged in money-lending or any full-time business activity, but was living like a gentleman on his income from property. We know from Winchester evidence that a sophisticated land market existed in cities. Properties could be freely bought and sold, and developed in several ways, especially by breaking them up and subletting. Rent-rolls could be purchased and there was mortgage business. Wealthy rentiers existed just as much in the towns as in the shires. It may be that Gilbert, with money received with his wife, had made some profitable trading ventures and then partly retired to live on his investment income and take an honourable part in the government of the city.[8]

Gilbert at the height of his fortune probably ranked just below the real heavyweights in London society. In 1166 Thomas answered Bishop Gilbert Foliot's taunt that Henry II had raised him from the dust by claiming that his ancestors were citizens of London, and by no means among the lowest – rather from the middle ranks who enjoyed a comfortable place in the bourgeoisie. By 1120 Gilbert could have been resident for about a decade and his standing is proved by his becoming for a term sheriff of the City. The office of mayor had not yet appeared. A sheriff was responsible, among other things, for paying to the king the sum of money, often fixed by bargaining, which was in lieu of all the financial rights the king had in that bailiwick. The sheriff expected to make a profit by collecting more than he had to render; but the king was a hard bargainer and there were, for the sheriff, the hazards of natural disasters. It was a very speculative business. Middlesex and London went together, and in the twelfth century usually a small group of citizens, either chosen by the king or elected by their fellows, jointly held the office. Thomas's biographers thought that Gilbert lost much of his wealth in later life largely because of the destruction of his property by fires. The first fire mentioned was on Thomas's birthday, when a conflagration spread from Gilbert's own house. A greater fire, in which St Paul's was damaged, occurred in 1133. As Gilbert lived until at least the 1140s, it may be that he was sheriff in the 1130s. If this was so, Thomas's childhood and boyhood were not clouded by his father's financial difficulties.[9]

It was an age of great opportunities. All the recent kings of England had been claimants who had seized their chance. Knights had become barons,

barons earls. There had been some extraordinary careers in the church. It was, of course, too, a time of great danger. In the competitive feudal society families rose and fell; in the cities fortunes were both made and lost. But, all in all, to have been born into a good home in the city of London was a lucky chance. Society was mixed and open: the English and Normans lived together in harmony; a colony of Jews was round the corner from the Beket house; long-established burghal dynasties existed; but newcomers easily found a place; the city and the royal palace of Westminster were cheek by jowl; and churches, great and small, were everywhere. At the wharves on the Thames lay the ships on whose voyages the merchants gambled. A talented and ambitious boy from such a background was unlikely to become a feudal magnate, but he could acquire great wealth or climb high in the service of the church or the king.

We are very badly informed about Thomas's life before he entered Archbishop Theobald's household in his mid-twenties. Among his biographers are men who could have heard him talk, or questioned him, about his youth – or, indeed, found informants after his death. But they chose to pass over this period as quickly as possible. It may not have been one of Thomas's favourite subjects, either as chancellor or as archbishop, and it must have furnished little grist for the hagiographical mill. His pious mother was credited with a few visions which presaged her son's future glory; and Thomas told Herbert of Bosham how, when a boy and ill with fever, he had had a vision of a tall and beautiful woman who promised that he would get better and presented him with the two golden keys of paradise which later would be in his charge.[10] But most writers were aware, if only from the others, that he had not been particularly studious, and some did the best they could by maintaining that, although he had behaved in most ways like an ordinary naughty boy, he had avoided the temptations of the flesh to which most were prone. But, although we are provided with very few hard facts and no dates, the scene can be reconstructed in outline and furnished here and there with some hazy detail. As we are concerned here with almost half his earthly life, the groundwork which underlay, perhaps determined, his later achievements, all that we can discover about it is valuable.

Thomas must have passed his infancy among women and girls. His mother is unlikely to have suckled him – his nursemaid is featured in one of her visions – but, if she was indeed a burgess's daughter, she was probably better educated than her husband and, like many women in medieval urban society, the driving force in the family. Thomas told 'Anonymous I', who knew him in exile, that his mother was particularly devoted to the Blessed Virgin Mary, and as a result he too, throughout his life, took Mary as his main guide and comforter. Matilda also used to provide him with food, clothing and money to give as alms to the needy in order to raise his credit with God and the Virgin. But his mother and the mother of God were apparently the only women of importance in his life. Although he kept in touch with his sisters, and may have helped them after his father's death, he does not seem to have been closely attached to them: he was no nepotist. And there is no evidence for women lovers, friends or confidantes.[11]

French would have been spoken in the family and it probably remained Thomas's first tongue. It was the language of the several households he later passed through, from Merton priory to the royal court. But in the bilingual urban society he would have learnt to speak English as well. It is quite likely that his nursemaid and other servants in the house would have been English speakers; and he would have heard much English on the streets. From his mother and nurse he would have learnt to recite nursery rhymes, the Lord's Prayer and other simple devotions. It is unlikely, even if his mother was literate, that he would have been taught at home to read or write; but he could have been familiar from an early age with the abacus, the counting frame, if only as a toy.

All that we are told about his schooling is that between the age of ten and twenty-one, that is to say, probably between 1130 and 1141, he was successively, but perhaps intermittently, a boarder at the Augustinian priory at Merton in Surrey, a pupil at one or more of the London grammar schools and a student at Paris. His mother is said to have been the parent who encouraged him to study, and it was her death, when he was twenty-one, which brought this phase to an end.

If he was not taught his letters at home, he must have gone to an elementary school, perhaps conducted by the parish priest, where he would have learnt to read and write, probably in both French and English, and become acquainted with the rudiments of Latin (grammar, as it was called). There would have been no shortage of such 'song-schools' in London at that time and elementary education may also have been given by some of the greatest establishments. Why Gilbert and Matilda switched him at the age of ten to Merton, some 15 miles away, in the archdeaconry of Surrey and the bishopric of Winchester, but within visiting distance, is not clear. It was no more and no less 'ecclesiastical' than St Paul's or the other city schools attached to minsters; but it would have had a different tone. It may have been considered more devout or socially superior; it was undoubtedly fashionable. Canons regular had lately become popular in those circles which founded religious communities, because these clerks, although observing a quasi-monastic rule, operated more in the world than Benedictine monks and included in their ministry the education of the people and the care of the sick. These aims were admired by the more progressive members of the English upper classes. The royal court patronized the Augustinians;

and the newer aristocracy, the rich citizenry and some bishops ensured the rapid spread of the order in the first half of the twelfth century.[12]

Merton, founded as recently as 1114 by Gilbert, sheriff of Surrey, Cambridgeshire and Huntingdonshire, and moved to a new site by the River Wandle in 1117, was still in a rather primitive state in 1130 when Thomas was sent there. Ambitious plans for replacing the wooden church, houses and cloister by stone structures had been abandoned in 1125 when Gilbert died five months after laying the foundation stone of a third church. The building of new residential quarters may have been started before 1132, but there was no stone church until much later. Nevertheless, although the buildings were flimsy and dilapidated and the endowments slender, it was probably an attractive place with its running water, mill, cemetery and vineyard.

Also in the 1120s and 1130s the tone was undoubtedly lively. The first prior, Robert of Tywe (1114–49), was taken by Gilbert from St Mary's Huntingdon where he had been for eight years and where there was a good school. The author of Merton's foundation narrative gave him an excellent testimonial: he was very well educated, wise and prudent, an elegant speaker and a man of great generosity, mercy and compassion. Perhaps his piety was taken for granted. The original schoolmaster at Merton, an Italian named Guy, a scholar of some distinction, who had been borrowed by other priories, had died about 1120; but it is unlikely that the pedagogic tradition had collapsed. The community had grown from fifteen in 1117 to thirty-six in 1125; and among the brethren were Stephen, formerly archdeacon of Surrey, and Serlo, the former dean of Salisbury, 'besides others distinguished by their piety, learning and noble birth'. By 1150 seven other priories had been founded from Merton, as widely spaced as Bodmin, Edinburgh and St Lô in Normandy. Thomas retained an interest in the house, helped it when he was chancellor and even took one of its canons, another Robert, as his chaplain and confessor, a man who was still with him when he was killed. He may have remembered kindly the prior's compassion for a reluctant scholar.

It is possible that the only English clerk of the period to have had an even more dazzling career than Thomas, Nicholas Breakspear, born at Abbot's Langley in Hertfordshire, the son of a clerk in the king's chamber, who rose to be Pope Adrian IV, had been educated before 1120 at Merton. Nicholas, too, caught a series of favourable breezes which kept him on a successful, if unpredictable, course. But we should beware of thinking that Gilbert Beket had in 1130 an ecclesiastical career in mind for his son. It was not usual to put an only son into the church; and Thomas was not, as might have been the case with a Benedictine monastery, given as a child oblate. The boy would have been tonsured, for almost all scholars were clerks; but the tonsure and even subsequent minor orders did not prevent a man from marrying or engaging in any other secular activity. From Gilbert's later behaviour it would not seem that in 1130 he was looking very far ahead. He was only making sure that the boy would be qualified to become a clerk in any kind of office or household. And it is most unlikely that Thomas gave any of his masters reason to believe that he had a vocation for the priesthood.[13]

When and in what circumstances he was removed from Merton to one of the London grammar schools is unknown. These might well have been, with their freer out-of-school life, more to his taste. William fitzStephen gives a vivid account of some aspects of the activities of the boys at the three principal minster schools, St Paul's, St Mary-le-Grand and St Mary-le-Bow. The last was just up the road from the Beket house, the others less than half a mile away, and he may have been entered in turn at them all. The names of the schoolmasters at St Paul's in Henry I's reign are known, but none had much reputation. In any case it does not seem that Thomas's schooling was continuous at this time, although the cryptic remarks of some of the biographers are open to different interpretations.[14]

It was, apparently, in the period between Merton and Paris that Thomas became attached to a nobleman, Richer II of Laigle, a scion of a distinguished Norman family and closely related to the neighbouring counts of Perche and Mortagne. Richer's father, Gilbert I, was the grandson of Engenulf killed at the battle of Hastings, and his mother, Juliana, was the sister of Rotrou II of Perche and Mortagne, a survivor of the First Crusade. Gilbert received from Henry I the English honour of Pevensey in Sussex after it had been forfeited by William of Mortain in 1106; and Richer made good his claim to this, despite a serious quarrel with the king, some time after his father's death in 1114–18, only to lose it once more during Stephen's reign. He finally recovered possession in the 1160s, during Henry II's reign, possibly at a time when Thomas was still influential. Consequently he was one of those members of the royal court who declared the Constitutions of Clarendon in 1164, the event which above all set Thomas on the road to martyrdom. His witness appears in the document high among the barons after the earls. Two of his younger brothers, Geoffrey and Engenulf, while serving in Henry I's military household, were lost with the king's heir in the White Ship disaster, Geoffrey clinging to a spar in the freezing water off Barfleur almost until rescuers arrived. By the 1130s Richer was a soldier of considerable experience, perhaps a little wild, but respected by his neighbour, Orderic Vitalis, the Anglo-Norman historian at St Evroult, as an honourable and God-fearing knight.[15]

Richer, we are told, lodged with the Bekets when he was in London; and, as we have noticed, Gilbert may have been born not far from some of the family's estates. As the baron lived until 1176 he may have been some ten years older than Thomas; and clearly he took a liking to the boy, who could have acted as a substitute for his dead brothers. He carried him off for holidays in the country, presumably in Sussex, where they seem to have passed their time in hunting and hawking. An incident remembered from this period illustrates, according to the version followed, either God's providence or Thomas's reckless courage. The youth, while out hawking with Richer, fell into a millstream and almost drowned, either because his horse slipped off a narrow bridge or because he plunged in to save a hawk which had pursued a bird into the water. He owed his life to the stopping of the millwheel and a helping hand. Edward Grim thought that the citizen's son learnt much from the baron; and this can hardly be doubted. Aristocratic manners were to stand him in good stead. He always had tremendous style.[16]

From William fitzStephen and the Icelandic Saga, following Robert of Cricklade, we learn that Thomas studied at Paris; and, although the latter puts it before, it was most likely after the Richer of Laigle affair, a story which fitzStephen omits. The mysterious Paris episode is an important crux for the interpretation of his career. Not yet a university, the schools of Paris were, however, already the most distinguished in the North-West and the goal not only of serious students but also of dilettanti. A good number of Englishmen attended them in this period, and friendships formed in that fabulous city were long-lasting. Ralf of Beauvais arrived there before 1140 and studied under Peter Abelard, and John of Salisbury was there between 1136 and 1147, sitting at the feet of all the most distinguished masters, of whom he wrote a most interesting account. If Thomas was there round about 1140, he, too, should have been part of that small and intimate society of scholars. It is possible that one of his masters was Robert of Melun, an Englishman, but, like Ralf of Beauvais, called after the place where he became a schoolmaster. John of Salisbury considered Robert one of the two leading *disputatores* of the age, that is to say of those who publicly disputed, using the arts of rhetoric and logic, controversial questions. Thomas could indeed have learnt something from him.[17]

It is most difficult, however, on the scanty evidence available, to be sure why Thomas went to Paris. The only anecdote concerning this period is furnished by the Saga and, since most of it is derived from an unrelated Mary miracle story, is in all parts a complete fabrication. When we consider the interest which the next generation of Paris masters took in the martyr and their sympathy for his cause, it is strange that we know of only one person, Everlin, abbot of St Lawrence at Liège (1161–83), who later claimed to have met the Londoner at Paris; even John of Salisbury seems never to have alluded to any acquaintance with him at this time.[18]

It was becoming usual to style a clerk who spent an adequate period in cathedral schools and qualified to teach others *magister*, master. The procedure had not yet been regulated: the term of years was unspecified and it is unlikely that the successful student was granted a formal *licentia docendi*, licentiate or master's degree. But the qualification was recognized and was allowed to such contemporaries of Thomas in Archbishop Theobald's household as John of Salisbury and William de Vere. Thomas was never styled master. Either, then, he was not a serious student at Paris, a dilettante, who, perhaps on Richer's advice, went simply to add more polish to his manners – even improve his French – or something went wrong.

The hagiographers incline to the latter explanation. Most are completely reticent; but Edward Grim, followed by Guernes and elaborated by Anonymous I, explains that Thomas's schooling was cut untimely short by family misfortunes: the loss of his father's wealth and then the death of both parents. Anonymous I stresses the effect of his mother's death. It was she who pushed him to study, and, when she died, he just gave up. Herbert of Bosham, however, thought that Thomas abandoned his studies because he was behaving foolishly at the time.[19]

There is no need here to be more indulgent than the hagiographers themselves. Even if there had been no serious intention that Thomas should qualify as a master and make a career in the church, his biographers, some themselves masters, were embarrassed by his lack of both interest and purpose. According to Abbot Samson of Bury St Edmunds, when he was a boy, towards the end of Stephen's reign, it cost £3-4 a year to keep a clerk at school, and he might have been thinking of Paris.[20] If Gilbert Beket could not afford that, he had really come down in the world; but, from what we know of Thomas's tastes, it might have cost his father a great deal more. It may be, however, that the biographers exaggerated the financial aspect. Most likely father and son, now that Matilda had died, agreed that it was time to take stock and make new plans for the future. Thomas was believed to have returned home after he had completed his twenty-first year, that is to say, after 21 December 1141.

Thomas's rather sketchy education caused the biographers some difficulty. They knew that, although he was extremely intelligent, he was never much of a scholar; and it was common knowledge that the boy had been passionately interested in rural sports and had retained that taste for almost the whole of his life. But here we may be a little more indulgent than those writers. Presumably, because he became an archbishop and then a saint, they do seem to have set their standards unnecessarily high. Even if he had been an inattentive schoolboy, in ten years he must have gone through the whole curriculum at a modest level and acquired some knowledge of the seven liberal arts: the *trivium* – Latin grammar, rhetoric (the art of public speaking and letter writing) and dialectic (logic, or the art of reasoning)

– and also the slightly more advanced *quadrivium* – the mathematical subjects which could have been more to his taste, arithmetic, geometry, astronomy and music. But clearly he had not mastered the subjects. Herbert of Bosham remarks, with reference to a 'miraculous' prophetic Latin hexameter which came into the archbishop's head one night when resting after nocturns during their exile at Sens, that Thomas could not have composed it even when awake, for he had not acquired the art of writing Latin verses at school – or hardly at all.[21] It is also clear that, in youth, he did not proceed beyond the basic curriculum. His legal and theological studies pertain to later periods of his life, to professions which required those special qualifications.

We can test his education by the skills he displayed later in his career. John of Salisbury stressed the acuteness and subtlety of his mind and his wonderful memory: he had total recall and could solve knotty problems with ease. He had also very sharp ears and an excellent sense of smell. With such natural gifts a little education went a long way. He was obviously literate and, as both an archiepiscopal clerk and royal chancellor, capable of reading and writing in Latin, although when he became grand he could, and did, have a clerk to read documents to him and probably translate them into French. Likewise, when archbishop, most of his private letters, together with the other administrative documents, were, as was usual, composed and written by secretaries and clerks. It was claimed by a contemporary that he had insufficient Latin to make one of the opening speeches at the papal council of Tours in 1163. But that was asking for a skill rare outside those educated in the cloister or specially trained to this end, and John of Salisbury reported in 1167 that he spoke eloquently and skilfully in Latin to the papal legates at the meeting at Gisors-Trie. In a vision experienced by Benedict of Peterborough shortly after the martyrdom, the monk questioned Thomas in French and was answered in Latin – presumably proof that his visitor was indeed in Heaven. Thomas was clearly a good and agreeable speaker in French, moving easily in the best society; and he could argue well enough. As a merchant's son, a banker's clerk and royal chancellor he must also have been numerate. The mysteries of the exchequer board would have posed no problems at all.[22]

After 1155, however, he operated at the directorial level where he hardly required detailed technical expertise. He always kept a large household to serve him and provide the practical skills. His contribution was judgement, vision and imagination. What can fairly be said is that he was at least as well educated as the average bishop who owed his position to having served the king as a clerk. He was equipped to succeed, after a little extra training, in all the posts he held before the archbishopric. That, of course, was another matter.

While Thomas had been finishing his schooling, the political scene in

England had changed almost out of recognition. Strong government and the *pax normannica* had disappeared. Henry I had died in 1135 and had been succeeded by his nephew Stephen, despite his own intention that his only surviving legitimate child, Matilda, 'empress of Germany', whom he had married, secondly, to Geoffrey, count of Anjou, should have the throne. In 1138, in support of her claim, Geoffrey had invaded Normandy, Robert of Gloucester, Matilda's half-brother, had brought west and south-west England out in rebellion and David of Scots, her uncle, had invaded the north. By the spring of 1139, however, Stephen seemed to have weathered the storm: Geoffrey and David had been repulsed and Robert had been contained. London and south-east England always stood firmly for Stephen. But the times were dangerous, and Gilbert Beket may well have thought that Thomas should stay with him and help to look after the family business.

There were also changes in the church which were to affect Thomas's career. The bishopric of London was going through a rather disturbed period. After Richard de Beaumais I had died in 1127, the king had made the eccentric choice of the Breton, Gilbert 'the Universal', a scholar of immense renown, but with many nephews and a dubious reputation. And after his death in 1134 the see, partly because of disputes over the succession, remained vacant until 1141, when Henry I's old clerk, Robert de Sigillo, was appointed by the empress, then temporarily in control of the city. The Bekets could not look to a bishop of London for patronage. In more than compensation, in 1138 Stephen had secured the election of Theobald, abbot of Bec, as archbishop of Canterbury in order to keep out his ambitious younger brother, Henry, bishop of Winchester and abbot of Glastonbury. Pope Innocent II had tried to solace Henry with a papal legation, and, by thus splitting authority in the English church, made certain that Theobald would have a rough ride.[23]

The new archbishop was, as we have noticed, a compatriot and possibly a distant kinsman of Gilbert Beket. It did not take the merchant long to bring this to Theobald's notice. Archbishops of Canterbury had a house and estate on the south bank of the Thames at Lambeth and a favourite manor at Harrow in Middlesex. In 1141 Gilbert and Thomas may have been depressed by their personal troubles and the uncertain political situation. But for a young man freshly returned from the schools of Paris, there was probably no shortage of opportunities. We are told, however, that he passed his twenty-second year at leisure.[24]

CHAPTER TWO

THE LOWER RUNGS OF
THE LADDERS, 1143–1154

All the memorialists who had known or seen Thomas thought him a most attractive man; and the truth of this is proved by his climb up the several ladders of patronage. Men of importance were pleased to hold out a hand, and Thomas responded eagerly. He also tried not to provoke his competitors. In such a situation he had to be ingratiating. There had been a series of these social mountaineers since the Norman Conquest, men of rare talent and usually of great physical presence, such as Ranulf Flambard under William Rufus and Roger of Salisbury under Henry I; and, although they were often resented as they pushed their way to the top, they were always accepted in the end.

The biographers tell us just enough about Thomas to give us some idea of his personal appearance.[1] Tall and slender, vivacious yet elegant, he was extremely good looking in youth and handsome when older. He had a fair skin and dark hair. His features were regular, although his nose was rather long and aquiline. His forehead was wide, his eyes were bright and his expression was calm and happy. It is obvious from his physical achievements in early manhood that his constitution was in essentials robust. But contemporaries considered that he had a congenitally 'cold stomach'; and this would seem to have made him susceptible to stress. Icelandic sources, to which we owe much of our information about Thomas's looks, drawn probably from the lost work of Robert of Cricklade, also contribute the interesting fact that Thomas had a slight stammer. This disorder is difficult to interpret at such a distance, for its causes differ from person to person. But it can be a neurosis arising from psychological conflicts, especially emotions of frustration. The sufferer fears both the danger of falling under the control of others and his own repressed feelings of aggression. Such a diagnosis would not be unfitting in Thomas's case – a proud man, usually in subservient situations, who in the end kicked over the traces.

Thomas was after 1145 always an outsider, and his struggle to succeed in every role he played could undoubtedly exert intolerable pressure on him. Occasionally he suffered disabling or weakening ailments. He had an attack of colitis at Northampton in 1164. He was sometimes prostrate during his exile. His delicate digestion is often noticed. A man named Jordan, who had been the groom in charge of Thomas's only horse when the clerk was in Archbishop Theobald's household, remembered in 1171–2 an incident when they were visiting Theobald's steward at Croydon in Surrey, the clerk Thurstan. Because his master could stomach no alcoholic beverage, like wine, cider or ale, he had scoured the district to find some whey for him to drink. Likewise Hugh of Meymac recalled that he had offered Thomas, when chancellor and riding through the Limousin, either in 1156 or 1159, whey in a silver cup. Thomas always responded to misfortune by pushing himself hard, obviously sometimes too hard. But until things went seriously wrong he was a charmer out to please. Even an impediment in speech can be attractive and, indeed, exploited by its possessor.[2]

There was likewise among the biographers, largely again due to copying, general agreement on his character and behaviour in this period. He pursued 'the shifting breeze of popular fashion'. He had a modest and pleasant turn of speech and engaging manners. He was prone to frivolity and ostentation in dress, enjoyed company and joined his friends in their buffooneries. He was particularly addicted to hunting and fowling. As Herbert of Bosham, once a fine fellow himself, remarked, 'Like Ephraim he fed the winds and ran after shadows.' And there are important omissions. No one who knew him indicates that he was warm and affectionate, that he had the gift of friendship. They preserved no intimate letter, hardly one which can be regarded as an ordinary communication between friends; they mention no tokens of his love, only ostentatious presents to men of the greatest importance. That Archbishop Theobald and King Henry, perhaps the young Henry too, loved him is undoubted. Thomas's own reciprocal feelings were probably a compound of several emotions. Although a few of his clerks stayed with him to the very end, indeed beyond the end, it was partly perforce. At Easter 1166 some of the closest were prepared to abandon him if Henry would grant them honourable terms.[3]

The muted criticism and tactful omissions of the biographers are, however, swept aside by their appeal to the example of St Brice (Britius) of Tours. He, although in youth proud and vain, safeguarded his chastity. It was a valid case in point. Thomas, although he detested lust, idle talk and avarice, like a wise man dissimulated his feelings so as not to offend those who went in for such things. His courtesy and generosity – he would share everything he had with his companions – made him an agreeable member of the fashionable world of which inwardly he disapproved. All commentators stressed his absolute truthfulness and chastity, to which Herbert of

Bosham added his faithful service to his masters.

It is not quite clear how his prudent dissimulation can be squared with complete veracity; and his perfect chastity raises a problem. When we consider the general pattern of Thomas's life, it is an unnecessary complication. Some of his sympathizers after 1164 regarded him as atoning in exile for his follies and sins as a courtier: it was a splendid opportunity to improve his behaviour and education.[4] There was, therefore, no absolute need for the hagiographers to whitewash his past. He could have stood with St Augustine of Hippo. Sometimes the greater the sinner the greater the saint. It could accordingly be argued that the case for Thomas's chastity is a strong one: its invention was unnecessary. But this is to overlook the change in attitude between 1164–70 and 1173. Thomas when alive could be treated as an ordinary human being and freely criticized. After his death even his greatest enemies had to change their tune; and, once he had been canonized, there was a temptation, almost a compulsion, to reconsider the whole of his life in the light of the unexpected ending. Many must have convinced themselves that much of his worldliness had been a mere appearance; and the theme of the secret ascetic amid the luxury, the hair shirt under the finery, could hardly be resisted.

The truth is unascertainable. But to think that the appearances may not in fact have been deceptive is not only reasonable but also in no way prejudicial to the case for Thomas's sanctity. Throughout his life he tried to play to the full the role in which he found himself. Before he took deacon's orders when made archdeacon, or, more realistically, until he was consecrated priest on becoming archbishop, he would not have been expected to display heroic virtues. He was not a monk, nor, as we shall see, was he much attracted or even sympathetic to monasticism until late in his life. As a banker's clerk he was part of a society where wild oats were sown with abandon, and even Archbishop Theobald's household was not a perfect model of decorum. As royal chancellor he was actively encouraged by his young master to debauchery. There seems to have been little of the prig in him, and until 1164, even if he discriminated, he was not averse to worldly pleasure. A little fornication would not have added much to a debit sheet which contained at the least military service, hunting, dicing, pride, ostentation, actions prejudicial to the church, and no doubt some other deadly sins as well. On the other hand, the lack of warmth, stress and repression may have combined to restrict intimacy with either sex.

Be that as it may, one year after his return from Paris, possibly shortly after his twenty-second birthday, Thomas left the parental home and entered the household of a greater London citizen, Osbert Huitdeniers (Eightpence).[5] He is said to have found his own house desolate after the death of his mother; his father's fortune had declined; and he needed to start on a career of his own. In this employment he remained for two or three years. Accordingly, if he was twenty-two in December 1142, he would have served Osbert from early in 1143 until some time in 1145.

Osbert, a kinsman, was, on the evidence of his surname, engaged in the city's money market, in effect a London banker. He was a man of some standing, holding a knight's fee in Kent of the royal bastard, the earl of Gloucester, and was known at the royal court. His wife, Rohesia, like Thomas's sister Agnes, became a benefactor of the Augustinian priory for women founded perhaps a year or so later at Clerkenwell, about a mile from Cheapside. Osbert had succeeded Andrew Buchuinte (Oily Mouth), another city magnate, as a justiciar or sheriff of London in 1139 and held the post until the end of July 1141. Thomas, therefore, could not on any reckoning have been in his household for more than a month or two while his master held one of these important royal offices. His main task was to keep Osbert's accounts; and it was believed that he acquitted himself well, that he learnt there those administrative and financial skills which later he was to display in wider fields; and that he behaved in the worldly fashion already described.

The years 1141–5 were a stormy period in London's history. The city fathers, by supporting the claims of Stephen of Blois against the Empress Matilda in 1135, had forged an alliance which conferred on them some relief from royal and baronial oppression, together with hopes of more self-government, and secured for the king their loyal support, both financial and military. It is, indeed, possible that they made at least tentative moves towards creating a commune, an oligarchical constitution. When the king was captured by the rival party at Lincoln in February 1141, the Londoners did the best they could for him. A council was convened by the papal legate, Henry, bishop of Winchester, to his episcopal city in April, with the purpose of transferring the allegiance of the English church from his brother to his cousin. The Londoners protested, and in June they tried to make terms with the empress before admitting her into their city. When she arbitrarily imposed a tax on the citizens, they took to the streets and drove her out, thus frustrating her hopes of a coronation at Westminster. They then sent troops to help Stephen's queen, Matilda of Boulogne, and contributed to the empress's defeat and the king's release and restoration. On 7 December 1141 Henry of Blois held another council, this time at Westminster, in order to reaffirm the church's recognition of Stephen.

Even more dangerous at the time was feudal, baronial power. In an insurrection in London in May 1141, perhaps caused by an earlier move by the Angevin party, a great ministerial magnate, Aubrey (II) de Vere, lord of Hedingham in Essex and hereditary royal chamberlain, was killed;

and in July the empress created his son and heir, another Aubrey, earl of Oxford. At the same time the younger Aubrey's brother-in-law, Geoffrey de Mandeville, lord of Pleshy in Essex, hereditary Constable of the Tower of London, and, since 1140, earl of Essex, took advantage of the situation to increase his power. The empress, while in control of London, made him sheriff and justiciar of the city and Middlesex, as well as of Essex and Hertfordshire; and, although she recognized in her charter that the Londoners were the earl's 'mortal enemies', Stephen on his release from captivity had to accept the situation and confirm Geoffrey in his offices. In the autumn of 1143, however, the king forced him to surrender all his castles and offices, a disaster which Geoffrey did not long survive. In 1145 London again sent troops to the royal army. Its exact status in the period 1143–54 is unknown; but it probably enjoyed a fair measure of self-government.[6]

Thomas of London is often portrayed as a very loyal man. But we should note that it was loyalty of a particular kind. He was, or like most ambitious men became, markedly egocentric. Even if he did not wear his heart on his sleeve, he discarded old loves fairly easily as he went on his way. For a start, he seems never to have displayed any sympathy later with the ambitions of London or with those of the House of Blois. He embraced the Angevin cause, in the person of Henry fitzEmpress, and championed royal government against such rivals as the towns and church, with enthusiasm. In the spring of 1170 he sent an extravagant eulogy of Robert, earl of Gloucester, to Robert's son, Roger, bishop of Worcester. And, although he was intimately involved, and for a long time, in the financial world of London, it does not seem that any of his city friendships survived his several changes of career. The clerk's wild friends were no doubt discarded when he left London. The great banker, Gervase of Cornhill, makes an appearance late in the story, but as an enemy. Andrew Buchuinte, Richard Bucherell, William Blemund (the eponym of Bloomsbury), and other such magnates are ignored by the hagiographers. There is, of course, nothing discreditable in any of this; and Thomas's exclusive loyalty to his lord for the time being can be put to his credit. In any case we have only a severely edited account of his life.[7]

John of Salisbury and Herbert of Bosham believed that Thomas switched from the financier's counting house to the archbishop's household because he had seen in the courts of the magnates of this world the many injuries done to the clerical order.[8] This does not agree with the acknowledged frivolity of his life as Osbert's clerk and as royal chancellor, and seems rather far-fetched. A religious conversion was not required as a preliminary to entrance into an archiepiscopal court. More likely Theobald was regarded simply as an alternative patron, an even greater lord, who for some reason or other had now come just within reach. What is clear is that Gilbert

Beket used all his influence and contacts to get his son into this most desirable post.

Two completely different explanations are given of how Thomas transferred to the archbishop's household.[9] Edward Grim attributes his entry to the invitation of a certain household servant of Theobald, whom he later identifies as a man surnamed Axe or Hatchet. Guernes develops the story a little: the servant was a marshal who used to lodge with Gilbert and bore the name Baillehache (Carry-Axe). And Anonymous I further embroiders the theme: one of the archbishop's officials, again identified as Baillehache, used to stay at Gilbert's house when he visited London on the archbishop's business and so knew Thomas from childhood. When he saw that the son had grown into an elegant young man, well educated and well behaved, he tried to persuade him to accompany him to his lord's court. Thomas thought it presumptuous to go without an invitation; but in the end, accepting that the servant had authority to take him, he went with him to the archbishop; and Theobald took an instant liking to him and invited him to stay. The story is strengthened by the fact that Baillehache was indeed Theobald's marshal, that is to say the official in charge of the horses and stables, who often was given messenger duties, as we can see from his witness to a charter of the archbishop which comes from the years 1150–3. In a list which begins with Roger, archdeacon of Canterbury, Thomas, clerk of London, Master John of Salisbury and John of Canterbury, he is noticed at the very end, after the archbishop's master cook, door-keeper and porter.[10]

Although it is unlikely that the 'Canterbury' story is completely untrue, William fitzStephen explains the mechanics of Thomas's move quite differently; and his evidence, which is just as circumstantial, is at least of equal authority. He identifies the intermediaries as two brothers from Boulogne, Archdeacon Baldwin and Master Eustace, who used to lodge with Gilbert and were also well known to Theobald; and he adds that Theobald was especially aware of Thomas because of those territorial connections which we have already discussed. As a result of this double recommendation, the archbishop enrolled him among his retinue, and later found him to be steadfast and true. Thomas first came to the archbishop at his manor of Harrow accompanied by a single squire, Ralf of London.

The stories cannot be reconciled by identifying the squire as Baillehache. A London merchant's son would not travel without servants; and it is the modesty of his retinue at this time – a single squire – that fitzStephen is emphasizing. Baldwin of Boulogne, who was archdeacon of Sudbury on the Suffolk–Essex boundary in the diocese of Norwich from before 1143 until after 1168, certainly was later in Thomas's circle, for he was with the exile in November 1164 at St Bertin's and in 1168 was the recipient, under a pseudonym, of one of John of Salisbury's letters. But the origin of the connection cannot be elucidated. The queen, Matilda, was countess of Boulogne in her own right, and as such had large English estates, including London properties. Gilbert Beket's trade or banking interests could have brought him into contact with men from that county. It is even possible that he ran a superior kind of guesthouse in Cheapside. The two stories are not mutually exclusive and can easily be conflated: Gilbert was eager to get his son into the archbishop's household and exploited all avenues open to him. The result was that Thomas was well established as an archiepiscopal clerk by 1146, and thereafter regularly witnessed Theobald's charters as Thomas of London.[11]

The connection with Canterbury may also have played a part in the marriages of Thomas's sisters. One, possibly Agnes, married the lord of Hills-Court, an archiepiscopal knight enfeoffed on the great manor of Wingham. And as Roheise settled in Canterbury with her sons Ralf and John after her brother's death, she could have had an earlier association with the city. After the proscription of his kin at Christmas 1164, Thomas did what he could for his nephews, the clerks Gilbert and Geoffrey. But his involvement with his sisters and nephews does not seem to have been close.[12]

Theobald's court, like all major households, was ambulatory, moving between his palace adjacent to Canterbury cathedral and the houses built by his predecessors on the archiepiscopal manors, and sometimes coalescing with the royal court. At first Thomas had a rough time. William fitzStephen is quite frank. In the archbishop's household were some very important and excellently educated clerks, many of whom were later promoted through the archbishop's favour to English bishoprics, and one, Roger of Pont l'Evêque, to the archbishopric of York. By their standards, he admits, Thomas was inferior in education. But, as good morals were superior to a good education, Thomas strove to excel them in virtue; and also he eventually became the best educated of them all. The biographer underestimates the distinction and influence of Theobald's household: it produced in fact four archbishops and six bishops. It was becoming common for high-flyers rising through episcopal households to serve an apprenticeship as archdeacon before promotion to the bench, for this official was essentially the bishop's administrative second-in-command, particularly in legal matters; and five of the ten, including Thomas, first held the lower office, while another was a disappointed candidate. Four of Theobald's clerks were promoted before Thomas and were probably his seniors: Walter, the archbishop's brother, whom he made first archdeacon of Canterbury and then bishop of Rochester, 1148–82; Roger of Pont l'Evêque, his replacement as archdeacon, 1148–54, archbishop of York, 1154–81; John of Pagham, bishop of Worcester, 1151–7; and John of Canterbury, an unsuccessful candidate against Ralf of Diss (Diceto) for the archdeaconry of Middlesex in 1152, but treasurer of York in 1153, bishop of Poitiers in 1162, and archbishop of Narbonne and then of Lyons in 1182, resigning in 1193, eleven years before his death, to become a monk at Clairvaux. Another of the seniors was John of Tilbury, scribe and notary.[13]

Probably junior to Thomas were another four, only two of whom were important in his life. Bartholomew became archdeacon of Exeter in 1155 and bishop of that see, 1161–84, and enjoyed a high reputation as a theologian and canon lawyer; John of Salisbury, after a brilliant but unrewarded career in the schools of Paris, entered Theobald's household through the recommendation of St Bernard, abbot of Clairvaux, in 1147–8 and became the expert on papal affairs, often absent on missions to the curia, perhaps for almost the whole of 1150–3. To complete the list, William of Northolt, who was in the household by 1154, became archdeacon of Gloucester in 1177 and bishop of Worcester, 1186–90; and Master William de Vere, a brother of Aubrey, the first earl of Oxford, and an archiepiscopal clerk by 1152, held the bishopric of Hereford, 1186–98. Arnulf, bishop of Lisieux, who played quite an important part in Thomas's life, expected a visit from William de Vere at Easter 1160, and warmly invited Ralf of Diss, archdeacon of Middlesex, the future dean of St Paul's and distinguished historian, who had recently arrived at the schools of Paris, to join the party. The bonds between Paris scholars were usually very close. Only Thomas seems to have been indifferent to the connection. That put him a little apart in this company.[14]

All these episcopal servants were clerks, men, until promotion to an archdeaconry or similar dignity, in minor orders. Of course not all of Thomas's contemporaries in Theobald's household obtained even an archdeaconry; and among these were some most interesting men. The earliest archiepiscopal document witnessed by Thomas was attested also by Jordan Fantosme, later a clerk of Henry, bishop of Winchester, and master of the school in that city, who wrote an account in French verse of the rebellion of Henry II's sons and the Scottish war of 1173–4. In 1149 a fellow witness was Master Ralf, son of Ranulf Flambard, the great servant of William Rufus and bishop of Durham. And we should also note the presence in Theobald's court since about 1143 of Vacarius, an Italian master who had studied Roman law at Bologna and who after 1154 joined Roger of Pont l'Evêque in the northern province, where he spent the last fifty years of his life. He and John of Salisbury were exponents of the most up-to-date and modish subjects of the most fashionable schools in the West, men who knew everyone of importance who had passed through Paris or Bologna, enormous fishes in a rather small provincial pool. It is probably merely an accident that Vacarius and Thomas are co-witnesses to no extant charter.[15]

About 1168 John of Salisbury, then for some years 'an exile and outlaw' at Rheims, in a letter to John of Tilbury recalled their idyllic days under Theobald. What with philosophic speculations, legal business, services to one another, literary seminars and useful but jolly arguments, there had never been a dull moment and the days had flashed by. He did not mention, but it has recently become clear, that the library facilities at Canterbury were first class and lay behind his great literary works, *Policraticus* and *Metalogicon*, both of which he was to dedicate to Thomas. John, a small and delicate man, warm, lively and playful, a joker with an eye to the ridiculous, the confident member of a learned élite, so sure of his scholarship that he could quote, to amuse his circle, classical authors and other embroideries of his own invention, was everything that Thomas was not.[16] Thomas probably found some of these men culturally, if not intellectually, intimidating. Whatever had happened at Paris, he bore some of the marks of an academic failure. He would probably have found monastic discipline even more daunting; but he was spared that, for, although his new lord was a monk, and, in theory at least, abbot of the cathedral convent of Christ Church, the archiepiscopal household could not have had a monastic tone or practised simple claustral piety. Theobald needed a companion monk, and he seems always to have drawn on the monastery for chaplains. One of these, Richard, prior of the convent Theobald founded at Dover, 1157–74, had an unexpectedly distinguished career, but very much later: a blameless mediocrity, in 1174 he succeeded Thomas as archbishop of Canterbury.

Theobald, once archbishop, seems steadily to have drawn away from his monastic past. Prior Jeremiah and the monks had not been consulted over his appointment, disliked his court of clerks, resented his nepotism and despised him for his initial failure to maintain the rights of his church. In return, Theobald treated them harshly. About 1143 he deposed Jeremiah, and in 1149 helped the new prior, Walter Durdent, to get the bishopric of Chester. In his place he secured the election of his chaplain, Walter Little, who was so appalled by the financial and administrative mess he found that he asked the archbishop to take over. Theobald, we are told, was at first unwilling, but, persuaded by his clerks (and these, of course, included Thomas), took the whole administration into his own hands, appointing his own men to all posts, putting the monks on very short commons, and, when they appealed to Rome against these measures, likened them to dogs, seized the prior's horses and posted soldiers to keep them within the close. Later Theobald had Walter deposed and imprisoned at Gloucester, presumably in the abbey. Theobald also fell foul of the traditionally difficult abbey of St Augustine's at Canterbury.

John of Salisbury, in a letter of rebuke sent to Christ Church from Rheims at the end of 1167, remarked that it was notorious that the monks, by a sort of hereditary right, detested their archbishops: see how they had treated Anselm, Ralf d'Escures, William of Corbeil and Theobald. No one says that Thomas as Theobald's clerk or archdeacon of Canterbury loved the monks of the cathedral city; and most likely the prevailing mood in the household encouraged him to indifference if not to hostility. The old-fashioned Benedictine ideals had gone very much out of fashion. Those educated in the cathedral schools, the bright young men of the new age, were inhabitants of a completely different world. With Thomas, Christ Church had only a posthumous honeymoon.[17]

Theobald recruited so many distinguished clerks because he faced exceptional difficulties.[18] He needed to withstand the challenge from the papal legate, Henry of Winchester, who tried to create for himself a third province in the kingdom; he had to navigate through the war of succession waged by Stephen and Matilda's party; and he had to deal with the many problems caused by the collapse of the traditional strong government in church and state. The pope was the key figure in most of these matters, and the special skills which Theobald looked for in his servants were diplomacy and legal expertise. At the beginning Thomas had no obvious qualifications in either of those fields: fluent spoken Latin was required for diplomacy at the papal curia. Either he was taken on as a financial expert or on the basis of his charm and intelligence. There can be little doubt that he quickly found favour with the archbishop and that his entry into the household caused resentment. He was not well received by Roger of Pont l'Evêque. Edward Grim and the others identify Thomas's introducer by name because Roger began to call the newcomer in derision 'clerk Baillehache'. The established clerk must have considered Thomas's method of entry in some way irregular, perhaps because of his 'advanced' age, perhaps because of his deficient education, probably because Baillehache was a layman and had a particularly inferior office. William fitzStephen says that Roger twice succeeded in having Thomas banished from the archiepiscopal court and that on each occasion the victim took refuge with Theobald's brother, Walter, then archdeacon of Canterbury (before 1148), who managed to effect a reconciliation.

William considered Thomas 'raw and modest' when he fell foul of Roger. The latter seems to have been neither. One of this company, most likely John of Salisbury, some twenty years later when the shock of Thomas's death caused him to reopen all old wounds, reminded William, archbishop of Sens, of a scandal in which Roger had been involved about 1152, to which the French archbishop was privy as he had been staying with his uncle, Henry of Winchester, at the time. It was alleged, John believed with absolute truth, that Roger had had a criminal homosexual relationship with a beautiful boy named Walter. When the youth grew up and began to spread stories about the archdeacon, Roger, by means of some undisclosed judicial procedure, had his eyes put out; and when the victim accused him of this crime, Roger persuaded some secular judges to condemn him to death. He was indeed hanged on a gibbet. These events naturally did not go unnoticed; but Roger escaped the punishment he deserved, largely because of Thomas's efforts. His fellow-clerk enlisted the help of their old colleague John, bishop of Worcester, and the legal expert Hilary, bishop of Chichester; and these persuaded Theobald to accept Roger's 'purgation', that is to say, his denial of the charges on oath, in the chapter house of Christ Church. (It is just possible that Walter could have been a Canterbury monk.) But this secret ceremony was not enough to silence all the archdeacon's detractors, for he next went to Rome and, with the help of Gregory, cardinal of Sant'Angelo, and great gifts made throughout the curia, cleared himself before Pope Eugenius III. Roger was indeed at Rome in 1152; and John of Salisbury should have known, for he was probably in residence at the curia at the same time.[19]

The whole story should not be dismissed as incredible and a mere fabrication of an embittered enemy. We cannot doubt that Roger had been gravely defamed of serious sins and crimes. But it is equally certain that he cleared himself of the charges. This does not mean that he had not committed the offences, but it does reduce the importance of the affair. It is likely that there had been some exaggeration. John of Salisbury revived the story in 1172 both to denigrate Roger and to demonstrate Thomas's extraordinary magnanimity. But it is possible that the two men were never such constant and implacable enemies as is sometimes thought. Indeed, it seems that they had become friends. William of Canterbury believed that three clerks, Roger of Neustria (i.e. of Normandy), who can be none other than the future archbishop of York, John of Canterbury and Thomas, formed an alliance, and contracted that each would protect and advance the interest of the others, especially in their absence from Theobald's court.[20]

All three did well. Thomas's biographers believed that he was employed often in diplomacy with the papal curia, and, if so, he must have brushed up his Latin. The first time he went abroad may have been his attendance at the Council of Rheims in March 1148 with Roger of Pont l'Evêque and John of Salisbury. Theobald made his way there – almost by swimming, as the admiring pope announced – despite Stephen's prohibition, and for his disobedience was punished by exclusion for a time from the kingdom. At Rheims there was much English business, both ecclesiastical and secular, before the council, and John of Salisbury describes some of the most interesting of the proceedings at length in his *Historia Pontificalis*, written probably in 1164–6, when he was in exile at that city. Thomas was being introduced to the great ecclesiastical world, where distinguished church leaders and savants were on show, momentous cases decided and issues of great intellectual and doctrinal importance debated. To have seen and heard, probably

even met, Suger, abbot of St Denis, Bernard of Clairvaux, Peter Lombard, Robert of Melun (perhaps Thomas's old teacher) and Hugh of Amiens, to name only the most famous of those concerned in the case of the orthodoxy of the Paris theologian, Gilbert of la Porée, later bishop of Poitiers, was a wonderful chance.[21]

Also connected with the Council of Rheims was an event which was to have a harmful effect on Thomas's career. When the saintly bishop of Hereford, Robert of Béthune, died at Rheims, Theobald managed to get his friend, Gilbert Foliot, abbot of Gloucester, who had accompanied him to the council, consecrated in his place. This was done in consultation with Henry fitzEmpress, the *de facto* duke of Normandy, who, from his stay at his uncle Robert of Gloucester's court at Bristol a few years before, would have known the abbot and whose supporters controlled the diocese of Hereford. Eugenius also colluded, for he was coming round to the Angevin side and took the opportunity to spite Stephen. Gilbert obtained possession of the see through some remarkable diplomacy; but one thing he could not fix: his ambition to retain his abbey in plurality, on the model of Henry of Winchester, was defeated by the monks.

Gilbert, of noble birth, a former clerk and master and then monk and prior of Cluny, a good scholar and theologian and an ascetic of the purest morals, indeed insufferably righteous, a man with wide connections in the Western church and known in high places, was to become the Doeg (1 Sam. 21–2), the Ahithophel (2 Sam. 15–17), the ruler of the synagogue, even the Judas in Thomas's life, according to the archbishop's supporters. Some men, including perhaps Theobald, possibly Gilbert himself, may have seen in the new bishop of Hereford a future archbishop of Canterbury. He was roughly in the tradition of Lanfranc, Anselm and Theobald. Anonymous II, who seems to have been connected with London, Gilbert's later appointment, thought that King Henry II too, until he was captivated by Thomas, thought of him as the natural successor to Theobald. Be that as it may, Gilbert's secure social position, impeccable career and traditional if rather 'black' churchmanship were to constitute a rebuke, and sometimes a threat, to Thomas's more unconventional career. Yet he too had his weaknesses. His behaviour in 1148 does not appear to have been entirely straight; and on some other occasions his actions could be looked at askance. But he was so high-principled that only the implacably hostile could suggest that lofty motives sometimes concealed self-interest. Despite all the dissimilarities, the two men seem, at least until 1163, to have been on excellent terms. Thomas is said to have had a high regard for Gilbert, and both as royal chancellor and as reforming archbishop could view him as a natural ally.[22]

At the end of 1149 or early in 1150 Theobald was at last appointed papal

legate by Eugenius; and Thomas may have played some part in this. In 1151 he was again at the curia, this time involved in the delicate matter of the proposed coronation of Stephen's son, Eustace, which Theobald wanted to avoid. The papal prohibition to the archbishop which he secured probably harmed considerably the prospects of the house of Blois. And in a letter he wrote early in 1166 to Cardinal Boso, papal chancellor and historian, perhaps an Englishman, reminding him of the constant faithfulness of Canterbury to Rome, he also reminded the cardinal that Roger of Pont l'Evêque had gone to the curia on behalf of the king and barons to try to obtain a release from the prohibition which Theobald steadfastly refused to disregard. In the summer of 1168, however, conveniently forgetting his own part and completely shifting his stance, he recalled how Gregory, cardinal-deacon of Sant'Angelo, who foresaw Henry II's tyranny, had wisely tried to persuade Eugenius to allow Eustace to be crowned, for it was easier to hold a ram by its horns than a lion by its tail.[23]

There is general agreement among his biographers that Thomas served the archbishop wisely and well. The only detailed remarks on this topic, however, come from Robert of Cricklade, through the rather opaque medium of the Icelandic Saga. Theobald, we are told, was an upright man, but quick tempered, and sometimes spoke far too rashly. He also, when dealing with powerful men, trimmed his speech according to how the business was received. Thomas's contribution was to remedy both those weaknesses: to turn away the archbishop's wrath with his own humility, and, when Theobald was at a loss when making a case, to come to his aid and supplement his arguments, rather as if he was glossing a text.[24]

It is also agreed that, through his charm and ability, Thomas became the favourite of the ageing archbishop. It seems, however, that most of his early preferments came from elsewhere. A few days before his death he reminded the abbot of St Albans that it was his monastery which had given him his first 'honour', the church of Bramfield in Hertfordshire, when he was young and poor. Probably a more substantial reward came to him by the gift of his former colleague, John of Pagham, bishop of Worcester (i.e. after 4 March 1151), in the shape of the church of St Mary-le-Strand in London, formerly the chapel of the Holy Innocents. He then obtained from Theobald the church of Otford in Kent; and from the bishop of London (possibly Richard of Beaumais II, 1152–62) and the bishop of Lincoln (Robert of Chesney) prebends in their cathedral churches. As chancellor and archbishop Thomas was to be deeply involved in the affairs of the bishopric of London; and one of his fellow-prebendaries at Lincoln was Philip de Broi, whose case precipitated his quarrel with the king. Another Lincoln dignitary with whom he may have had close relations was Richard d'Ameri.[25]

Theobald must also have had his clerk's promotion in mind, for he granted

him leave of absence for a year to study law at Bologna and then at Auxerre. John of Salisbury believed that he studied both roman and canon law in those schools and that the purpose was to equip him as a pleader and judge in the ecclesiastical courts. The choice of Bologna needs no explanation; and another Englishman studying there in the early 1150s in the school of Hubert Crivelli, the future Pope Urban III, was the much younger man, Baldwin, later one of the greatest English decretalists, progressively arch-deacon of Totnes, abbot of Ford, bishop of Worcester and Richard of Dover's successor as archbishop of Canterbury, who died on the Third Crusade. Thomas himself may have met Hubert at this time, for when in exile (1164–70) he attracted him, then archdeacon of Bourges, into his circle as a legal adviser. Auxerre was possibly chosen because Gilbert, later bishop of London, had taught there in the 1120s. But, as usual with Thomas's schooling, we have no details and scant proof of his attainments. He was not another Gilbert the Universal or Baldwin of Ford. Nor are we told that he was coached in law in Theobald's household by Master Vacarius, perhaps simply because this expert later went over to the 'other side'.[26]

Although Thomas was doing well, he was still in the years before 1154, when he reached his mid-thirties, merely a man of promise, a household clerk who had acquired little of substance or dignity. To depend on favour had its risks, as he had learnt at the beginning; and few suitable vacancies occurred in the English church in the period 1148–54. In Thomas's circle John of Pagham got the one plum, the rich see of Worcester, in 1151. London, which remained vacant until 1152, and Durham were impervious to Theobald's influence. St Asaph was suited only to the romancer, Geoffrey of Monmouth, the inventor of the Arthurian legend. But Theobald had a great success in June 1154 when William fitzHerbert, Stephen's nephew, who had had such a chequered career, died soon after his restoration by the pope to the archbishopric of York. It was rumoured that he had been poisoned; and the miracles he worked at his tomb earned his canonization in 1226. Theobald secured the election of Roger of Pont l'Evêque to the northern see, and appointed Thomas to the vacant archdeaconry of Canter-bury. Moreover, Roger, then or later, gave his former colleague and quite clearly friend, the valuable provostship of Beverley. In 1166 the exiled primate answered the taunt of Gilbert Foliot, by then bishop of London, speaking for 'the clergy of England', that he was guilty of ingrati-tude to the king who had raised him up from poverty, by retorting that he did not think that the archdeaconry of Canterbury, the provostship of Beverley, many churches, quite a lot of prebends, and not a few other things which he possessed when made royal chancellor exactly represented in worldly terms poverty. William fitzStephen believed that the arch-deaconry was worth £100 a year. Thomas himself may have boasted in 1166 that it had brought him in 300 marks or pounds a year.[27]

The relationship between Thomas and Roger became difficult after the younger man was elected to Canterbury. The *ex officio* rivalry and Thomas's and Canterbury's misfortunes pulled them apart. But there seem never to have been any personal difficulties and as late as the summer of 1170, when Roger was threatening to injure their 'common mother' and his former colleague, Thomas wrote respectfully and peaceably to him. It was after the martyrdom that the full fury of the victim's clerks was unleashed against him.

Thomas may have taken the minor orders which followed the tonsure up to subdeacon after entering Theobald's household; the archbishop, as was usual, consecrated him deacon as a preliminary to collating him to the archdeaconry. He was now precluded from marrying, bearing arms and pursuing other unsuitable activities. FitzStephen thought that this office put Thomas next in dignity in the English church to the bishops and abbots; and he was probably right. Thomas retained the archdeaconry until 1163, but held it alone only for the three months before his appointment as royal chancellor in January 1155. To judge by the reticence of his biographers, he must have been an absentee, delegating his duties to an unidentified deputy. Anonymous I says that, although he was very splendid, he was never arrogant, and distributed his great wealth in alms to the poor. Herbert of Bosham admitted with regret that, when he became chancellor, he neglected his deanery. He did not, however, neglect its profits. There was some trouble in 1156–7 over aids levied by the archdeacon on Theobald's churches; and Theobald, as an act of restitution and penance before his death, abolished the bad custom of 'second aids' which his brother Walter had imposed on the churches of the archdeaconry, and forbade their collection in future under pain of anathema. But Thomas, to the great grief of the archbishop, objected to this arbitrary reduction of his income; and we do not know how the sorry story ended. It was also remembered in the diocese of Lincoln that Thomas had taken money from sinners in commutation of penance. But when the archdeacons cited this in their own defence, Bishop Hugh of Avalon (1186–1200) replied smartly, 'Believe me, it was not that which made him a saint.'[28]

In the one surviving administrative document, composed in typical chancery style, the royal favourite is entitled 'Thomas, royal chancellor and archdeacon of Canterbury'. His personal seal, which he had probably acquired while in Theobald's household, was an antique gem showing a naked figure, helmeted and resting against a pillar, with the legend 'Sigillum Tome Lund.' – the seal of Thomas of London. Such antique gems were reaching western Europe in large quantities in the twelfth century, to be used mostly as personal signets. Thomas is most likely to have acquired his in Paris or Bologna.

The figure on the intaglio has been identified as Mercury, but may be the Argive hero, Perseus, 'the destroyer', or the young Mars. His predecessor in the archdeaconry, Roger of Pont l'Evêque, had a gem with a triple-faced mask of Greek comedy engraved on it and the legend, 'Caput nostrum trinitas est' – our head is a trinity. It might be unfair to describe Thomas as the worst type of medieval archdeacon; but no one seems to have thought much of his behaviour.[29]

Before we leave the archbishop's clerk and then archdeacon, we should note the width of his ecclesiastical experience. As Theobald's confidential agent he knew Canterbury and the whole English church, its personnel and institutions, inside out; and, through his association with John of Salisbury and Vacarius and his diplomatic missions to the papal curia, he had acquired not only a good knowledge of the Western church at large but also of its mainspring, the papal household. When seven years later Thomas became, to most people's surprise, archbishop of Canterbury, he was not an innocent intruded into a strange world.

Moreover, he would have learnt from Theobald a style of archiepiscopal government which had been proved successful. Theobald had recovered from a most unfavourable start which was in no way of his own making. His, too, had been an unexpected and considerably resented appointment. But, through patient diplomacy, perseverance, sometimes dignified resistance to superiors and often overbearing behaviour to inferior authorities, he had restored Canterbury to its traditional position and raised himself to the undoubted ruler of the English church. Aided by the strength of conservative feeling in that body, he had survived or defeated the revisionist ambitions of Henry of Winchester. He had profited from the misfortunes of the rival metropolitan church of York and in the end had made his own clerk its archbishop. He had served Stephen loyally, but had managed to secure the succession of the 'rightful heir', Henry fitzEmpress, duke of Normandy, the future Henry II. He had protected the liberties of the church as best he could whenever the secular powers had threatened them. All this he had done with the help of an able household. He had also benefited from his realization that the pope had become an important power, and was as likely to help the humble as the proud. Henry of Winchester, although he seemed to have every advantage – the highest birth, wonderful connections and influence, great wealth – usually overplayed his hand and alarmed the curia.

But, although Thomas could have learnt the virtues of patience and caution, he may rather have considered them the hateful penalties that the weak had to pay for survival. He himself, supported neither by kin nor by office and making his way by his wits, had a position of servitude which he had to endure, but from which one day he might perhaps be able to escape. As a merchant's son he may have thought that the dazzling Henry of Winchester was more to be admired than the knight's son from Thierville, and, remarkably, it was probably Henry who of all the English bishops was most affected by Thomas's death. It is clear, however, that Thomas served Theobald faithfully up to 1155 and held his master in respect. But in some ways the ten years he spent as his clerk were a fairly lengthy interlude in what by 1162 he may have considered his true vocation. In 1172 William, monk of Canterbury, when recording the martyr's miracles, remarked that Thomas had always, both in the world and now in heaven, been most partial to the knightly order. And it is noticeable that as a saint he was much involved in the cure and recovery of hawks as well as of their masters.[30] Although some of his erstwhile friends and most of the hagiographers thought that he reneged in 1155, to all appearances he escaped to freedom, to a world in which the young eagle could really spread his wings.

CHAPTER THREE

ROYAL CHANCELLOR, 1155–1162

In 1153–4 Theobald was much involved in settling the dynastic war between Stephen and his young cousin-once-removed, Henry fitzEmpress, whose star was rising fast. In 1152, Henry, already duke of Normandy and count of Anjou, became also duke of Aquitaine in the right of his wife. In January 1153 he invaded England, and, although he had little real military success, luck began to desert Stephen, and with it much baronial and ecclesiastical support. Queen Matilda had died in 1152, and on 17 August 1153 died suddenly Stephen's son and heir, Eustace, a fine soldier on whom he had set all his hopes. By the end of the year Theobald had arranged that Stephen was to keep the crown for the rest of his life, but was to adopt Henry as his heir instead of his second son, William, earl of Surrey. At Easter 1154, when Henry returned to the Continent, the compact seemed to be breaking up. But on 25 October Stephen himself died unexpectedly, and on 8 December Henry returned and took over the kingdom without hindrance.

The reuniting of England with Normandy, even if there was now association also with Anjou and Aquitaine, seems to have been popular, if only because it brought the expectation of peace to a very disturbed kingdom. And there was a similar attitude towards the new ruler. The senior grandson of the king whose death had closed what was beginning to be considered a Golden Age, he was undoubtedly the most suitable of the great-grandsons of the Conqueror to wear the English crown. But Henry's succession also signified a sort of Angevin conquest; the youth was little known in England; and his few military interventions in the civil war had usually been disastrous. Moreover, he had no reputation for trustworthiness or good judgement. All the same, there had always been a small devoted 'Angevin' party in the kingdom, and the young prince, now in his twenty-second year, had recently become fortune's darling. Men were not only attracted by the legitimacy of his claim but also were looking to the future, opting for promise. What Henry's English backers now wanted was to get him under control, provide him with wise counsel and educate him in the ways of the Anglo-

Norman kingdom, in order to minimize his Angevin heritage and, in so far as the church was concerned, check any anti-clerical prejudices he might have inherited from his haughty mother and brutal father.

In Normandy Henry's chief ecclesiastical adviser had been Arnulf, bishop of Lisieux, a man in his late forties, a well-connected and well-educated prelate who had been on the Second Crusade, was known at Rome, and who enjoyed a literary reputation which was only to be surpassed by John of Salisbury. But the English church wanted its own man close to the king; and the agent chosen by Theobald was his clerk and archdeacon, Thomas of London. Henry, in one of his rages against his former friend in December 1170, was believed to have exclaimed that this proud traitor was the very man who had first pushed his way into his court on a panniered and limping nag.[1] Thomas had entered Theobald's court attended by a single squire and it may be that he considered a modest approach to a new master the proper thing to do.

Henry was crowned at Westminster by Theobald on 19 December 1154 and spent Christmas at Bermondsey. Arnulf of Lisieux remained in attendance; but from some point in January Thomas began to witness royal charters as chancellor. Stephen's chancellor had been Robert of Ghent, dean of York, and there could have been no question of his remaining in office. Thomas's appointment was generally regarded as Theobald's work; but William fitzStephen thought that Henry of Winchester was another advocate, while Anonymous I believed that Theobald associated Arnulf of Lisieux and Philip of Harcourt, once Stephen's chancellor and since 1142 bishop of Bayeux, with his representations. The chancellor was the chief ecclesiastical servant in the royal household and received the largest salary of all the household officials, 5s. a day. He was in charge of the chapel royal and its subsidiary, the *scriptorium*, or writing office, and so was responsible for the church services at court and for the secretariat and royal archives. Among the clerks he inherited or recruited were Ernulf, Herbert of Bosham, Gervase of Chichester and probably William fitzStephen. The chancellor travelled with the king in the ambulatory court and was in frequent personal contact with him. It must be remembered, however, that the greatness to which Thomas temporarily raised the office was mostly due to the friendship which developed between him and Henry. The royal chancellor was essentially and historically merely a royal chaplain and chief clerk, who had traditionally been rewarded with a bishopric on retirement. Moreover, under Stephen his position had probably deteriorated with that of the king, for in 1140 Stephen had failed in his attempt to appoint Philip of Harcourt, then dean of Lincoln and archdeacon of Evreux, to Salisbury. No previous chancellor, except Roger le Poer, who held the office for only a couple of years at the beginning of Henry I's reign, had been a man of any great importance at court or anything beyond a trusted servant.[2]

The office had in the past often, perhaps usually, been purchased, and for a very considerable sum of money. The transaction was on a par with the fine or relief which, in the case of a secular office, an heir paid to the king for succeeding to his father's position; and the Pipe Rolls are strewn with the records of such bargains. In 1166 Gilbert Foliot, bishop of London, ingeniously turned Thomas's alleged purchase of the chancellorship into a charge of simony against him: the archdeacon had made a definite bid (the implication is that he had rivals) and had paid several thousand marks for the office, and with it the expectation of the archbishopric. Ralf Niger, a pupil of John of Salisbury and in his circle, thought the same. This, however, is almost certainly untrue. Even if we take with a grain of salt fitz-Stephen's answer to the charge – that, since the chancellor could become a bishop or archbishop, if he wished, the office was not for sale – when we consider the matter in the context of all Thomas's financial dealings with the king, it is impossible to believe that he ever paid a penny. Like most of the lucrative custodies which he received from Henry, it was never recorded as a debt on the Pipe Rolls; and, even more to the point, it does not seem to have been reactivated by the king during the financial wrangling which followed Thomas's resignation of the office. There appear, therefore, to be only three possibilities: that Thomas had paid Henry some five thousand marks in some unrecorded way before 1164, that the debt had been quickly and irrevocably cancelled, or that it had never existed. Of these the first seems the most improbable. Most likely Theobald and Thomas paid for the office by their untiring support for Henry's cause and interests. Perhaps even Gilbert Foliot would not have considered that a heinous simoniacal bargain.[3]

Thomas's change of master may not have been quite as sudden as the bare notice of the event in the biographies would suggest. He must have taken some part in the negotiations which led to Henry's succession and could have been one of Theobald's diplomatic agents. The biographers' concealment of such a role is only to be expected. Thomas's charm and other personal qualities no doubt appealed to Henry in the same way as they had attracted Theobald some ten years earlier. At first sight, however, it is the disparity between the two men which is the more obvious, their birth, profession and age, the king twenty-one, the clerk at least thirty-five. But they also had things in common: Henry as much as Thomas had been an adventurer, with his fair share of reverses; he too was a man of considerable intelligence with a rather sketchy education; both were athletic, with a passion for field sports, and Thomas added warfare enthusiastically when he got the chance. King and chancellor, although always master and servant, became great friends; but again this intimacy may have taken time to develop. Some biographers, but not William fitzStephen, who was in the best position to know, mention the difficulties Thomas experienced at the royal court. John of Salisbury, followed by Anonymous I, puts these at the beginning of his service; Herbert of Bosham makes them a standing feature. They speak of the envy of the courtiers and their tale-bearing. This was only to be expected and was similar to what he had suffered in the beginning at Theobald's court. It was the way of the world. The first two writers also thought that the chancellor complained tearfully to Theobald and other old friends of the burden of his new office and used to say how happy he would be if only he could give it up. Such protestations also are not unusual and can be variously explained.[4]

All observers were impressed by the grandeur, ostentation and apparent worldliness of Thomas's life once he had fully established himself at the royal court and become the king's best friend. Typically, he imitated Henry, bishop of Winchester, and King Henry I in keeping wild animals, including monkeys to adorn his cortèges and a couple of wolves to be used in hunting their own kind. Contemporaries stress the great wealth (mostly the king's) at his disposal, the magnificence of his household and retinue, the sumptuousness of his furnishings and apparel, the crowds of servants, the throng of guests at his table, including, according to Guernes, even harlots and lechers, the lavishness of his alms, the squadrons of choice knights, the six or more ships, some his own, required for his household when he crossed the Channel. His custody of the honour of Eye gave him the service of at least eighty knights, Berkhamsted about twenty-three. Magnates, not only English but also from the neighbouring lands, put their sons to be educated in his household or sent them to be knighted, and Thomas retained the best of these in his own service. One of those he knighted was Baldwin, son of Arnoul, count of Guines, near Boulogne, in Flanders, and his successor in 1169, who later was to show his gratitude. To crown all, Thomas was even entrusted, probably in 1162, with the king's son and heir, the young Henry. Many – fitzStephen says 'innumerable' – barons and knights did him homage, saving the fealty they owed to the king; and among these, he claims, were William de Tracy, Reginald fitzUrse and Hugh de Morville, three of his murderers.[5]

Thomas gloried in all the pomps of the world. FitzStephen, who saw less fault in all this than did some of the others, and devoted many more pages to it, depicts the king and his chancellor as boon companions, in and out of each other's apartments, gaming, fowling and hunting together, as close off duty as on. He tells the famous story of how, when riding together through London one winter's day, the king noticed a poor old man shivering in the cold, and, as a merry jest, forced Thomas to give in alms his brand new scarlet cloak lined with miniver, the two men, having

dismounted, wrestling together until Thomas gave way. Obsequious attendants, of course, then offered the chancellor their own. It was thought
that Thomas outshone the king in his magnificence; and it is probable that
both men, brought up in relative poverty, revelled in the great wealth of
England, and that Henry took pleasure in indulging his 'low-born' favourite
in his extravagance. For Thomas, the bottomless purse, the limitless credit,
the satisfaction of all his caprices, his freedom from everyone but the king,
must have been pure heaven. He was even able to lavish presents on his
master. Once he gave Henry three ships which he had had built and fully
equipped.

Inevitably the biographers tried to explain the appearances away. Most
considered that he had done his best for the church in very difficult circumstances; some averred that he had the good of the kingdom at heart and
influenced the king to act justly. William fitzStephen believed that he had
ensured that vacancies in the bishoprics and abbeys were kept short and
were filled gratis with the best candidate. He had poor scholars recalled
from France and suitably endowed in England. There were in fact only
four episcopal vacancies during his chancellorship, and these lasted at Worcester in 1157–8 for a year, at Coventry–Chester in 1159–61 for sixteen
months, at Exeter in 1160–1 for a year and at Canterbury in 1161–2 for
fourteen months. This was, indeed, a pretty good if not impeccable record.
The evidence from the abbeys, although less precise, seems even better:
vacancies appear usually to have been for less than a year, except at Ramsey
in 1160–1 and possibly Tewkesbury in 1161–2.

The two repatriated scholars named by fitzStephen are William, prior
of St Martin-des-Champs, Paris, given Ramsey in 1161, and the Paris master,
Robert of Melun, appointed to Hereford in 1163. This policy, therefore,
would seem to be associated more with Thomas's visit to Paris in 1158
and with his custody of, and then promotion to, Canterbury than with
his chancellorship. FitzStephen also informs us that Thomas interested Henry
in Merton priory and persuaded him to complete at his expense the building
of the church from the transeptal crossing westwards, to increase the monastery's endowments and once to spend the three penitential days before Easter
in retreat there.[6] The clerk's supporting evidence, therefore, shows Thomas
patronizing his own particular interests and cannot really be stretched to
support the case alleged, however good that might be.

With evidence for great ecclesiastical zeal in short supply, and faced with
a few awkward matters, most biographers took the line that the outward
show was a necessary camouflage for the continuing integrity of his private
life. He did good works secretly and remained chaste. He was a second
Joseph at the court of Pharaoh. John of Salisbury thought that he became
the perfect courtier so that he could recall his colleagues from error. Herbert

of Bosham testifies to his chastity at great length. But Edward Grim, one of the earliest investigators, also reported that some men thought otherwise.[7]

A few stories were told to prove the hidden purity of his life. Robert of Cricklade, according to the Icelandic Saga, related how a close kinsman of his, when he went to the royal court on some business, decided first to approach the chancellor, and, setting off at dawn for his lodgings, passed him in the twilight prostrate before the doors of a church. William fitz-Stephen thought that, although Henry deliberately put temptation in his way, Thomas was so occupied with his duties that he had no time for such distractions. He also attested that he had heard from the very lips of Thomas's confessor, Robert, canon of Merton, that from the day he became chancellor he abstained totally from sexual activity. As a confessor was bound to secrecy, and would not have babbled to anyone as unimportant as the chancellor's clerk, this revelation is unlikely to have been made before 1171, and is of less value than would at first appear. On a par is the evidence of Anonymous I, derived, he claims, from men who had been twenty years or more in Thomas's service, that, even when doctors had advised their master to indulge in sex for the sake of his health, he had refused that sort of medicine on the grounds that, rather than healing, it polluted both body and soul.

That Thomas had strong passions can hardly be doubted, and is supported by two other disclosures made by fitzStephen. One of the chancellor's clerks, Richard of Ambli, a man of high birth, seduced the wife of a colleague who had been long abroad and who, he suggested, must have died. Such was Thomas's hatred of unchastity that he had Richard imprisoned in chains in the Tower of London. FitzStephen may be right; but the punishment, even if sharp, must have been short. A Richard of Ambl(ia) appears on the Pipe Rolls, sometimes in association with the chancellor, from the beginning of the reign until Michaelmas 1159, and again at Michaelmas 1161, as the recipient of various royal favours. Moreover, he may well be the distinguished clerk, Richard d'Ameri, who appears similarly at Michaelmas 1160 and 1162, thus filling the gaps. In 1161 and 1162 the entries are connected with Thomas's custody of Berkhamsted. This Richard, from the Oxfordshire family of Amory or Damory, succeeded his kinsman, Roger, as precentor of the cathedral of Lincoln in 1160–1 and became also archdeacon of Stow. With an even more famous clerk, Richard of Ilchester, he was royal custodian of the vacant bishopric in 1166–74.

FitzStephen also reveals that the chancellor used often, but secretly, to accept discipline, that is to say scourging, on his bare back, at the hands of Ralf, prior of Holy Trinity, Aldgate (1147–67), when he was in the vicinity of London, and of Thomas, priest of St Martin's, Canterbury, a rectory in the archbishop's collation, when he was near that city. Discipline of this sort was, of course, intended either to tame or to punish the flesh; but, as is equally well known, is not always effective. In any case, fitzStephen may have been antedating the habit.[8]

Finally in this context a story which originated with William of Canterbury, but is retold with additional, and once discordant, detail by Guernes, concerns Thomas and the beautiful Avice of Stafford, a former mistress of the king, who may possibly have been the sister or daughter of Robert II, lord of Stafford and sheriff of the county at that time, a member of the large and important Tosny family. When Thomas visited Stafford, or, according to Guernes, was lodging with Vivian, the clerk at Stoke-on-Trent (some 15 miles north), Avice sent him gifts. The landlord suspected that she was trying to get a new lover, and secretly inspected his lodger's bedroom in the middle of the night to see if he had indeed gone to visit her. Everything looked so undisturbed that Vivian thought at first that it was deserted. But then, raising his lamp, he perceived Thomas lying on the floor by the bed, his feet and legs naked. He had fallen asleep exhausted after arduous prayers.[9]

Herbert of Bosham, reflecting in old age on these matters, produced the most elaborate defence, from the ecclesiastical standpoint, of Thomas's behaviour. Granted that the archdeacon had been forced into royal service for a laudable purpose – the reconciliation of church and state – he justifiably followed at court the path of prudence, and wisely dissimulated, so that he should seem to do what he did not do, and seem not to do what he did do. Hence a series of paradoxes: in the interests of charity he often acted contrary to charity, against the law for the sake of law, against religion for religion's sake. He was like David feigning madness at Gath in order to escape (1 Sam. 21 : 13–15), Judith playing the harlot so as to save Jerusalem (Judith 10–13). And so Thomas in the royal court put off the archdeacon for the time being, diligently heeding the times rather than reason, vanity rather than truth. It was as though he cried out daily to his fellow courtiers that verse of St Paul (2 Cor. 12 : 11), 'I am become a fool in glorying; ye have compelled me.'[10]

But before Thomas became archbishop it is doubtful whether any defence at all was needed for the clerk's behaviour. A basic feature of medieval life was man's servitude, and the constant aim of the careerist was to find a more important lord. By the twelfth century, as a result of the several ecclesiastical reform movements in the eleventh, the propriety of clerks and priests serving a secular lord could be questioned and could pose problems for tender consciences. Archbishop Anselm of Canterbury had been disturbed by some aspects of his feudal subjection to Kings William Rufus and Henry I, and the ambitious Henry of Winchester had raised the flag of clerical independence during his brother Stephen's reign. But the rank

and file of the bishops and abbots held fast to Jesus's, 'Render unto Caesar
...' and to the late fifth-century Gelasian expression of the two powers
in this world, each with its proper place. Towards the end of Henry II's
reign, Peter of Blois, archdeacon of Bath, wrote two rhetorical exercises,
one condemning the practice of clerks serving a king, the second condoning
and even justifying it. For was not the king the Lord's anointed and entrusted
by God with thaumaturgical powers? It was a problem of which John
of Salisbury became increasingly aware. He knew how hard it was for a
Christian, a stranger and pilgrim amid a bewildering maze of paths, to
choose the right road to salvation, and in his *Policraticus*, which he dedicated
to Thomas, tried to chart for courtiers this perilous world, to distinguish
between *nugae* and *seria*, trifles and matters of importance. It is of interest
that he seems never to have been outraged by married archdeacons.[11]

Such problems were, however, for the elect and the morbid, and before
1162 Thomas of London seems not to have been troubled by them at all.
He was simply on the make. But when as archbishop he suddenly became
scrupulous, his previous indifference became a weapon in the hands of his
enemies, an embarrassment to his supporters. Some loyal servants of the
church found his behaviour as chancellor hard to forgive. John of Salisbury
was one of the most outspoken. Edward Grim, even after the martyrdom,
drew attention to the dangers and temptations into which the chancellor
had fallen.[12] The biographers, therefore, as a whole, looked askance at his
achievements as chancellor. But what exactly those achievements were is
not easy to assess.

Thomas was in the king's company, apart from brief missions out of
court, from Christmas 1154 until May 1162, when Henry dispatched him
from Normandy to England in order to be elected archbishop of Canterbury.
He was, therefore, mostly out of England, for Henry in the first eight
years of his reign spent only the initial year and the sixteen months from
April 1157 to August 1158 in the kingdom. Henry's security in England
had to be assured; but the business of his French fiefs was of most concern,
for he had been at war with Louis VII since 1152. William fitzStephen stresses
that Thomas was a member of the king's council and did not need an invitation to attend its meetings. But he was, of course, one of many, and,
although used from the start to greet foreign embassies, could never have
become a real expert on foreign affairs. He was one of a fairly constant
group of household officials which travelled with the king: the co-justiciar,
Richard de Lucy; the chief steward or seneschal, Manasser Bisset; a chamberlain, Warin fitzGerold; a constable, Richard de Humet; and a knight, Jocelin
de Balliol. All these, except Lucy, were in Henry's service before he became
king. Henry was usually accompanied also by his youngest brother William and
by several earls and barons. Bishops Philip of Bayeux and Arnulf of Lisieux

always rejoined him when he was in Normandy. In England Archbishop Theobald (Roger of York less often), together with other bishops, was usually at court. And the king, as he perambulated his dominions, must also have relied on the local officials and aristocracy for advice.[13]

Thomas, however, was the most 'familiar' of these *familiares* and *curiales*, the closest to the king, the most trusted. In financial matters he was allowed a freedom from account which was to prove dangerous. Naturally Henry did not always take his advice – he was not besotted: he remained shrewd and fundamentally cautious; but Thomas soon became a man of power and influence. Once, probably when the king and chancellor were in England, perhaps as early as 1155, Arnulf of Lisieux wrote a revealing letter to his 'venerable and dear friend'. The theme was friendship, a key twelfth-century topic, and the difficulty of keeping friends and trusting colleagues in the ambitious and emulous society at court. The young king, he feared, might be inconstant, and he relied on Thomas to keep him in royal favour during his absence. He was not writing to Thomas in this vein in order, as they say, to teach Minerva her letters, but felt free with a true friend to let his words run away with him. The warm and slightly indiscreet letter shows that Arnulf recognized and accepted the influential position that the chancellor had acquired to his own detriment, but still had confidence in him.[14]

Thomas was making new friends and becoming forgetful of some from the past. Geographical detachment must have contributed to the weakening of old allegiances. By the autumn of 1156 he had already distanced himself in every way from Canterbury and its affairs. At that time John of Salisbury, whom he had left in charge of his interests at the archbishop's court, incurred the king's anger, apparently as a result of stories told by Arnulf of Lisieux about his conduct at the papal curia. And when the terrified clerk begged Thomas for help, he ventured to approach him only through his secretary, Master Ernulf. Nor is there on record any expression of John's thanks for the chancellor's services in this matter.[15]

It was believed that Thomas played some part in the restoration of good order and regular royal government in England in the period immediately after Henry's accession. He was not, of course, responsible for either the policy behind or the contents of the royal documents he issued, as the dispute in Lent 1155 over whether Henry should confirm Battle abbey's royal charters makes perfectly clear. These Battle privileges were not only of doubtful authenticity – one was a brand new forgery – but also prejudicial to the rights of its diocesan, the bishop of Chichester, who was supported by the metropolitan. When it was learned that the king had ordered Thomas to have his confirmation sealed, Theobald objected, and Henry sent for Thomas and countermanded the order. But, while the king was trying to hear Mass, back came the abbot to protest against this change of policy, and Henry once again sent for his chancellor so as to reaffirm his original order, a decision to which he held firm even when it next brought in the indignant Hilary of Chichester. But Thomas was instructed to retain the charter until it could be scrutinized in the presence of the archbishop; and, when it received a hostile reception at Lambeth, he took it back with him and deposited it in the chapel royal. Finally in July Henry yielded to the abbot and allowed him to take the sealed charter away. That, however, was not the end of the story.[16]

In this initial period, in which Henry established his authority in England, Thomas accompanied him on his campaign against dissident northern and Welsh marcher barons in May 1155 and could have been engaged in the expulsion of mercenary soldiers and the slighting of unauthorized castles, the aftermath of the civil war. But if he was involved in the measures which led to Henry of Winchester taking refuge at Cluny, the great bishop took no lasting offence. FitzStephen relates that Thomas also, and here we may think that his interests were fully engaged, had Rufus's Westminster Hall, which had become ruinous, repaired between one Easter and Whitsuntide (either in 1155 or 1158), by using an army of carpenters. As chancellor he had duties at the royal exchequer, the board of officials which scrutinized and accounted for the English crown revenues. But he could have discharged these in person only at Easter and Michaelmas 1155 and at the two Easter and one Michaelmas sessions in 1157–8. In any case it was Nigel, bishop of Ely, whom Henry appointed to reconstruct the financial administration and the exchequer after the 'anarchy'. Thomas became a spending, not an accounting officer. He also, when in England, sat occasionally, usually with a more senior royal official, like the justiciar, the earl of Leicester, or the constable and sheriff, Henry of Essex, as a judge; but clearly only as a stop-gap.[17]

One case in which he was involved, the abbey of Battle v. the bishop of Chichester in May 1157, which is described at length in the Battle Chronicle, is of considerable interest for the light it sheds on Thomas's attitude. In the twelfth century, bishops, when attempting to establish orderly diocesan government, came up against claims of exemption from their jurisdiction, usually advanced by monasteries; and by 1123 the papacy had switched its support from the monasteries to the episcopate. We have already seen how Theobald, no doubt helped by Thomas, exerted his authority over Christ Church and St Augustine's, Canterbury. Similarly, Hilary, bishop of Chichester, a most experienced canon lawyer, supported by papal authority and by his metropolitan, Theobald, was attempting to break the independence of the royal foundation (*Eigenkloster*), St Martin's Battle. The abbot defended himself with the help of a series of royal charters of doubtful authenticity, which, as we have seen, he managed to get confirmed in 1155, and also, most impudently, by some new forgeries specially designed to meet the objections to his case which had been raised in that year. Not only were royal charters in question but the abbot, Walter de Lucy, was the brother of Richard, the royal justiciar. Thomas was now firmly in this other camp.

Many of his duties at the hearing of the case at Colchester, mainly before the king in person, were administrative: he served as the court's clerk, reading out the evidence, calling on the parties in turn to plead, and generally controlling the procedure. But after Henry had taken offence at Hilary's indiscreet questioning of the validity of royal authority in such ecclesiastical matters, he instructed Thomas to act as the abbot's advocate, an office he performed enthusiastically and successfully. In the end Hilary was forced to submit. It is possible that Theobald was hurt by his protégé's failure to influence the king to favour the bishops. But he should not have been surprised; and there is no place here for moral reflections. Moral issues were not involved: Hilary's introduction of great principles probably embarrassed all others concerned; Thomas was a royal servant and in this case was acting for the crown. It is unlikely that he had the slightest twinge of conscience. In the summer of 1168, however, in a letter to the pope, he cited this case as an example of how royal authority, aided by a servile court, frustrated papal authority. But he did not mention that, when Hilary had challenged Henry's competence in the matter at issue and had remarked *inter alia* that a bishop could not be deprived of his see except by the judgement or permission of the pope, the king had extended his arms and replied, 'Very true; he can't be deposed; but look (and at this he gave a violent shove with his hands), he can be given the push.' In 1157 this sally had been received with sycophantic laughter. Thomas did not think it so funny in 1168.[18]

Thomas's services to the king were well rewarded. The chancellorship itself was a profitable office, attracting gifts of all sorts as well as fees. Thomas when archbishop is said to have prohibited all venality to his own chancellor, Master Ernulf, although, no doubt, only going, as elsewhere, from one extreme to another. In the years after 1154 he had obtained, probably from a variety of benefactors, a number of church benefices, including the deanery of Hastings; and these, with his archdeaconry, would have provided him with a useful basic income. But most important were the crumbs from his lord's table. One of the chancellor's perquisites – and one which he shared with many other royal servants, both great and small – was immunity from all common burdens on land, namely danegeld, scutage and other royal taxes, the *murdrum* fine and so on; and for these liabilities he and his fellow beneficiaries received 'pardons', which were recorded on the Pipe Rolls, the records of the annual exchequer audit. We can, therefore, discover that in the period 1155–62, although not necessarily at the same time, Thomas held unidentified taxable estates in London–Middlesex, Surrey, Essex, Hertfordshire, Buckinghamshire–Bedfordshire, Northamptonshire, Gloucestershire and Yorkshire. However, to judge by the amounts excused, most of these were small or modest holdings. Until he became archbishop, he was never a territorial magnate in his own right.[19]

Far more valuable were the custodies which Henry assigned to him. William fitzStephen states that Thomas was granted the Tower of London, the castlery of Eye (Suffolk) and the castle or town of Berkhamsted (Hertfordshire). The most likely date for such grants would be 1155, when Henry resumed important castles from baronial hands. And Herbert of Bosham believed that Thomas retained possession of his castles and other honours until he was disgraced after the Council of Clarendon in January 1164. Also, according to fitzStephen, at his trial at Northampton later in the year he was required to account for £300 that he had received from the castleries of Eye and Berkhamsted; and to this the archbishop replied that he had spent the money on repairs to the palace of London (i.e. Westminster Hall) as well as to the two castles mentioned.[20]

To understand the problems presented by Thomas's custodies it is necessary to know the basic rules of the business. The traditional system was for custodians to 'farm' the estates entrusted to them, that is to say, they paid the king, in addition to any entry fine, an agreed 'farm' (rent), and retained for themselves anything surplus to this. The farm, instead of being paid into the royal treasury, could be spent on behalf of the king – as Thomas claimed in respect of Eye and Berkhamsted. But most of such disbursements had to be authorized, the warrant serving to acquit the debtor at the exchequer audit. If, therefore, Thomas shared the profits with the king, he would have had two kinds of quittance to put against the farm: tallies issued by the treasurer, which were receipts for cash paid into the royal treasury, and evidence of some sort to prove legitimate expenditure on behalf of the king. In this way a balance could be struck at the final exchequer audit at Michaelmas. The farmer (the debtor) was either quit, in debt or in credit. And, moreover, such a custody at farm would be given an individual entry on the Pipe Roll.[21]

Thomas's custodies are, however, poorly recorded on the Pipe Rolls. He seems to have farmed Berkhamsted for £76 p.a., and by Michaelmas 1163 his agent, William fitzAlfred, had squared the account. But the honour of Eye is only represented by a single entry revealing that in 1162–3 his serjeant, Carham, had paid £150 3s. 8d. into the treasury, but had rendered no account. His other custodies are almost invisible. FitzStephen states that a good part of the chancellor's fifty-two clerks were employed on administering his own benefices and his ecclesiastical custodies, and believed that he had the custody of all bishoprics, abbeys and baronies which came into the king's hands. Herbert of Bosham shared his belief. In September 1160 John of Salisbury wrote to Thomas about Theobald's candidate for Exeter and said that rumour had it that the king had granted Thomas the revenues of all three vacant bishoprics (i.e. Exeter, Worcester and Chester–Coventry). There are, significantly, no accounts on the Pipe Rolls for Worcester (1157–8, 1160–3), Coventry (1159–61) or Exeter (1160–1). And, as the sheriff of Worcester in 1162 paid Thomas, or remitted, the sum due from the bishop's lands for danegeld, we know that the chancellor had had the custody of that bishopric and retained it when archbishop.[22]

Herbert of Bosham discloses, apparently correctly, that Thomas also had the custody of the archbishopric after Theobald's death. Although it is recorded on the Pipe Roll for 1160–1 that two of the dead archbishop's men, a clerk, Pain of Otford, and a lay servant, Philip of Tonge, had paid £420 into the treasury and that William fitzAdeline had acquitted the scutage of the archbishop's knights (£80) by presenting two tallies, there is no suggestion that these men, or anyone else, were farming the archbishopric. The £420 may well represent the value of Theobald's chattels, to which the king was entitled. On the next Pipe Roll (1161–2) the end of the Kent entry is unfortunately in part illegible, but there seems to be no reference to the archbishopric or to Pain and Philip.[23]

The case of the bishopric of London is more complicated. Richard de Beaumais II became incapacitated some time before his death on 4 May 1162; and Thomas, who may have been a canon of St Paul's, invited Gilbert Foliot, bishop of Hereford, to assume the administration and, after taking care of the expenses of the bishop and his household, dispose of the remainder as the king directed. Foliot was to be, apparently, bishop–coadjutor and collector, not farmer, of the revenues, possibly as a first step towards succeeding to the bishopric. But, doubtless because he was more scrupulous than Thomas, he begged the king to excuse him; and he and the bishop of Lincoln persuaded the new dean and the archdeacon of London to take on the unpopular task. The bishop was heavily in debt and the collectors ran the risk of being held responsible. However, when Richard died, shortly before Thomas's election to Canterbury, Henry replaced the collectors by two custodians, who at Michaelmas 1162 accounted at the exchequer for £123 11s. 11d., the farm for six months.[24]

On this evidence Thomas did indeed usually have custody of the vacant bishoprics while he was chancellor, although when he became archbishop-designate the situation changed. If fitzStephen is proved right over the bishoprics, it is unlikely that he was wrong over the vacant abbeys and escheated secular honours, which likewise, except for Berkhamsted, are missing from the Pipe Rolls until 1160–1, when some begin to appear. Hence Thomas was granted by Henry between 1155 and 1162 a series of most profitable custodies for which he did not account at the royal exchequer. It could be that he paid the farms into, and accounted to, the royal chamber (*camera curiae*), the finance office in the ambulatory court. But, when asked in 1164 for his accounts, he did not make this answer. He may have said that the king had often 'heard' his accounts, but this suggests no more than informal reports. It would seem, therefore, that he had not farmed these custodies. The profits would have been enormous. Henry had diverted an important source of royal revenue into his chancellor's hands. In 1164 he asked Thomas to account for £30,000, probably an arbitrary amount, but representing £3,000–4,000 a year, in respect of custodies other than Berkhamsted and Eye, for which he claimed £300. The archbishop replied that all the money in question had been disbursed on behalf of the king. This was probably substantially true. But, when the favourite fell from grace and the benefactor turned nasty, the tallies of receipt and the warrants for payment could not be produced.[25]

Thomas may have been careless, but that is all. It was notorious, and he appealed to common knowledge, that his enormous expenditure had been solely on the king's account. Clearly by the standards of the age, indeed by most standards, he had done nothing wrong. He had not secretly embezzled royal revenues in order to create a private fortune; he had not amassed freeholds, built mansions, established a dynasty, even enriched his family and friends. The splendour of his life-style was to honour the king, for the greatness of a master lies in the grandeur of his servants, and Henry had encouraged Thomas in his extravagance. Moreover, as both master and servant fully knew, the servant was completely at the mercy of his master. Thomas had no important kin or following: he was simply a creature who could be broken at any time. And the chancellor must also have known from his connection with the exchequer how the Angevin king, like his Norman predecessors, used debt as a political weapon. Those in favour enjoyed unlimited credit; those who fell were called to strict account. It was a system designed to encourage faithful and pliant service. Thomas had made hay while the sun shone in an almost totally innocent way. But he could not have been surprised at the damage he suffered when the storm broke, even if it caused him great pain.

Only a youthful prince, strong, courageous and light-hearted, could have coped with the multifarious difficulties that faced Henry in 1155. The border problems, from Scotland and Wales all the way across France to the Pyrenees, were many, and Henry knew that, when rectifying his frontiers, he would be obstructed by his overlord, Louis VII, who had been alarmed when Geoffrey of Anjou, Henry's father, had taken Normandy from Stephen, and dismayed when Henry had married Louis's divorced wife, Eleanor of Aquitaine. The two princes had been at war from 1152 to 1154. Usually the Capetian was in natural alliance against Henry with the family of Blois-Champagne, in the person of Count Theobald v, the late King Stephen's nephew. It was Henry's policy when king to do everything possible, short of abandoning any of his 'just' rights, to conciliate his feudal lord. He therefore did homage to Louis for his French fiefs on 5 February 1156 before going to crush his younger brother Geoffrey, who held some strategic castles in Touraine and claimed that, since Henry had now obtained his mother's lands, Normandy and England, he should have the paternal fief, Anjou and its dependencies. In 1157 Henry brought Scotland under control and then invaded first north Wales and then the south. In the years after 1158 he gave his full attention to his Continental lands.

In the first four years of the reign Thomas received a thorough grounding in Henry's ideas and practices; he may even have helped to form them. He, too, was active, brave and adventurous, intelligent, resourceful and cheerful. In the following period, 1158–62, he played a rather more public part in Henry's schemes. In August 1158, at a conference on the River Epte, the old Norman–French boundary, Henry and Louis made an alliance. Henry's eldest surviving son, another Henry, then aged three-and-a-half, was betrothed to Louis's infant daughter Margaret, the child of his new wife, Constance of Castile. Louis's two elder daughters from Eleanor of Aquitaine were, of course, out of the reckoning. To prepare the way for this agreement, or to settle the terms of the contract, Thomas was sent on an embassy to Paris which is gloatingly described in all its magnificence by his clerk, William fitzStephen.[26]

Thomas used all possible means to impress the French king with the wealth of his country and master. He took with him on the embassy a household of some two hundred men of all ranks, each with his own attendants, and all dressed in new livery. Thomas himself had twenty-four changes of clothes (perhaps one for each day), many of silk, and almost all destined to be given away as presents. He displayed all the elegance of vair, miniver and foreign furs, and of drapes and tapestries fit for the bedchamber of a bishop. His hounds and hawks were of the kinds kept by kings and men of great wealth. In the cavalcade were eight five-horse waggons, each drawn by animals equal to warhorses. Each horse was attended by a sturdy groom in a new tunic; and each groom had his own cart with its horse and driver. With each waggon and cart went a great and terrible hound capable of overpowering a bear or a lion. On two of the waggons were loaded iron-hooped casks of beer to provide strange, but much appreciated refreshment for the French; on others were the equipment of his chapel, bedchamber, dispensary and kitchen, on the seventh a modicum of food and drink, and on the eighth horse-cloths, coverlets, portmanteaux of nightclothes and all other sorts of baggage.

Thomas also took twelve packhorses, eight with coffers containing his cancellarial gold and silver plate – vessels, pots and pans, goblets and cups, ewers, basins, salt-cellars, spoons, salvers and dishes. In other baskets and panniers was cash sufficient for his daily expenses and alms, as well as his clothes, some books and such like. The leading beast carried the utensils of his chapel, the altar ornaments and the service books. Each animal had a well-appointed groom at its head and a monkey on its back.

When they entered a French town the concourse made an orderly procession. First went footmen, some 250 in groups of six or ten, singing English songs as was the English custom. Then came leashes of hunting dogs and greyhounds with their handlers and other hunt servants. Behind these were the iron-tyred waggons, covered with great sheets of leather, rattling along the cobbled street, followed at a distance by the packhorses, with a groom kneeling on the rump of each. When the astonished inhabitants learned that it was the household of the chancellor of the English king on an embassy to their king, they exclaimed, 'What a wonderful king he must be to have such a great chancellor!' After the sumpter-beasts followed squires carrying the knights' shields and leading their warhorses; then came other squires, pages and men with falcons; then stewards and the masters and servants of the household; then knights and clerks riding two by two. The chancellor, riding with a few of his intimates, brought up the rear.

We may be at the court of Petronius's Trimalchius, a text certainly known to John of Salisbury, or anticipating the gargantuan scenes of François Rabelais; but it is clear what impression fitzStephen wanted to make on his readers. And he had even greater marvels to tell. As Thomas travelled to Paris by way of Meulan in the French Vexin, the hospitable king forbade anyone to sell provisions to his approaching guest. But the chancellor, anticipating the edict, sent ahead servants in disguise to the markets of Lagny, Corbeil, Pontoise and St Denis to buy bread, meat, fish, wine and other victuals in great quantity. And when he reached his lodgings in the house of the Templars, situated in the north-east suburbs of the city, his men informed him that they had procured three days' rations for 1,000 men. Moreover, the chancellor's table was not only ample, it was sumptuous. On one day a single dish of eels put before him had cost 100s. (£5) sterling. This marvel was for a time on every man's lips.

The embassy was, naturally, a complete success. Royal host and noble guest vied in the honours they paid each other. Thomas also held a reception for English scholars at Paris, their masters and their creditors. Everyone, the French nobles, barons and knights, the schoolmasters, scholars and better citizenry, he stuffed with gifts. He gave away all his gold and silver plate, all his changes of clothes, his cloaks and furs, as well as palfreys and war-horses. And he got all that he had come for – whatever that may have been. Of greatest importance to him was the friendship of Louis VII, which was to be his salvation after his quarrel with Henry. On the return journey Thomas even captured a rebel baron, Guy of Laval, and had him imprisoned at Neuf-Marché on the River Epte, north of Gisors.[27]

Henry put his new alliance with Louis to immediate use. Thomas had, apparently, secured the confirmation of Henry's claim, as count of Anjou, to be the French king's seneschal; and armed with this authority he entered Brittany, not so much perhaps to quell the disorder there as to obtain Nantes at the mouth of the Loire, a frontier town with Anjou, which his brother Geoffrey had held at the time of his death on 27 July 1158. Henry then met Louis at Le Mans and conducted him home through Brittany and Normandy. Both kings paid a visit to Mont St Michel on 23 November. As usual Thomas was in attendance. In December Henry received the surrender of the frontier towns of Amboise and Fréteval from the count of Blois and, farther north, captured Thouars and was ceded Moulins-la-Marche by the count of Perche. It must have given the chancellor much pleasure to see his master taking immediate profit from the treaty with Louis in the shape of the rectification of the frontiers of Anjou and southern Normandy.[28]

But Henry, perhaps influenced by Thomas, then overplayed his hand. The dukes of Aquitaine had a long-standing claim to lordship over the border county of Toulouse. Louis himself had, in 1141, when married to Eleanor, tried to enforce the claim, and Henry now decided to follow suit. Louis, however, who had given his sister, Constance, the widow of Eustace, once King Stephen's heir, in marriage to the count, and no doubt resented Henry's apparently insatiable border claims, could no longer stand idly by. And when Henry, having raised an army in the spring of 1159 and invaded in July, set siege to Toulouse, Louis, although with only a small escort, threw himself into the city. John of Salisbury regarded Thomas as the architect of the campaign; William fitzStephen claims that he had a household contingent of 700 picked knights; and his military ardour apparently knew no bounds. He advocated an immediate assault on the town in the hope of taking the French king as well, arguing that Louis, by a hostile act contrary to the treaty, had forfeited his title to be Henry's lord. But Henry took a more cautious line. He was reluctant to attack the person of his feudal superior, to whom he owed fealty and reverence, and he probably attached great importance to the marriage contracted between their children. Toulouse – like Ireland – was not of immediate importance and could wait. Henry abandoned the siege and departed, leaving Thomas and a royal constable, Henry of Essex, behind in charge of the conquests, Cahors and some other towns. Henry of Essex had fled from Henry's disastrous battle with the Welsh near Hawarden in 1157, for which loss of nerve he was to pay a heavy penalty in 1163.

FitzStephen says that in the autumn of 1159 all the earls in Henry's army refused the Toulouse command. Thomas took the opportunity to achieve his wildest dreams of secular glory. Clad in armour and at the head of his troops, he captured three fortified towns. As a result of a campaign across the Garonne, on which stood Toulouse, into the eastern part of the county, he received the surrender 'of the whole province'; and then he too withdrew. It may well be that the recapture of Cahors on the River Lot, well to the north, was the only lasting success of the war. And there were for Thomas some sour consequences. The method he found for financing the war was fiercely resented by the English church; and after his disgrace in 1164 he was required by Henry to repay sums of money lent him during the campaign. Thomas had thought they were gifts.[29]

While Thomas was fighting in Aquitaine, Henry invaded France south of the Seine in the Beauvoisis area, but made a truce in November followed by a peace in May 1160. By the treaty, which was witnessed by, among others, Arnulf of Lisieux, Philip of Bayeux, the Master of the Temple and Thomas the chancellor, Henry was to have all the territories which his grandfather Henry I had possessed on the day he died, except for the Vexin. Three fiefs held by his vassals he was to keep; the rest, including the castles, was to be Margaret's dowry, to be held for three years in trust by the Knights of the Temple. If during that period Margaret were to die, the dowry should revert to Louis; but if, with the permission of the church, the marriage should be celebrated, it would pass to the bride and bridegroom. As for Toulouse, Henry was to keep his conquests, but was to make a year's truce with the count.[30]

Thomas was also involved in two other political marriages, no less irregular. The death of King Stephen's last surviving son, William, earl of Surrey and count of Boulogne, during the retreat from Toulouse in October 1159, led to proposals, one quite amazing. The county of Boulogne passed to his sister, Mary of Blois, abbess of Romsey, and Henry arranged that she should marry Matthew, a brother of his ally Philip, count of Flanders. Thomas, according to Herbert of Bosham, strenuously opposed this plan, but was overruled. Who granted the dispensation is unknown. Only Theobald's incapacity and the papal schism made the marriage possible. It was also necessary to arrange for the remarriage of the widow, Isabel of Warenne, countess of Surrey. Henry wanted to marry her to his brother William, who was still without a proper endowment. This matter, however, Thomas dealt with after he had become archbishop.[31]

Thomas's behaviour, his pride, extravagance and military exploits, were not necessarily repulsive to the church at this time, for, although he was an archdeacon and well beneficed, he was rated as a *curialis*, a courtier. He was pre-eminently a 'secular' clerk, for which there were different standards of conduct. John of Salisbury, in his *Policraticus* (1159), although in a satirically farcical passage, drew attention to the fact that St Martin of Tours had been a soldier under the Emperor Julian. What specially rankled in the church was that Henry, abetted, perhaps instigated, by his chancellor, had begun to impose scutages (in effect an extraordinary tax) on those who owed him military service, but whose services he did not require, in order to pay for his foreign wars. There was one in 1156 in connection with Henry's campaign against Geoffrey, and in 1159 the even more notorious scutage of Toulouse. The latter was levied at the rate of 2 marks for each knight owed, so that, for example, the bishops of Worcester, Winchester and Lincoln had to pay £80, as did the abbot of Peterborough, for their *servitium debitum* of sixty knights. But it is likely that these sums could be recovered from the knights themselves; and scutages in 1161 (again at 2 marks) and in 1162 (at 1 mark) seem to have caused no overt trouble. What really hurt in 1159 was that the king, besides demanding 'gifts' (*dona*) from the cities and boroughs, the knights of the shire, Jews, moneyers and even the sheriffs who collected the money, also required large sums from the bishops and abbots. Five bishops (York, Durham, Lincoln, Bath and Winchester) were each assessed at 500 marks of silver (£333 6s. 8d.), three at 200 marks (London, Norwich and Worcester), Exeter at £100, and Chester at 100 marks. The clerks of Carlisle, which was vacant, were charged £16. Nineteen abbots and four abbesses were assessed at sums ranging from 220 marks (St Augustine's Canterbury) and 200 marks (Bury St Edmunds) to £5 (Pershore, Winchcombe, Abbotsbury and Shrewsbury). In total the bishops paid £2,233 and the abbots and abbesses £904.[32]

They were unused to this sort of thing: when the land-tax, danegeld, was imposed, they were invariably 'pardoned'. And that some of their number apparently escaped in 1159 could have inflamed the general anger. Missing entirely from the record are the archbishop of Canterbury and his vicar, the bishop of Rochester, together with the bishops of Chichester, Salisbury, Ely and Hereford and their brethren in Wales. Thomas may well have looked after Canterbury and Rochester (in contrast, St Augustine's was heavily assessed); Ely was the royal treasurer; and the Welsh bishops were too poor. But it is not clear why Hilary of Chichester, Jocelin de Bohun of Salisbury and Gilbert Foliot of Hereford should have been pardoned. Fewer abbots who owed military service seem to have escaped the net: perhaps only Westminster and Tavistock. Resentment in the church was all the greater because it was felt that Thomas should have protected the prelates from the exaction.[33]

His involvement in scutages did his reputation lasting harm. Even John of Salisbury could hardly find an excuse for his behaviour, and he thought that Thomas's future tribulations were God's punishment for this crime. In 1171 or 1172, at some assembly of the English magnates, one of Thomas's former clerks, Henry of Houghton, had a conversation with a nobleman who had been one of the archbishop's enemies, probably Richard de Lucy. The baron was marvelling at the cures taking place at the martyr's tomb and asked the clerk how it was that Thomas, who when he was chancellor had been the most severe of them all against the church, now surpassed all the saints they knew in the number and magnitude of his miracles. Henry replied that Thomas had suffered almost seven years of exile and a great number of injuries culminating in his cruel death. If St Peter and the thief on the Cross could get God's pardon for their sins, surely Thomas had more than atoned for his, lesser transgressions.[34]

Once good relations between the English and French kings were restored in May 1160, they collaborated in tackling the problem of the papal schism which followed the death on 1 September 1159 of Adrian IV, the only Englishman ever to sit on St Peter's chair and a close friend of John of Salisbury. One party of cardinals had elected Octavian, cardinal–priest of St Cecilia (Victor IV), who was friendly to the German emperor, Frederick I, Barbarossa. Another party had elected the chancellor, Roland Bandinelli (Alexander III), a great canon lawyer, who favoured an alliance with the Lombard communes and Norman Sicily against the emperor. Frederick failed to secure Alexander's attendance at Pavia in February 1160, when he attempted, in the traditional imperial way as 'advocate of the Holy Roman Church', to adjudicate between the two candidates; and the council decided for Victor. The Gallican church, however, was won over by Alexander, and in Normandy Arnulf of Lisieux, mindful of his support of Innocent II in 1133, immediately and enthusiastically championed his cause. But the English church, although anxious to be orthodox, waited cautiously for a lead. By the autumn of 1160 ecclesiastical councils in England, Normandy and France had decided in favour of Alexander, and Henry, once he had extracted all possible diplomatic advantage from the situation, joined Louis in a formal acknowledgment. In this business Thomas seems simply to have followed the king. But he did what he could to protect Arnulf's friends, Hugh of Amiens, archbishop of Rouen, Hugh's nephew and archdeacon, Giles de la Perche, and William, bishop of Le Mans, when, to Henry's extreme anger, they recognized Alexander before the king's permission had been given.[35]

Alexander was most grateful to Henry for his recognition and was anxious to reward him. He sanctioned or tolerated his legates' dispensation to enable the royal children to be married, as envisaged by the treaty concluded in

May, and he looked favourably on Westminster's petition, supported by Henry and the whole English church, and likewise endorsed by the legates, for the canonization of Edward the Confessor. On 7 February 1161 at Anagni, dispensing with the need for a formal inquiry into Edward's claims, he issued the necessary bull. It was a gracious and suitable reward for a faithful church and king. But it was not by any means the last favour that Henry expected him to grant.[36]

From May 1160 until his death on 18 April 1161, Archbishop Theobald, through letters written by John of Salisbury, who was bearing the heavy burden of his master's incapacity, begged Henry to go back to his duties in England and also demanded the return of his archdeacon. The archbishop was anxious that Alexander should be recognized, eager that Archdeacon Batholomew should be elected to Exeter and most desirous of seeing both his lord and his servant before he died. Theobald even threatened Thomas with excommunication and loss of his benefices, and in the end wrote with much bitterness of his ingratitude. Neither king nor archdeacon went to see their father in God: both pleaded necessity. The executors to Theobald's will were his brother, Walter, bishop of Rochester, his chancellor Philip, Master Ralf of Lisieux and John of Salisbury. John was at the deathbed and was greatly affected by his master's death. He always remembered Theobald with great respect and gratitude – indeed, during his exile at Rheims the years spent in his household seemed a golden age. Thomas, although he too in later years referred respectfully to Theobald, did not write with the same warmth. Theobald had been, perhaps, not the first, and certainly was not the last, to accuse his protégé of ingratitude.[37]

Henry and Thomas were certainly busy in those months. In October 1160 the young Henry did homage to Louis for Normandy and on 2 November Archbishop Hugh, at Le Neubourg, 38 kilometres south of Rouen, made use of the dispensation and married the prince, by then five years nine months old, to the even younger Princess Margaret. The prize was her dowry, the strategic Vexin castles, which Henry took over from the Templars. Just before or just after this marriage, Louis VII married, thirdly, Adela of Champagne, the sister of Theobald of Blois, both to strengthen his position against Henry and in the hope of begetting a male heir. Henry then attacked and captured Theobald's castle of Chaumont on the Loire, which screened Blois, and by May 1161 Henry and Louis were again at war, mainly in the Vexin.[38]

In the fighting between Gisors, Trie-Château and Courcelles-les-Gisors Thomas had, according to fitzStephen, besides his 700 household knights, another 1,200 hired cavalry and 4,000 serjeants under his command for forty days. Each of the mercenary knights was paid 3s. a day, in the coinage of Rouen, for his horses and squires, and was fed at the chancellor's table.

This cancellarial contingent was always in the van of Henry's army, and, with Thomas instructing it, leading and urging it on, it was always the most daring in its schemes, the most effective in action. It was by the trumpets of his troops that the advance and the retreat were sounded, and their calls were familiar to every soldier in both armies. Once, fitzStephen adds, Thomas, clerk though he was, jousted with a valiant French knight, Engelram of Trie, overthrew him and took his charger as prize. Such were the chancellor's feats that, although an enemy and a destroyer of the land by fire and sword, he earned the love of the king of France and the French magnates. For courage is admirable even in an enemy; and Thomas displayed the noblest virtues.

So William fitzStephen. Edward Grim was more censorious. Who, he asked, could count the number of those whom Thomas had condemned to death or loss of all their possessions? With powerful military forces he had wiped out towns and fortresses; without mercy he had burnt down farms and properties; resolutely he had been an enemy to all enemies of the king, in whatever quarter they had arisen. To please or obey the king there had been no one whom he would not injure. The only saving grace was his chastity. An unknown monk or clerk in central France, presumably from the Angevin dominions, when reading in Lactantius's *Divinae Institutiones* about Christian beneficence (VI. 12), was moved to rebuke Thomas – in marginal jottings – for his inordinate and mis-directed largesse. Among the un-Christian extravagances noted are the purchase of wild animals, the arming of soldiers and the ransoming of military prisoners. Thomas should abandon the wicked Henricians and their shameful deeds.[39]

There were factors at this time which may have discouraged Thomas's flamboyant pursuit of worldly glory. Towards the end, or just after, the Vexin campaign he fell seriously ill and went into hospital at the church of St Gervais, a cell of the ducal abbey of Fécamp, in the north-western suburb of Rouen. There he had the honour of a visit from both kings at the same time, probably after they had made a truce in the middle of June (1161). Theobald was dead, but Henry was still in no mind to end the vacancy at Canterbury for at this very moment he sought and obtained papal permission to use any bishop he chose to crown his now married eldest son. He then went south into Gascony, leaving his chancellor to get well. It was at St Gervais that Thomas probably formed that friendship with Nicholas, canon of the neighbouring Augustinian leper hospital of St Jacques on Mont-aux-Malades (now Mont St-Aignan), which was to be so useful to him during the first years of his exile. And it was here that one day, while he sat playing chess dressed in a cloak with sleeves, an old friend, Ansketil, prior of the Augustinian abbey at Leicester, arrived from the king, who was still in the south. 'What's this?' the prior joked.

'So you go in for capes with sleeves now, just like fowlers when carrying hawks! And you a clerk – unique, I know, but plural in your benefices. Archdeacon of Canterbury, dean of Hastings, provost of York, canon here and canon there, custodian of the archbishopric and, as court rumour has it, archbishop to be.' To which chaffing Thomas replied in the same vein, saying among other things that he knew no less than three, moreover three poor priests in England whom he had rather see raised to the archbishopric than him. 'For if it should come about that I am promoted, I know the king so well, indeed inside out, that I would either have to lose his favour or, God forbid!, neglect my duty to the Almighty.' Thomas was in a good position to know that Henry usually collected his debts, and often on the nail.[40]

Nevertheless, it is possible that he was beginning to rehearse a new role. He asked Peter, abbot of Montier-la-Celle, near Troyes in Champagne, John of Salisbury's friend, for a copy of the sermons of Master G., no doubt Gebuin, precentor of Troyes cathedral, of whom he may have heard from John. Such reading would get him into the proper frame of mind. And he could have thought that he was making a sacrifice. By the winter of 1165–6, Herbert of Bosham was prepared to claim, in a letter he composed for Stephen de la Chapelle, bishop of Meaux, to send to the pope on behalf of Thomas, that the archbishop was especially meritorious, for he had been nurtured in a palace, mixing with and learning from the great, and had thrown all that splendour up for the sweat of pastoral chores.[41]

CHAPTER FOUR

ARCHBISHOP OF CANTERBURY,
1162

After Theobald's death on 18 April 1161, Walter, bishop of Rochester, who happened to be the deceased's brother, assumed the duties of vicar-general in matters spiritual. The Canterbury monk, Gervase, not only records in his Chronicle that, by the decree of the prior and convent of Canterbury and of Bishop Walter, Bartholomew was consecrated bishop of Exeter by Walter in Canterbury cathedral, but also adds that at this time Thomas, archdeacon of Canterbury and royal chancellor, was the most powerful man in England, glorious in the sight of all, extremely wise, and admired by everyone for the nobility of his soul; he was also most formidable to his enemies and rivals since he was the king's friend and deputy, indeed his tutor and almost his master. As we have seen, Thomas was granted by Henry, probably immediately after Theobald's death, custody of the temporalities of the archbishopric.[1]

It was generally held in the English church that the archbishop of Canterbury, its metropolitan and primate, should have outstanding qualities; but there was less agreement on what those should be. Although no one would have disputed that only a man of the highest moral reputation and stature was worthy of consideration, most would have stressed the need for prudence, even perhaps some degree of worldliness. The primacy of the saintly and uncompromising Anselm (1093–1109) had been painful and disastrous. Canterbury tradition, almost unbroken since the mid-tenth century, required that the archbishop should be a monk, and since the Conquest three, including Theobald, had been taken from Bec. This intensified the problem, not only because monks were usually without suitable experience or sufficient standing, but also because Benedictine monasticism had lost much of its esteem. Moreover, Theobald had not behaved particularly like a monk–bishop: certainly his own monks thought that he acted more like a secular clerk; and the time had perhaps come when a man who had been educated in some distinguished French cathedral schools and had risen through service in a cathedral church, for example, an archdeacon, would not be considered scandalous outside a small circle, principally the monks of Christ Church. According to Robert of Cricklade, at Thomas's election at Westminster, Bishop Hilary of Chichester smartly put down Master Laurence, abbot of Westminster, who objected to the election on the grounds that he was not a monk with the reply, 'Do you think, my lord abbot, that in the eyes of God there are no good men except monks?' Hilary was at the time sheriff of Sussex.[2]

There was, however, in England one man who met most of the traditional requirements, Gilbert Foliot, bishop of Hereford. And there can be little doubt that he himself thought in 1161–2 that he was the right man for the job. But to what extent his candidature was considered by the others most concerned – the king, the bishops and Canterbury priory – is unknown. Gilbert was a difficult man and many of the bishops may have thought that he would make a harsh master. Besides, he was something of a fanatic, and probably all the bishops were agreed that it was essential to have an archbishop who could get on with the king, deal with him tactfully and prudently. Men could see that Henry was on the way to becoming a very strong ruler – the Toulouse scutage of 1159 had given a sharp warning – and feared that all the church's gains since 1120, when Henry I became pious, could easily be lost if the wrong man got Canterbury. With this in mind few bishops could have felt much confidence in Gilbert Foliot. But they could hardly have preferred either of the other monk–bishops in England, Henry of Winchester and his protégé Robert of Bath, both in any case past middle age. And they were unlikely to have welcomed a bishop from another church, even the Norman.

John of Salisbury, an excellent witness, attests that Theobald wanted Thomas to succeed him. This may have been one of the reasons why the archbishop was so anxious to see both his archdeacon and his king before he died. The confidence he had shown in Thomas in 1154–5 had not been completely destroyed by the events of the next six years: his belief that Thomas would be able to influence, if not control, Henry had been amply confirmed; and he must still have thought that this influence was, on the whole, for good, and, if Thomas were archbishop, would be directed even more obviously to the benefit of the church. Even in moods of disenchantment, Theobald may have felt that of all the possible evils Thomas would be the least. Moreover, Thomas was the best fitted to protect the metropolitan see itself: he would be able to withstand the ambitions of York and Winchester and the restored papacy, keep the suffragan bishops in their place, and stand no nonsense from the Canterbury monks. Theobald also was undoubtedly swayed by his feelings for Thomas.[3]

Given the general situation, together with the rivalry among the bishops, their general disrespect for monks, and the partiality of Theobald, the emergence of Thomas as a possible candidate for the primatial see is not so unlikely as could at first sight appear. All the same, there were some obviously scandalous features, on which Gilbert Foliot was to harp so often and at such length. Never before, except on one unfortunate occasion, had the mother church of England been given to a royal clerk. Indeed, since 1120 such men had almost ceased to be appointed to any English bishopric. Besides, whatever view is taken of Thomas's alleged secret life of piety, on the surface he was not only completely identified with Henry's policy and actions, but was seen to glory in some of those which were most unsuited to the clergy. To elect as archbishop a worldling who only two years before had commanded troops on campaign and had taken part in the fighting was almost inconceivable. In his schooling, his career, his conduct and his general demeanour, Thomas was all that an archbishop should not be.[4]

The procedure for electing an archbishop of Canterbury was not precisely or uncontroversially formulated at this time. In the past, 'elections' had usually taken place at a meeting of the king's council, which, as regards this business, could also be regarded as a national assembly of the English church, clergy and laity. In 1164, however, in the Constitutions of Clarendon, which purported to reveal 'ancient custom', it was declared that the election of a bishop should be made in the chapel royal with the assent of the king and the counsel of those persons whom the king had summoned for the purpose. In the case of Canterbury, even the identity of the electors was doubtful. The convent of Christ Church was claiming – and in the end established its right – to be the essential and exclusive electoral body; but the bishops of the province had claims to be involved and could not easily be denied a part. Also the king always had a large say – if he wished, the principal voice. But he took advice, and on one occasion even Henry I had been dissuaded by the magnates from pushing his own, generally unpopular, candidate. In this triad the cathedral monks were the weakest element, all the more since the king and bishops usually came to an agreement which disregarded their particular and limited interests. And the king could be defeated only if the bishops united against him, a most unusual event.[5]

What is more, in 1161 Henry, like the Conqueror in 1070 and Stephen on the last occasion, made use of papal authority. He was at the time in very close contact with Pope Alexander's legates in France, Henry of Pisa, cardinal-priest of St Nereus and St Achilles, and William of Pavia, cardinal-priest of St Peter *ad vincula*, who had been involved not only in the recognition of Alexander as pope but also in Anglo-French relations. They had, as we have seen, given a dispensation for the children to get married, and they co-operated with Henry at Le Mans on 1 March 1161 in the business of the resignation of the archbishop of Dol. Henry of Pisa, perhaps in

September, baptised at Domfront Henry and Eleanor's new child, Eleanor, and he was with the king at Fécamp early in 1162 for the translation of the bodies of some of the dukes of Normandy. Henry also consulted him about Canterbury and made use of his services. At this time he was imagining a fruitful collaboration between king, pope and archbishop of Canterbury, which he would exploit to his advantage.[6]

In the end, possibly after a period of indecision, undoubtedly after he had sounded out some of his advisers, Henry decided for Thomas. It is possible that, although they were still firm friends, some of the earlier intimacy had disappeared. In any case, it was generally believed that Henry intended to turn his faithful chancellor into his faithful archbishop. Moreover, as he would have known, Alexander had encouraged Louis VII's chancellor, Hugh of Champfleury, to retain his office after his election in 1159 to the bishopric of Soissons – and was to keep him there until 1172, when Hugh quarrelled with his royal master. Probably even more in Henry's mind were the German emperor, Frederick Barbarossa, and his faithful and warlike servant, Rainald of Dassel, in 1156 his chancellor, in 1159 archbishop of Cologne. As Ralf of Diss remarks, in this very Canterbury context, in Germany the archbishop of Mainz and in Italy the archbishop of Cologne served that ruler as arch-chancellor; and in the chronicler's opinion Henry thought it a very convenient arrangement. Certainly to have an archbishop as chancellor would enhance his dignity. His sons, first Richard with William of Longchamps, then John with Archbishop Hubert Walter, perfected this scheme. Although it was said that Henry obtained Alexander's permission for the plurality, we are not told that he had discussed the matter with his chancellor. It is possible that he took for granted that so arch a pluralist would be delighted at such a plan.[7]

Henry was also thinking about the government of England and the future of his heir, the young Henry, in 1161 six years old and married to a princess who might turn out to be the heir to the kingdom of France. Seven was the age at which a nobleman was taken from his nurse and mother and entrusted to men for his education, both physical and scholastic. Although Henry had not allowed his brother Geoffrey a share in the Angevin lands and had done nothing on a grand scale for his other brother William, he was from the start anxious to establish the position of his own children, and, more generally, secure his dynasty. What the Capetians did regularly for their heir, what Stephen had failed to do for his sons, Eustace and William, Henry was determined to do for his.

He had made an early start. On 10 April 1155 at Wallingford he had required the magnates to recognize his sons, William and Henry, as in the line of succession to England. William had died in the next year; but two more sons came after Henry, Richard on 8 September 1157 and Geoffrey on 23 September 1158. The young Henry had done homage to Louis VII for Normandy in October 1160 and had been married in November. While Canterbury was vacant (April 1161–June 1162) Henry II obtained two papal bulls, one allowing him to have his son crowned by any bishop of his choice, and the other, addressed to Roger of York, and dated 17 June (1161), announcing the permission and ordering Roger, who had the right to perform coronations, to carry it out when the king required him so to do. The archbishop was to render the new king due obedience and reverence, saving in all things the authority of the senior king, and see that all other men did likewise. And on the Pipe Roll in the financial year 1161/2 is recorded under Berkshire a payment to the great financier, William Cade, of £38 6s. for providing gold for a crown and other regalia for the king's son. As gold was probably still around 15s. the ounce, some fifty ounces had been bought. Clearly Henry had the coronation of his son in mind. He himself intended to cross to England at Whitsun (27 May) 1162.[8]

Great schemes were on foot. Many of the biographers, from John of Salisbury on, associate Henry's choice of Thomas as archbishop with some royal scheme for the heir to the throne.[9] Some of Henry's actions, seen in the context of earlier and later moves, suggest that he was contemplating setting up a subordinate government in England, with the young Henry as nominal ruler, and power delegated to a regency council under the chancellor-archbishop and one of the justiciars, probably the earl of Leicester. Possibly Queen Eleanor, who was often in England with her children, would also have a part to play; perhaps the purpose of the new scheme was to release her for other duties, presumably in her own duchy of Aquitaine. At all events, Thomas would have a key role. If so, things went very wrong. Thomas, like Theobald in the last reign, was to get deeply involved in the status of the king's heir, and with even more disastrous results. In the end it appeared to the royal court that he had constantly thwarted Henry's attempts to establish his son's position in England.

In looking for a faithful archbishop, Henry also had one other, no less important, aim. He was anxious to recover everywhere his 'just' rights, many of which he believed had been lost during Stephen's reign. He was especially anxious to withstand and push back notorious ecclesiastical encroachments. The English church, in step with most others, had since 1100 become more distinct as a separate order, more self-sufficient in government, more connected, although not always willingly, with the reformed papacy, less subservient to the lay powers, more vocal, more self-confident. In their different ways Theobald and Henry of Winchester exemplified the new type of bishop; and Alexander III, the former papal chancellor and distinguished scholar, particularly in jurisprudence, pointed the way to the

new bureaucratic superpower which was emerging out of the reform movements of the eleventh century. Henry II, before old age, was not an exceptionally pious man; but neither was he irreligious. He was an autocratic
ruler who wanted the obedience of all his vassals, ecclesiastical as well as
lay. Bishops, thanks to the Compromise of Bec of 1106, still did homage
and swore fealty to the king before receiving their lands from him and
their consecration from the church.[10]   At what point between April 1161
and May 1162 Henry decided to make Thomas archbishop cannot be said.
The two men seem for some of the time to have been apart. Henry was
mostly in his southern dominions between June and Christmas 1161; and
Thomas's movements after he lay ill at Rouen in the summer are obscure.
He appears to have travelled with Richard de Lucy by way of Southampton
to Winchester before 29 September, and the two men may indeed have
been sent to attend the exchequer audit on that day.[11] But he still had no
standing role in England, for he and the justiciar seem to have returned
to Normandy to rejoin the king some time before Christmas.

Edward Grim and William of Canterbury thought that Thomas was finally
sent to England for a variety of reasons, and Herbert of Bosham mentions
Welsh affairs. It would seem that it was at this time that the young Henry
was put in his charge and he was given the task of assembling the magnates
to do homage to the boy. Herbert also relates that it was only when Thomas
was taking leave of the king at Falaise that he was informed that he was
to have the archbishopric. But, although Henry was notoriously secretive,
it is over-rigorous to understand this as meaning that the gift came out
of the blue. The court had been buzzing with the matter for months. In
the spring of 1162 Henry summoned some English bishops to meet him
in Normandy, including Roger of York, Hugh of Durham, Robert of Lincoln and Hilary of Chichester. Although Henry of Winchester was missing,
this was a senior group whose support for a royal nomination to Canterbury
was essential. Either then, or a little later, arrived also Bartholomew of
Exeter, Walter of Rochester and Walter de Lucy, abbot of Battle, the justiciar's brother. Norman bishops, including Arnulf of Lisieux, probably had
a say; and at hand was the papal legate, Henry of Pisa. By 17 May Alexander
was expecting the return of his two legates and a visit from the bishops
of Bayeux and Evreux, Henry's nuncios. The king is reported to have claimed
that he had received permission from the pope for Thomas to be both chancellor and archbishop. All this is the immediate background to Thomas's election. Henry was making sure that there could be no effective opposition
to his schemes. We may think, therefore, that Herbert's words mean only
that the king had made the necessary arrangements and had decided that
Thomas should wait no longer.[12]

Most biographers followed John of Salisbury in thinking that Thomas had carefully considered what he would do if offered Canterbury, that he was fully aware of many of the problems that might emerge, that he hesitated, and that it took Henry of Pisa to bring him to accept the office. He may well have warned the king that it would not be all plain sailing. But no one thought that he made a fierce or protracted resistance. It was not like Anselm in 1093.[13]

It is likely that the chancellor travelled to England with Lucy and the prelates and magnates assigned by the king to secure his election, primarily the bishops of Chichester, Exeter and Rochester and the abbot of Battle; and the company must have left Normandy by the end of April at the latest. Thomas's first task in the kingdom was to obtain a general recognition of the young Henry as the king's heir and to get all the magnates and royal officials to do him homage and swear fealty. This he carried out with complete success, he himself leading the way. But, although it is possible that the boy wore a gold circlet for the ceremony, there was no coronation. The southern bishops must have dissuaded Henry from using the papal bulls of June 1161, and the decision to appoint Thomas to Canterbury could have been bound up with this. Once the mother church had a pastor there would be no need for York or any one else to intrude. But the change in plan wrecked the whole scheme. The disgruntled Roger petitioned the pope for confirmation of his ancient privileges of having his cross carried before him and of crowning kings. And the required bull was issued at Montpellier on 13 July 1162, probably at the same time as Thomas was granted the pallium, a balancing act typical of papal policy. With both metropolitans claiming the right to crown, a coronation was difficult, and after July 1163 Henry and Thomas were no longer friends. Early in 1164 John of Salisbury reported, probably jokingly, from France that people were saying that the boy's coronation had been postponed so that it could be performed by the pope on a visit to England. It was eventually performed on 14 June 1170 by Roger of York.[14]

In 1162, although the transformation of the young Henry was botched, the machinery for making Thomas archbishop functioned perfectly. The bishops and justiciar persuaded the reluctant Christ Church monks to make the formal election of their archdeacon, and then summoned a council of bishops, abbots and cathedral priors, earls, barons and royal officials to Westminster on 23 May, the Wednesday before Whitsun. Henry of Winchester took the chair in his capacity as subdean of the province – the dean, the bishop of London, having died on 4 May. The monks' election of Thomas was debated. Of the bishops only Gilbert Foliot publicly demurred, but even he, it seems, did not make a formal protest. The archbishop's apologists thought that he was motivated by private ambition and envy. In the end the monks' action was approved *nemine contradicente*, and Bishop Henry read out the formal record of the election in the monastic refectory. The archbishop-elect was then presented to the young Henry, who had been empowered by his father's writ to give royal consent to the election. It was left to Foliot to make the sour jest that Henry had indeed worked a miracle, for he had transformed a layman and knight into an archbishop. But two of the biographers, both well-placed, disclose the widespread reservations, even dismay, among the electors. At the time probably no one doubted that the king's choice had, for better or for worse, been imposed on the church. A quarter of a century later, Herbert of Bosham put it like this: a man full of vainglory had been transferred from the royal court (*aula*) into the church, contrary to every rule of law, grotesquely and irregularly. Yet, immediately after the martyrdom, John of Salisbury, who had probably been present at the ceremony in 1162, together with Herbert of Bosham and William fitzStephen, was able to comment that, despite all appearances, Thomas had been pre-elected by God to be archbishop and a future martyr.[15]

The electoral procedure as depicted by the biographers leaves two matters, both of future importance, inadequately explained. Bishops-elect were required to do the king homage and fealty. Theobald, to his great distress, had been unable in his last illness to consecrate Bartholomew as bishop of Exeter because the elect had not yet become the king's vassal. Bartholomew had to be sent to Normandy for the purpose. But no one mentions a specific act of homage by Thomas in connection with his election. In January 1169 at Montmirail, however, Thomas, when negotiating with Henry the terms on which he and the king could be reconciled, made a great feature of the oath of fealty he had made to him, 'to preserve his life, limbs and earthly honour, saving his order'. In the *aide mémoire* drawn up by the papal commissioners and in the archbishop's own report to the pope, homage is not mentioned. But, when John of Salisbury described the negotiations to Bartholomew, he, no doubt correctly, referred to the homage and fealty Thomas had done the king. Since Thomas could not have done this after he had been consecrated and would not have saved his order in 1155, the occasion must have been when he took leave of the king in Normandy. Such feudal acts by ecclesiastics were among the bad customs barely tolerated by the church, and the matter was inevitably obscured by the biographers. But at Montmirail, and again in September 1169, it reappeared as a useful archiepiscopal debating point.[16]

On the other matter, almost the converse of the first, there seems to be, no less significantly, undue emphasis and unwarranted detail. Five of the biographers were aware that Thomas, at some point after the general approval of his election at Westminster, and either just before or after the royal consent, obtained from the young king some form of acquittance from all secular obligations. It was demanded by Henry of Winchester acting on behalf of the rest, and the move may have been provoked by Gilbert Foliot's jibes about Thomas's worldliness and unsuitability for the office. The release is variously described. William of Canterbury thought that he was freed from all secular business; William fitzStephen, from any secular judicial proceedings (*querelae*); Guernes, from any rendering of account; Herbert of Bosham, from all obligations to the royal court. Anonymous I, in an obviously inflated version, accords Thomas release from every imaginable obligation or claim against him.[17]

Verbal transactions are almost invariably unsatisfactory, and some of the formulations may be due to hindsight. But even a limited release from his various ties with the royal court raises problems of interpretation. It may be asked whether Thomas had already decided, or was being pushed by the bishops, to resign the chancellorship. It is difficult to see how he could continue in that office quit of all accountability to the king. On the other hand, it could be imagined that all that the bishops were demanding was that the slate should be wiped clean so as to allow a new and more prudent start to be made. It is even possible to make light of the whole affair: it was a neat answer to Gilbert Foliot. But it had a symbolical importance which gathered meaning as the events unfolded. On 23 May Thomas became a new man. The French *trouvère* Guernes has Bishop Henry referring to Saul and Paul.[18]

Finally, in this context, it may well be asked why the king had abandoned his intention, almost obligatory in the circumstances, to travel to England for the recognition of his heir and Thomas's election. His movements on the Continent are poorly attested for these months; but that is itself some indication that nothing much was happening. He may have been on the alert, but he was not at war. One possible reason for his absence is that he had decided to give pride of place to his favourite. These should be Thomas's great days. Ironically, it is by no means unlikely that, had he been in London in May, personally in charge of all the proceedings, the results would have been far different, for much less would have been said at the council about Thomas's worldliness and his need to cleanse himself of his contamination by the royal court.

Be that as it may, Thomas was successfully elected to the archbishopric, and no time was wasted in completing the business. On the Saturday after Whitsun (2 June) he was ordained priest at Canterbury by Walter, bishop of Rochester, and on the following day he was consecrated bishop in his cathedral church. This was the magnificent romanesque edifice built by Lanfranc in 1070–7, and dedicated to the Holy Trinity, as modified during the first three decades of the twelfth century by the lengthening of the choir and the decoration of the whole. By 1162 it was probably considered somewhat old-fashioned. Destroyed by fire in 1174, only fragments of the earlier church now remain.[19]

Thomas's consecration was a splendid affair. As this was basically an ecclesiastical ceremony, kings seem seldom to have attended; but on this occasion Thomas, dressed in a black cope and (white) surplice 'as befitted a clerk and archdeacon', was conducted to the church not only by the nobles but also by the justiciar Richard de Lucy and the young Henry. And in the presence of all his fourteen suffragan bishops – London and Worcester were vacant and the northern province was unrepresented – he was ordained by Henry of Winchester, the subdean, acting *vice* London. Both Roger of York and Walter of Rochester had claimed the right; but the former was refused by the bishops because he would not first make his profession of subjection to the see of Canterbury, and the latter was gently eased out. The only mishap in the proceedings was when the Gospels were, as was usual, opened at random, and the chance text proved to be the 'terrifying' Matthew 21 : 19, Christ's cursing of the barren fig tree, ' "Let no fruit grow on thee henceforth for ever." And presently the fig tree withered away', a *prognosticon* which Gilbert Foliot considered amply fulfilled by 1166. His own prognostic in 1148, however, had hardly been more auspicious; and in 1162 the mischance could be shrugged off. Thomas appointed that memorable day, the octave of Pentecost, as the principal feast of the Holy Trinity.[20]

After the consecration the next step was to solicit the pope for the pallium, the symbol of archiepiscopal authority. Although it was accepted custom that the archbishop should go in person, and Theobald had gone to Rome in 1139, there had been exceptions, and no doubt the king forbade a visit in 1162. Thomas's own wishes are unknown. He sent a distinguished embassy, composed mostly of men attached closely to him, and to one another: John of Canterbury, treasurer of York and just about to be appointed by the king bishop of Poitiers; John of Salisbury; Adam of St Liz, the influential abbot of Evesham, formerly prior of Bermondsey; Jordan of Melbourne, archdeacon of Lewes; Simon, monk of Canterbury; and the archbishop's secretary, Master Ernulf. They found Alexander at Montpellier, in the county of Toulouse; and the pallium was duly conceded. On 10 August Thomas received this token of his papal vicariate barefooted and prostrate, and then took it up with his own hands from the high altar of his cathedral before it was arranged as a yoke around his neck. Step by humble step he was entering into the service of the church. Herbert of Bosham thought that he was about forty-four years old, and he should not have been far out. There was ample time for great achievements.[21]

CHAPTER FIVE

THOMAS AT CANTERBURY: THE FIRST YEAR, 1162–1163

Thomas's achievements at Canterbury were a surprise to all. Unexpectedly he remained in possession of his see for only two-and-a-half years. This extraordinary swing in the wheel of fortune is the crux on which all appreciations of his life and career depends. The succession of events is well documented and presents no great problems. Nor are the public attitudes of the actors in the drama in much doubt: indeed, they were to be copiously, even tediously, explained. Where there is room for difference of opinion – and always has been – is over the rights and wrongs in the matters at issue and also over the motives of the participants in taking their particular stands. Herbert of Bosham, when justifying his paying so much attention to theology in his biography of the saint, exclaimed with the Psalmist, 'Give me understanding, oh Lord!' (Ps. 119: 34, 73, 125).[1] And indeed, in the case of Thomas, understanding is usually rather more profitable than judgment.

All the biographers agree that Thomas, once consecrated, put off the chancellor – they forget to mention that he retained the archdeaconry – and put on the archbishop. On the very day he refused money to jongleurs and gave it to the poor instead. Herbert discloses that, immediately after the election, on the road to Canterbury, Thomas had asked him to keep an eye on his comportment and also listen to what others said about it, so that he would know how to behave. On migrating from the court (*aula*) to the church some change was indeed necessary: it was a new office, with a completely new set of duties. As Herbert reminds us time and again, Thomas was not only a new archbishop, he was also a new priest, a new celebrant of Mass, a new ordinator. He had to learn a new way of life; and the steps he would take to equip himself for the new duties would determine whether there would be a complete transformation of character. Among those to whom Thomas announced his elevation, and whose prayers he solicited, was Maurice, ex-abbot of Rievaulx, a much esteemed Cistercian monk whom his fellows regarded as a second Bede. His messenger was his knight, Hugh de Morville, who received an encomium from the monk for having deviated 20 miles from his road, no doubt to his castle at Burgh by Sands, near Carlisle, in order to carry out the commission. Maurice urged the new prelate to reform the glaring abuses in the English church, especially those caused by secular oppression. It would entail renunciation of all worldly pomp and popularity. Eight years later, Hugh, although he himself did not strike a blow, was one of the gang which killed Thomas for eventually following this course of action.[2]

Thomas held his first ordinations in the Ember Week following his consecration (Sunday, 16 September), and his address to the ordinands was on the text of St Paul's admonition to Timothy, 'Lay hands suddenly on no man, neither be partaker of other men's sins' (1 Tim. 5 : 22). Herbert believed that Thomas, with his own unsuitability in mind, was most conscious of the need to refuse unsuitable candidates; yet also realized, again thinking of himself, that even sinners could, by the grace of God, be rendered acceptable.[3]

The more scrupulous writers chart the transformation or reveal the progression. The difficulty is once again that for most commentators the externals were merely a cloak to hide the secret life. Influenced by John of Salisbury, who not surprisingly was unusually expansive on this topic, several biographers distinguish two layers of concealment. And these were perfectly demonstrated by the clothes he wore: a hair shirt next to the skin, followed by a monastic layer, and both concealed by the decent aspect of a regular canon that he presented to the world. This, however, would seem to be nothing more than a projection back by the biographers of an interpretation of the garments he was supposed to have worn on the day of his martyrdom. Moreover, the interpretation itself is, if not completely mistaken, undoubtedly open to question. Even Herbert of Bosham did not accept it in all respects. John of Salisbury's rhetorical claim that Thomas on becoming archbishop also put on the monk and hair shirt, and variations on this theme by other hands, must be rejected.

It is certain that Thomas at first continued to dress largely as before – Herbert thought that he wore light-coloured clothes for the whole of the first year – and that the offended monks of Christ Church murmured and complained about his visiting the cloister in such a rig. In the end, possibly only after the Council of Clarendon in January 1164, he made a change to an enveloping dark full-length robe or mantle, and used as furs nothing more costly than lambskins. This style was generally considered suitable and unremarkable – 'honest' – neither ostentatiously rich nor ostentatiously squalid. It also gave him the appearance of a canon regular; but Herbert categorically denied the suggestion made in some quarters that he became a professed canon: he remained always a secular clerk. Thomas also, it is said, wore the priestly stole on his shoulders, both day and night.[4]

The underclothes, however, were not for all to see. When they were finally glimpsed at the time of his death and burial, they came, we are told, as a shock to everyone except his chaplain and confessor, Robert of Merton. It had been a closely guarded secret. But even if the archbishop was wearing some rough garment next to the skin in 1170 (and estimates of its asperity varied), it is difficult to imagine its use antedating the anguish after Clarendon or even his exile and the years of humiliation. And the 'monastic' tunic may, as we shall see, have been acquired only in 1165.

Thomas's dinner table likewise had its outward appearance and supposed concealed austerities. The magnificence of his entertainment when chancellor is attested by William fitzStephen; its splendour when archbishop is no less gloatingly described by Herbert of Bosham. At the archbishop's table, where the cross-bearer read edifying literature throughout the meal and there was also serious discussion of the lecture, Thomas's band of scholars, to which Herbert belonged and which we will presently view more closely, sat on his right, monks and such like on his left. Knights and secular guests, even men of importance, were placed at separate tables, lest they be inconvenienced by the reading. Table service was performed by the noble boys and youths in the household, led by the king's son and heir, who served the archbishop. Herbert believed that, just as the king had the right to the service of the eldest sons of the nobility, so the archbishop of Canterbury had a right to the second-born; and Thomas claimed and enforced this privilege.

Herbert says that the table decorations were superb and the food incomparable. He mentions boars, all kinds of venison, pheasants and chickens. And Thomas was a splendid host, carefully watching over the proceedings, attentive to all men and all things. Herbert admits that there was some criticism of the luxury: the provisions could have been sold and the proceeds given to the poor; but he dismisses such churlishness. The fact was that Thomas himself, although he appeared to be feasting with the revellers, ate and drank with moderation. And he ate only the most delicate foods. He had been accustomed to fine fare from youth, and his health would have suffered had he broken suddenly with habit. Water in particular was harmful to his stomach, which had a cold complexion; he had been advised by his doctors never to drink it, and cider but rarely: always wine in moderation. Herbert imagines his master toying with a pheasant, while others ate grossly of coarser dishes. Thomas's temperance in food and drink amid the feasting was asserted by John of Salisbury and accepted by later writers. Anonymous 1 excused the grandeur as an English custom which the new archbishop could hardly discontinue. Thomas undoubtedly maintained a great household until October 1164, when he fled the country.[5]

One anecdote about the conversation at his dinner table is told by Walter Map. After the reading of a letter from St Bernard, abbot of Clairvaux, to Pope Innocent II condemning Master Peter Abelard and Arnold of Brescia, two Cistercian abbots, who sat next to the archbishop, took the occasion to tell of Bernard's wonderful miracles. This was too much for Thomas's clerk, John Planeta, who had been a pupil of Abelard, and he rejoindered with a scurrilous story of how at Montpellier he had seen the saint fail to work a miracle. Thomas rebuked him for his levity, but, according to Walter, the clerk added a few barbs for good measure and got away with it. Thomas's clerks were not overfond of monks.[6]

John of Salisbury, in an influential chapter, lists the main features of Thomas's changed behaviour as archbishop, and was repeated, sometimes verbatim, by several of his successors. The greatest elaboration comes from Herbert of Bosham, one of the party which had transferred with Thomas from the royal chancery, a man very much to his master's taste, tall and handsome, intelligent, scholarly, high spirited and stylish, and one of the closest to him. According to Herbert, there were several distinct and mutually exclusive groups in the household. Besides the knights and secular officials, there were two sets of clerks: the experts in secular law, whom the archbishop needed for his operations in the secular courts, and his advisers in God's law, who aided him in the courts spiritual and were also his 'table-companions in religious studies'. Herbert belonged to this latter exclusive band of scholars; and in an appendix gives a 'catalogue' of them, based on the list of David's mighty men, thirty-seven in all, in 2 Sam. 23: 8–39 and 1 Chr. 11: 10–47. He accordingly saw them as the archbishop's spiritual warriors, the equivalent of the choice knights he had recruited when chancellor.[7]

Herbert gives the names of twenty-two of Thomas's *eruditi*. It is a very unsatisfactory schedule. On the one hand, there are a few obvious additions, such as Edward Grim, a purely honorary fellow, and some whose membership of the household is doubtful or intermittent and confined to the period of exile. On the other, there are curious omissions. John Planeta does not make it. Nor do two ex-chancery clerks. The archbishop's chancellor, Master Ernulf, because of his title perhaps a Paris scholar and addressed by John of Salisbury at Christmas 1156 as his dearest friend, was to be cast off by the archbishop in exile. William fitzStephen was the arch-deserter. It is clear that there were jealous divisions in the archbishop's court; and it must be allowed that, although Herbert lists many who abandoned their master for one reason or another, others, some faithful to the end, he simply ignored.[8]

About seventeen of his list would seem to have been members of the household for some of the period 1162–4. Of those who came with Thomas from the chancery, Herbert mentions, beside himself, only Gervase of Chichester, another theologian. Likewise only two on the list, John of Salisbury and John of Tilbury, can be proved to have been Thomas's fellows in the household of Archbishop Theobald. But, although it is possible that the former archbishop's household had dispersed during the vacancy, it would be rash to think that Thomas had made so clean a sweep. The background of some of his clerks is unknown. Nevertheless, it is tempting to think that, just as Thomas claimed the sons of barons as his pages, so he called on some bishops to provide him with suitable clerks.

Three men, Jordan of Melbourne and Matthew and Gervase of Chichester, were protégés of Bishop Hilary and probably his pupils in jurisprudence. Jordan was archdeacon of Lewes and later dean of Chichester, while Matthew also became dean. From London came Philip of Calne, of whom fitzStephen naturally has something to say, and Hervey of London. From Winchester hailed Gunter; from Wales, Alexander-Llewelyn, Thomas's cross-bearer and reader at dinner; and from Lisieux, Bishop Arnulf's nephew and archdeacon, Hugh de Nonant, bishop of Coventry in 1185, and Gilbert de Glanville, later archdeacon of Lisieux and in 1185 bishop of Rochester. Herbert omits here another of Arnulf's nephews, Silvester, treasurer of Lisieux. Robert Foliot's name connects him with the bishop of Hereford–London, although he was archdeacon of Oxford in the diocese of Lincoln before becoming bishop of Hereford in 1173. Gerard la Pucelle, auspiciously named and a nursling of Thomas's household, after a distinguished teaching career in France and Germany, became bishop of Coventry in 1183. The last of this group, Reginald Lombard, was the son of Jocelin de Bohun, bishop of Salisbury (1142–84), and a nephew of Richard, bishop of Coutances (1151–80). Jocelin was a product of Henry of Winchester's household, and his son, whom he made his archdeacon, was the result of a liaison while he studied law in Italy. Reginald was appointed bishop of Bath in 1173, and elected to Canterbury in 1191. John of Salisbury was always friendly to both son and father, an alliance which divided him sharply from the archbishop.

We can also probably take here Master Lombard of Piacenza, who, although not noticed in the household until November 1164 at St Bertin's, most likely had been recruited earlier to help Thomas in his case against the king. He was Master Vacarius's replacement. Lombard, a fine canon lawyer, a subdeacon in the papal curia, who later became a cardinal and archbishop of Benevento (1171–9), was respected by both John of Salisbury and Herbert of Bosham.[9]

On examination these seventeen *eruditi* prove to be not quite what might have been expected from Herbert's words. Four were archdeacons and another was a member of a cathedral chapter; six (including three of the archdeacons) became bishops. True, in the schools canon law was a branch of theology. But Herbert admits that Gunter of Winchester was not very learned, and only about half would seem to have had much reputation as scholars. Besides John of Salisbury, Herbert and Lombard, Gervase of Chichester was a commentator on the Bible and a homilist, and Gilbert de Glanville was 'a master of both canon and civil law'. Gerard la Pucelle acquired a fine reputation as a canonist. William fitzStephen tells us that Philip of Calne studied at Tours for two years before Thomas went into exile (he could hardly have spent much time in the household), attending lectures on theology and giving instruction in jurisprudence. He may have advised Thomas at the papal Council of Tours in 1163. And lastly, John of Tilbury is described by Herbert as an excellent scribe. He was probably the author of *Ars Notaria Aristotelis*, which was dedicated to King Henry.[10]

If Thomas took Theobald's household as model, it would not seem that in the two-and-a-half years available to him he came anywhere near to equalling, let alone improving on it. Moreover it is clear that he looked for men skilled in ecclesiastical administration rather than for pure scholars, for usefulness rather than for holiness. Many of his recruits were, like him, careerists, and Herbert, by classifying them according to their future achievements, tacitly accepts this standard. Herbert does not mention specifically the archbishop's chaplains and confessors or assign monks an important place in the daily round. The omission of Robert of Merton, who was still with Thomas at the martyrdom, must be due to jealousy. But in the circle that Herbert chose to describe there was but one priest, and he a beginner, the archbishop himself. The archbishop's enemies used this feature as a charge against him after he had abandoned his see at the end of 1164, when we learn that they had some unspecified shameful name for his 'well-born *eruditi*'. It is to be hoped it was not catamites.[11]

Herbert expands John of Salisbury's sketch by taking us through the archbishop's day. Generally speaking, men used the hours of darkness for sleep, so that the working day expanded or contracted according to the season. In the following reconstruction of Herbert's scheme it is the summer *horarium* which is followed; in winter it would have been more compressed.[12]

First Thomas carried out his Maundy duties (John 13 : 34), which he strove to do, not once a year, but every day. After Nocturns (about 2 a.m.) his almoner secretly introduced thirteen poor men into a closet, and the archbishop, under cover of night, stripped to his hair shirt and stole, washed their feet and gave them 4*d*. apiece. At Matins (dawn), however, it was his almoner who washed the feet and fed a second group of twelve paupers. And at Tierce (about 8 a.m.) two monks tended and fed one hundred of the archbishop's poor 'prebendaries'. In the ninth century two thousand seems to have been the conventional figure for Canterbury's poor. John of Salisbury believed that Thomas also sent food and clothing to the homes of the indigent and sick, and that he devoted a tithe of all his revenues to alms, thereby doubling Theobald's expenditure, itself a doubling of previous custom. When, after Christmas 1164, the archbishopric was in the king's hands, the custodian accounted annually for £16 10s. 4d., representing established alms debited to the archiepiscopal manors, and, usually, £140, on the authority of a royal writ, for the 'infirm' of Canterbury. As the farm of the archbishopric was £1,562 15s. 5½d., Henry was ensuring that a tithe of this was spent on charities. But whether this represented Thomas's gifts in full cannot be said.[13]

To revert to the archbishop's daily routine. After his Maundy duties and a resumed sleep in bed, he turned to the study of the Bible with Herbert as tutor, for the archbishop, because of his background, was rather at a loss in this field; and then, shut away in his closet, he meditated alone until Tierce on what they had read and discussed. So keen a student of theology did he become that he often took lessons from Herbert as they rode on their journeys; and he also kept edifying literature up his voluminous sleeves so that he could learn it by heart.

John of Salisbury, in connection with Thomas's new devotion to study, stresses also the time he found for private devotion and prayer. He cleansed his life from sin. Anonymous II and fitzStephen believed that he underwent frequent scourgings on his bare back. The latter adds that, whereas as chancellor he had never exceeded the bounds of chastity and decorum, he was now filled with the greatest sense of modesty. Herbert remarks that, although he drank a little wine and took adequate nourishment, his confessors knew – and it was to them both a miracle and joy – that rarely, even after meals, did he experience any 'rebellion of the flesh'. It was a singular grace that he could live as pure as an angel while still in the prime of life.

After these preparations Thomas celebrated Mass at Tierce (about 8 a.m.), but not every day, and, although with the utmost reverence, briskly. Even though he studied St Anselm's prayers during the ante-Communion, he rarely included more than one collect in the service. These features gave Herbert some trouble. He himself had had doubts over the Eucharist (presumably over the real presence); but Thomas, he thought, had simple faith: so great a reverence that he could not stand such a disturbing experience as frequently as priests who had become careless through habit. In any case there was no law on the subject. John of Salisbury associated Thomas's reverence for the sacrament with the gift of tears.[14]

Between Tierce and None (about 8.30–2.30) the archbishop devoted himself to business, and sat in the audience chamber as a judge. Archbishops of Canterbury in their several capacities as barons and ecclesiastical magistrates held various types of court; but the differentiation was marked not by the place but by the law under which the case was heard, by the procedure, and by the status of the 'judges' and officials. Herbert states expressly that, when Thomas heard ecclesiastical cases, the *eruditi* were his assessors. He also, no doubt following John of Salisbury, stresses Thomas's incorruptibility and fairness as a judge and his efforts to root out all improper fees and bribes. He allows that advocates may have been allowed salaries, but asserts that all other court officials were absolutely forbidden to accept anything. Even the keeper of his seal and the notary were to charge nothing for their services, even for the parchment, the wax, or imposing the seal.

Thomas, who had almost certainly not bought the chancellorship from the king, and certainly not the archbishopric, obtained a posthumous reputation for hatred of simony which was not confined to the biographers. Peter the Chanter, who in 1171 was a canon and professor of theology at the cathedral school at Paris and a great supporter of Thomas's sanctity, when dealing with simony in his *Verbum Abbreviatum*, twice reported the archbishop's injunction when he instituted his own chancellor, Master Ernulf. He bound this official by oath never to accept anything, even unsolicited or as small as a knife, in return for cancellarial services. Peter thought that this was as far as anyone could go: he himself did not consider professional fees simoniacal.

Four original deeds (*acta*) issued in Thomas's name during the period 1162–4 have been preserved and about twenty-two copies. Only six have witness-lists. Robert Foliot, archdeacon of Oxford, witnesses three; Herbert of Bosham, John of Tilbury and William of Leicester attest twice. Geoffrey Ridel, John of Salisbury, Master Philip of Calne, Master Arnald of Otford, Robert of Beaufai and Stephen of Ecton and the chaplains Robert (? of Merton), William and Richard (? both of Salisbury) appear once. These twenty-six deeds from two-and-a-half years can be compared with Theobald's three hundred or so from twenty-two years.[15]

At None (2.30 p.m.) Thomas rose and retired to his chamber, where, while often talking with Herbert, he prepared himself for dinner. His dinner table has already been described. The meal was completed with the singing of a hymn; and then Thomas returned to his chamber, accompanied by his band of scholars, any suitable guest whom he invited by name, and sometimes household officials. This conclave engaged in religious discussion and also acted as the archbishop's privy council.[16] Sometimes, however, the archbishop took a short nap immediately after dinner. This post-prandial session would take us, although Herbert does not mention it, to bedtime, about 8 o'clock.

John of Salisbury concentrates on the archbishop's inner life, Herbert on his eagerness to adapt himself to the requirements of his new office or vocation. Herbert probably exaggerates less than John. But it must also be recognized that the routine which Herbert describes could have been observed only when Thomas was residing in his palace at Canterbury. There must have been modifications when he was on the move or staying on one of his manors. Unfortunately his itinerary is unknown. But even in the peace and quiet of 1162 he was probably never at Canterbury for long.

Thomas's progression from chancellor to archbishop, in appearance, conduct and heart, can be elucidated by considering when and in what circumstances he divested himself, or was divested, of his existing offices, benefices and honours. He retained all the secular honours he had acquired as chancellor until stripped of them by the king in October 1163. He seems to have kept all the ecclesiastical benefices he held in plurality, except one, until he fled the country at the end of 1164. The exception was the archdeaconry of Canterbury which he continued to hold – at Henry's express desire, so it was said – until before 8 March 1163, when he surrendered it to Geoffrey Ridel. This clerk, later if not then a married man, was one of Thomas's protégés and, as keeper of the king's seal, his deputy in the chancery. It was believed that Thomas had obtained this office for him.[17]

Unfortunately we do not know exactly when Thomas gave up his office in the royal household. Since all the biographers, except William of Canterbury and Guernes, ignore the matter, it would seem that they regarded Thomas's physical separation from the king, which prevented him from carrying out the duties, and his enfranchisement on election from all royal financial claims against him, as constituting at least *de facto* resignation. This is a reasonable view, all the more since in the past the granting of a bishopric to the chancellor had always marked his retirement from the office. Indeed, unless Thomas was to remain a member of the royal household and follow the royal *iter*, he could retain the chancellorship only in some titular or honorary capacity. It may be that this was a position he had already reached before 1161 – that the ordinary duties of the chancellor were being carried out by a deputy – for Henry did not appoint a new chancellor *eo nomine* until after the archbishop's death. Geoffrey Ridel remained acting-chancellor.

William of Canterbury says that Thomas asked Henry to appoint a new chancellor when he found that his pastoral duties were too heavy to allow him to serve two masters. Guernes embroiders this by making Thomas send Master Ernulf (his own keeper of the seal) to return the Great Seal to Henry, then beyond the sea, and that the king was greatly offended. If this event occurred as described it would have been in the autumn of 1162, just before Henry decided to return to the kingdom. It could have been a direct result of the receipt of the pallium.[18] And, if Henry was angered, he could have forced Thomas to hand over the archdeaconry to Geoffrey.

The two men became bitter enemies. It would seem, therefore, that the only office that Thomas surrendered willingly was the chancellorship, and that this was not because he had been converted to austerity or humility, but because as archbishop he was so grand and so rich that he had no need of that office, which would now bring in little revenue and which he may have considered beneath his dignity. He did not want to hold an office of the king. Obviously Thomas as archbishop was in appearance much more splendid than ever before. No wonder that the biographers had to make him hide his changed character from public view.

These writers regarded Thomas's change of life-style as the direct cause of his quarrel with the king: as he began strictly to observe the laws of God he had to disobey the royal laws. The interpretation is, of course, far too simple. Almost every newcomer into office causes an unwelcome disturbance. But, despite Maurice of Rievaulx's plea for a moral reform drive, Thomas was in that respect no Anselm. Indeed, he continued on his predictable worldly path. He considered that his primary task at Canterbury was to put the archiepiscopal estates in order. Within living memory these had suffered greatly from the ambitions first of the house of Godwin, then of Odo of Bayeux. Both Lanfranc and Anselm had struggled to recover losses. Moreover, Theobald had been a nepotist. Inevitably Thomas turned his administrative and financial skills from the royal interest to his own. There was nothing improper in this. He was no more avaricious than Anselm. Nor was he attempting to make undue provision for his own kinsmen or special friends at the expense of a former set of beneficiaries. But his loyalty to the existing set-up had been weakened by his eight years' virtual absence from England and Canterbury. As a seemingly rapacious absentee archdeacon it is unlikely that he was much liked in the diocese. And as the king's right-hand man he had acquired an offensive authoritarian style.

William fitzStephen, who must have been deeply engaged in this business, says that the archbishop obtained a royal writ authorizing him to recover lands wrongfully alienated by his predecessors or usurped by laymen; and Thomas may have been advised by his canon lawyers that a grant of a fee-farm (lease) at too low a rent was tantamount to its alienation. Several writers give examples of his remedial actions. He revoked all leases of archiepiscopal demesne, dismissed the 'farmers' and took the estates back into direct exploitation, but perhaps simply in order to renegotiate the terms and halt the drift to hereditary ownership. From Roger de Clare, earl of Hertford, a man of considerable importance, he claimed homage and other duties for the town and honour of Tonbridge. And from the king he claimed custody of the castles of Rochester, Saltwood and Hythe and lordship over William of Ros with his service of seven knights.

No doubt in all these actions the archbishop had an arguable case; but the rights and wrongs were then as now extremely obscure and his behaviour was arbitrary. The dismissed lessees argued that he should have proceeded by legal process. The aggressive policy and the abrasive way in which it was carried out had unfortunate results. The property owners in Kent became alarmed; Thomas made many enemies in his diocese; and complaints streamed across the Channel to the king. One of his 'victims' was an important royal servant, John the Marshal, whose attempt to recover land at Mundham, pertaining to the archbishop's demesne manor of Pagham in Sussex, played a large part in Thomas's quarrel with the king. And it seems that because of that quarrel most of the hereditary farmers, including John, regained possession.[19]

How the archbishop behaved in purely ecclesiastical affairs within his province cannot be judged because his short period of ordinary government is poorly documented. For his official acts he assumed the humble style of 'Thomas by the grace of God the humble servant of the church of Canterbury'. But in March 1165 Arnulf of Lisieux informed him that his enemies were accusing him of pride and of continuing to behave as imperiously as when he was chancellor. Metropolitan powers were, however, few, and it is unlikely that Thomas was given much opportunity to throw his weight about before he became embroiled with the king.[20]

Despite all the complaints against Thomas, Henry, according to Herbert, remained loyal and postponed all action on them until he should return to England. And, when he and his family arrived at Southampton in the latter part of January 1163, he greeted Thomas and Prince Henry, who had gone to meet him, boisterously and with the utmost joy. Next day king and archbishop rode off together, talking happily in private for the whole of the journey. In the following two months Thomas was often at court. On Palm Sunday (17 March) Henry visited Canterbury and Thomas then accompanied him to Dover to meet Count Philip of Flanders and confirm their treaty of alliance. On 6 April he was at the royal court at Windsor, where the trial of Henry of Essex for cowardice was being held. A composition made in his presence there between Geoffrey de Mandeville and Ramsey Abbey was witnessed by Hilary, bishop of Chichester, and five archiepiscopal clerks, Robert Foliot, archdeacon of Oxford, John of Tilbury and three others.[21]

When Thomas, towards the end of April, left for the council which Alexander III had summoned to Tours, on the frontier between the French and English kingdoms, a good deal of important English church business was nearing completion. Three bishoprics were being filled. In 1162 Henry had petitioned the pope, undoubtedly with Thomas's full and warm support, for the translation of Gilbert Foliot from Hereford to London. The promotion was not only compensation for his having been passed over for Canterbury, not merely an acknowledgment of his leading place in the English church, but also to meet Henry's, and possibly Thomas's, wish to have him London-based for reasons of state. Thomas, however, had to miss his enthronement, possibly on 28 April 1163. He was represented by the bishop of Rochester and Geoffrey Ridel, by then archdeacon of Canterbury. To Hereford and to Worcester, vacant since 1160, Henry made appointments in March 1163. And if the choice for Worcester of Roger, son of Earl Robert of Gloucester and the king's first cousin and friend, was Henry's, that of the schoolmaster Robert of Melun for Hereford was Thomas's. But we should notice that Roger had been Robert's pupil in theology at Paris about 1158 and that in June 1166 Thomas reminded both that the pope had procured their election.[22]

One other bit of ecclesiastical business, the completion of the rites for the canonization of Edward the Confessor by the festive translation of the body to a new shrine in Westminster Abbey, was in suspense. It had been postponed from 1161 until Henry should return to England and a great ceremony could be organized. For the canonization of Edward was a triumph for the monarchy, and was so regarded by English kings. Significantly, Thomas went to Tours with the intention of securing the canonization of Anselm, one of his predecessors at Canterbury. That would be a triumph for the church, and particularly for Canterbury.[23]

Herbert of Bosham, who accompanied the archbishop to the council, presents the visit as the zenith of Thomas's earthly career, a pinnacle from which he was so suddenly to fall. From the port of Romney in Kent to Gravelines in Flanders, through Normandy and Maine to Tours, where they arrived, he thought, about three days before the opening session, it was triumph all the way. In Flanders Thomas was welcomed by the count and his nobles, and as he travelled through the royal dominions he was treated as though he was the king. On their approach to the city of Tours they were received by the citizens, by those attending the council and even by all the cardinals, save two who remained in attendance on the pope. So great was the welcoming crowd that Alexander had himself to move from his chamber in the palace into the hall for the reception. What is more, he rose and advanced towards his visitor. Thomas and his suite then retired to the nearby royal castle, where they were to lodge.

During the sitting of the council, which opened on 19 May, participants and royal officials paid Thomas assiduous court; and the Roman church treated him as though he was its eldest son, showering him with privileges for his own church. The business of the council, the reforming decrees, especially those concerned with the recovery of possessions usurped by the laity (Canons 3, 10), and the sentences of excommunication against Rome's enemies, including the Emperor Frederick I and William I, king of Sicily, may well have impressed, indeed elated, the new archbishop. The return journey was just as fortunate as the outward; and in England the king, as usual, welcomed Thomas joyfully and eagerly, like a son greeting his father.

Herbert remembered the visit to Tours as the closing scene in that glorious first year of Thomas's reign at Canterbury. He allowed it to be disfigured by no bad days, shadowed by no premonitory signs. He omitted to mention that not only Thomas but also Roger of York and all the English bishops, except those of Winchester, Lincoln and Bath who pleaded their infirmity, together with abbots and priors were present. He overlooked the 'torrential' sermon preached at the opening session by Arnulf of Lisieux. He ignored Thomas's failure to persuade the pope that Gilbert Foliot ought to renew his profession to him as bishop of London. And he forgot that the longstanding dispute between Canterbury and York over the primacy, which had last been ventilated at the Council of Rheims in 1148, which Thomas had attended, had flared up again, apparently over the seating arrangements for the English delegation.

Roger of Pont l'Evêque seems to have been the aggressor, and claimed, on the authority of Pope Gregory the Great's famous letter to St Augustine, that, as the senior by consecration, he should have the primacy. After a lengthy debate, in which the awkward complication of the status of the bishopric of London came up, Alexander is said to have awarded the two English archbishops parity at the council. But as Canterbury and his suffragans were put on the pope's right, York and his single suffragan on his left, Thomas lost nothing here. Nevertheless, the public dispute before the great concourse of cardinals, archbishops, bishops and others may have given him a painful reminder of Roger's superiority as a Latinist and ecclesiastical lawyer and reopened some old wounds. It may be that he had not had such a personal triumph on that distinguished stage as Herbert alleged; and he could have realized that he had still much to do before he attained the professional standards of his peers.[24]

The other set-back may not have seemed important at the time. Thomas presented a book on Anselm's Life and Miracles, presumably John of Salisbury's short version of Eadmer's, in support of his petition for his predecessor's canonization. But he suffered a double discomfiture. So many similar petitions, including one for Bernard of Clairvaux, were presented at the council that his, like Bernard's, was crowded out. And, although he obtained a papal bull dated 9 June authorizing him to summon a provincial council with power to act, it is unlikely, because of the quarrels in which he became involved, that the process was completed. It was Henry who made use of Anselm's sanctity. On at least one occasion during their disputes he referred to the more acceptable behaviour of Thomas's predecessors, some of whom had been much holier than him. In this matter, of course, it was Thomas who was the better historian: Anselm had defended the church against royal 'tyrants', including Henry II's revered ancestor, Henry I. But it is doubtful whether Thomas, in championing Anselm, was trying to score against the monarchy. More likely, in his new tactless way, he was simply aiming to advance the interests of Canterbury against all rivals; but in so doing once again he gave Henry food for thought.[25]

It is, therefore, possible that Thomas returned to England in June 1163 ruled by conflicting emotions. On the one hand, he may have been exalted by contact with the general-staff of the church militant, inspired to defend at all cost the liberties of the *ecclesia anglicana* and Canterbury that were imperilled by secular aggression. And, on the other, he may have felt some dissatisfaction with his own performance so far both in the kingdom and at Tours. This was a very explosive mixture.

CHAPTER SIX

THE QUARREL WITH THE KING,
1163–1164

Almost immediately after Thomas's return from Tours he had a serious dispute with the king. On 1 July 1163 Henry, following his military expedition into south Wales, on which he had captured the rebel Rhys ap Gruffydd, held his court at Woodstock, near Oxford, one of his favourite hunting lodges. In attendance were Thomas and the bishops of London and Lincoln (Robert de Chesney); William the king's brother; Earl Reginald of Cornwall, his uncle; William, earl of Gloucester, his cousin, and various officials and barons, including the constable Richard de Humet, the co-justiciar Richard de Lucy, the chamberlain Henry fitzGerold, and Simon fitzPeter, one of the royal justices. This was a close 'family' group, to which Thomas himself had until recently belonged. Important visitors were, besides Rhys, Owain Gwynedd, prince of north Wales, and Malcolm IV, the Maiden, king of Scots. The three 'foreign' rulers were there to do homage to Henry and to his son and heir. Henry had become titular overlord of almost the whole of Britain.[1]

With Henry's increasing responsibilities and greater involvement in administration went less extravagance. The removal of Thomas's 'bad' influence may also have contributed to the onset of the new mood. Henry began to believe that more money was going into the coffers of tax-gatherers than into his own: his subjects were being fleeced by a multitude of rapacious officials, both royal and ecclesiastical (he seems not to have interfered with baronial administration); and this he greatly resented. At Woodstock he turned his attention to the general land tax, danegeld, an unpopular levy, since Henry I's reign only intermittently imposed and last collected in 1161–2. In 1163 Henry proposed that a traditional supplementary payment by landowners to the sheriffs and their staffs, sheriff's aid, should be levied at 2s. the hide and paid, not to the sheriffs but into the royal treasury. It would seem that he was proposing to levy danegeld under a new name and at the same time reduce the sheriffs' profits. As Thomas knew full well,

Henry had taken an aid from sheriffs in connection with the Scutage of Toulouse. But an expedient which, as chancellor, he might easily have suggested or supported, as archbishop he resolutely opposed. Sheriff's aid, he said, was a free-will offering to deserving officials, not a royal rent or due. The argument got out of hand. Henry, swearing as usual *par les olz Deu*, by the eyes of God, ordered that these sums should be entered as shrieval debts on the Pipe Rolls. Thomas declared by those very same eyes that not a penny should be paid from his estates or church lands. Thomas carried the day, presumably because the king received little support from the other courtiers present; and Henry was furious.[2]

Although for Herbert of Bosham the break between king and archbishop was at the time an experience both shattering and completely unforeseen, much later he moralized that no stable personal relationships could be expected at the royal court, in a society rife with envy, falsity and intrigue. Yet Woodstock must have been the occasion when a long-developing rift could be concealed no longer. Henry had been patient. He had allowed Thomas to get a firm grip on Canterbury and establish his authority in the English church. This was a necessary stage in the royal schemes. But he must have been alarmed and saddened by some actions which he would have thought wayward and ungrateful. Thomas cannot be blamed for seeking to be an excellent archbishop. But he was impelled to extremes by two factors. One was his own character. He had obtained an independent power base at last. No more need he be a courtier, a slave to his master's caprice. His pride, even if now put to the service of the church, gave him a dangerous audacity. He had all the failings of the typical parvenu. The other factor was the need, because of his admitted episcopal deficiencies, to out-bishop the rest. He would give Gilbert Foliot no further opportunity for well-directed jibes. He would be *curialis* no longer. Herbert maintains that Thomas would have no clerk in his household who had sworn fealty to the king. He required undivided loyalty. When Henry's patience ran out there would be trouble.[3]

It is significant that, when Henry confiscated Henry of Essex's lands after his defeat in the ordeal by battle in April, he also retained the honour of Saltwood which the constable had held of the archbishop. One consequence, although possibly not until 1164–5, was the expulsion of the rector of Saltwood, Master Edward Grim, the archbishop's future biographer. After Woodstock Thomas, because of the king's ill-will, lost two important lawsuits. On 22 July Roger de Clare successfully pleaded before the 'Common Bench' at Westminster that he held Tonbridge in chief of the king, and, perhaps later, an inquest found that William de Ros was a royal vassal. Thomas was still trying to recover these three losses in 1170.[4]

Henry also prepared to collect the debts he thought he was owed for making his chancellor an archbishop. What he required from Thomas was support for the reform of certain abuses he had discovered in the English church. He was particularly dissatisfied with ecclesiastical justice. A vital ingredient in the 'Gregorian' reform movement of the late eleventh century had been the elucidation and enforcement of the law of the church, canon law. And an important aspect of the twelfth-century Renaissance was the development, especially in the church, of organs of government. Law and government grew up together, each nourishing the other. By the middle of the twelfth century the bishop, through his household of clerks and his agents, archdeacons and rural deans, was governing his diocese, both the clergy and the laity, in a much more systematic and purposeful way than ever before. But hardly had he established his authority when he began to lose some of it through the development of appeals to the papal curia.[5]

This new feature was not the result of papal aggression. Although the papacy had become more active in government, and had been using general councils (like that at Tours in 1163) and legates, either resident in a province or dispatched from Rome, to establish and enforce the law and papal policies, it rarely initiated legal proceedings. The pope, as the successor to St Peter, the cornerstone of the whole church and the principal guardian of the law, was appealed to by a growing number of men. The clergy mainly sought the confirmation of their privileges; but judicial appeals from episcopal and archiepiscopal judgments, or in anticipation of them, became increasingly frequent. Even an English baron, Richard of Anstey, at this time (1158–63) pursued a matrimonial case to Rome. But few of these appeals to the papal curia were actually heard and determined at Rome. Usually they were remitted by the pope to be heard by local churchmen, skilled in the law, acting as judges-delegate. In Normandy, Arnulf of Lisieux often acted in this capacity; in England, Roger of York, Gilbert Foliot, Hilary of Chichester, William of Norwich, Bartholomew of Exeter, Roger of Worcester, Laurence, abbot of Westminster, and Baldwin, archdeacon of Totnes.

By 1164 Henry was nursing various grievances about ecclesiastical jurisdiction. The principle was generally acknowledged that the church had a monopoly of authority in cases 'pertaining to religion'. This meant that the whole body of the clergy, including men in minor orders, was subject, almost exclusively, to its own law in both civil and criminal matters. Clerks were to be disciplined for any kind of sin, offence or crime, and also were to litigate, according to canon law in ecclesiastical courts. In addition, the laity was answerable to the church for any infraction of the moral code. There were, of course, disputed areas; and in practice the king drew the boundaries. William I had done so at Lillebonne in 1080. He had both enjoined the Norman church to enforce its laws more stringently and also warned it off certain matters. That was typical. King and bishops worked together to bolster up each other's authority. If there was a dispute it was over detail, and the king had the last say.[6]

Under Stephen's weak rule, however, there had occurred a considerable and unplanned expansion in the fields of ecclesiastical government and jurisdiction. The old framework had been shaken and was threatened with demolition. By 1164 Henry had become convinced that unlawful encroachment on royal preserves had occurred since the death of his grandfather, Henry I. In particular he resented church courts hearing land cases. He also did not care for the way in which the church was exercising its jurisdiction. He shared with many bishops and frustrated litigants their dislike of appeals to the papacy. He was at one with the people in his belief that archdeacons and deans were exploiting sin as a way to wealth. And he had come to the conclusion, held also by some of his justiciars, that clerks in holy orders who were guilty of secular crimes were punished too leniently by church courts. These could pass quite severe sentences, including flogging and imprisonment. Their awards of pilgrimage, especially to Jerusalem, came close to outlawry and banishment. But they were debarred from ordering the spilling of blood, which excluded sentences of death and mutilation, as well as, by extension, blinding and branding. Henry probably also thought that the usual method of exculpation awarded to accused clerks – denial of the charge on oath, either unsupported or supported by a specified number of helpers – allowed many clerical criminals to escape punishment altogether. Preoccupied with the problem of law and order in his dominions, he was anxious that more criminals should be convicted and then drastically punished.

Some of these matters seem to have been on his mind for a long time. In 1158 a burgess of Scarborough had complained to him at York of a rural dean and archdeacon who had taken 22s. from him for withdrawing a charge of adultery which they had brought against his wife. Richard de Lucy had pointed out that Henry's own enactment on the way in which an accusation should be brought had been flouted; and Henry was enraged when John of Canterbury, then treasurer of York, asserted that the king could not punish the dean because he was a clerk. Henry raised the matter with Theobald, but was prevented from pursuing it by more urgent business abroad. He did, however, declare that archdeacons and deans extorted more from the people than he himself drew in revenue; and at Falaise in 1159 he repeated his enactment about the procedure for accusations. More generally, he reissued the decrees of the Council of Lillebonne (1080) probably at Rouen on 25 February 1162.

In return, John of Salisbury in his *Entheticus* (1156–9) and *Policraticus* (1159), both dedicated to Thomas, had drawn attention to the danger to the church from evil ancient customs and to the attacks which tyrants, particularly King Stephen, had made on the jurisdictional privileges of the clergy (*privilegium fori*). John, however, would confine the privileges to priests and exclude the mass of the clergy in inferior orders. Thus warning shots had been fired by both sides shortly before Thomas became archbishop. He was fully aware of the controversy. Indeed, in 1154–5 he must have been involved in the great dispute over how Archdeacon Osbert of York, accused of the murder of his master, Archbishop William, should be tried. Theobald, although claiming jurisdiction, had been forced to inform the pope, by a letter written by John of Salisbury, that in such cases, 'according to the custom of our nation', trial was in the royal court. But, after Stephen's death, Henry had allowed an ecclesiastical trial. What line, if any, Thomas took is, however, unknown.[7]

The problem of how to treat criminous clerks, that is to say priests and clerks defamed or accused of committing a serious secular crime, a felony, for which, in the case of the laity, the penalty was death or mutilation as well as confiscation of their land and chattels, was becoming tricky. Two contentious issues were emerging: how should they be tried and how punished? In the past bishops had not exerted themselves unduly to protect clerical malefactors haled before a secular tribunal. Of many cases they would have heard nothing; to some they may have turned a blind eye. When necessary, they stripped the criminal of his clerical orders and left him to his fate as a layman. Sometimes, especially when it was an ecclesiastical crime, such as heresy or rebellion against ecclesiastical authority, they actually invited or required the lay power to inflict a corporal punishment. By the second half of the twelfth century, however, some of these attitudes were less easy to maintain. The clergy was becoming more distinct as a separate order in society; theologians were inclining towards the view that holy orders were indelible; knowledge of canon law was spreading; and there was greater administrative efficiency. But, as soon as 'benefit of clergy' emerged as a useful plea for clerical criminals, it not only frustrated and irritated royal and other secular justiciars but also created the impression that the number of criminous clerks was growing fast.[8]

Thomas's biographers cite some cases in which the archbishop was involved and which came to the king's angry notice. According to William fitzStephen, Thomas refused to allow a clerk of Worcester, who had killed a respectable man in order to rape his daughter, to be tried in a lay court and had him put in the bishop's prison so that the royal judges could not get hold of him. Similarly he protected a clerk who had been arrested for the theft of a silver chalice from one of his own churches, St Mary-le-Bow (of the Arches) in Cheapside, London. But he deprived him of his orders and, to mollify the king, had him branded. Herbert cites a case which led the archbishop to make a general rule. A priest in the diocese of Salisbury, accused by the bereaved relatives of homicide, was taken by them and royal officials before the bishop, Jocelin de Bohun. The accused denied the charge, but failed in the proof decreed by the bishop (probably he either made a mistake in the clearing oath or was unable to produce sufficient oathhelpers). The bishop then prudently consulted Thomas about the next step. The archbishop ruled, and made it a general rule for his whole province, that in no case should a convicted clerk suffer death or mutilation. Instead he should be deprived of all his ecclesiastical benefices, imprisoned in a monastery and there carry out enjoined penances. The duration of the penalty should depend on the rank of the offender and the gravity of the crime. In this case Thomas advised the maximum sentence, life.[9]

In 1163 Henry began to press hard. John of Canterbury, consecrated bishop of Poitiers at the Council of Tours, was already complaining before the end of June of royal restrictions on his jurisdiction. In England the *cause célèbre* occurred immediately after the Council of Woodstock, and was widely reported. Philip de Broi, canon of Bedford and a man of noble birth, when accused of the murder of a knight by the victim's relatives, had purged himself of the crime in the court of his diocesan, the bishop of Lincoln, and the king had accepted the verdict. In 1163, however, Simon fitzPeter, a royal itinerant justice, while holding an assize at Dunstable, attempted to reopen the matter. The canon lost his temper and hurled abuse at the judge; and Simon rode post-haste to London to complain to the king. When Henry threatened immediate and drastic secular penalties for the crimes, Thomas moved to protect his fellow prebendary, whom he must have known quite well. In the end it was agreed that the archbishop should try him for both offences and that a party of bishops and barons chosen by Henry should act as judges or assessors. The canon pleaded guilty to insulting a royal judge, but denied the charge of homicide and protested that he should not be tried a second time for an offence of which he had been acquitted. The archbishop's court accepted both pleas. It sentenced him to the loss of his prebend and all other revenues for two years, with the profits to be distributed to the poor at the king's discretion, to a public whipping in the presence of the judge he had insulted, and possibly to one or two years' banishment. Henry was outraged by the leniency. Here was another clerical criminal saved from the death penalty by his cloth, or, to use the common expression of the time, by his order.[10]

Thomas also offended the king in another matter which was to be pronounced on later at Clarendon. The archbishop, in virtue of his claim, obviously contested, to appoint to all vacant churches on the lands of his barons and the convent of Christ Church, gave the church of Eynsford (Kent) to a certain clerk named Lawrence. The lord of the manor, William, objected and expelled the clerk's agents. Thomas, without consulting or even notifying Henry, excommunicated William, who complained to the king. Henry, by means of a writ, ordered Thomas to absolve William. The archbishop replied that absolution, like excommunication, was a matter for him not for the king. Henry answered that it was a royal prerogative that tenants-in-chief should not be excommunicated without his consent. There was a blazing quarrel over this, and in the end Thomas gave way. He had violated an undoubted 'ancestral custom'.[11]

By the autumn of 1163 Henry had three main grievances against Thomas and sometimes the other bishops and their officials: the protection of clerical criminals from their 'proper', i.e. lay, punishment; inordinate and irregular persecution of the laity for moral offences; and, more generally, disregard for the ancient customs which governed relations between the royal and ecclesiastical authorities. He was taking advice from his experts in the three branches of law considered relevant, ecclesiastical, civil (i.e. Roman) and royal; and his main legal argument was to be that English royal laws or customs were not repugnant to divine law. This he undertook to prove by reference to the ecclesiastical law books. The most recent and systematic compilation of canon law was the monk Gratian's *Concordia Discordantium Canonum*, more briefly his *Decretum*, published about 1140 at Bologna. A typical product of the twelfth-century Renaissance, it was an encyclopaedia of the old law of the church, organized according to the latest scholastic methods, the citing of apparently discordant authorities, followed by a magisterial resolution of the problem. Important commentaries on it, *summae*, had been provided by Roland (Alexander III) and Rufinus (*c*.1157–9). It, therefore, furnished texts for all occasions and every point of view, and during the quarrel was cited by Thomas and Henry alike. But also by that time it was in some parts being superseded by new case law being created by judicial opinions and judgments issued by the pope and his curia, known as the decretals, a movement in which Alexander also played a large and formative role. With ecclesiastical law changing rapidly in order to meet new conditions in government and society, litigants had much room for manoeuvre.[12]

Henry's indignation was aggravated by Thomas's 'betrayal' and 'ingratitude'. He had been grossly deceived and badly let down. Thomas's defence for his changed stance was that he was defending the rights of the church, in all its parts, against evil customs, abuses and the violence and injustice of secular power. As long as he kept matters under control and did not provoke the king too far, he could be assured of the support not only of his professional advisers, the *eruditi*, but also of the other bishops and higher clergy. They accepted the basic principles on which he was taking his stand and were anxious not to lose the liberties they had gained during Stephen's reign. But very few of the beneficed clergy who had sworn fealty to the king and few even of the archbishop's clerks were prepared to go to extremes.

The bishops suspected Thomas's motives and competence, and, because of his background, regarded him as an unsuitable leader. They would follow him only warily. But nothing had yet got out of hand. Gilbert Foliot supported his metropolitan strongly in his attempt to prevent Roger of York having his cross carried before him in the southern province.[13]

In October Henry summoned an old-fashioned general assembly of the church to Westminster. It may well have opened with the translation of St Edward the Confessor to his reconstructed shrine in the abbey church, an ecclesiastical ceremony which took place on 13 October. The king and some of the greatest nobles carried the coffin on their shoulders through the cloisters in the presence of Thomas and all his suffragans, except the old Robert of Bath, reinforced by three Norman prelates, Rotrou of Evreux, soon to be archbishop of Rouen, Achard of Avranches, an English theologian, and Arnulf of Lisieux. At the end of this ceremony, a triumph for the abbey and for the monarchy, Thomas took as fee the only useful trophy he could find, the gravestone to which, it was believed, St Wulfstan of Worcester's staff had adhered when he was unjustly threatened with deposition by a Westminster synod, driven by William the Conqueror. It might defend him too against enemies, traitors and tyrants.[14]

When the council opened its proceedings, Henry aired his grievances; and, when he was heard unsympathetically, he asked the bishops if they would observe the ancient customs of the realm. This was the plank on which William Rufus and Henry I had taken their stand against the innovating Anselm; and it did, indeed, provide a firm position for the royalists. But also, as Anselm had shown, it could be challenged in argument and deed. Ancient customs were probably bad customs: they had to be tested against the laws of God. No bishop could give his assent to royal customs repugnant to those. And at Westminster the bishops stood firm behind Thomas and would only agree to the customs, 'saving their order', that is to say, with the reservation that anything contrary to canon law was excluded from their assent.[15] The council lasted for one day, and next morning Henry disgraced Thomas publicly by removing Prince Henry from his tutorship and depriving him of all the custodies and honours he had received as chancellor. He then left London suddenly for the Midlands. The break was still not absolute. Soon Thomas was summoned to an interview at Northampton, where they met in a field. As their horses were frisky and they could not get close enough to each other to talk, they had to change mounts. But there was no change of heart.[16]

The complete loss of royal favour must have been a great blow to Thomas's pride. The biographers, however, are not much concerned with his personal feelings at this time. Indeed, they deal with the events of the year which preceded the Council of Northampton (October 1164) in a rather muted and juristic way. None of them, it seems, not even Herbert of Bosham, believed that the issues, at least in detail, justified so great an upheaval: given the will, they could have been settled by compromise. The personal quarrel, which had taken over, was not necessarily to Thomas's credit or to the advantage of the church. With Thomas hurt and defiant and Henry embittered and revengeful, an honourable solution was out of the question.

Henry, advised by Arnulf of Lisieux, brought every possible pressure to bear on Thomas so as to force him to accept the ancient customs of the realm. By approaching the bishops individually he attracted many, perhaps most, of them to his side. The biographers name no exception. The aim of the moderates was to support or devise some scheme whereby clerical criminals could be severely punished without contravening canon law; and some of them were more expert in the subject than Thomas. Hilary of Chichester visited him at his manor of Teynham (Kent) to explain their attitude and attempt a reconciliation, but without success. On at least two occasions the pope appealed to Gilbert Foliot to work for a settlement.[17]

There also started after the Council of Westminster that web of diplomacy and litigation which is charted in the collections of Thomas's correspondence, and which involved principally the pope and cardinals and Louis of France, and also the German emperor and the princes of the Netherlands. In 1163–4 Henry used Arnulf of Lisieux and the bishop's friend, a royal clerk, Richard of Ilchester, archdeacon of Poitiers, as envoys to the papal curia at Sens. Thomas employed his clerks, Masters Henry of Houghton, Hervey of London and John of Salisbury, and also relied on John, bishop of Poitiers. The negotiations of both king and archbishop were conducted in secrecy; but if Henry's behaviour was underhand, Thomas's was close to treasonable. For an archbishop of Canterbury to conduct clandestine negotiations with the pope was contrary to the ancient customs of the kingdom; to establish an understanding with the king's enemy, the king of France, was even more criminal.[18]

As the secret diplomacy was concealed by fairly unrevealing letters of introduction and credence, its ramifications can only be reconstructed in outline. The main aim of the royal envoys in 1163–4 was to destroy Thomas's position, by obtaining from the pope toleration, if not recognition, of the English customs and a legation for Roger of York, by virtue of which he would be Thomas's superior. Thomas's agents sought to combat this and all other aggressive moves, including Roger's presumption in having his cross carried before him in the province of Canterbury, Gilbert Foliot's refusal to repeat his profession of obedience to Canterbury and Clarembald of St Augustine's refusal to make one. In addition, Thomas had begun to prepare to go into exile. He corresponded with Henry, archbishop of Rheims, the brother of Louis VII. The king and the count of Soissons offered him a refuge; and John of Poitiers wrote of joining him in exile. It is likely that Thomas, by dramatizing situations, by foreseeing the worst and making provision for it, helped it to come about.[19]

Only the secular sword was sharp. The great efforts made by both sides to manipulate papal authority rarely came to anything. Alexander, born at Siena of a noble Tuscan family, and roughly a contemporary of Thomas's, was a distinguished canon lawyer and theologian and a man of fine intelligence. As pope, with at first only fragile authority and slender resources, he was anxious to keep every possible friend, and certainly his more important supporters. Faced with new disasters in Italy, he could not afford seriously to offend Henry, but doled out concessions as sparingly and belatedly as he could. He was prepared to disappoint everyone, some a little, some a lot, in order to preserve the *status quo*. Fully aware of his long-term objectives, he nevertheless was forced to look for non-committal temporary solutions. Resourceful and diplomatic, he answered Henry's indignant appeal to history and Thomas's reliance on principles with dilatory evasiveness. In this he was helped by that effective brake on action, the judicial appeal. It was a labour of Sisyphus to obtain a definitive judgment in an ecclesiastical case. This is a standing feature of 'the Becket affair'. None of the issues which arose between the parties in 1163 came to final solution before the martyrdom. To take as an example the case of Roger's cross. In July 1162 he obtained papal confirmation of his right 'as exercised by his predecessors'. In 1163 Thomas secured a papal prohibition preventing Roger from having his cross carried in the southern province. Roger then appealed to the papal court against this action. In January 1164 Alexander suspended Roger's right, until the case should be concluded. But after Thomas's death he reversed that ruling, although again pending a definitive sentence. Disputes could become conveniently entangled in the labyrinth of jurisdictional procedure.[20]

From the point of view of the papal curia, Thomas was a liability, even a menace. There was little merit in his cause and all could see that he was a trouble-maker. He had to be restrained. All the same, Alexander was not going to deliver an archbishop bound and gagged to a king who was intent on using papal difficulties to strengthen his own authority at the expense of the church's. Thomas could be of some use to the pope as well as to Louis VII. Alexander could always hold him in reserve, even if on meagre rations.

In 1163 Alexander played desperately for time. On 26 October he advised Thomas to go to Canterbury and remain there quietly instead of dashing round the country. He then sent to England a Cistercian abbot, Philip of Aumône in Blois, who had been prior of Clairvaux under St Bernard, to urge moderation and flexibility on Thomas; and Philip, armed with letters from the pope and cardinals, and taking with him Robert of Melun, elect of Hereford, who might be expected to have some influence over Thomas, and John, count of Vendôme, one of the king's military captains, at a meeting at Harrow begged him not to rock the boat when it was already in danger of shipwreck. In the circumstances he could properly dissimulate and temporize. Thomas was also given, in order to save his face and spare his pride, various assurances, principally that Henry required only his verbal assent to the customs. Overcome by all this pressure, he went with the abbot to the king at Woodstock and promised, without expressed reservation, to observe the customs of the realm. Henry seems to have been on his best behaviour, and to have spared Thomas any humiliation. But it was the last flicker of royal goodwill. On 22 December Thomas at Canterbury performed his first episcopal consecration, Robert of Melun to Hereford. Henry, with typical cruelty, chose to spend his Christmas at Berkhamsted, which he had taken from Thomas.[21]

The king had decided – perhaps he had given Thomas full warning at Woodstock – that, because the archbishop had opposed him publicly on the customs at Westminster, he must likewise signify his adherence to them in public. A council of the magnates was therefore summoned to Clarendon, east of Salisbury, late in January 1164. It was probably as complete a collection of the higher clergy, major barons and royal officials as could be assembled. All the archbishops and bishops were there except Walter of Rochester, the old Robert of Bath and Hugh of Durham. Ten out of a theoretical total of fifteen earls were present, and the roll of barons is impressive. The council was in no way packed. Names prominent in Thomas's story are Prince Henry, the two justiciars, the earl of Leicester and Richard de Lucy, Simon fitzPeter, Richer de Laigle, his former patron, John the Marshal, Alan de Neville, who was to imprison one of his chaplains in 1166, and Hugh de Morville, one of his murderers.[22]

Henry demanded that, because disputes had arisen between, on the one hand, the clergy and, on the other, royal justices and the barons about their various rights and dignities, all the bishops should give their assent, expressly, absolutely and unconditionally, to the customs and privileges which his ancestor, Henry I, and his barons had observed. This uncompromising demand was greeted with dismay, and Thomas prevaricated. But he was gradually worn down. Henry was furious at his reluctance and made terrible threats. Two earls, the justiciar, Robert of Leicester, and Reginald of Cornwall, the king's uncle, used menacing words. Then two Knights Templar, Richard of Hastings, the English provincial master, and Hostes of St Omer, the same men who had delivered the Vexin castles to Henry in 1160 and had been expelled from France by Louis for this 'treachery', used the soft approach. Like Philip of Aumône, they said he must bow to necessity for the general good of the church. Although Gilbert Foliot in 1166 maintained that all ten bishops supported their metropolitan unswervingly, it is possible that Jocelin of Salisbury and William of Norwich begged him to submit lest they, who were already in Henry's bad books, should be further punished by the king; and it is unlikely that the others offered him much comfort or active support. They must have felt that the situation was entirely of his making; he had led them into this impasse and must now get them out of it. The barons, it seems, were hostile to a man. Not surprisingly the archbishop gave way. In 1166 Gilbert Foliot taunted, 'Only the leader fled the field.' John of Salisbury, followed by several other biographers, thought that he surrendered because he feared imprisonment, even death. Thomas made a solemn declaration in the hearing of the whole council that he would observe the laws and customs of the kingdom in good faith. He then, as Henry required, ordered the other bishops to do likewise. And this they did.

The king then decreed that a party of the more ancient and wiser barons should go apart with some royal clerks and 'make a recognition' of the customs – discover and declare what were the usages which the bishops had promised to observe. Such sworn recognitions were a familiar part of Anglo-Norman judicial and administrative proceedings, and the procedure would have surprised no one. Towards nightfall, which in January would have been about 4 o'clock, the elders emerged with a preliminary list of customs. We are not told whether they had had before them a draft, prepared in advance by the clerks; but this seems the only possible *modus operandi*. Their findings were then recited to the council. Part way through the recital Thomas interrupted. He said he was too young to know the ancient customs and was also only a recent archbishop. He would have to take advice on the findings and think about them. An adjournment to the following day was then agreed, perhaps so that a written record of the customs declared could be produced.[23]

This was done. In 1166 at Vézelay Thomas named, and excommunicated, Richard de Lucy and Jocelin de Balliol for having been 'promoters of royal tyranny and the fabricators of those heretical iniquities'. However that may be, royal clerks duly presented the recognitors' report in the form of a chirograph, dated 29 January. With this type of document, which was appropriate for a settlement or treaty, the text was written out two or three times on the same parchment, with the word CYROGRAPHUM separating the copies. By cutting horizontally through the segregating word, two or three authentic and identifiable copies became available for distribution among the interested parties. As a chirograph was usually drawn up after the 'final concord', it was not sealed. But at Clarendon the schedule of sixteen clauses recorded on the chirograph had not been agreed in advance;

and at the resumed meeting of the council Henry asked Thomas to append his seal.[24]

It is almost certain that the bishops managed to dissuade Henry from requiring them to seal the document. But their argument was that they were already bound hand and foot. It was never disputed at Northampton in October, or thereafter, that the two archbishops and the bishops had given their solemn undertaking on their word as priests, in good faith (*bona fide*), without deceit, and according to law (*legitime*), to observe the customs of the kingdom, especially as declared at Woodstock, and that they had done so on Thomas's personal order. They had also seen him accept a copy of the Constitutions; and everyone knew that acceptance of a document meant its recognition and approval. Hence their outrage and lasting grievance when Thomas reneged. He had forced them to act against their consciences, and then, adding insult to injury, had wriggled out of his own obligation. They were not impressed when at Northampton he explained that he had merely accepted the document so that he could study it and reject anything that was harmful to the church, for, he claimed outrageously, the reservation 'in good faith, without deceit, and according to law' meant 'saving the honour of the church'. Nor were they moved by his admission that perhaps also his flesh had been weak.[25]

Most of the biographers agreed with the archbishop that, in consenting to the Constitutions, he had done wrong. But, with hindsight, they could see that he had fallen only so that he could rise again. He was like St Peter who had denied Christ, David who had committed adultery and murder. But, if we renounce hindsight, it is clear that this was probably the lowest point Thomas ever reached. He had let everybody down, the king, the bishops, the church, above all himself. It was at this time that his clerks began to ask permission to leave his service. The first to go were Robert Foliot and Jordan of Melbourne, both archdeacons. As the dejected party rode from Clarendon to Winchester, Thomas was upbraided by some of his company. He suspended himself from priestly duties, imposed penance on himself and sent an account of the events to the pope. It may well have been at this point that he completed the change in his garments and demeanour which most of the biographers, but not Anonymous II, place earlier in his episcopate.[26]

The sixteen ancient customs declared at Clarendon are expressly recognized as being only a few of the important customs and dignities possessed by holy mother church, the lord king and the barons of the kingdom. They were selected presumably because they had a bearing on current matters at issue between the church and the secular authorities, and they form a heterogeneous and badly organized anthology. The declaration that clerks who held baronies of the king owed him all the usual feudal services, particularly attendance at court, except those irreconcilable with their order (clause 11) may have been a useful reminder to Thomas and any other prelate who was becoming too independent of the king. Henry referred to it at the Council of Northampton in October.[27] Some other of the Conqueror's regulations, which had already been disputed by Anselm in the reigns of William II and Henry I, reappear. The immunity of barons and royal officials from sentences of excommunication without prior royal consent is reaffirmed (7, cf. 10), and they were protected from loss of manpower by the custom that sons of villeins should not be ordained without the consent of the lord of the manor (16). Royal control of traffic between the kingdom and the papal curia (14) is made even more pointed by an attempt to limit judicial appeals to Rome (8). Henry I's concordat with Paschal II underlies the procedure laid down for episcopal elections, and the royal right to the custody of vacant bishoprics and abbeys is clearly stated (12).

Some of the judicial clauses redefine the boundary between the two authorities, warning the church off hearing disputes over land, except when held in free alms (9), and over advowsons (1) and cases of debt (15). Others attempt to reform abuses prevalent in church courts, especially archidiaconal, by a return to ideal earlier practices (5, 6, 10, 13, 14). Of these, clause 5, as a result of the sentences of excommunication promulgated by Thomas in 1166–70 and the penalties imposed by the pope after the murder, became especially contentious: to obtain (conditional) absolution excommunicates should not be required to give any sort of security, particularly on oath, for their future good behaviour, only security that they would submit to the judgment of the church.

Of more immediate importance, clause 3 regulates the procedure for the trial of criminous clerks. It is extremely concise, but can be safely expanded and expounded as follows. A clerk accused of a felony is to appear in the royal court when summoned and plead (make an answer) to the charge. If he pleads (instead of the normal Guilty or Not Guilty) that he is a clerk and should not be tried by a lay court, the court will decide where he is to stand trial. If it is decided to hand him over to the bishop (*traditio curiae*), so that he may be tried according to canon law, a royal official will go with him to watch the proceedings on behalf of the king. Finally, if the accused pleads or is found guilty in the ecclesiastical court, he is no longer to be protected by the church (i.e. he is to be degraded from his orders, rearrested and taken back to the king's court for imposition of the secular penalty).[28]

There are here two threats to clerical immunity. There was to be no automatic release of the clerk to the church christian; and, as we know from later practice, on some charges, for example breach of the forest laws, the clerk would be tried and punished in the royal court. But, more important, a procedure was envisaged which circumvented clerical immunity. The guilty clerk was to be degraded and then punished as a layman.

The most useful approach to any of the clauses of the Constitutions is to try to answer two questions: was it a true record of an ancient custom, and was it contrary to canon law? A fairly satisfactory blanket answer can be given to the first. Thomas had pleaded that he did not know the ancient customs of the kingdom. Herbert of Bosham pointed out that the king was even younger and probably even more ignorant. The recognitors had been asked to cast their minds back more than thirty years; and, although it is unlikely that they simply invented some of the customs in order to harm the archbishop and enslave the church, as Herbert alleges, their recollection may have been influenced here and there by current disputes. All the same, the historicity of the customs declared was never seriously challenged by Thomas and his adherents. Thomas may have been a new archbishop, but as an archiepiscopal clerk and archdeacon and as royal chancellor and justice he must have had a good working knowledge of legal practices over at least twenty years. It is, therefore, most significant that he and his supporters contented themselves with stigmatizing the ancient customs as ancient abuses and quoting Gratian's dictum that the Lord never said, 'I am the custom', but 'I am the truth'.[29]

In general, then, the Constitutions were genuine ancient customs of the realm. And, even if some of the more controversial clauses were contrary to canon law as currently expounded, they could, as in the past, continue to be tolerated by the church, or could be allowed, in whole or in part, to the king by papal dispensation. This is how the investiture quarrel had been settled by Paschal II and Henry I in 1106. If we direct our attention to clause 3, which was at the heart of the quarrel in 1164, it would seem that Thomas took not a strictly legal stand but rather a moral or theological one. And for a very good reason: he was unable to base his case squarely on the legal authorities. In defence of the custom, royalists could have appealed to Justinian's 83rd and 123rd Novel, available in Vacarius's textbook of Roman law, *Liber Pauperum*. And they found Gratian's *Decretum*, as then interpreted, almost equally comforting.[30]

Gratian states unequivocally that clerks were not to be tried in a secular court. But English custom only breached that rule exceptionally, and with ecclesiastical connivance. Gratian himself allowed exceptions and also drew the important distinction between ecclesiastical and secular crimes. The former were the exclusive preserve of the church, but the latter could lead to punishment by secular judges, and roughly by the method acknowledged to be English custom. Consequently, the Bolognese decretists, Gratian's pupils and followers, in the coherent theory of clerical immunity they created between 1140 and 1170, allowed a clerk, convicted of a secular crime in a church court and deprived of his orders, to be handed over to the lay authority for punishment (*traditio curiae*), particularly if the crime was enormous. For example, Alexander III, when Master Roland, argued in his *Summa* on the *Decretum* that, in the case of a clerk accused of a secular crime, no one should drag him before a secular judge until the clerk's bishop had deposed him. It would seem, therefore, that the only objection a Bolognese master of the period could have made to clause 3 of the Constitutions was the initial arraignment of a clerk in the secular court, an event which, owing to the development of royal sweeps for criminals, could hardly be avoided and in any case was a matter of minor importance.

Thomas, however, opposed the procedure sketched in clause 3 very strongly and, advised no doubt by one or more of his *eruditi*, most likely Herbert of Bosham, relied on the prophet Nahum, 1: 9. As he quoted this in the Old Latin version of the Greek Septuagint (LXX) text, 'Non judicabit deus bis in idipsum' (God himself will not judge twice in the same business), he was most likely drawing on a section in Gratian's *Decretum* concerned with penitence, where the text occurs repeatedly.[31] It is used by the canonist to support the thesis that penitence washes away sin, and that those punished sufficiently in this world will not be punished again in the next. Almost always, it seems, in Gratian and the Gloss the reference is to a second judgment or punishment after death, not in an earthly tribunal. But the principle could be variously applied. It can be read elsewhere in Gratian that, for this reason, a man on the gallows should not be refused the last sacrament. In 1149 Pope Eugenius III had forbidden Archbishop Theobald to take money from some lay servants of St Augustine's, Canterbury, for absolving them from a sentence of excommunication he had imposed, 'for men should not be punished twice for the same offence'.[32] Thomas's application of Nahum 1: 9 to the handing over of a man from one court to another was, however, an innovation; and experienced canon lawyers, like Alexander III, were at first astonished and sceptical.

Indeed, the archbishop's formulation did not attract much support in his lifetime and has at all times been ridiculed by commentators favourable to the king. It does not seem that the procedure declared at Clarendon involved a double trial or judgment, although it certainly required a double punishment: the clerk found guilty in the ecclesiastical court was to suffer first the ecclesiastical penalty of degradation and then the secular penalty of mutilation or death. Thomas and his apologists held that unfrocking was a sufficiently severe punishment by itself. The only concession they would offer was that, if the degraded clerk should offend again, he could this second time be treated as a layman.

Double punishment is a common feature in many societies (e.g. loss of job and punishment in a public court); but in modern times the first penalty is often cited in court in mitigation of the second, and objections on principle are not uncommon. In the twelfth century, however, double punishment by church and state was the basic feature of their co-operation. The theory of the Two Swords was accepted by everyone. The king expected the church to excommunicate his enemies before he could get at them himself; and the church required the king to provide physical means for enforcing its spiritual penalties – in the case of heretics and sometimes rebels, to eradicate them by combustion. Thomas had been present at the papal Council of Rheims in 1148 when the heretic Eon de l'Etoile and his followers were tried and condemned. Eon was sentenced to life imprisonment, but his followers were delivered to the lay court and then to the flames.[33] To abolish the possibility of a second secular punishment would be most inconvenient to the church, as everyone in 1164 not blinded by passion could see. If the king were to withdraw his co-operation with the ecclesiastical authorities, refuse to unsheathe his sword, the church's government would be almost entirely ineffective.

Yet Thomas did right to hesitate before accepting the procedure laid down in clause 3. A custom which may in the past have been sporadic and operated usually only when to the advantage of the church, was being turned into a rule. In the light of the new theology, it was hard to tolerate the execution of a priest who earlier that day had had the power to perform the miracle of the Mass. It was a very sudden change of character. In a case like that of Philip de Broi's, it could have shocked. But Thomas's precipitate and unqualified rejection of the procedure was not only unwise; it was also unrealistic. Most clerical criminals subject to the regulation were not beneficed priests, but men indistinguishable from laymen until they advanced this useful plea, clerks in minor orders, married men, engaged in secular business. There was room for discrimination. Subtlety, however, was not one of Thomas's qualities; and the legal case he developed against the procedure, although clever in its use of an impressive text as a slogan, was ill considered and, when considered, unconvincing.

The wisdom of Henry's actions can also be questioned. His requirement, probably after semi-official assurances to the contrary, that Thomas and the bishops should assent publicly to the customs was provocative, and his committal of these to writing was rash. His mother, the Empress Matilda, is reported to have expressed the view, when shown the Constitutions at Rouen the following Christmas, that, although the church needed reform and some of the customs were sensible, Henry had been unwise to publish them since it was an innovation to force bishops to swear to observe the customs of the realm. Yet, we may think, once Thomas had agreed to observe the customs, the recording followed inevitably. If there was to be a real settlement, it would have to be based, not on diplomatic evasions, but on definite terms; and, if the king meant business, the customs had first to be elucidated. Any canon lawyer could have told him that: it was what the church had been doing for a century. Wherever government was reactivated, unwritten custom was being replaced by *ius scriptum*. It was an age of record, and it was quite unrealistic of Thomas's biographers to quote the legal tag, 'Only things published (*expressa*) can cause injury; those remaining unpublished do not.'[34] Henry must be given credit for seriousness of purpose. The Constitutions presuppose, and give several instances of, fruitful co-operation between church and state. But they were intentionally old-fashioned in outlook. They view the king as the real head and master of the English church. The ultimate decision always lies with him; the liberties of the church are what he concedes. Moreover, because in 1164 Henry was also motivated by ill-will and the desire to humiliate Thomas, and because he regarded the situation, with the archbishop isolated and the pope in dire straits, as exceptionally propitious, an opportunity which might never recur, he overplayed his hand. It would have been more prudent to try to get his way on a few important, but limited, issues, especially technical matters like criminous clerks, which were amenable to practical solutions, rather than produce a wide-ranging schedule of royal prerogatives and baronial rights as a sort of offensive manifesto. But it is common practice to claim a lot in order to gain something. Litigants have to make a choice. Medieval man never understated his case. With hindsight Henry too can be vindicated.

The Council of Clarendon ended untidily with Thomas racked by the problem of whether or not to confirm and seal the Constitutions. Further pressure was put on him by the arrival of Rotrou de Beaumont, bishop of Evreux and royal justiciar in Normandy, to advise the king on a number of matters.[35] Rotrou, uncle of the then earl of Warwick and cousin of the earl of Leicester, the justiciar in England, was a man of great influence, who, when archbishop of Rouen, played an important part in Thomas's affairs. King and bishop travelled from Porchester to Woodstock, and it was probably there that they interviewed Thomas and persuaded him to write to the pope asking him to confirm the English customs. Although this action clearly worried the biographers, it was the only possible escape route open to Thomas, and can hardly be considered cowardly or dishonourable. But it was also, for all the parties, a desperate manoeuvre. And, although Alexander avoided the trap by neither confirming nor officially condemning the customs *en bloc*, Thomas was as a result left in an even worse position. He decided to stand and fight on his own. And it may well be that it was at this point that he suspended himself from service at the altar as punishment for his earlier weakness.[36]

It was also the point of no return for Henry. Not only had the events at Clarendon and their aftermath hardened his attitude towards Thomas, he had also had to swallow the bitter fruit of another of Thomas's ungrateful obstructions. On 30 January his brother William, his constant companion and close friend, but disliked by Thomas, died at Rouen, broken-hearted it was believed because the archbishop had refused, on the grounds of consanguinity, to allow him to marry the countess of Surrey, the widow of William of Boulogne, King Stephen's younger son. In 1164, perhaps in April, Henry gave her in marriage instead to his illegitimate brother, Hamelin. But it was a grievance which was never forgotten by the royalists. Richard le Bret struck the final blow at the martyrdom 'in memory of his lord, William the king's brother'.[37]

Henry began to injure Thomas in all ways he could. In 1163–4 Thomas had neither a papally confirmed primacy nor a papal legation. Therefore, if either office, especially the latter, could be obtained for York, Thomas could be put in humiliating subordination to his rival. But Henry's negotiations with Alexander during the winter months through Arnulf of Lisieux and Richard of Ilchester came to nought, and the royal clerks, John of Oxford and Geoffrey Ridel, were hardly more successful at the end of February 1164. They drove Alexander to pronounce on some matters, but the pronouncements were of baffling insufficiency, in detail and in sum, to all concerned. The pope refused to confirm the Constitutions, but in compensation granted a legation to Roger of York and declined to declare Canterbury's primacy. Moreover, he did nothing about the 'disobedience' to Canterbury of the bishop of London and the abbot of St Augustine's. But he also excluded Thomas's person, and perhaps more, from the new legate's authority. Consequently, towards the end of May, a fresh set of royal emissaries returned the legatine commission unused in an unsuccessful attempt to better its terms. On that day, however, Alexander heard that the antipope, Victor IV, had died and was in no conciliatory mood. All the same, by 1170 Roger was certainly 'legate of the Holy See' and had probably held the office continuously.[38]

Diplomatic failures did not deter Henry from enforcing observance of the Constitutions in the kingdom, particularly clause 3. He dispatched itinerant justices to sweep for criminals, probably using juries of presentment in a way which anticipated the Assize of Clarendon of 1166, and demanded the degradation and return to the secular court of all priests and clerks caught in the net. Thomas, driven to defiance, forbade this practice on pain of excommunication.[39]

King and archbishop still met occasionally on great ceremonial occasions; and one such was the dedication of Reading Abbey on 19 April 1164. This foundation of Henry I's, where he was buried, and where Henry II had his infant son William interred in 1156, was regarded by the Plantagenet as a family shrine. It also had a relic of the highest class. In 1125 the widowed empress Matilda, Henry I's daughter, had brought back from Germany among her treasures the hand of St James, once at Venice and more recently in the imperial chapel. This she gave to Reading. In 1157 Frederick Barbarossa had asked Henry for its return. But on 17 July of that year, at a great council at Northampton, where, incidentally, Silvester, abbot of St Augustine's, had made his profession to Theobald, Henry and Thomas had concocted a splendid letter of refusal, and dispatched, through the agency of Master Heribert and the royal clerk William, an enormous tent instead. As Master Heribert was almost certainly Herbert of Bosham, the clerk must have had interesting thoughts as he attended Thomas at the dedication of Reading seven years later. Perhaps he was already affecting German fashions in dress, in the circumstances a strange eccentricity. Also present at the ceremony, besides the king and the nobles, were ten English bishops, including Henry of Winchester, who had purloined the hand of St James during his brother's reign. Thomas granted an indulgence of twenty days to all those who visited the shrine.[40]

In the winter of 1163–4 John of Salisbury had left Thomas to go and live in France. The affair is cloaked in secrecy; but, reading between the lines, it would seem that he went on the archbishop's instructions to act as his agent, to spy and recruit allies, while posing as a scholar at Paris. He may well have been paving the way for Thomas should he decide to go to the papal curia at Sens to defend his cause or escape from the Angevin dominions. John was always a moderating influence on the archbishop. In what may have been his earliest report from France, he begged him to seek the king's grace if he could do it without offending God; and his absence from the household helps to explain why Thomas, in the hands of zealots like Herbert of Bosham, rushed to his doom. John's light-hearted gossip on royal and papal affairs in France and the doings of others who might be involved in the archbishop's fate is a pleasant relief. There was talk, he said, of the pope coming to England and carrying out a belated coronation of the young Henry, even pushing Thomas out of Canterbury. He had had an interesting chat with Louis VII about his daughter in England. And Paris was as marvellous as ever. It is clear that John would not spend his exile in sackcloth and ashes.[41]

Another of Thomas's clerks, Reginald, archdeacon of Salisbury, 'the Lombard', Bishop Jocelin's son, likewise had gone to live in France by June 1164. By November he was well in with the French king and the pope, and, according to Guernes, had been made by Louis abbot of Corbeil. It would seem that the archbishop's diplomatic activity in France was even greater than the king's, and, because illicit, distorted by all the paraphernalia of espionage, secret messengers, coded names, lost or destroyed communications, guarded news, misinformation and rumour. Two letters to Thomas from the summer of 1164, one from John, bishop of Poitiers, the other from the archbishop's nuncio, possibly Hervey, show these features well.[42]

Thomas's last recorded public engagement as archbishop in this period was the consecration of Roger as bishop of Worcester on 23 August at Canterbury. It was probably after this, and possibly provoked by having the gates of Woodstock shut in his face when he tried to have an interview with the king, that he decided to follow John and Reginald to France and consult the pope. From his manor of Aldington, near Hythe, he went with a few companions down to Romney, where he managed to hire a small boat. But the sailors, led by Adam of Charing, hereditary farmer of that episcopal manor, whom Thomas was to excommunicate in 1169, soon repented of what might turn out to be a treasonable act; and the wind too may have been unfavourable. At dawn Thomas found himself once again on the Kentish shore. After this he was admitted, perhaps summoned, to Woodstock, where Henry is reported to have asked reproachfully, 'Why do you want to leave my land? Don't you think it can hold us both?'[43]

Thomas, by attempting to leave England without Henry's permission, had, of course, violated one of the ancient customs as recently declared at Clarendon, and was clearly 'in the king's mercy'. By losing patience he had delivered himself into the king's hands. Edward Grim and his copyists were no doubt right in thinking that Henry was relieved that the escape bid had failed – even if their suggestion that he had feared a papal interdict on his kingdom if the archbishop had managed to reach Sens seems far-fetched. Thomas in England could be tormented; Thomas in France would be of use to Louis and Alexander. Henry, unlike William Rufus and Henry I, who did little to prevent Anselm going into exile, did all he could to stop Thomas escaping.

For reasons unknown, Henry did not charge Thomas with this breach of the customs, but used a feudal case and then financial suits to bring the chastened archbishop down. As we have noticed, Thomas had fallen foul of an important military servant of the Angevins, John fitzGilbert the marshal, one of the witnesses to the Constitutions of Clarendon. This brave soldier had lost an eye in the empress's service, and his son, William the Marshal, the mirror of chivalry, was to rise through royal favour to become earl of Pembroke and one of the greatest magnates in England. John had brought a suit in the archbishop's honorial court for possession of a parcel of land pertaining to the archbishop's demesne manor of Pagham in Sussex. When he failed to get judgment in his favour, he appealed, on the grounds of denial of justice, to the court of the archbishop's feudal superior, the king. Thomas, however, when summoned to answer the charge in the royal court on 14 September, did not put in a personal appearance, and, although most of the biographers tried to minimize the matter, clearly did not send a proper or adequate excuse (essoin). He was then cited through the sheriff of Kent to answer John's complaint at a council of the magnates summoned to meet at Northampton on Tuesday, 6 October, with the original purpose, it seems, of dealing with the rebellion in Wales. As he did not receive a personal summons to this assembly, he was from the start treated not as an archbishop or royal counsellor but as a baron accused of wrongful behaviour.[44]

Thomas's trial on various charges at the council held in Northampton castle had as precedents the trials of William of St Calais, bishop of Durham, at Salisbury in 1088 and of Archbishop Anselm at Rockingham in 1095. In each the outcome depended on where the sympathy of the magnates, both secular and ecclesiastical, lay: in 1088 William Rufus had an easy run, in 1095 he was less successful. In all cases the defendant disputed the competence of the court to try him; in all there were procedural difficulties; and in 1095 and 1164 the bench of bishops groaned at being placed between the anvil and the hammer. All the cases aroused great interest and were well reported by sympathizers of the accused. Among Thomas's biographers, William fitzStephen and Herbert of Bosham were in attendance on their master throughout the proceedings, and later described them in detail. Ralf of Diss (Diceto), the chronicler, then archdeacon of London, was also present, and wept abundantly on the final day; but his account of the court is noticeably dry.[45]

Thomas took a large retinue from Harrow to Northampton. He is reported as having almost forty clerks besides chaplains and monks as well as his military escort of knights and the noble boys of his household. On his arrival on the appointed day he found the king away hawking and his own lodgings occupied by royal squires under William de Courcy, a royal steward and seneschal of Normandy. He himself took up residence in the Cluniac priory of St Andrew. His first action was to ask the king to order William de Courcy out, and Henry obliged. As John the Marshal was also absent from court on royal business, nothing could be done on the Wednesday. But the court got down to business on Thursday, 8 October, when Thomas was charged with contempt of the king because he had ignored the royal summons to attend court on 14 September. There seems to have been a general feeling among the bishops and barons that Thomas was at least technically in the wrong, and he was condemned for his contumacy to forfeiture of all his moveable possessions at the mercy of the king. After a dispute over who should declare the judgment, the duty was imposed on Henry of Winchester. Thomas was only brought to accept the sentence by the unanimous pressure of the bishops, who wanted the whole business settled with the minimum of fuss and were willing, except for London, to stand surety for payment of the fine. No doubt they expected that it would be commuted to a 'reasonable' monetary penalty, as was usual in such cases. But when Thomas had recovered from the shock of his condemnation, he complained bitterly of the monstrous severity of the sentence, and was so outraged by the conduct of the bishops that he said privately that he would in due course suspend them all for having had the temerity to pass judgment on their own archbishop.[46]

Eventually, probably early in 1165, Alexander quashed this sentence on the general grounds that a superior should not be judged by inferiors, particularly subordinates, and that the church should not suffer loss through the fault of an individual. Moreover, confiscation of all moveable property was contrary to justice and ecclesiastical custom, especially since Thomas possessed no moveables beyond those belonging to the church. Gilbert Foliot, however, in 1166 blamed Thomas for having submitted to the judgment of a secular court.[47]

To return to Northampton, after this defeat Thomas had his one and only success. When called upon to answer to the charge of denying justice to John the Marshal, he refused on several grounds, probably those which he had pleaded by proxy when originally summoned: that John had no good claim to the land, that he had failed in his proof, that the appeal was a novelty and that John's oath in support of it was null, because he had sworn it not on the Gospels but on a service book. In this matter the sympathy of the magnates, who would not have cared for such appeals from honorial courts, was with Thomas. And Henry was forced to let the case drop. This should have ended the proceedings against the archbishop. But Henry, either because of a deep-laid scheme or, much more likely, because he would not accept defeat, began to air a series of other grievances – Thomas's failure to repay royal loans and his retention of royal revenues while chancellor, and, finally, his contempt for the oath he had taken at Clarendon to observe the ancient customs of the realm. The court sat on Friday and the following Tuesday, 13 October. On Saturday the parties took counsel; Sunday was a holiday; and on Monday Thomas was ill of some stomach disorder.[48]

It is possible that Henry asked as early as Thursday for the accounts of the custodies which Thomas had held as chancellor. The archbishop replied that he had not been cited on this matter and was unprepared. He refused throughout on those grounds to make a formal answer to this charge, but said, off the record, that he had spent all the profits and much more on the king's business, and everything he had done had been with the king's authority. Moreover, he had been given acquittance before his consecration of all claims against him as chancellor. Everyone knew by this time that Henry intended Thomas's humiliation and ruin. If judgment on these debts should be given against the archbishop, the debtor would have to produce sureties for payment, and, indeed, starting with the bishops, he provided a series of pledges. The machinery for enforcement was distraint, first on the debtor's (or sureties') moveable goods, then, if necessary, on his or their land, and finally on his person, that is to say he could be imprisoned. As the royal pressure grew, many courtiers, including Thomas, believed that Henry was aiming at his arrest. Before the end there were rumours of penalties even more severe.

The king seems to have started with two successes. William fitzStephen believed that he got the court's judgment in respect of £300 owed from the custody of Eye and Berkhamsted, and that Thomas named William, earl of Gloucester, the king's cousin, the magnanimous William of Eynesford, and one other as his sureties. As regards the royal loans and guarantees on the Toulouse campaign, which Thomas claimed had been gifts, Herbert of Bosham thought that on the Friday both barons and bishops decided that Thomas should repay one sum of £500, and that five men offered to stand surety at £100 apiece. But when Thomas was required to account for all the custodies which had passed through his hands, and the amount involved was estimated at £30,000, some bishops thought that Thomas could escape only by throwing himself on Henry's mercy and offering to pay a heavy fine. But they seem to have been proved wrong. According to William fitzStephen, on the Saturday Thomas offered the king 2,000 marks which Henry of Winchester had offered to find, and the king refused it.[49]

Thomas consulted his suffragan bishops as a body on several occasions. They were unanimous in declining to support him actively. Most thought that he had brought the disaster on himself and that he was paying for his vainglory and arrogance as chancellor. Just as in 1088 and 1095, prudent colleagues urged the 'martyr' to submit, in 1164 in order to save the church and them from even worse treatment. Why should they, the English church and the papal cause have to suffer because of Thomas's secular and sinful past? Some bishops, including a few who wished him well, advised him to offer the king his resignation: this humiliation would satisfy the tyrant. A few, principally Gilbert of London and Hilary of Chichester, who had been his friends, became his enemies. Roger of York played as discreetly as possible for his own hand. Thomas's household was naturally split between a minority of fanatical supporters and the main body of moderates and time-servers. Among the former was Herbert of Bosham, among the latter William fitzStephen. After Friday Thomas was no longer visited in his lodgings by nobles and knights.[50]

The hiatus between Friday and Tuesday only exacerbated the quarrel. Henry became more and more impatient, and he believed that Thomas's illness on the Monday was put on. The archbishop was warned that the king was threatening imprisonment or death and that some courtiers were plotting to kill him. It is difficult to know how seriously the threats were intended. No doubt Henry made some rash and angry remarks (as at Christmas 1170), doubtless there were irresponsible courtiers who talked even more foolishly. But it was almost unheard of for a bishop to be imprisoned by a king, especially on a trumped-up 'civil' charge, and out of the question for an archbishop to be sentenced by the royal court to death. And though it is possible, although most unlikely, that the highly contentious clause 3 of the Constitutions of Clarendon might have been invoked, Arnulf of Lisieux informed Thomas in March 1165 that Henry had not had the slightest intention of going beyond threats – indeed, it was because he did not intend to proceed to extremities that he was forced to such mimic violence. Thomas, however, isolated and undoubtedly abused, believed in the truth of the rumours, and during the weekend he must have put the final touches to his contingency plan to escape abroad. He was to use the services of Gilbert of Sempringham's order of canons, and recruited two guides, Robert de Cave and Scaiman, possibly from the Gilbertine priory at Lincoln. His life was to assume clandestine features from which he could never completely break free. But if the threats caused his nervous prostration on the Monday, by Tuesday he had recovered his strength and nerved himself for battle. Convinced that he could not make peace on honourable terms, he resolved to go down fighting.[51]

Tuesday, 13 October, started with Thomas meeting the bishops, presumably in the priory where he lodged. He found them dispirited, full of warnings that he was about to be charged with perjury and treachery for violating the royal customs, particularly the Constitutions of Clarendon, and desperately anxious that he should submit to the king. Thomas complained angrily of their desertion and of their having twice passed judgment on him. He forbade them to do so again, especially on a criminal charge, and appealed to the pope against the possibility. He also ordered them, if he should be subjected to physical coercion, to excommunicate the aggressors. Gilbert of London immediately made a counter-appeal to the pope. Then all the bishops, except Henry of Winchester and Jocelin of Salisbury, who remained to comfort him, left for the king's court.[52]

Thomas's next act of defiance was to celebrate a votive Mass to the protomartyr St Stephen, with its Introit, 'Princes also did sit and speak against me' (Psalm 118=119: 23), and afterwards to secrete the Eucharist on his person. He also proposed going to court still fully vested and girt with the pallium, but was dissuaded by some Knights Templar. Instead, he took his cross from the bearer when he reached the castle and advanced with it in his hands. The bishops who awaited his arrival recognized the gesture as provocative – unsheathing the spiritual sword – and tried to disarm him.

Worcester offered to carry it for him, London tried to snatch it from his hands. But to no avail. Gilbert Foliot in his exasperation exclaimed, 'A fool he always was, and a fool he'll always be.' Thomas then sat as usual in the outer chamber, attended by a few clerks, including Herbert of Bosham, John Planeta, Hugh de Nonant and William fitzStephen, while the king conferred with the bishops and his other counsellors in an upper room.[53]

The bishops told Henry what had taken place at St Andrew's earlier that morning, and the king sent down earls and barons to ask Thomas whether he had indeed made that appeal and prohibition, and to remind him that he was the king's liege vassal and had sworn him fealty. He had also sworn at Clarendon to preserve the royal rights and dignities and had recognized that bishops should take part in all judgments in the king's court, save those which involved the shedding of blood. Further, they asked if he was ready to give surety that he would render the accounts of his chancellorship and accept the court's judgment in the case. Thomas refused this demand, elaborating the reasons he had already given; and he admitted that he had made the appeal and prohibition, which he justified and renewed. He placed his person and the church of Canterbury under the protection of God and the Holy See.

The biographers believed – they were deprived of firsthand information – that, when these answers were reported in the upper chamber, the barons were indignant and the bishops dismayed. The Constitutions of Clarendon were invoked and it was decided that the court should condemn the archbishop. But since no formal judgment was declared in open court, the biographers were uncertain of what was decided. Most likely it was intended to condemn Thomas both for refusing to render account and for violating his oath to observe the Constitutions. The latter judgment would have made the archbishop – as in the case of the bishop of Durham in 1088 – guilty of perjury and treason, and would have justified – as with Odo of Bayeux in 1082 – a sentence of imprisonment. Indeed, Roger of Howden believed that this was the judgment of the barons. The bishops, therefore, their reluctance intensified by Thomas's prohibition, tried to escape further participation in the court's judgments. Henry agreed to a dual procedure. The bishops, for their part, were to appeal to the pope against Thomas on the grounds of his perjury and were to do their best to persuade Alexander to depose him. They went down to initiate their ecclesiastical process, and Thomas accepted it, but justified his behaviour, very much like Anselm when placed in a similar position in 1097, by arguing that he had accepted nothing at Clarendon except bona fide, by which he meant 'according to his conscience', and that there was always in such clerical undertakings the inescapable reservation 'saving the honour of the church'.[54]

When, however, the barons, led by the justiciar, the earl of Leicester, went down in their turn, Thomas refused to accept their judgment. He had been cited to court only in the case of John the Marshal; there had been no pleading in any other case; and, anyhow, barons were incompetent to judge an archbishop. While the justiciar faltered, Thomas rose, went out of the chamber and passed through the hall to shouts of 'perjurer' and 'traitor'. Among his revilers were Hamelin, the king's illegitimate brother, Ranulf de Broc and Hugh Wake of Bourne. Ranulf, hereditary doorkeeper of the king's chamber and keeper of the royal whores, was, with his clan, the *Brokeis*, to play an important part in the archbishop's life and death. Thomas answered their taunts with abuse: Hamelin was a servile bastard; a kinsman of Ranulf had been hanged for a crime. Miraculously Thomas and his clerks managed to escape from the castle through a locked gate, for which his servant, Peter *de Munctorio*, found the key. Mounting their horses, they reached the sanctuary of St Andrew's. William fitzStephen remembered that in the confusion Herbert of Bosham could not get on his horse and that Thomas carried him away on his. Herbert himself does not mention this mishap.[55]

The trial had come to a tumultuous end. In the months that followed king and archbishop shaped their views of what had happened. For Henry, the ungrateful and forsworn archbishop had been tried for financial embezzlement while in his service, had refused to produce accounts and had therefore been justly condemned. He was a convicted criminal on the run. On the very eve of their reconciliation at Fréteval in July 1170, Henry, when discussing the matter with the king of France, referred to Thomas as a thief. Thomas, for his part, was outraged by the unheard of humiliations to which an archbishop of Canterbury had been subjected: he had been treated as a layman, judged and condemned by his sons in God and persecuted by those who were seeking to destroy the liberties of the church by invoking evil customs which they claimed were 'ancestral'. In short, he was a martyr for the liberty of the church. Neither view can be dismissed out of hand. Both were held by respectable observers before the martyrdom.

To redress the bias of the biographers and chroniclers who wrote after that event, attention should be given to an account of the reign completed in 1169, the poem *Draco Normannicus* by Stephen of Rouen, a monk of Bec. The hero is Henry and one of the villains is Thomas. As chancellor he was guilty of peculation. As archbishop he was a rogue plantation, not only insufficiently educated but also 'the faithless heir of that triple cheat, Simon Magus'. He bought his pallium, and, it is suggested, other sacred offices too. When he fled to France, because accused of theft, he told lies to the pope at Sens and then adhered to and encouraged Henry's greatest enemies. In short, he was a criminal and traitor. The patriotic Norman monk could not stand him.[56]

Although after the conclusion of the trial at Northampton, Henry, at the request of the bishop of Hereford, had it proclaimed that no one was to do Thomas harm, rumours of intended violence were rife. While the archbishop was at dinner, the bishops of London and Chichester, still convinced that the king could be bought off, arrived with a new proposal. If Thomas were to offer him his manors of Otford and Wingham (in 1086 worth £60 and £100 a year respectively) as sureties for paying the fines, everything could be arranged. Thomas replied in fury, 'The king is holding the manor of Higham, which rightly belongs to Canterbury. And although I have not the slightest hope of recovering it, I would not offer even that in order to recover his favour.' The two bishops indignantly withdrew. After dinner all the archbishop's knights tearfully renounced their homage and, with the archbishop's permission, left his service. The noble boys being educated in his household also departed. Herbert of Bosham did not blame any of these, but could not condone the desertion of some of the clerks. Thomas then sent the bishops of Rochester, Hereford and Worcester to Henry to ask for a safe conduct for his journey from court. When they reported that the king, whom they had found in a good humour, had replied that he would consider the matter on the following day, Thomas concluded that all was lost and put into effect the escape plan he had prepared.[57]

Herbert of Bosham was dispatched to Canterbury to collect as much as he could of the archiepiscopal rents which had been due at Michaelmas and then go with the money to St Bertin's monastery at St Omer, where he was to await his master. At Northampton fresh horses were obtained and held ready; the town gates were reconnoitred; and a bed was prepared for Thomas behind the high altar of the priory church. After the office of Prime and the recital of the litany, that is to say, about 7 o'clock, just before dawn on Wednesday, 14 October, Thomas was ready to go. He deliberately left behind his usually inseparable priestly stole (temporarily suspending himself from priestly functions) and took only his pallium and seals, symbols of his governmental authority.[58] Under the additional cover of a rainstorm, the small party, the archbishop with one servant, Roger de Bray, and the two Gilbertine lay-brethren,[59] left the town by the unguarded north gate and rode hard for Lincoln. This was doubtless to put his enemies, who would have expected him to travel south, off the scent. After a few hours sleep at Grantham, the party did the last 25 of the 83 miles' journey, and went into hiding with James, a fuller, a friend of one of the guides, who probably lived by the river. Thomas then travelled by boat down the Witham towards, or to, Boston, a distance of some 35 miles, lurking in Gilbertine priories and granges, including 'the Hermitage' (perhaps Catley) and Haverholme, in the fenland to the west of Boston. When he was confident that his trail had not been picked up, he moved cautiously towards the Channel ports, disguised as a Gilbertine lay-brother, and answering to the name of Christian or Dereman. When he reached the Gilbertine priory of Chicksands in Bedfordshire, he recruited the chaplain Gilbert, presumably to serve as a guide on the most dangerous section. They now rode only at night and laid up by day. Finally they reached the Canterbury manor of Eastry, close to Sandwich, the archiepiscopal port he intended to use. On Monday, 2 November, almost three weeks after he had fled from Northampton, a little before dawn he embarked in a small boat, and in the afternoon landed on the beach at Oye, between Marck and Gravelines, not far from Dunkerque, in the county of Flanders. He was outside Henry's jurisdiction. St Omer was some 40 kilometres south. He was on the road to Sens. Royalist bishops, such as Arnulf of Lisieux and Gilbert Foliot, maintained that Thomas had never been in danger and had not been pursued. Henry himself always protested that Thomas had simply bolted. Intentions are seldom consistent and justifications rarely entirely true.[60]

CHAPTER SEVEN

THOMAS ON THE DEFENSIVE, NOVEMBER 1164–APRIL 1166

It had not been unusual since the death of Lanfranc in 1089 for an English archbishop to go into exile. Anselm had taken leave of William Rufus in 1097 and of Henry I in 1103. Thurstin of York had gone abroad in 1116. In 1148 Stephen had banished both archbishops from England, and in 1152 had driven Theobald out. In all these cases the prelate had been defending the rights of the church, or of his own church, against a 'tyrant'. In most there had also been personal or political differences between archbishop and king. In none, however, except possibly in 1152, had the archbishop fled because of the threat or fear of violence to his person.

All these precedents were familiar to Thomas, and he could have taken comfort from the fact that none of the exiles had lasted more than three years – most had been considerably shorter – and that all had ended satisfactorily for the archbishop. No one involved in the quarrel between Thomas and Henry in 1163–4 would have expected it to have lasted so long or to have ended so tragically: Henry was regarded, even in Thomas's household, as a much better king than Stephen, the arch-tyrant. But it had a feature absent from all the other cases: the personal animosity which Thomas's conduct had aroused not only in the king but also in several of the bishops and even more so among the barons. They did not think that he was too holy or too idealistic to be a successful archbishop of Canterbury. On the contrary, they thought that the causes he championed were harmed by his support.

Deserted subordinates are inclined to believe that their leader has failed in his duty towards them. Anselm had been blamed, and Thomas was to attract even more censure. Things had gone dreadfully wrong. At any point between 1162 and the martyrdom it was, and is, not unreasonable to take the view that Thomas's career had peaked as chancellor. He had done extraordinarily well in that office. But as archbishop he had floundered and then panicked. The difficulties he had to face would have tested any incumbent

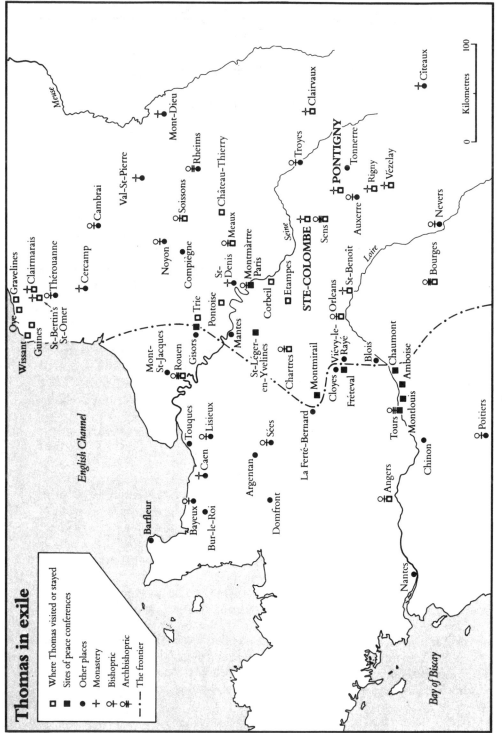

Thomas in exile

Where Thomas visited or stayed
Sites of peace conferences
Other places
Monastery
Bishopric
Archbishopric
The frontier

English Channel

Bay of Biscay

Thomas in exile

of the see, and he was not given much time for growing into the office before he had to meet the challenge. Thomas's past – his dependence on the king and his worldliness – doomed him to failure. Nevertheless, if we accept that he had not actively aimed at the archbishopric and that the scheme was entirely Henry's, he was more a victim of circumstances than an Icarus. Everyone had expected him to be a worldly archbishop, and would have tolerated its consequences, some of which would have benefited both church and king. It is ironical that, by trying to refashion his way of life, he disappointed even those who had disapproved of his appointment and satisfied few beyond some zealots in his household. If he aimed at joining the ambitions of a Henry of Winchester to the single-mindedness of an Anselm, he forgot the solid foundations on which both of those built and which were to preserve their careers and reputations.

When the small party of fugitives landed on the open beach at Oye early in November 1164 they were in a sorry state, weary, dishevelled, dejected, short of money and uncertain of their welcome, indeed fearful of capture by authorities whom the English king could have enlisted. Only by mounting the exhausted archbishop on a miserable nag they hired for a penny could they get him the 8 kilometres to Gravelines and the comfort of an inn. But, although there were moments of alarm – the archbishop could still be aroused by the sight of a hawk – their disguise held; and next day they set off for St Omer, a hummock in the wetlands, probably by boat. A complication was the simultaneous arrival of an embassy dispatched by Henry to the same princes whose favour Thomas had to seek, the count of Flanders, the king of France and the pope. This grand company, which included the archbishop of York, the bishops of London, Chichester, Exeter and Worcester, the earl of Arundel, the royal clerks Richard of Ilchester, John of Oxford and Guy Rufus, dean of Waltham, the royal chamberlain Henry fitzGerold and other barons and ecclesiastics, had crossed from Dover to Wissant or Boulogne, a more southerly course than Thomas's, and was likewise making for St Omer. Both parties wanted to avoid an embarrassing encounter, and the archbishop first went into hiding and then cautiously followed in the others' wake.[1]

Thomas had appointed the Benedictine abbey of St Bertin's at St Omer, the usual staging-point, as rendezvous with his supporters. And there he was awaited anxiously by Herbert of Bosham, who had managed at Canterbury to lay his hands on only a few silver vases and 100 marks (£66 13s. 4d.) in cash, the sole provision for their journey. But while the royal embassy remained thereabouts, Thomas hid once again in marshes, this time at the Cistercian abbey of Clairmarais, 4 kilometres north-east of St Omer, and then in a water-girt hermitage (Oldminster) belonging to St Bertin's. There, or more likely later in the abbey itself, he received one unwelcome visitor,

Richard de Lucy, who was returning from either a pilgrimage or an embassy to the count. The justiciar begged his old friend to return to England with him, promising that he would settle all his differences with the king. And when Thomas refused, they had a violent quarrel which culminated in Richard's renunciation of the homage he had done the archbishop – paying it back, the exile remarked angrily, as though it was a loan he could settle at his pleasure. This interview is recorded by the biographers without comment. But it marks for Thomas the point of no return. It also shows how bitterly men loyal to the king viewed his desertion.[2]

An exchange of letters with Hugh, probably Hugh de Nonant, Arnulf of Lisieux's nephew, reveals how bewildered and desperate the archbishop was. Thomas had written to his clerk (possibly as a channel to Arnulf) asking for advice on what to do. Hugh answered that, although he was the most unimportant of those who had incurred the king's wrath, he intended, unlike many others of Thomas's men, to stand by him loyally. He was ready to undergo imprisonment, even death. But, as he was only a boy, he could hardly advise his lord. Nevertheless, he thought that the archbishop would be better advised to wait and discover exactly what Henry's intentions were before turning to a foreign prince.[3]

After a few days in the marshlands Thomas received a warm welcome from Abbot Godescal of St Bertin's, and was soon joined there by some of the clerks he had left behind at Northampton and by a few others. Of his companions on the journey from England only the chaplain Gilbert and Scaiman can be identified. From Northampton or Canterbury came, besides Herbert, the archbishop's chaplains, Robert, canon of Merton, and Richard of Salisbury (possibly a relative of John of Salisbury), his cross-bearer, Alexander-Llewelyn, the keeper of his seal, Master Ernulf, his clerks Baldwin of Boulogne, archdeacon of Norwich, Gunter of Winchester, and Theold, canon of St Martin's, Canterbury. Also at St Bertin's were Master Lombard of Piacenza, the future cardinal and archbishop of Benevento, and Silvester, treasurer of Lisieux, a nephew of Bishop Arnulf. None of this company would seem to have been a monk. Notable absentees were John of Salisbury and William fitzStephen.[4]

Thomas was also visited and befriended by Milo II, bishop of neighbouring Thérouanne, an Englishman by birth. It was known that the royal embassy to Philip of Alsace, ruling as count in the place of his Crusading father, had requested the prince not to harbour the 'fugitive from justice', even, perhaps, to arrest him and return him to England. So it was decided to send two abbots, perhaps those of Clairmarais and St Bertin's, to ask for the count's safe conduct. But when Philip gave an equivocal reply, the bishop and Abbot Godescal personally conducted Thomas out of Flanders that very night, the archbishop riding a great white horse provided by Milo.

They got safely across the border south of Cambrai, and Thomas made for Soissons which he had named as the next rendezvous with his clerks. Also he dispatched Herbert of Bosham and one other to follow and spy on the royal embassy; and this they did successfully, trailing always one day behind, picking up the news and then attempting to undo any harm the royalists had done.[5]

Henry's envoys met Louis at Compiègne, north-east of Paris, and asked him too not to give asylum to 'the former archbishop'. They pointed out that the recent peace treaty between the two kings had envisaged that neither would harbour the other's enemies and had provided for the extradition of fugitives from justice. But Louis was evasive, and, instead of writing to the pope on Henry's behalf, as requested, wrote on behalf of Thomas. Next day Herbert appeared at court, told the archbishop's story, and obtained a safe conduct for him. The clerk then followed Henry's embassy south towards Sens, and may, like the royalists, have passed through Corbeil, where the former archiepiscopal clerk, Reginald fitzJocelin, tried to intervene.[6] Meanwhile Louis travelled the short distance east to meet Thomas at Soissons, assured him of his favour and offered financial aid during his exile.

Thomas's fortunes were improving. But his fate depended on the attitude of the pope and curia. The least biased account of the royal embassy is given by fitzStephen; but it is unlikely that the 'Canterbury' writers did much more than heighten the discomfiture of the ambassadors. Speeches on behalf of the king were made at Sens by the bishops of London, Chichester, York and Exeter, in that order, and then by the earl of Arundel, speaking in French. Gilbert Foliot and Hilary of Chichester, normally eloquent and elegant speakers in Latin, are said to have made errors in grammar, quantity and pronunciation, which the congregation ridiculed, and revealed an absence of charity, which the pope rebuked. York did better; Exeter was brief; and the earl did best of all. As, however, the scale of misfortune corresponds closely with the degrees of hostility felt by the reporters towards the actors, the story cannot be taken too seriously. The general points the ambassadors made in open session were Henry's benevolence towards the church and pope, the disaster of this unfortunate quarrel and the king's hope, with Alexander's help, for a just settlement. The Holy Father was thought by fitzStephen to have remarked in reply to each, 'We are glad that the king is so good. May God make him even better.' It was perhaps in more private sessions that the envoys made their requests and offered the rewards. Henry wanted the pope to order Thomas to return to England and to send legates there with power to hear and determine the appeals and counter-appeals that had been made at Northampton. The key word was 'determine' and this needed to be reinforced by the disallowance of the right of appeal against their judgments (*omni appellatione remota*). In return he offered to increase the yield of Peter's Pence, England's annual tribute to the pope. The envoys also distributed bribes among the cardinals.

A number of these, led by William of Pavia, supported Henry. Alexander did not wish to offend the king. But Herbert and his companion had arrived at Sens, and a small party of the archbishop's supporters, although not allowed the right to answer the royal envoys, was active behind the scenes. The stumbling block was the clause disallowing appeals to be included in the commission appointing the legates *a latere*. All suspected that Henry would be able to buy or intimidate the judges. In the end the pope would not agree to entrust final judgment to his legates, quoting Isaiah, 'My glory will I not give to another' (42: 8); and the embasy left Sens empty-handed. Although some biographers believed that Alexander dismissed the envoys, Herbert probably correctly reports that the pope said that he could not make a final decision except in Thomas's presence and after hearing his side of the case; and that the embassy decided not to wait. The truth may be that they had become convinced that they were not going to get papal legates with the required plenary powers and had been instructed not to conduct the case in the papal curia. As they crossed a river on their way north, they saw waiting on the other side 'more than 300 horsemen' of the archbishop's retinue, and they detached the dean of Waltham to return to Sens and watch the proceedings on behalf of the king.[7]

When Thomas arrived a few days later, he was met, according to fitz-Stephen, by most of the cardinals who rode out to greet him, and was warmly welcomed by the pope, who rose to embrace him. However that might be, he seems to have lost his nerve. Conscious that he was far inferior to the royalist bishops in rhetorical skills, and hardly reassured by stories of their discomfiture, he tried to persuade one of his clerks to present his case for him. These, however, to the archbishop's grief, but correctly and wisely, refused. Thomas's formal audience on the morrow with pope and cardinals was in private in the papal chamber; and Thomas, forced to undertake his own defence – for he was in a sense on trial – seems to have performed well. The biographers agree on the main points. The archbishop presented Alexander with the copy of the Constitutions (the chirograph) which he had been given at Clarendon. These evil laws, he declared, were the cause of his exile, and he confessed that, like the rest, he had sinned by agreeing to them. Thomas then took the court through the document clause by clause, revealing the iniquity of each in turn. William of Pavia represented the king and defended the customs. Finally, at the end of a long and exhausting day, the pope pronounced on the Constitutions. None of the laws was good, but some were tolerable. Others were directly contrary to canon law and must be condemned. But this snap judgment was never put into writing; and many years later Thomas also complained that Alexander on this occasion had refused to give judgment in his case against his rebel suffragans.[8]

Most of the biographers believed that at some point Thomas resigned his office into the pope's hands.[9] Edward Grim and William of Canterbury place the resignation at the beginning of the session when Thomas confessed to having agreed to the Constitutions. FitzStephen reports that Thomas confessed in secret to the pope that he had sinned by allowing himself to be intruded into Canterbury by the lay power and by agreeing to the Constitutions; furthermore, it was said that he resigned the archbishopric and that the pope let him sweat for three days before restoring it. Alan of Tewkesbury and the Saga seem to echo this version. The English theologian and jurist, Ralf Niger, who had excellent sources, believed that Thomas resigned his office because he had obtained it through the chancellorship, which he had bought. Herbert of Bosham, however, goes out of his way to insist that Alexander blamed Thomas only for his assent to the customs, but, although he says nothing of a resignation, he was capable of suppressing such a weakness. Thomas was partial to the grand gesture, and it is likely that he did offer his resignation to the pope – to the dismay of his clerks. Moreover, after this episode, he regarded himself as absolved from any public errors he had committed as archbishop. He could agree with his episcopal detractors that there had been, in his former life, wasted years. He dutifully professed that he was a great sinner, now in a hermitage atoning for his transgressions. But he admitted no fault in his behaviour with regard to the king or the bishops.

Herbert also tells of a session Thomas had on the following day with the college of cardinals, when he was blamed for rocking the boat when it was already shaken by the storm of schism. The text for the debate was St Paul's Epistle to the Ephesians 5: 15–16, 'See then that ye walk circumspectly, not as fools, but as wise men, redeeming the time because the days are evil.' Thomas's reply to the advocates of expediency is reported in something more than 3,000 words, and would seem to owe more to Herbert than to the tyro scholar.[10]

Although Thomas had not lost his case, indeed had scored some points, and had retained his title and office, he could not return to Canterbury until either he climbed down or Henry relented or died. Like Anselm he had to prepare for a long exile. In discussions with the pope and curia he and his clerks expressed a preference for the Cistercian order and, in particular, for Pontigny, the second daughter of Cîteaux, situated in the duchy of Burgundy, some 55 kilometres south-east of Sens. Founded in 1114 by Theobald IV, count of Blois, the brother of King Stephen and Henry, bishop of Winchester, patronized by Louis VII and with Hugh, count of

Macon, as its first abbot, it no doubt had an aristocratic tone which Thomas found congenial. Outside both the royal French demesne and Angevin territory, with a temporal ruler, Hugh III, still or recently a minor, it was not too distant from the papal court and the courier routes. It also had an abbot, Guichard (1136–65/7), who had been recruited in June by John of Poitiers to act on Thomas's behalf at the curia; and John had informed the archbishop that, if Angevin tyranny should make it impossible for him to remain at Poitiers, he intended to take refuge at Pontigny.[11]

Towards the end of December Guichard, by then the Alexandrine candidate for the archbishopric of Lyons, and some of his senior monks were summoned to Sens and agreed to accept Thomas and a small household. These were given scattered lodgings within the monastic compound, 'little rooms in Noah's Ark (mansiunculae)', according to Herbert of Bosham, lonely in a wooded solitude between the monks and the stones.[12]

Herbert clearly disliked the place. Pontigny was 20 kilometres from the 'civilization' of the episcopal city of Auxerre, where Thomas had read law some ten years earlier and where now Herbert soon bought himself a suit of fine new clothes. Like all Cistercian monasteries, it was situated in a wilderness, in this case on the wet heavy clay by the slow-moving Serein, a tributary of the Yonne, in a densely forested area. To be dumped between monks and rocks was indeed a sad lot, although what these stones were is not clear. Pontigny has no rocks: the stone for building the church had been brought from Tonnerre, some 30 kilometres to the east. Perhaps Herbert was alluding to the imprisoning walls, possibly he was joking sourly about the white monks and the heaps of white limestone, the debris of the building operations or the stones for work in progress. The church, however, should have been of some consolation to the exiles. Radiantly white, lofty, simple, with clean and elegant lines, it is Cistercian architecture at its best. But it may have seemed to Herbert too cold and austere. He, like the other clerks, could take a critical view because he was an innocent victim and, moreover, a very secular clerk. Thomas, however, appears to have regarded the incarceration as part of his penance. He seems never to have alluded in his letters to the physical deprivations of his exile or taken notice of his environment. After the shock of his relegation from palaces to a hermitage, he bore his wretchedness with stoicism in public.

Not all of Thomas's household could be accommodated at Pontigny, and in the spring of 1165 more refugees began to arrive. Henry's embassy to Sens reported its failure to the king on Chistmas Eve 1164 at Marlborough in Wiltshire, one of his favourite hunting lodges. On Boxing Day Henry started to take his revenge on Thomas and his supporters, real and presumed. He ordered the confiscation of all Thomas's possessions and the forfeiture of the archbishopric. But in December 1170 Thomas blamed not Henry but the archbishop of York and the bishop of London for these measures.[13] The archbishopric was granted retrospectively from Michaelmas to a trusted royal servant, Ranulf de Broc, with whom Thomas had bandied insults at Northampton, for an annual farm of £1,562 5s. 5½d., and he retained the custody until Michaelmas 1170. The day-to-day administration he entrusted to his clerk and kinsman, Robert de Broc, alleged to be a renegade monk, who built a house at Canterbury out of timber taken from the archbishop's woods. William of Canterbury describes him feasting there with his friends at Christmas 1170 and sharing the food with their dogs. Ranulf and Robert were efficient custodians, only £13 8s. 6d. in debt to the king at the hand-over; and this was pardoned by Henry at Michaelmas 1172. Thomas was accordingly deprived of something over £9,000 from the temporalities of the archbishopric alone. He also complained that the archiepiscopal estates were ravaged (the estates and revenues of the monks were unmolested until the death of Prior Wibert on 27 September 1167). There were usually complaints against the exploitive management of royal custodians, eager to extract the maximum profit – Thomas would know all about that – and the degree of iniquity at Canterbury is hard to judge. Even more detestable, in the eyes of the archbishop's supporters, was the decree that Thomas was not to be given any aid, even by prayers. William fitzStephen describes the changes made in the liturgy in the chapel royal and the diocese of London.[14]

At Christmas 1164 the king also ordered the seizure of all the churches and revenues of Thomas's clerks. The confiscated benefices were put in the custody of the several diocesan bishops and, in the case of Canterbury, of the bishop of London. William fitzStephen believed that, in respect of the church's treasures, Gilbert Foliot behaved quite unlike St Laurence and St Sebastian, but his clerk and official, Robert Housecarl, who was an honest man, put the churches out to farm at a modest rent and a large entry fine, so that small sums were chargeable to the royal treasury while large sums were available for religious purposes. In the autumn of 1166 Gilbert, when proposing to surrender their custody, reported to Henry that he had received from them, in respect of the oblations of the faithful, alms for the poor and tithe (the spiritualities), £180 14s. 6d. The profits of the temporalities had, presumably, gone to the king. Well-endowed archiepiscopal clerks, like John of Salisbury and Herbert of Bosham, were seriously harmed.[15]

It may also have been at Christmas that Henry began to demand payment from some of those who had stood surety for the archbishop at Northampton. John of Poitiers believed that Jocelin of Salisbury had to sell almost all the stock on his demesne manors in order to satisfy the king. William of Eynesford paid in full in 1165–6, but, with the help of the pope, actually recovered the sum in the 1180s from the gifts at St Thomas's tomb. Henry, however, spared those sureties who were in his favour.[16]

On Boxing Day Henry also ordered the proscription and exile of all Thomas's relations and members of his household, both clerical and lay, together with their families. In order to stifle opposition, all appeals to the papal curia were prohibited. Richard de Lucy witnessed at least one of these edicts. On Sunday 27 December Ranulf de Broc and other royal servants travelled to London, and, taking possession of the archiepiscopal residence at Lambeth, ordered the arrest of all Thomas's relatives, clerks and servants and of all those who had given him aid during his flight from Northampton. A few of the proscribed were allowed to buy immunity. Stephen of Everton and Alfred of Walthamstow paid £100 each, Thurstin of Croydon, after a day's imprisonment in a vile thieves' gaol in London, 100 marks. Some fines entered on the Pipe Roll for Kent in 1164–5 may be the punishment of archiepiscopal servants who had either helped Thomas escape or aided Herbert of Bosham to collect funds. Pain of Otford and Philip of Tonge, each fined £200, were probably Thomas's stewards. Adam of Charing, fined 100 marks, was one of the crew, perhaps the skipper, of the boat in which Thomas had tried to escape in the autumn. However, William of Salisbury, an archiepiscopal chaplain, went unmolested until the summer of 1166.[17]

William fitzStephen made his peace with Henry in the chapel of the hunting lodge at Brill in Buckinghamshire by presenting him with a royal prayer to God, which he had composed in elegant verses and which he proudly displayed in full in his biography of the saint. It tells us much about both men that the clerk could offer such an unexpected gift, in which Henry is made to confess some very serious and relevant sins, especially vainglory, adultery, anger and covetousness of other men's possessions, and that the king should be pacified by such an offering. Perhaps the only admission that the clerk made, and that in code, was the prayer that God would grant that the king's clergy, by espousing sound divine and human law and loving God with all their souls, might show themselves to all as models of good behaviour. Nor does Thomas seem to have borne his ex-clerk much ill-will. When he met him next, perhaps by chance, at Fleury-sur-Loire, they discussed the events at Northampton, and in 1170 he welcomed him back into his household.[18]

These were the lucky ones. Ranulf de Broc compelled most of those he arrested to take an oath that they would leave the kingdom immediately and proceed directly to the archbishop at Pontigny. The exiled kindred included women, children and servants, clearly whole families. Among them was at least one of Thomas's married sisters, perhaps Roheise, and several of his nephews. It was generally believed that the numbers involved were considerable. Not all the exiles, however, reached Pontigny. Some, particularly the aged, poor and sick, were absolved from their oath by papal authority

and remained in Flanders. Thomas's sister and her children were sheltered
by the abbey at Clairmarais and the nephews were then scattered widely.
But enough fellow-sufferers arrived at Pontigny to inspire one of Herbert's
longer excursions. Although he never says so, it is possible that among
the fugitives were his own kin. Thomas, although greatly moved by the
plight of these innocent sufferers for the cause of God, remained, with the
help of his *eruditi*, steadfast in his resolve.

Even if we allow for exaggeration and the emotive introduction of preg-
nant women and those with infants at the breast or in the cradle, the persecution was real enough. Henry's failure to secure Thomas's effective
condemnation at both Northampton and Sens and the archbishop's escape
to safety triggered severe reprisals. But, in Herbert's opinion, Thomas did
not allow his former great love of Henry to turn into hatred. His love
survived tribulation, suffering and persecution. He felt great sorrow for
Henry, driven as he was by false friends and the archbishop's rivals along
the road to tyranny. Thomas remained hopeful of a change of heart.[19]

Most of the exiles he had to disperse among well-wishers, and some,
Herbert believed, even improved their lot abroad. Gerard la Pucelle taught
at Paris until he defected to Germany at the end of the year. Philip of Calne
and Ralf of Sarre were recommended to the dean and chapter of Rheims,
Richard of Salisbury to the dean and chapter of Thérouanne, Richard the
chaplain to the dean and chapter of Orleans. Some were maintained by
the king of France, the Empress Matilda, Henry's mother, and the count
of Flanders. A few may have reached Norman Italy. John of Salisbury's
relatives and friends did best. Among the disappointed was Ernulf. From
Rouen, probably in the summer of 1166, he wrote a pathetic letter to Thomas,
complaining of his neglect. He did not ask for material aid – he was content
with his poverty – but his unemployment and isolation, his enforced separation from his master, would be a little more tolerable if Thomas, for
whom in the past he had written so many letters, were to heed one written
in Ernulf's own name and be good enough occasionally to take notice of
him and send him a few scraps of news. The archbishop's messengers passed
by quite often, but were always engaged in more important business.[20]

Thomas settled down to a life of religious observance, utilitarian study
and the prosecution of his case through correspondence and diplomacy.
To what extent he conformed to the monastic rules and horarium is deb-
atable. It was generally, and inevitably, believed that at Pontigny he lived
religiously and austerely, even ascetically, as an atonement for his sins.
There is a story that he subdued the rebelliousness of his flesh in an icy
stream which flowed through the compound, and two of the monastic biographers believed that he petitioned the pope for a monastic habit, and
that Alexander had one made and sent it with his blessing and the cryptic

remark that it was not what he would have liked to send but such as he had. We may well ask what he would have wished to provide. Moreover, no one explains why Thomas should have approached a non-monastic pope, and not the abbot, for a religious dress.

A subsidiary anecdote, although hardly clearing the matter up, does afford us a glimpse of the archbishop's underwear, a matter of some importance in his legend. The garment sent by the pope was of thick woollen cloth. Thomas's clerk, Alexander-Llewelyn, disapproved of it, and thought in particular that the hood (*caputium*) was disproportionately small. 'I don't know if it's according to the rules,' he remarked, 'but it seems to me that the lord pope has rather inappropriately removed the hood from a cowl (*cuculla*).' To this his master replied with a smile, 'He has done this so that you can't make fun of me again as you did the other day.' And went on to explain, 'The day before yesterday, when I was robing for mass and, with my belt tied, looked rather padded out, you asked how it was that my backside was puffed up. So, if I were to have a great hood hanging down my back causing a protuberance there, you could taunt me with being a hunchback. The pope has providentially spared me from such insults.' Alan of Tewkesbury explains that Thomas wore, unknown even to his closest servants, a hair shirt which stretched from his neck to his knees and that this, because of its rigidity, protruded when his belt was tight. He has also probably unwittingly revealed by this description of the strange garment sent by the pope the origin of the black *colobium* without a hood which Thomas wore in later years over his hair shirt and which the monks in 1170 identified as a monastic cowl.

But, although the abbot was supposed to have invested Thomas with this costume in a secret ceremony attended by Alexander-Llewelyn, no one, except perhaps Alan of Tewkesbury, claims that the archbishop took the monastic vows or was formally professed a monk. The pope's suggestion in August 1165 that a bishopric or abbey might serve as provision for the exile is by no means decisive evidence, for in the circumstances an irregularity would not have been considered scandalous. Herbert of Bosham, the best witness, states explicitly that the visitors were granted, immediately and voluntarily, dispensation from the rules regarding the eating of meat and some other things. It is likely that Thomas went through a disturbed period and may well have been tempted at times to follow the monastic road to salvation – even become a monk *in petto*. Undoubtedly he would have entered into the life of his hosts as far as he could. Gervase of Canterbury believed that he worked in the fields with the monks and helped with the hay harvest even when sick. But it would also seem that he remained always an archbishop in exile, a clerk among his clerks.[21]

It was, indeed, Herbert of Bosham – keenly aware of being a stranger at Pontigny, 'amid the rocks and the monks', as he often joked – who this time kept his master from his usual habit of overdoing things. When Thomas's attempt, after the arrival of the exiles, to follow the Cistercian diet made him ill and interfered with their studies, Herbert produced a nice sermon on the evils of excess and how for some men extreme abstinence could be the work of the devil. Herbert believed that the Cistercians fed like horses and that Thomas, delicately nurtured from infancy, was simply incapable of surviving on such gross fodder. Fortunately the archbishop soon saw the error into which he had been tempted to fall. John of Salisbury, in a letter to Baldwin of Exeter, joked that Thomas had been granted the opportunity to improve his Latin as well as his character. But it was not to the classical *auctores* that the archbishop turned but to the books of law, the Bible and the compilations of canonical and roman jurisprudence. It would seem that the clerks, the *eruditi*, present at Pontigny formed a study group, and that the chief instructor in theology was Herbert, in the more specialized field of canon law Lombard of Piacenza. Herbert maintains that the archbishop, conscious of his lack of qualifications as a 'ruler of souls', grasped the opportunity eagerly and made much progress in his studies. He was specially attached to the Psalms and the Epistles, the two eyes of the soul, the one providing material for spiritual contemplation, the other moral philosophy. And it was at Pontigny that Herbert started, at Thomas's request, his edition of his master Peter Lombard's Great Gloss on those parts of the Bible. Both John and Herbert tend to be affectionately condescending on the topic of Thomas's pursuit of moral improvement and learning.[22]

The study of the law of the church was the necessary preparation for the maintenance and prosecution of the archbishop's cause. William fitzStephen believed that Thomas assembled a large and serviceable library, seeking books throughout France and having them transcribed for his use. Thomas also, and this was the fruit of these labours, petitioned for every possible papal privilege for his church. FitzStephen thought that none of Thomas's predecessors had provided Canterbury with a finer collection of books and privileges. John of Salisbury, however, who saw little hope of a settlement in the existing political situation, begged Thomas to spend his time in prayer rather than legal studies. These would only encourage him to rash and counter-productive measures. Later he reported to a friend that Thomas was doing penance at Pontigny for his life at the royal court. But John's call for humility, although reinforced by the other John at Poitiers, fell on deaf ears.[23]

Thomas was always a fighter. He took up the struggle immediately and pursued it to the end. He quickly established a widespread intelligence network. Herbert was probably his spy-master and the outstations were at Rheims (John of Salisbury), which was well placed to get news from Germany, especially through Gerard la Pucelle, Rouen (Nicholas, prior and guestmaster of the hospital of Mont-St-Jacques) and Poitiers (Bishop John). The main apparent weaknesses (it has to be remembered that some secret sources may have been successfully concealed) were the lack of really productive agents in the papal and royal courts. Although Master Lombard joined the curia probably at the beginning of 1169 there was never a great flow of top-level information. And, although Thomas always had sympathizers in the royal court, Walter de Lisle was uncovered at the end of 1166 and the trickle of news seems never to have been sufficient to give the exiles a full understanding of the royalist plans and manoeuvres. Also, Nicholas soon pulled out and in the end the two Johns were discouraged. Thomas then relied increasingly on William, archbishop of Sens, and other French bishops and supporters. The dossier of this largely secret, and from the king's point of view treasonable, correspondence is enormous: some 700 items; and most business was done by word of mouth.[24]

The organization of Thomas's household in exile received little attention from his biographers, even from Herbert of Bosham, who was probably his major-domo. The direction of the limelight, particularly after the canonization, was on Thomas alone and Herbert's egocentricity conceals most of the services of the other household clerks and chaplains. Herbert was proud of being one of the *eruditi*, that band of scholars which Thomas had recruited, and he listed some of them and their careers in a separate section at the end of his work. It is, however, a selection made primarily on the basis of subsequent achievement, and he had to explain, rather lamely, how it was that he had included so many backsliders and renegades at the expense of more faithful, but less distinguished, members of their society. It is also noticeable in the *Catalogus* that he is studiously vague about the precise services which the individuals rendered the saint.

John of Salisbury's situation, although quite different, led to similar results. The very fact that, although a fellow-victim and a staunch supporter of the archbishop's cause, he chose to live at Rheims is revealing. He rarely approved wholeheartedly of Thomas's behaviour; he must have been out of sympathy with Thomas's immediate entourage; and he too, in his literary works, neglects most of these clerks, including Herbert. In the autumn of 1167, when he disliked the tone of a letter composed in the household, he sent his own suggested version for the archbishop's judgment alone and begged that it should not be exposed to the ridicule of the others, although it could be shown in secret to Lombard and Alexander. The pointed exclusion of Herbert speaks volumes. Herbert placed John third in the *Catalogus* – inferior only to the archbishop himself and Master Lombard – and allowed him wisdom and knowledge and faithful service. He could hardly have done less. John's own circle of friends merely overlapped Thomas's. It may be surmised that there was no love lost between John and Herbert: men of completely different interests and outlook, they were rivals for the archbishop's ear. No doubt the jealousies and tensions of medieval courts were intensified by those prevalent in émigré societies. The only one of Thomas's clerks to pay much attention to the others was completely detached from them – William fitzStephen, who had returned to royal service.[25]

The exact composition and organization of Thomas's household in exile are difficult to discern. The company has been glimpsed at St Omer in November 1164 and we have a list of those present at Gisors-Trie three years later. Of the seventeen *eruditi* who may have been in the archbishop's service in England, five did not go into exile. Of the surviving twelve, another five, for a variety of reasons, left his service. These were Reginald, archdeacon of Salisbury, Gerard la Pucelle, Hugh de Nonant, Philip of Calne and Master Lombard. Four of those gathered at St Omer also departed: Silvester, treasurer of Lisieux (Hugh de Nonant's brother or cousin), Baldwin of Boulogne, archdeacon of Norwich, the chaplain Richard of Salisbury and Theold, canon of St Martin's. Master Hervey of London died on a mission to the papal curia during or after the summer of 1166, and Master Richard likewise in 1168.[26]

Herbert names seven *eruditi* who remained to the end: himself, Gilbert de Glanville, Gunter of Winchester, Alexander-Llewelyn, Roland and Ariald of Lombardy and Humbert (*alias* Hubert Crivelli), archdeacon of Bourges. He was, however, thinking as much of loyalty to Thomas's cause as physical presence. Master Gilbert, possibly at the time a canon of Lisieux, although one of Thomas's nuncios to the curia in January 1164, then disappears from view. He interceded for Jocelin and Reginald of Salisbury in March 1167 and would seem to be based mainly on his cathedral church before rejoining Thomas when, or after, the archbishop returned to England. Likewise the archdeacon of Bourges, 'among the last of the recruits' and a *quasi* member of their society, probably only gave occasional help to the exiles, but secured a place in the list because he was a celebrated canon lawyer who was elected archbishop of Milan and then Pope Urban III in 1185. Thomas's one known contact with him is a rebuke delivered in October 1167 for not having sent news of the papal legates. Roland and Ariald are merely names. We are told that they were recruited for their literary skills and worldly wisdom and that the one was paid 10 marks (£6 13s. 4d.) and the other 100s. a year, apparently throughout the exile, but their activities have left no trace.

If, however, Herbert inflated the list of *eruditi*, he also omitted some important chaplains and clerks. Nowhere does he mention Robert, canon of Merton, Thomas's chaplain and constant companion. Among those present at Gisors-Trie were the clerks Henry, John the Cantor, Alan and

Richard. Henry, although he has sometimes been equated with Hervey of London, is more likely to have been Master Henry of Houghton. He was one of those sent to Sens in September 1163, when he was described by Thomas as a close and confidential clerk whom the pope and cardinals knew well. He was still at the curia early in 1164, but is not noticed again in the archbishop's company until 1169. John the Cantor was another most confidential clerk, entrusted with important business at the curia in February 1167 and, with Alexander, in 1167–8 and in 1169–70. He may have been that John Planeta, a pupil of Peter Abelard, whom we have glimpsed ridiculing St Bernard at the archbishop's dinner table in 1162–4 and is noticed by William fitzStephen in the archbishop's service at Northampton in October 1164 and again at Canterbury at Christmas 1170. Richard may be 'of Salisbury', the master, not the chaplain. Alan cannot be identified.[27]

Thomas's cross-bearer Alexander and Gunter of Winchester are likewise, except in the *Catalogus*, neglected. Herbert describes the former as well educated and a great and amusing talker, but also a man of action, constantly braving great dangers in the archbishop's service, and, something rare in a Welshman, completely loyal. He was, as we have seen, with Lombard the only one in the household whom John of Salisbury respected and really liked. He was 'the prince', 'of the race of Merlin and the interpreter of his prophecies'. Besides going to the curia in 1168 and 1170 with John the Cantor, he was sent with Herbert at Christmas 1170 to France and then with Gunter went on to the pope with news of the martyrdom. Gunter is mentioned by Herbert once or twice and in the *Catalogus* is described as simple and upright, timorous and uncomplaining; his conduct made up for his defective education. Like the short Zacchaeus (a rich publican) he climbed up a tree in order to see Jesus. Gunter had been to the curia early in 1164 and may have been sent on other unrecorded missions.[28] Finally, there is Herbert of Bosham himself. We have seen him sent to Canterbury in October 1164 and then to the French king and the pope. Six years later he was sent with John of Salisbury to King Henry. In between he seems to have acted as the archbishop's *chef de cabinet*. He may have kept the seals and organized what must have been a relatively informal office. He sometimes records the hard-line advice he gave his master. John of Salisbury may have considered him Thomas's evil genius.

The paucity and obscurity of Thomas's household should not be allowed to minimize its importance. Its main function was the furtherance of the archbishop's cause through propaganda, diplomacy, politico-legal moves and espionage. We know from Herbert's description of the life of the household at Canterbury and from occasional later glimpses that the *eruditi* formed the archbishop's council and would meet with him at least once a day in order to discuss all matters of concern, give technical and general advice and make plans. Letters were an essential tool of almost all their activities, and these ranged from simple letters of credence for nuncios to elaborate manifestos. The language of government and diplomacy was Latin, and by the second half of the twelfth century the form of letters was governed by elaborate rules. The style depended both on the quality of the sender and his business and on the rank of the recipient, and, except in the simplest business documents, a rich ornamentation was expected. It was a task only for highly educated and specially trained scholars, *dictatores*. Celebrated exponents of the art at this time were Arnulf of Lisieux, John of Salisbury and Peter of Blois.

Thomas, who had not had a good grounding in grammar and rhetoric and did not have the poets or the Vulgate embedded in his memory and at his fingertips, was certainly incapable of drafting anything beyond the simplest letter. And, although he probably improved his Latin, both written and oral, while in exile, we cannot doubt that he was more at home in the vernacular. As only the more elaborate epistles were normally preserved in letter collections, we cannot gauge how much correspondence was carried out in plain Latin. Ironically, the best example of such a letter in the 'Becket collections' is the one written in Henry II's name, probably by a chancery clerk, to the pope in January 1171 exculpating him from Thomas's murder.[29] But in the archbishop's case, when something beyond his own skill was required, all he had to do was to instruct his clerks on the content. It was their job to transform what was as a rule quite a simple message into a work of art. Very occasionally Thomas's own words come through; but mostly the letters issued in his name are highly professional and often long-winded productions.

William fitzStephen had been a *dictator* in Thomas's chancery, possibly even before 1162. Master Ernulf claimed to have written most of the archbishop's letters when they were at Canterbury. He was probably discarded in exile because he had not the skills necessary for the type of letter then required. Sometimes an individual clerk, Herbert or Lombard, wrote a complete letter, or John of Salisbury, the only one of them trained in the papal chancery, was called in or volunteered his services. Sometimes there may have been co-operation or a series of revisions. But it is unlikely that anything of importance went out without its having been read to, and approved by, the archbishop himself. There was, therefore, plenty of work at times for a number of scribes. Copies had to be made not only for the record but also for multiple addressees and other interested parties.[30]

Besides this company of chaplains and clerks were some lay servants, including the archbishop's valet Brown, probably under the command of Thomas's marshal, William de Capes. William's primary responsibility at Canterbury would have been the archiepiscopal stables at Stablegate, adjacent to the palace. But it was he who had successfully protected the archbishop's household after Thomas had fled from Northampton and he seems to have rejoined his master shortly afterwards. At Pontigny and Sens he was probably in charge of all secular matters, such as messenger service and transport. It is interesting to see that his nephew Richard was one of those involved in the delivery of Thomas's sentence of excommunication on Gilbert Foliot at St Paul's on 29 May 1169. Herbert of Bosham remarks, in connection with the diplomacy of 1168, that there were frequent deaths and replacements among the archbishop's messengers and that the multitude of exiles formed an inexhaustible pool of helpers.[31]

Thomas and his companions stayed at Pontigny for almost exactly two years and were to remain in exile for a further four. Once he had fled to France and put himself under the protection of Louis VII and Alexander III, his case became merely one of the minor side-issues in two major contests – the papal schism and the rivalry between Henry and Louis. It was the former which appeared to govern his fate. Although the imperial popes (or anti-popes), Victor IV and his successors, Guy of Crema, Paschal III (1164–8), and John of Struma, Calixtus III (1168–78), were unable to widen their support beyond Germany and Poland and those parts of Italy under Frederick I's control or influence, Alexander's landslide victory in the West did not give him a clear winning position. The Emperor's dignity and power were paramount, and neither Louis nor Henry, without whose recognition Alexander's cause would have collapsed, was committed to the papal side by either firm principles or strong emotions. Louis, susceptible to imperial pressure, almost went over to Frederick in 1162, shortly after the pope had taken refuge in France, and Henry always regarded a switch of allegiance as a diplomatic card up his sleeve. After all, Frederick was his natural ally against Louis. He was, however, shackled by the loyalty to Alexander of the English and French bishops. In ordinary circumstances he would have found it impossible to transfer the allegiance of the fifty or more bishops he was credited with to the other side. Indeed, in neither contest had the protagonists much freedom of action, and the checks and balances produced an inertia which helped to prolong Thomas's exile seemingly without end.[32]

Typically, although Thomas depended almost entirely on Alexander and Louis, he could not rely on either of them. For both he was a useful, but small, diplomatic asset, of value mostly because they could sacrifice him if it was in their interest so to do. That neither in fact ever abandoned him completely owed as much to the necessity never having arisen as to their unshakable loyalty. Moreover, neither had the power or the will to do much positively for him. Only in exile was Thomas of much use to Louis, and Alexander's usual aim was to avoid provoking Henry. In general, therefore, Thomas was an embarrassment to the pope, and Alexander aimed at keeping him secluded and quiet by supplying him with the minimum diet of encouragement. As for Thomas, he gradually became disillusioned, full of his wrongs, with time for incessant complaints and manoeuvres, a sore trial to some of his friends. Unlike Anselm, he could not settle down humbly and patiently to a subordinate pastoral ministry and the composition of a great work of theology while waiting for God's will to be done.[33]

John of Salisbury's attitude is noteworthy. He too was in exile, but mostly at Rheims, and he carefully distinguished his own case from his former master's. He maintained that he had committed no crime against the king, and until at least 1167 was both ready and anxious to make his peace with Henry if this could be done on honourable terms, that is to say, without having to subscribe to the Constitutions of Clarendon or renounce the archbishop. He believed quite passionately that Thomas was defending the liberties of the church against the wrongful actions of the king and his supporters. But he was far too intelligent to see the matters at issue simply in terms of black and white and too sensible ever to approve wholly of Thomas's conduct whether as courtier, prelate or exile. He stayed in touch with his pupil, Ralf Niger, still at Paris, who remained on good terms with the king. He could even write affectionately to Gerard la Pucelle after his old friend had left Paris for Cologne, but drew the line when invited to join him there. By 1166 John had come to realize that there would not be a quick settlement and began to lose interest in the intrigues and diplomacy. His love of France and acceptance of exile led in 1176 to the bishopric of Chartres.[34]

Thomas in the first months of his exile tried to recruit supporters. The king of Scots and the count of Flanders interceded for him, but others approached, such as the Empress Matilda and Arnulf of Lisieux, were unwilling to commit themselves publicly. In March, however, Arnulf sent the archbishop a long letter, in which he balanced the hostile views of Thomas's enemies, which he outlined, against his own compliments, assessed the strengths and weaknesses, mostly the latter, of Thomas's position and offered some sensible advice. He reported that all the English bishops and barons were supporting the king, while sympathy for the archbishop was confined to the lower clergy, and was of the opinion that foreign assistance would tend to dry up. This would seem to be a fair assessment of the situation, for in the course of that year even Robert of Melun, bishop of Hereford, earned a papal rebuke for neglect of the exile's cause. Arnulf saw little immediate hope for Thomas. But nothing was immutable, and Thomas should seize every opportunity for a reconciliation, particularly the present, when Henry was at hand in Normandy and beset by many problems. The archbishop should be prepared to be humble and ascribe any peace move to the magnanimity of the king. With regard to terms, he should at all cost avoid

135

minutiae and should agree to accept the Customs and so forth with only unobjectionable reservations. This he could safely do because, after a reconciliation, the king would be reluctant to reopen all the old wounds while Thomas, having learnt by experience, would proceed more cautiously.[35]

Probably later in the year, Thomas received not entirely dissimilar advice from John of Poitiers, who was a more genuine friend. John agreed with Thomas, possibly with reference to the silence imposed on the archbishop, that the pope put his own interests first. He also agreed that ideally it was essential that the terms of a settlement should be spelt out in detail before Thomas returned to England. However, he criticized some of the archbishop's suggested terms – which included the case of William de Ros – on the grounds that the injustices complained of concerned the archbishop's regalia rather than the liberty of the church, and that he had not included the grievances of the other sufferers for the cause. Really, John thought, it was impossible to see how so many different issues could be reduced to a manageable schedule. One possible solution would be for both king and archbishop to submit to a small body of independent arbitrators; and he thought that Thomas could honourably and safely return to England if that were agreed. If there should be a meeting under an acceptable safe conduct, Thomas should go with only a humble retinue and should take John of Salisbury with him because the clerk was not only wise and skilled in such matters but also had a great reputation. It is clear that not only Thomas's enemies but also his friends bewailed his pride and lack of judgment.[36]

In the spring of 1165 Henry crossed to Normandy for diplomatic reasons. He was visited by the count of Flanders at Rouen and on 11 April met Louis on the frontier at Gisors. The archbishop of Sens, Hugh de Toucy, and Ralf, bishop of Bethlehem, were in attendance on the French king; Alexander was in Paris (12–20 April); and Thomas had been brought to Pontoise in the hope of a reconciliation. But, basically no doubt because Henry would not offer acceptable terms, no meeting between king and archbishop took place. Afterwards Henry turned to the negotiations he had started in 1164 with the Emperor Frederick, receiving the imperial ambassador Rainald, archbishop of Cologne, and then dispatching Richard of Ilchester and John of Oxford to Germany, where they attended the Council of Würzburg on 23 May. At the beginning of the year, as can be seen from an intemperate letter he sent to Rainald, Henry was saying that he was about to renounce Alexander and his treacherous cardinals because of their support for Thomas and refusal to accept the English customs; and at Würzburg the English legates swore on his behalf that he would abandon 'Roland' and accept Paschal. But by that time Henry's fury had subsided a little and his tangible aims had perhaps been reduced to a marriage alliance with the emperor. The 'oath of Würzburg' had become something to deny or explain away. Nevertheless Louis and Alexander had been alarmed, had learnt the lesson and were discouraged from doing overmuch for Thomas. Moreover, the pope's plans to return to Italy portended the removal of the archbishop's only possible saviour. Thomas did, however, make one useful new friend at this time. Ralf Niger, the pupil of both John of Salisbury and Gerard la Pucelle, then studying and teaching at Paris, introduced Thomas at Sens to Conrad of Wittelsbach, the noble archbishop of Mainz, who had recently defected from the emperor. In 1182 Ralf reminded Conrad, by then cardinal-bishop of Sabina, how useful that connection had been to the German. It had also been of considerable help to the less favoured exile.

In the spring of 1165, however, Thomas's position seemed hopeless. In April, perhaps in panic, he accompanied the curia as far south as Bourges, but returned to Pontigny when Alexander went on to Clermont in Auvergne. It may have been on this occasion that he temporarily recruited John, a monk of St-Satur, near Sancerre, either as companion or guide, a trip which cost the monk 6d. in Angevin currency.[37]

Thomas responded to these various misfortunes by appealing to all possible supporters for help. He wrote to the earl of Leicester to complain of the treatment he had received at Northampton, and the pope obligingly quashed the sentence imposed on him in the John the Marshal case, although this was the one in which he was generally considered guilty. Alexander also wrote several times to Gilbert Foliot, first asking him to intercede with Henry for the exiles and reminding the bishop that he owed Canterbury obedience, next, on 8 June from Clermont, giving him fuller instructions. He was to go with Robert of Hereford to Henry, then on a Welsh campaign, and protest against the king's restrictions on appeals and visits to the papal curia, his negotiations and intercourse with schismatics (i.e. the emperor and his men), his expulsion of Thomas and his ill-treatment of the church. Also he was to collect Peter's Pence, dispatching, if possible, the total amount (£200) before 1 August, even if he had to anticipate the collection out of his own pocket or from loans. It may be thought that the latter commission would have had a dampening effect on the former.[38]

Gilbert replied to Alexander at some length. He had clearly had further, perhaps verbal, instructions that he was to warn the king that the pope was losing patience with him and might proceed to a punitive sentence. Henry, he reported, had received the papal reproofs modestly and had replied that, if recently he had not been as reverent to the pope as usual, it was because his embassy to Alexander (in December) had been turned away empty-handed. He had not, and would not, impede visits to the pope, but appeals to the curia were limited by the ancient customs of the kingdom. As regards Frederick, he was unaware of his excommunication. As for Thomas, the archbishop had not been expelled from England but had departed of his own free will, and was free to return in peace provided that he would answer to the charges outstanding against him and observe the royal dignities which he had sworn to uphold. Gilbert advised Alexander to be patient and not impose a sentence of interdict or excommunication. It was better to tend a sick limb than amputate it. If the pope took severe measures, there was the real danger of England going over to the anti-pope. As for Peter's Pence, everything depended on the king's goodwill: he himself had no authority to collect it, and there was no question of an advance as he had no money of his own and could not raise a loan. Alexander climbed down. In reply he expressed his great love for Henry and hoped that the king would graciously agree to what he had requested, for he preferred to overcome his stubbornness by patience and gentleness than by harsh measures, although there was a limit to his tolerance. Gilbert was to send Peter's Pence as soon as he could to St Bertin's. This eventually Gilbert did, but subtracted the £9 5s. still owed by the bishop of Exeter.[39]

In October Thomas sent to the pope an answer, composed by Herbert of Bosham, to Gilbert Foliot's excuses for the king. At inordinate length, but with considerable skill, Herbert ridiculed Gilbert's arguments – 'It is shameful for a woman spinning in the house to blame a soldier fighting on the field of battle' – and begged the pope, commander of the army of Christ, to draw his sword. There were, however, at this time but few crumbs from Alexander's meagre table for the exiles. On 10 July at Montpellier the pope ordered Clarembald, abbot of St Augustine's, to make his profession to Thomas and Canterbury, just as his predecessors had done (an escape clause), although without prejudice to future litigation on the matter. On 6 August he asked Louis to provide Thomas with a bishopric or abbey should one become available, a provision which John of Poitiers advised the archbishop to refuse: he would be better living in modest retreat at Pontigny. Probably later in the year he asked the monks of Christ Church to give Thomas suitable financial aid, and the bishop of Troyes to transfer the provostship of his church from William aux Blanchesmains, bishop-elect of Chartres, to Herbert of Bosham.[40]

But at some point, probably before he left France for Italy (late August), Alexander imposed serious restrictions on Thomas. As the times were evil, he was not to provoke the king in any way before Easter 1166. When the times improved, the archbishop and pope could decide what steps should be taken. This was understood as withdrawing for the time being the king, the kingdom and the English prelates from the archbishop's jurisdiction. Thomas's cause had been shelved. Alexander was not going to have the papal galleys rocked by any of Thomas's wild gestures while he ventured into difficult Italian waters. He would be, for a time at least, at greater risk at Rome than at Sens, even more in need of friends.[41]

The pope's return to Rome also re-established his normal remoteness and inability to meddle in the ordinary affairs of the English church. From 22 August 1167 until 24 February 1170 he was even some 150 miles farther off at Benevento. The wheel of diplomacy around the exiled archbishop continued to rotate, but at an even slower speed. Although an express courier could, under the most favourable conditions, make the journey from the north of France to Rome in just under a month, with another three days for Benevento, an ordinary traveller would allow at least seven weeks for Rome with a further week for Benevento. Nor was the curia geared to rapid business. A return trip within three months would be quite exceptional, six months was usual. This slowness of communication is one reason why Thomas's exile lasted so long. When there was no will to settle the dispute, there were endless means of delay.[42]

If, however, Alexander could govern Christendom from Rome and Benevento, Thomas saw no reason why, except in the area prohibited to him, he should not govern the province of Canterbury from Pontigny. Vexatious business in which he was involved from 1165 were the longstanding vacancy at Bangor, the rebellion of the lay-brethren of Sempringham, the Pentney affair and the case of the deanery of Salisbury. Bangor remained without a bishop from August 1161 until 22 May 1177. The pope took the Sempringham business out of Thomas's hands in 1166, preferring to employ two sets of judges-delegate, the bishops of Norwich and Winchester and those of York and Durham. The earl of Norfolk's attempt to re-site the Augustinian canonry of Pentney, south-east of King's Lynn in Norfolk, led to the earl's excommunication by the pope, the imposition of an interdict on the earldom and the discomfiture of the bishops of London and Norwich, who were expected by Alexander and Thomas to enforce these measures despite Henry's prohibition. Hugh Bigod eventually submitted in October 1170. The case of the deanery of Salisbury, which became vacant in 1164 or 1165, when Henry de Beaumont was made bishop of Bayeux, agitated Thomas the most. Jocelin of Salisbury, at Henry's request, gave the vacant dignity to John of Oxford, the royal clerk and envoy who had taken the oath at Würzburg. Thomas and John of Salisbury were greatly affronted by the appointment, the latter could even have had disappointed hopes. But their legal case was shaky and Alexander was not prepared to oppose the king on this. He confirmed the royal clerk in the office at the end of 1166. It will be seen that Thomas's attempts to interfere in the domestic affairs of the province of Canterbury were ineffectual.[43]

Early in 1166 Henry issued at Clarendon an important assize designed to rid the kingdom of notorious robbers and other evil-doers. No franchise was to impede the measures, and, although benefit of clergy is not instanced, it was unlikely to have been regarded. It was also decreed that no one in the kingdom was to harbour any of that schismatic sect (Flemish Cathars) recently condemned at Oxford. Henry was working for good order in both church and state. A letter to him from Thomas probably at this time is surprisingly warm in tone. Although the archbishop protested against the wrongful detention of Canterbury property, he made it clear that he was eager for a just settlement of the quarrel.[44]

In March Henry crossed to Normandy and went to the queen's help in Maine. The term of silence imposed on Thomas by the pope, and in practice on himself, would expire at Easter (24 April) and Alexander had established a firmer position in Rome and Italy than could have been expected. Henry, however, was in no hurry to make peace with Thomas. He had made Gilbert Foliot, who was dean of the province of Canterbury, the virtual head of the English church, and they saw eye to eye on many things besides the 'impossible' archbishop. Gilbert was not a pliant tool of the king. He had very strong principles and was an unabashed papalist as well as a great believer in the liberty of the church. He had influence over Henry and must be given credit for keeping Henry's inclination to violence under control. Really, Gilbert must have thought, all was just as it should have been. And with the situation in many ways advantageous to both Gilbert and Henry, neither could see any need to make concessions in order to buy Thomas's return to the country.

Henry celebrated Easter at Angers, the capital of his ancestral county, where he had arranged to meet his overlord. Louis arrived with Thomas and some of the archbishop's principal clerks, including John of Salisbury, Herbert of Bosham and Philip of Calne, for whom he was interceding on the grounds that they were innocent parties in the quarrel. He was anxious, of course, to get the cost of their maintenance off his back. Once again no meeting between king and archbishop could be arranged, although the Easter deadline was about to be passed; but, apparently a week later, Henry gave an audience to the clerks which is vividly described by William fitz-Stephen, who was either there or had the story from Philip of Calne.[45]

The clerks were introduced one by one into Henry's presence. First John of Salisbury, who had never been in royal service, petitioned for the king's peace and restoration of his ecclesiastical benefices. He pleaded that he had committed no offence against the king and stated that he was prepared to submit to him and serve him devotedly and faithfully as his earthly lord, saving only his order. Henry, however, answered that, since the clerk was born and bred in England, he must take an oath that he would be faithful to the king as to his life, limbs and earthly honour against all men, and especially that he would lawfully preserve his recorded customs and the royal dignities, whatever the pope, the archbishop or his bishop might do.

John demurred solely on the matter of the customs and the archbishop. He was an alumnus of the church of Canterbury and had sworn to obey the pope and the archbishop. Hence he could not desert the church of Canterbury or his lord the archbishop, nor observe any customs against the pope or the archbishop. He was prepared to accept only those things which were acceptable to them. This was not acceptable to Henry and John was dismissed. He complained to his friends that his journey had not only been a complete waste of time but had also cost him £13 and two horses.

The case of Herbert of Bosham, the next to be summoned, was rather different. He had been a royal clerk and was well known to Henry. 'Now we shall see a proud fellow', the king remarked as the clerk came in, dressed in all his finery. FitzStephen remembered that on this occasion the tall and handsome man was very smartly dressed in a tunic and cloak, which hung from his shoulders to his heels in the German fashion, both of green cloth of Auxerre, and adorned with all suitable accessories. Herbert replied at first to the king's conditions in words similar to John's and found the same stumbling blocks. But he went further. He praised Thomas's honest life and faithfulness to the king and declared that true faithfulness was to be found not in a time-server but in the servant who spoke up and tried to prevent his master from doing wrong. Since he knew that the king could not tolerate such behaviour he could not swear true fealty to him. He also echoed John on the customs, but added that he was astounded that Henry had had them written down. There were evil customs in respect of the church in all kingdoms, but they were not in writing, which gave more hope that they would be abolished by the kings. Henry followed this up and asked what he would specify in the French kingdom. Herbert told him, and for good measure added the bad customs of Germany. Henry took offence at Herbert calling Frederick king, not emperor, of the Germans. When Herbert put him right on Frederick's correct title, Henry cried out indignantly, 'For shame! It's come to a pretty pass when this son of a priest can upset my kingdom and disturb my peace.' 'Quite untrue', Herbert replied, 'and also that I'm the son of a priest, for I was born before my father became one. Like you can't be the son of a king if your father wasn't one.' The impudent thrust went home, and Henry was for a moment speechless. He then ordered Herbert to leave, and out the clerk went.

The third petitioner, Philip of Calne, was again in a different position. He had been a student in theology at Tours since 1162 and in poor health, so he had never thereafter been in Thomas's company, on a mission to Rome or involved in any way in the quarrel between him and the king. He had useful advocates who reminded Henry of these things and also told him that when Philip was informed that because of the archbishop's flight he had been despoiled of his goods in England, he had exclaimed,

'Dear God, why should the good king want to take something from me?'
Henry, urged to perform at least one act of mercy, granted Philip peace
and restoration of his goods, without requiring the oath he had demanded
from the others. He then got up and turned to other things. Later John
of Salisbury complained that he himself had not been offered these quite
acceptable terms.

This is a very instructive episode. There can be no doubt that all three
clerks, even Herbert of Bosham, were prepared to make their peace with
the king, provided, as in the case of Philip, it was granted unconditionally.
They were aware that the long-running dispute was about to enter into
a new and more bitter phase, and they could not see that they were under
any obligation to fight to the death with their lord. Although Herbert's
insolence doomed his suit to failure, by then he had probably decided that
if John of Salisbury could not succeed, he himself stood no chance at all.
Henry, no more than Thomas, could not stomach divided loyalty in his
servants. It would seem that it was in Henry's interest to pardon these
clerks and thus weaken the archbishop's position. But since he would not
stoop even an inch to conquer, it is clear that he was still completely implacable. If men of fine intellect and attractive personality chose to rot in exile,
so be it. All the same, as all involved in the dispute fully accepted, it was
a tragedy. The clerks knew full well that Henry was no monster. As we
can see from Herbert's behaviour they had complete trust in his safe-conduct.
Since 1163 Henry thought himself long-suffering and at times provoked
beyond bearing. But he was a conventional man at heart and drew the
line at enormities.

CHAPTER EIGHT

THOMAS ON THE ATTACK,
APRIL 1166–MAY 1167

In 1166 Thomas hit back. When he had learnt in the previous autumn of his virtual suspension by the pope until Easter 1166, he had not only protested but also petitioned for additional weapons to be used against his enemies. Alexander, as usual, procrastinated, but in April, feeling more secure now that he was back in Rome and angry because of Henry's contacts with the emperor, began to re-arm the archbishop and, unusually, to indulge him. Hence at the end of May or early in June a portfolio of privileges, measures against Thomas's opponents and letters in his support was delivered to the exile. For once Thomas had got most, if not all, he had asked for. Needless to say, Alexander quickly regretted this careless generosity, a change in attitude, which, although resented, Thomas would have expected.[1]

The pope stated his standing difficulties quite frankly in a letter to Thomas dated 10 September 1170, just before he received news of the archbishop's reconciliation with the king at Fréteval. 'Among the many cares which force themselves on our attention in these evil times', he wrote, 'the harassment you have suffered while protecting the liberty of the church moves us most deeply, since our yearning to show you greater favour is hampered by other cases which come roaring in from every direction. For the mind, when besieged by horrors, cannot easily perceive in what direction to turn, especially when it cannot see which course offers the greater advantage and the better chance of avoiding trouble and danger. When even sailors can be so baffled by the inconsistency of the winds that they cannot agree among themselves whether they should keep on course for their intended destination or turn back to their port of departure, there would seem to be no grounds for surprise or censure if, in this immense ocean, where countless serpents impede our course and the danger is not so much to earthly bodies and worldly merchandise as to souls and spiritual qualities, the captain of the ship of the church should not find it easy to decide to which proposal he should agree when conflicting interests produce conflict-ing advice.'

'Inevitably', the pope continued, 'there is disharmony between the views of the promoter of an individual case and of him who has to take care of society as a whole. Wherefore, dearest brother, if we should seem to have acted remissly in your case and that of the English church and have not responded to your petitions exactly according to your desires, it is not because we do not believe that you and we, together with the English church, do not have a cause in common or because for some reason or other we want to let you down. It is because of our belief that we ought to be patient and overcome evil by goodness. We also have been anxious that, if a major schism should develop in the church, it could not be attributed to our rigidity.' This was about as forthcoming as any pope could be expected to be, even at the end of the day.[2]

One of Thomas's standing difficulties was that he was fighting for his own and Canterbury's privileges as well as for the liberties of the English church and so on behalf of the church as a whole. The wider objects of his campaign, if not always the methods, aroused considerable sympathy, particularly in the Gallican church, where few of the harmful effects could be felt, and in the Cistercian Order. The English prelates, however, since they experienced the full inconvenience of the conflict, were, when not hostile, lukewarm. They thought that the struggle need not have happened, and, but for Thomas, would not have occurred. They tended to blame his intransigence and pride. Thomas was painfully aware of their 'selfish and short-sighted' attitude, which he intended to correct by punishment. He never made the slightest concession, even a gesture of compromise or of mercy, to any of his opponents of inferior status.

In the circumstances Thomas began his campaign in the spring of 1166 with commendable caution. Until the papal letters arrived towards the end of May he confined himself to warning shots. Henry, aware that the truce was running out and expecting trouble, looked to his defences. He began to exact oaths that men would not accept letters or messengers from the exile; and among those forced to swear was Walter de Lisle, the keeper of the king's seal under Geoffrey Ridel, probably a canon of St Paul's and certainly a secret supporter of the archbishop.[3]

In May Thomas began to warn the king. He informed the Empress Matilda, through Nicholas of Mont-St-Jacques at Rouen, that he was about to unsheathe the sword of the Holy Ghost against her son and his land. He also sent at least three letters of mounting severity to the king. In two of them he asked for a personal meeting with his lord, and in one, perhaps the last, he avowed that he was prepared to serve Henry faithfully and devotedly as his most dear lord and king to the utmost of his power, saving only the honour due to God and the Roman church and his own order. If Henry would not make peace and restitution on these terms he would surely incur God's revenge in all its ferocity. The first two letters were delivered by Urban I, abbot of Cercamp, a daughter house of Pontigny in Artois, the last, insultingly, by Gerard 'Barefoot', a 'squalid monk'. And at the end of the month Henry, at Chinon, protested to the Cistercian Order about this.[4]

Thomas was in despair when Henry disregarded his overtures and warnings and considered resigning his bishopric. His advisers, as usual, dissuaded him from this 'cowardice'; but it was probably the arrival of the package of papal letters which reanimated him. On 8 April Alexander had confirmed Thomas's primacy in the English church. Ever since Calixtus II's grant on 16 November 1103 to Anselm and his lawful successors of a primacy 'as has been enjoyed by your predecessors', archbishops of Canterbury had a standing claim to the privilege on those terms, and sought confirmation only as and when they thought it advisable. Thomas maintained that Alexander had confirmed his primacy verbally at Sens in November 1164; but he thought it expedient to impetrate for it at this juncture. It would not seem, however, that the primacy conferred on the metropolitan (which Thomas was by virtue of his pallium) any additional powers, unless it was the right to crown the king – a right which had been in dispute with York and was confirmed to Thomas independently in a letter to Roger and all English bishops on 5 April. But although a primacy was not something to be abandoned, it had become so small a thing compared with a papal legation that Thomas seems never, either before or after June 1166, to have used it in his official style.[5]

The grant of a papal legation, announced on Easter Sunday, 24 April, but dated 2 May, was quite another matter. Coveted and fought for by Theobald, who eventually held one from 1149 or 1150 until the death of Adrian IV in 1159, by its delegation of papal powers it reinforced an archbishop's authority considerably. But because of its potency it was carefully controlled. In 1166 Alexander excluded from Thomas's jurisdiction the diocese of York; and a legation lapsed on the death of the grantor and could be suspended at will, especially when legates a latere were dispatched from the curia.[6]

In 1166, however, Alexander did not exclude Henry's person; and in a separate authorization, likewise repeated to all the bishops, abbots and other prelates in the province of Canterbury, Thomas was empowered, after lawful warnings and proceedings, to punish all those who had done violence or injury to him and his men in respect of the goods and possessions of his church. 'Also we do not give you a special mandate concerning the person of the king, nor in any way deprive you of any of your pontifical rights.' John of Salisbury, in a letter in July, explained this as meaning, 'the pope added that he had not ordered him to excommunicate the king, nor had he forbidden it, for he should not deprive him of that power.' Alexander also authorized Thomas to take measures against invaders of his property, a letter he repeated to all bishops, abbots and other prelates in England, and especially to Gilbert Foliot in respect of the despoilers of Thomas's clerks. Moreover, in a letter to the archbishop of Rouen, repeated to Bordeaux and Bourges, he complained of Henry's overtures to the emperor and treatment of Thomas and urged them to exhort the king to mend his ways under threat of ecclesiastical censures.[7]

The award of a papal legation gave Thomas's authority a new dimension. Although in much correspondence he continued to use his standard style, 'by the grace of God the humble servant of the church of Canterbury', without embellishment, in letters addressed to England, particularly to ecclesiastics, he usually included 'legate of the Holy See' in his title. The new office undoubtedly encouraged him to take action against his enemies in June 1166. But he thought it wise to proceed deviously. He decided, as Herbert of Bosham repeatedly complains, to keep his plans secret not only from the pope, whom he feared might frustrate them, but also from his closest and most confidential friends, whom he knew would disapprove. Besides, since Angers, he evidently had less confidence in the loyalty of these.[8]

He began to go on pilgrimages, no doubt as a form of relaxation, but also to enlist the saints for his cause. Towards the end of May, presumably after he had heard that he was to be appointed papal legate, he travelled north to Soissons, some 200 kilometres from Pontigny, and seems to have met John of Salisbury, coming from Rheims, at Château-Thierry, on the outward or return journey. At Soissons he spent three nights in vigil, one at the shrine of the Virgin, one at the shrine of St Gregory, the founder of the English church, and one at the tomb of St Drausius, the seventh-century bishop of the place, who was the patron saint of champions, those about to wage the ordeal by battle. Thomas was not only being punctilious, he was also signalling his intentions, although Herbert asserts that all the archbishop's companions still remained completely in the dark.[9]

Meanwhile, on 1 June, Henry, alerted by the three letters he had received from Thomas, held a council at Chinon in Touraine, attended by the archbishop of Rouen and other Norman bishops, to discuss how the threat of ecclesiastical censures should be countered. Arnulf of Lisieux advised making an appeal to the pope against such sentences, naming 16 April 1167 as the term; and it was decided that he and Froger bishop of Sées, together with the archbishop of Rouen, should go to Pontigny to make the appeal. They arrived, fruitlessly, on 3 June, probably the day on which Thomas left Soissons. He had decided to travel to Vézelay, 72 kilometres south of Pontigny, and there on Whit Sunday (12 June) pronounce sentence on his enemies. As he needed the maximum publicity, Pontigny would not do. In any case he wanted to spare the Cistercian Order. But why he chose the ancient Cluniac, but at that time semi-independent, abbey of Vézelay, with its beautiful church full of radiant light on the top of a hill, rather than Soissons, Sens or Auxerre, cannot be said with certainty. Perhaps he went impatiently to intercept his nuncios returning from Rome with the legation. But St Bernard had preached the Second Crusade there on Easter Sunday 1146, and once again the symbolism may have been important for the crusading archbishop, although if he had known that Arnulf of Lisieux, as well as King Louis and Waleran count of Meulan, had taken the Cross on that occasion, he might well have had second thoughts.[10]

On the journey south from Soissons Thomas may have avoided Pontigny, for on Friday 10 June he was a little to the south-east at the Cistercian abbey of Rigny, near Vermenton, on the River Cure, 28 kilometres downstream from Vézelay. It was there that he learnt, from a courier of the French king, that Henry had fallen seriously ill and had had to abandon a meeting he had arranged with Louis. Possibly a proposal to meet Thomas had also been jettisoned. According to John of Salisbury, it was because of the archbishop's compassion for his stricken lord that he decided to give him a reprieve. From Rigny Thomas and his companions went on to Vézelay, and on Whit Sunday, at the invitation of Abbot William de Mello and the convent, Thomas celebrated the main, public Mass. After the Gospel he went up into the pulpit and preached to the congregation. He started on a familiar note, explaining the cause of his quarrel with the king and describing his sufferings. And then, to everyone's surprise, including Herbert of Bosham's, he began to pronounce sentences of anathema and excommunicate some of his enemies by name. First he condemned the Constitutions of Clarendon and anathematized, although not personally, all those who observed and enforced them. He quashed the written document and condemned specifically the clauses which controlled intercourse with the papal curia (8, 4), restricted the church's power of excommunication (7, 10) and diminished ecclesiastical jurisdiction (6, 15, 3, 1), that is to say, although the practices condemned by Thomas do not coincide exactly with the Clarendon schedule, about half of the sixteen clauses.

He then excommunicated by name John of Oxford, for communicating with the schismatic Rainald of Cologne, taking the oath at Würzburg and usurping the deanery of Salisbury; Richard of Ilchester for communicating with Rainald; Richard de Lucy and Jocelin de Balliol for promoting royal tyranny and fabricating the Constitutions, 'those heretical iniquities', and Ranulf de Broc, Hugh de St Clair and Thomas fitzBernard (the master forester) for usurping the goods and possessions of the church of Canterbury.

All future usurpers were likewise condemned. Thomas added that he had not yet pronounced a personal sentence on the king, but would do so unless he came to his senses and mended his ways. It is noticeable that he did not bring Henry's illness into the matter.[11]

Although Thomas believed that Stephen had been defeated in 1152 by papal sentences of personal excommunication and interdict on his kingdom, and at Vézelay could undoubtedly have sentenced Henry, he chose not to. He behaved similarly at Fréteval in 1170. On each occasion he was prepared to shelve his grievances against the king in order to get at the royal servants who were directly harming him and his clerks, and especially at his suffragan bishops whose treachery caused him the greatest pain and anger. There were good reasons for this policy. For maximum effect it was for the pope, not his legate, to act. Most of his advisers, with their reverence for monarchy, awareness of Henry's power and lack of confidence in Thomas's statesmanship, counselled patience and caution. There was widespread fear, shared by the pope, that if Thomas and Alexander should expel Henry from the communion of the faithful, he would simply go over to Pope Paschal and the emperor; and Thomas may have received secret orders, or at least advice, from the pope on this matter. Moreover, Thomas, who never completely extinguished the embers of his former great love for the king, began to view Henry as somewhat outside the war he was waging: the king was ill-advised, misled, the victim of circumstances. Although this was probably wishful thinking, the pope too came to share the opinion. It was the charitable view of Henry's selfishness and willingness to sacrifice the bishops, or anyone else, if it served his purpose. In any case, Thomas could excuse his forbearance by the argument that if the king was indeed a willing participant in the condemned practices, and if he should willingly communicate with excommunicates, he was likewise *ipso facto* infected. He was leaving Henry with a choice.[12]

The policy of sparing the king allowed Thomas to wage limited campaigns against his more accessible enemies, which, if seldom remunerative and never decisive, at least kept him occupied. It became a way of life. All the same it increased, if that was possible, his unpopularity among the bishops and royal servants. They found it intolerable that all the burdens and penalties should fall on them, who were not principals, indeed were not parties to the quarrel. It was all very well for the Gallican church, if John of Salisbury was to be believed, to be amazed at the behaviour of the English bishops.[13] In the arena things looked rather different. It is also possible to question the wisdom of Thomas's strategy. If in 1166 he had excommunicated Henry by name and put an interdict on England, the violence could have broken the deadlock. In any case, the results could hardly have been worse than those which followed his half-hearted attack. But if we were to think that

1. Archbishop Theobald's seal. The archbishop full length, standing on a corbel, vested for Mass, holding his crozier, his right hand raised in blessing. Legend: SIGILLUM TEOBALDI DEI GRATIA ARCHIEPISCOPI CANTUARIENSIS. Thomas's would have been similar, with TOME for TEOBALDI.

2. Thomas's personal seal, made from an antique gem engraved with the figure of a Roman god or hero, perhaps Mercury, Mars or Perseus. Legend: SIGILLUM TOME LUND. See pp. 38–9. Here used as a counterseal: see Pl. 16. No genuine example or satisfactory representation of Thomas's official seals as archdeacon or archbishop have survived. But the latter would undoubtedly have been similar to those of his predecessors and successors: for Theobald's, see Pl. 1.

(Latin manuscript text)

3. (above) Writ of right of King Henry II addressed to Earl Hugh of Chester and his wife, in favour of Gloucester abbey. Dated Worcester (20 April 1158) and witnessed by Thomas the chancellor. Sealed with the great seal.

4. (left) Font in the Romano–British church of St Martin, outside the walls of Canterbury on the Sandwich road, where Thomas when chancellor is said to have been scourged by its priest, another Thomas. See pp. 46–7. The font is a composite structure consisting of a stone base and three rows and a rim of carved stones – the lower two and the rim Anglo-Saxon work, the third Norman romanesque.

5. (opposite) Drawing of Thomas, robed as primate, with the pallium conspicuous. It prefaces John of Salisbury's Prologue to his Life of St Thomas, *incipit, Sacrosanctam ecclesiam.* This forms the introduction to Alan of Tewkesbury's collection of the 'Becket correspondence' made in 1174–6.

eccliam iugit iupugnat hostis antiq.
ti q ipam cruore ipo redeturo di fili
ea sanigne imbroz suoz, in uera asse
tio & puehit libtate. In qbz pminen
glosus aploz chorus & seoz marti
rus purpurar exerar. quru doctina
copaca quru exeplo roborata quoz
sanigne uelut cemeo & qsi glutino
ecla cosolidati su una lapides in edi
ficio corporis xpi, ut pficiens ecclia
dilatet & crescat numo fidelui &
uirtue, in templu scin in dno s, cum
oni marturi prerogatiua habeat
gtie sempitne, uirulus uirtlloz illus
tride e cetiu & corona clari radiat, q
duplici honore digni doctoz fun
gut officio forma gregis ex aio fat
ti, & tepore necessitati ponetce aiam
p ouibz suis. Sic eni stella a stella dif
fert in clartate, sic in resurreccioe seoz
singli in ordine suo iusti fulgebut ut
sida, & q ad uirta iusti erudiut, ut
ut firmamti splendos in ippetuas ef
mitates. Quibz iure & merito ses can
tuariox archiepc thomas associan
dus e, ut q certus soc p xpo luela
tioiis & patientie sr eis in ipo cohe

...des ...iui...a in uitam beati

...martinis thome secundum Johar

...reu duschler...

6. (left) Seal of Christ Church, Canterbury, 1155 x 8, showing the angel steeple and the towers surmounted by cockerel weather vanes. Legend: SIGILLUM ECCL[ESI]E XPI CANTUARIE PRIME SEDIS BRITANNIE.

7. (below) The city of Canterbury in the sixteenth century, looking north. The cathedral close is within the walls (top). The London road enters across the River Stour by Westgate (left) and in the centre is joined by Palace Street from Northgate (top). Burh Street skirts the south wall of the close and exits by Burgate, where it becomes the Sandwich road, with St Augustine's abbey (upper right) and St Martin's church to its north. The Dover road leaves by the next two, more southerly, gates (lower right).

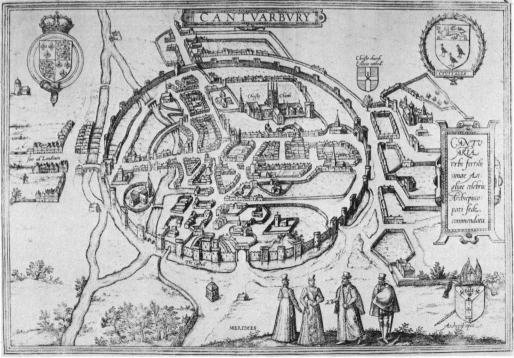

8. (right) Execution, by order of Bishop
Theodred of Elmham (late tenth
century), of eight robbers who had
broken into the abbey of Bury St
Edmunds. For this 'unpremeditated
sentence' he did penance for the rest
of his life. It was from that fate
that Thomas wanted to save
criminous clerks. Miniature from
Abbo of Fleury's *Life and Miracles of
St Edmund, King and Martyr*, dated
c. 1130.

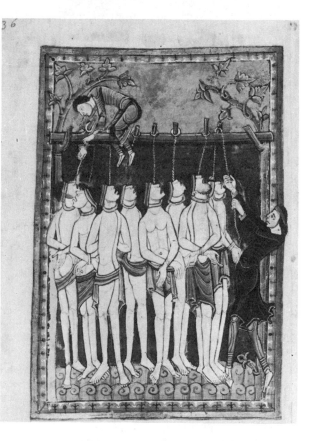

9. (below) Clarendon 'palace', about
three miles south-east of Old Sarum
(Wilts), the centre of the forest of the
same name. It was a favourite
hunting-lodge of Henry II, who
greatly extended and improved it.
Walls were of flint rubble with stone
dressings. It was here in January
1164 that the Constitutions of
Clarendon were drawn up. See p. 98.
The photograph shows the
excavations of 1933–9.

10. (above) Notification by Archbishop Thomas of the amends promised by Earl
Geoffrey of Essex to Ramsey abbey for the injuries done to it by his father,
Geoffrey de Mandeville, in time of war. Settlement dated Windsor, 6 April
1163, and witnessed by Hilary bishop of Chichester and the archbishop's clerks,
Robert (Foliot), archdeacon of Oxford, John of Tilbury, Robert of Beaufai,
Stephen of Ecton and William of Leicester. See p. 84.

11. (below) Writ of King Henry II to Robert bishop of Lincoln ordering him to
restrain the prior and canons of Launde: failing which Thomas archbishop of
Canterbury will act. Dated Woodstock (1 July 1163) and witnessed by John
of Oxford. For the council of Woodstock, see p. 88.

12. (left) Silver matrix of Exeter
city seal, *c.* 1200, made by Luke
at the expense of William Prudum.
Legend: SIGILLUM CIVITATIS EXONIE.

13. (below left) Seal of Robert
(II), earl of Leicester
(1119–68), to be dated
perhaps soon after 1119. The
earl carries a long shield and
wields a lance overarm.
Legend: SIGILLUM ROBERTI
COMITIS LEGRECESTRIE. On the
reverse (not shown) is a gem
counterseal, 'Victory holding
a rudder'.

14. (below) (Second) seal of
William de Mandeville, earl
of Essex (1166–89), to be
dated *c.* 1180. Imitated from
the seal of Philip of Alsace,
Count of Flanders, with
whom he had crusaded,
1177–8. Legend: WILL DE
MANDEVILLA COMES ESSEXIE.

15. (above) Henry of Blois, bishop of Winchester (1129–71), depicted on one of
a pair of plaques, copper, engraved, enamelled and gilded, made by a Mosan
goldsmith for this great patron of the arts. The bishop is shown making a gift,
possibly of an altar set with decorated roundels, to a church.

16. (below) Confirmatory charter of Archbishop Thomas for the Priory of Holy
Trinity, Aldgate, London, addressed to Walter bishop of Rochester *et al.*, to
be dated probably 1162–4. Face of seal lost. For the counterseal, see Pl. 2.

17, 18. The exterior and nave of Pontigny abbey (Yonne), Thomas's home from December 1164 to November 1166. The church was then newly built. See pp 123 ff.

19. (above left) Letter of Pope Alexander III to King Henry announcing the appointment of William and Otto as his legates, to be dated *c*. 1 January 1167. *Incipit, Magnificentię tuę petitionibus: Mats.*, no. 273. From Alan of Tewkesbury's own copy of his collection of the correspondence, for which see Pl. 5, fo. 142 v. For the letter, see p. 163.

20. (above right) Letter of the Pope to Thomas, dated 10 September 1170. *Incipit, Inter multiplices curas: Mats.*, no. 699. Provenance as Pl. 19, fo. 332 v. For the letter, see pp. 143–4.

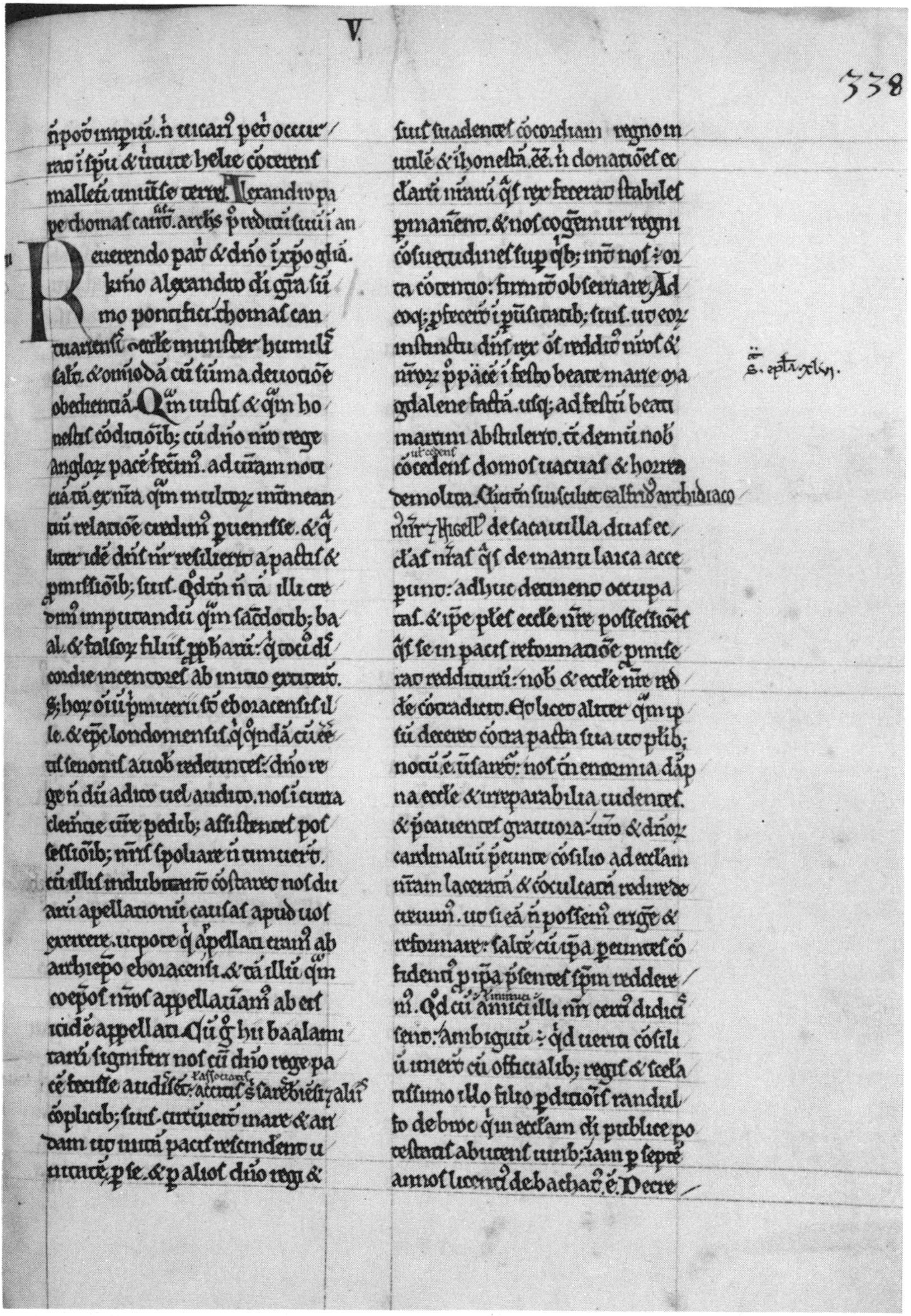

21. Letter of Thomas to the Pope, reporting his return to England, to be dated early December 1170. *Incipit, Quam iustis: Mats.*, no. 723. Provenance as Pl. 19, fo. 338r. For the letter, see p. 228.

22, 23. The church of
Vézelay abbey
(Yonne), (left) the
nave, (below) museum
cast of the narthex
tympanum, where on
12 June 1166 Thomas
first excommunicated
his enemies. See pp.
146 ff.

24. (right) Sens cathedral (Yonne), the nave, in construction while Thomas was living at the nearby abbey of St Colombe, November 1166–November 1170. Its architect, William, was to rebuild Canterbury cathedral after the fire of 1174. See pp. 158 ff.

25. (below) Château de Chinon (Indre-et-Loire), on a spur overlooking the River Vienne. It is composed of three separate fortifications. Fort St-Georges, built by Henry II and where he died in 1189, was on the far right.

28. (opposite) Architectural plan (south at top) of the waterworks installed by Prior Wibert (1152/3–1167) at Christ Church, Canterbury. As regards the martyrdom it shows (top right) the cellarer's range and the square cloister beneath the cathedral, but omits the archbishop's palace, which is off the picture top right. From the 'Eadwine Psalter', a Canterbury MS to be dated *c.* 1150–60.

26. (above) A mitre (back view), formerly at Sens, which in the nineteenth century was associated with Archbishop Thomas and is indeed of the period. It is of white silk twill with red bands and embroidered with silver-gilt thread.

27. (right) Late twelfth-century high relief of the archbishop, said to be from a house at Sens where Thomas once lived and now let into the wall of the ambulatory of the cathedral.

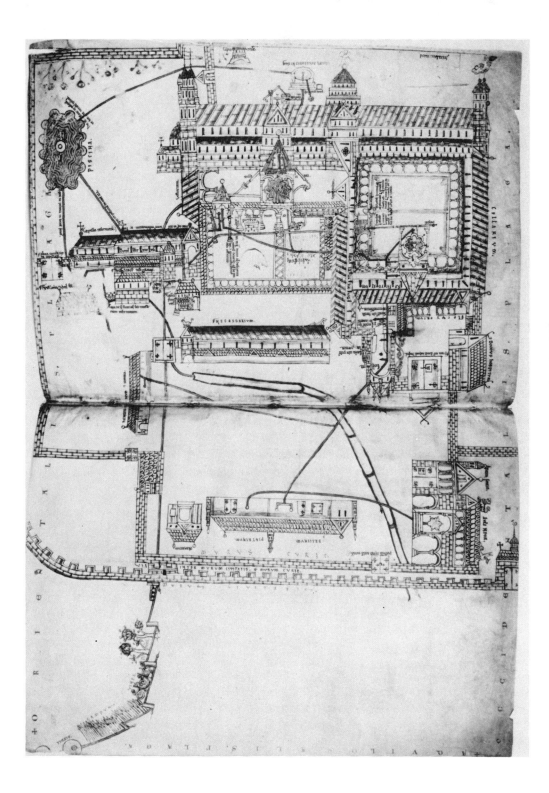

29. (left) The site of the martyrdom, the lower north transept of Canterbury cathedral.

30. (right) The earliest known representation of the martyrdom. In the upper register the arrival of the four knights is announced; below (left) Reginald fitzUrse strikes the first blow; (right) the murderers do penance at the tomb. The miniature prefaces John of Salisbury's letter *Ex insperato* (no. 305), to be dated early 1171, in Alan of Tewkesbury's collection, for which see Pl. 5, fo. 341r. For the event, see pp. 245 ff.

31. The martyrdom as depicted on a fresco in the church of Saints John and Paul at Spoleto, Italy, considered by Tancred Borenius to be of the late twelfth century. It seems to show Henry II, seated left, issuing orders to knights, one of whom holds the archbishop while he strikes at his head. Edward Grim is in attendance.

32. (left) The martyrdom as
    shown on the counterseal
    of Stephen Langton,
    archbishop of Canterbury
    (1207–28): four murderers
    and Edward Grim, with a
    dove descending. Legend:
    MORS EXPRESSA FORIS TIBI
    VITA SIT INTUS AMORIS, a
    rhyming hexameter,
    meaning 'may the picture
    of an external death be for
    you an inner life of love'.

33. (below) The murder and
    (on the top) the burial,
    depicted on a late twelfth-
    century Limoges enamel
    gabled reliquary (*châsse*).
    The roof is set with three
    rock crystals and two
    enamelled studs.

34. The burial. The lowest of three roundels in a decorated capital I, from Alan of Tewkesbury's collection of correspondence, for which see Pl. 5, fo. 214v.

35. The burial place. The ambulatory of the Norman crypt. The massive column is a post-1174 intrusion.

36. (top) Pilgrims at the tomb. This is the original low tomb in the eastern crypt, 1171–1220: the marble sarcophagus within a stone box pierced by four oval portholes. See pp. 249–50, 267. Thirteenth-century stained glass in the south aisle of the Trinity chapel in Canterbury cathedral.

37. (above) The burial, shown on a late twelfth-century silver reliquary, with niello decoration and surmounted by a simulated ruby. The interior is divided to hold two phials. Possibly made in the Rhineland. It has been suggested, but on mistaken evidence, that it may have been the one given by John of Salisbury to Chartres.

38. (opposite) St Thomas, as shown in a thirteenth-century stained glass panel in the north aisle of the Trinity chapel in Canterbury cathedral.

res cõsolatiõis & gtic. Cui̧ ut ṁna cla
ri dulcescanti̧ uma ueler latiõis ei̧
succinctê & admodū breui̧ sermo
p̃ curra. Nam gestoꝝ ei̧ serie nosse
si tui̧ forte malcto eꝛ a magui̧s ꝗ ab
illo & de illo uoluminib; s̃pta sīt eni
mutuanda, ut cõstat ad cõmdati

onē gṙe di̧ q̃ ut uult spirat: qm̃ breui̧ in
tuallo uariaꝝ occupationū expletū
tẽpora multa. Indicant hoc eṗ́le ei̧ ꝑ śp
ta alioꝝ fide plena, & digna relatu: q̃
tam presentes quam posteros si di
ligenter inspiciantur ad uirtutē
poterunt ammarẽ

THOMAS

LONDONIENSI. VRBI INDIGENA
patꝛū mechocū pietͣ illust̃: à p̃mis ado
lescẽtie annis gṙa multiplici ditat͛ e. Erat
enī statura pꝛoceᷣ decoᷣ forma ingenio ꝑspicax
dultͣ & iocūdus eloꝗo. & uenustate moꝛ ꝑ
erat amabilͥ: tantoꝗ; iuuenͥs urgebat acu
mine, ut ꝓdeūt ianduras & difficilͥ soluter
q̃stiōes. adeoꝗ; feliciter gan

39. (left) Decorated *Incipit* to John of Salisbury's *Vita et Passio*, reading *Predictus igitur beatissimus Thomas Londoniensis urbis indigena*, prefixed to Alan of Tewkesbury's collection of correspondence, for which see Pl. 5, fo. 2v.

40. (below) Back of a gold reliquary pendant (49 × 31 mm), made perhaps *c*. 1176 for Reginald 'the Lombard', bishop of Bath, to present to Margaret of Navarre, queen-mother of Sicily (died 1183). It shows the bishop blessing the queen. The transparent front and the relics contained are lost. The relics listed are portions of the martyr's blood and of his blood-stained garments, pelisse, belt, cowl, shoe and shirt.

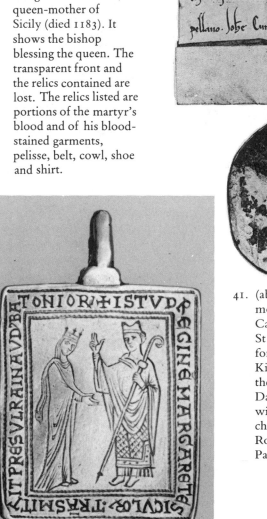

41. (above) Henry II grants to the monks of Christ Church, Canterbury, for the love of God and St Thomas the Martyr, free passage for a hundred *muids* of wine which King Louis of France has given them annually for the same reason. Dated Marlborough (1179 × 80) and witnessed by Godfrey de Lucy, the chaplain Nicholas, John Cumin, Roger Bigot and Reginald de Pavilli.

42. Henry II's painted wooden effigy on his tomb in the abbey church of Fontevraud (Maine-et-Loire), where he was buried in 1189.

Alexander would most likely have countermanded, or at least weakened, his legate's measures, the course of events would have been little changed.

A legate's actions only became completely firm when acknowledged by the pope, and Thomas lost no time in sending a report of his sentences to Alexander with a request for confirmation. His mission returned with the crucial ratification, although rather grudgingly displayed, shortly after the archbishop's move to Sens in November. Thomas also circulated his report, with minor variations, to various cardinals and archbishops, together with the news that the archbishop of Rouen had told Henry that he himself would communicate with none of those sentenced and would observe sentences against the king and the kingdom if ordered to do so by the pope. To his suffragan bishops Thomas gave a few more details about the despoilers of Canterbury and asked his subordinates to observe his sentences. Gilbert Foliot was to see to it.[14]

Thomas also singled out one bishop, Jocelin of Salisbury, for exemplary punishment. Because he had irregularly intruded the 'damnable heretic' John of Oxford into the deanery and maintained him there despite papal and archiepiscopal prohibitions, he was sentenced to suspension from his episcopal and priestly offices and should appear before Thomas within two months in order to make amends. Jocelin's offence was soon compounded by his failure to secure the release of the archbishop's chaplain, William of Salisbury, who was imprisoned by a royal marshal, Alan de Neville, for some six months in Corfe Castle in the diocese of Salisbury because of something he had done in consequence of the Vézelay sentences. Thomas worked exceedingly hard for his release. In October or November he put the diocese under an interdict until the chaplain should be freed. He pursued a vendetta against Jocelin until the very end of his life, although unsupported by John of Salisbury and given the barest assistance by the pope. There would seem to have been something personal in the affair. It may not be irrelevant that both Jocelin and Gilbert Foliot came from baronial families.[15]

Henry's response to the Vézelay sentences was not only to send the Norman bishops to make an appeal to the pope against them but also, through the keeper of his seal, Master Walter de Lisle, and Richard de Lucy, to require the English bishops to do likewise. This they did unanimously on about 24 June at London and probably again on 6 July at Northampton. Jocelin of Salisbury and his chapter also appealed on their own behalf, giving as term 23 April 1167.

At the Council of London Gilbert Foliot organized the proceedings and drafted the two letters which were sent in the name of the bishops and dignitaries of the province, and sealed by them, to the pope and archbishop. In the letter to Alexander the bishops recalled how reasonably Henry had responded to the papal mission of the bishops of London and Hereford to him in Wales and how splendidly he was behaving. He was a most Christian king, a most faithful husband, an incomparable preserver of peace and justice who strove with all his heart to cleanse the kingdom of every kind of sin and establish good order and sound government. When the kingdom was disturbed by some licentious clerks, with his usual reverence for the church he referred their crimes to the ecclesiastical judges, the bishops, so that the one sword should aid the other and the church secure that peace among the clergy which he was establishing among the people. This laudable purpose led to the recording of the customs and dignities of the realm, to the present conflict over them and to the archbishop's contumacious, irreverent and inordinate behaviour. Now the archbishop had excommunicated royal servants who had not been cited or allowed any defence, who were even unaware, they claimed, of having committed any crime, who had neither confessed nor been convicted. The proper order of justice had been perverted. And Thomas had since then committed a similar injustice against the bishop of Salisbury. In order, therefore, to prevent this upsetting of the church and kingdom, they appealed to the pope and designated Ascension Day (18 May 1167) as the term for the hearing.

The parallel letter to the archbishop was no less shrewd. Gilbert included a few passages intended to wound its recipient. The bishops were pleased to hear that Thomas at Pontigny was atoning for the earlier wasted years by fasts, prayers and tears, and begged him to persevere in that penitential mood so that his well-wishers might secure a negotiated settlement of the quarrel. They recalled Henry's great benefactions to the chancellor, including the gift of Canterbury against the advice of the empress and despite the sighs and groans of the church. They could not claim that Henry had never sinned, but they could say that he was always ready to make amends to God for his transgressions. When John of Salisbury read these letters he found them all the more insulting because they echoed, malevolently, some of his own criticism.[16]

Because of the royal blockade, Thomas was unable to publish his legation, the other papal letters and his own punitive mandates until after the Council of London. The Salisbury sentences were delivered by a monk. It was on 30 July, St Paul's day, that a complete stranger – a calculated insult – served the letters on Gilbert Foliot as he stood at the altar in his cathedral celebrating the Mass of its patronal saint. And the bishop, a faithful servant of the pope, was put in great difficulty by the receipt of the letters. He wrote to Henry in evident distress to report the event. He had been ordered to secure the restoration of all the confiscated benefices within two months under threat of anathema and without the right to appeal. He was to collect Peter's Pence (due on 1 August). And he was to publicize the legation and Thomas's several demands. In Gilbert's view the appeal already made by the bishops was powerless against the papal mandates, and he asked for permission to obey them. He also suggested that if there was anything in the archbishop's letter contrary to the customs of the realm, the king should order the bishops to appeal against it to the pope or any legates whom he might send. It seems that the English bishops and abbots met at Northampton on 6 July, and they probably renewed their appeal against Thomas on this occasion.[17]

Northern France was buzzing with rumours. Optimists like John of Salisbury and Nicholas of Mont-St-Jacques still thought that terms could be found for a reconciliation, possibly through the efforts of the empress or the archbishop of Rouen – neither, as it happened, by any means eager supporters of the exile. Nicholas had heard, however, that Thomas was to be appointed Louis's chancellor and intended to excommunicate Henry by name on St Mary Magdalene's Day (24 July). In England there was no less confusion. As the Vézelay sentences were not properly published in the churches, nor, of course, enforced by royal officials, they were outwardly ineffective, and none of the royal agents in Kent seems to have been deterred. But some of those involved were uneasy.[18]

The appeals and counter-appeals had started on 13 October 1164, when Thomas himself had been first in the field. None had yet come to term, and probably no one expected a final legal judgment. In the late summer of 1166 both the archbishop and the king had embassies in Rome, the one seeking confirmation of the Vézelay sentences, the other, well-furnished with money, pursuing their appeals against them. Both were jockeying for position. Thomas rejected the appeals on various technical grounds. And arguments could be circular. After the Vézelay sentences most agents of the other side could be regarded as excommunicate, either *ipso facto* or by contamination, and so incapable of valid legal action. Step by step with the growth of the custom of appeal had developed a repertoire of counter-measures. What the royalists were looking for were papal legates *a latere* who would supersede Thomas and might be persuaded to decide against him. What all were waiting for was the death of one or more of the actors. Although John of Salisbury disapprovingly quoted the *Disticha* of Cato, 'Place not your hope on another man's death', a new archbishop, a new pope, a new king would break the deadlock.[19]

Meanwhile Thomas tried to enforce his measures. He had cited the bishop and chapter of Salisbury to appear before him, and, advised by John of Salisbury, in July and August summoned several English ecclesiastics to go to meet him. The purpose was partly disciplinary, partly consultative. Among those cited to appear at Pontigny within forty days were Bartholomew of Exeter and Geoffrey Ridel, archdeacon of Canterbury and acting royal chancellor. He also tried to detach from the royalists Robert of Melun, bishop of Hereford. He had written, perhaps in 1165, to 'his eldest son', the one whom above all the rest he would have expected to join him in exile. And in August 1166, prompted by John of Salisbury, two leading Paris scholars, Ernis abbot of St Victor and his prior Richard, admonished Robert for having reneged on the principles he had held and taught when he himself was in the schools. John even remarked rather tactlessly to Thomas that Robert had always been a hypocrite, avid for fame and money. But no one undertook the journey to Pontigny.[20]

It was in the summer and autumn of 1166 that the rival parties exchanged the heaviest epistolary salvoes of the whole campaign. Once Thomas had received in July the two letters of appeal (written by Gilbert Foliot) he and his clerks got down to preparing answers. At least four were drafted, one by Herbert of Bosham, another by Lombard, neither of which was used, and a further two which were issued under Thomas's name, on which they probably all collaborated. Herbert's was in little short of 5,000 words, Lombard's in rather less, and the final versions, one to the bishops collectively in some 5,600 words, and the other to Gilbert Foliot personally in some 2,350. The key word among these 16,000, and in many of Thomas's letters, is *expectavi*, 'I have been waiting'; and while he waited he had plenty of time for explaining what he expected.[21]

The English bishops had made a definite legal move – an appeal against Thomas to terminate on 23 April 1167. Thomas's two replies were not technical legal instruments. They answered the bishops' allegations one by one, and they contained some, Lombard's much, legal argument and quotations from the *Decretum*. But they rested mostly on the Bible, and the general tone, characteristic of Herbert, was theological and moral. The main theme was, of what possible validity were appeals made in order to protect the persecutors of the church and harm its defenders? And indeed Thomas had no charge of much substance to answer. The bishops had raised a series of separate grievances against him based on alleged misdemeanours or failures of duty. They were serious men and their complaints were not frivolous. But no moral enormity was alleged, no legal irregularity of any great moment and no crime except against a secular ruler. Accordingly, in his answers Thomas simply took his stand on different ground: his priestly order and his offices as bishop and metropolitan. He justified the actions of which the bishops complained by moral necessity.

The two letters of appeal and Thomas's two replies are, therefore, manifestos and do not constitute a debate since they start from different premises. With regard to Thomas's ingratitude to the king, his 'illegal' flight from Northampton and his sentences at Vézelay, there were, after all, simple answers available based on his bounden duty to defend the liberty of the church and punish sinners; and by harping on the enormity of inferiors passing judgment on their superior some moral advantage was to be gained. Insinuation was answered by insinuation. If the bishops suggested that Thomas had been unworthy of the archbishopric and had been forced on the electors by the king, Thomas could claim that he was being persecuted by men who had coveted his office. Each side presented its champion as engaged in, or ready for, repentance. According to Herbert, Thomas was being pursued and judged as though he was still Saul. Daily the exile prayed to God, 'Do not remember the faults of my ignorant youth.' He was now Paul, with clean hands and eyes unveiled. And, Thomas's party asked with every excuse, in what sense was Henry repentant for his sins, in what practical way did he intend to make amends, and when?

The one positive, but completely unhelpful, move made by Thomas in this correspondence was to lay down his conditions for a reconciliation. Henry was to permit the English church to enjoy peace and liberty and the Roman church to have all those rights and liberties it enjoyed in other kingdoms. He was to restore to the church of Canterbury and its archbishops all those rights, liberties and possessions he had taken from them, and to Thomas the full peace and security which would allow him to fight for God under the king. In return Henry would have the use of all Thomas's services, but saving the honour of God and of the Roman church and of Thomas's own order. As Thomas required Henry's total surrender on all the matters at issue, this too was more a manifesto than a realistic offer.[22]

Thomas's resentment at Gilbert Foliot's behaviour is understandable. Not only was the bishop of London responsible for the spiritualities of the 'vacant' diocese of Canterbury and for the confiscated benefices of the archiepiscopal clerks, he also, as dean of the province, was acting-head of all the bishops, except York and Durham. Moreover, as one of Henry's leading supporters and advisers, he had assumed that role in England which Henry had originally intended for his chancellor. And the irony in the situation was that it was administratively necessary for Thomas, when acting as papal legate, to use Gilbert as his agent in England as regards the whole bench of bishops except York.

Thomas had every excuse to be bitter. He had opened his letter to Gilbert with the words, 'I am amazed and astounded that a wise man like you, a biblical scholar, above all a monk, should so obviously (I almost wrote, irreverently) and without fear of God, oppose the truth, resist justice and, with a view to confusing right and wrong, seek to overthrow the institution of the church which God himself has founded.' It was, however, an inadvisable exordium. Gilbert sat down and composed a famous and masterly reply (*Multiplicem nobis*). In elegant Latin, yet simply and clearly, at length but without the distraction of too much ornament and appeal to authorities, he explained exactly what he thought of Thomas's performance as archbishop and why it was necessary to oppose him and render him powerless. His version of the events of the last four years is, of course, selective and biased, but probably no more so than the interpretation offered, at much greater length and from many more hands, by Thomas and his supporters. Gilbert's also gains by its apparent coolness and moderation, its reasonableness, its avoidance of vituperation. Even if he had stumbled in his speech at Sens in 1164, and that is barely credible, he hardly put a foot wrong in this indictment.[23]

Gilbert started by denying that he personally had ever coveted the archbishopric: his dismay at Thomas's nomination was caused exclusively by the denial of freedom to the church and the royal candidate's unsuitability. Thomas, by buying the chancellorship, had effectively purchased a bishopric. Richard de Lucy, now rewarded with excommunication, had forced the electors to elect the chancellor and Thomas had wielded against his opponents the sword which previously he had used against the church in the matter of the scutage of Toulouse. Like a thief and a robber he had entered the sheepfold not by the door but had climbed up some other way (John, 10: 1 ff.). The terrible *prognosticon* at his consecration showed this all too clearly. Hitherto Church and State, except for the disgraceful Toulouse business, had been fruitfully at peace and the church had flourished. Any hope of improvement under Thomas was dashed when the archbishop, instead of stamping on a spark of discord with the king, had fanned it into a great fire. The result was the inquiry into the royal dignities (Constitutions of Clarendon) and a threat to the liberties of the church. In the face of this all the bishops had stood firm behind Thomas, but at Clarendon they were abandoned by their leader who made an abject surrender, and then tried to flee the kingdom, although he had just sworn in good faith to observe the customs which prohibited such a departure without royal licence. At Oxford Henry had welcomed the returning fugitive with kindness. But the archbishop had then flouted royal authority in the case of John the Marshal, and, not surprisingly, was called upon to answer at Northampton for contempt of the royal summons. There the archbishop, contrary to canon law, accepted and submitted to the jurisdiction of the royal court – perhaps he considered that Henry, because he was an anointed king, was an ecclesiastical person.

At this point Gilbert digresses to consider the relationship between church and state and royal and sacerdotal authority, and advances the moderate Gelasian attitude widely held in the church at that time: each was a legitimate power, but bound to work together in a common purpose. Therefore it was especially valuable for the church to have prelates, who, because of their temporalities, played an important part in the king's counsels and courts. Thomas, when transferred from the court to the church, was probably by that very act absolved from all entanglements with the court, but if later some question arose over his financial accounts, this could have been settled quietly in a civil action. Instead, he was arraigned at Northampton over his debts to the king. Thomas claimed that it was unheard of for an archbishop of Canterbury to be tried in a royal court on such a matter. But it was just as unheard of for someone who one day was involved with hounds and hawks and other jolly sports in the court, the next day to be standing at the altar and administering spiritualities to the bishops and priests of the whole kingdom. Thomas had raised his cross threateningly against the patient king and had then fled in disguise at night, although with no one in pursuit. Now he was trying from exile to govern the church which he had deserted and left unprotected.

Gilbert then turned to the difficulties in which the English church and bishops were placed as a result of Thomas's flight. It was the cause, not the penalty, which made the martyr (St Augustine). What reason had the bishops to follow such an untrustworthy leader? Why should they make sacrifices in order to recover his revenues for him? Was he not playing the part of Judas? They were being asked to lay down their lives for the sake of the English church. But that church was in a most flourishing condition and all its members were strong supporters of Alexander. All this fuss about the king wanting to observe some of the customs which his ancestors had observed! Even if some of the practices were bad, they were all deeply rooted and would have to be eradicated gradually. The king himself was devout and a good family man, even a prospective Crusader, yet Thomas pictured him as a tyrant oppressing the church. What sort of a doctor is he who, to cure one wound, inflicts another even more severe? Was the evil of the customs so great as really to justify Thomas's desertion of his church, the rebellion against his king, the disturbance of both the kingdom and the church and the neglect of the salvation of his subjects in body and soul? Henry would probably abandon the bad customs when he decently could, that is to say of his own free will. He would certainly not act under compulsion. The bishops had been forced to appeal to the pope in order to avert the dangers to them caused by Thomas's misguided policy. Gilbert begged his father in God to contain his zeal within the bounds of modesty and stop trying to disallow the appeals. Humility, the monk-bishop thought, was the only key which could open all doors.

There was really no answer to this long and detailed indictment except that which Thomas had already made and which, on its own terms, was entirely valid: that he was defending the liberty of the church not only against a royal tyrant but also against those who were tolerating the measures which would reduce them to slavery. And Thomas apparently made no reply. John of Salisbury, however, answered it, obliquely and not entirely satisfactorily, in a letter to Baldwin, archdeacon of Totnes, the future arch-bishop of Canterbury. At too great a length, with too many quotations, hampered, like the true intellectual he was, by his acceptance of the truth of some of the charges, he produced a diffuse apologia for the archbishop. The contrast between Gilbert's *Multiplicem nobis* and John's *Expectatione longa* could not be greater. John does not seriously challenge Gilbert's chronicle of events, he re-interprets some of them from Thomas's point of view, others he discreetly passes by.[24]

He opens his letter by expressing regret that his messenger had returned from Exeter without a single word in writing. Everyone in the kingdom seemed to be cowed. Some, however, like 'the ruler of their synagogue' (Gilbert Foliot), were aiding 'the thief' (Henry) by deceitfully misinterpret-ing the law and perverting the truth. Gilbert claimed that there was no need to fight for the liberty of the church, although this was the most righteous cause there could be. If we consider, John continued, those aspects of Thomas's behaviour cited by Gilbert, it is true that the archbishop yielded at Clarendon, but only because he was persuaded by some bishops and seduced by some cheats, as well as succumbing to a fear which could have overcome the bravest of men. You know full well that later he repented of having done this wrong, confessed and was absolved by the pope, and that he also secured from the pope the English church's absolution from the Constitutions of Clarendon. Why do not the bishops, who joined him in this wrong-doing, likewise repent?

As for Northampton, it is quite untrue to say that he was frightened of the financial case, he was merely afraid of the corrupt judges who were completely under the king's thumb. Were these, unlike everyone else, not aware that the king had freed Thomas from all obligations as chancellor so that he could become an archbishop, had urgently obtained a pallium for him and had made all sorts of promises to get the acceptance of those abominable ancestral customs? Was he not treated irregularly and unlawfully in several particulars by the judges, who, although they may have acted mostly according to an appearance of legality, must have given judgment against their consciences? As all know, the pope has quashed their judgment (in the John the Marshal case). In these circumstances surely Thomas was justified in fearing that worse would follow when he was put on trial con-cerning his accounts as chancellor and, to prevent that, in appealing to the Holy See. By this action did he not spare the bishops from either doing further evil or being punished by the king? Is it not common knowledge that the archbishop and his followers have been unjustly outlawed? And do not the bishops now sing the praises of the barbarous persecutor of the church?

When Thomas was a haughty trifler in the king's court, when he appeared to despise (divine) law and the clergy and joined the magnates in their low pursuits, he was greatly honoured and respected, indeed, considered by one and all the most suitable person to be made archbishop. But as soon as he became a bishop and tried to carry out his duties seriously as befitted a priest, they turned against him. He is persecuted because he tells God's people their sins and summons the princes of Sodom and the men of Gomorrah to hear and obey the law of God. Thomas and his followers are prepared to stand to judgment – in a just tribunal. The only matter now at issue is the validity of the evil Customs, for the financial charge was only trumped up and has been dropped. What causes most sorrow to the exiles is that they are being persecuted by those for whose cause and liberty they are fighting. All they can do is trust in God and in the meantime give thanks to him for all his mercies and for allowing them to be numbered among those who suffer persecution for righteousness' sake. All they ask from their friends is their prayers.

Henry is unlikely to have been much influenced by the higher flights of rhetoric in which the clerical proponents were engaged. But, like them, he was inclined to answer injury by injury. The Cistercian abbeys of Pontigny, Cercamp and Rigny had in different measure given help to Thomas, and Henry decided to deprive the exile of that assistance. The Emperor Frederick had, probably in 1165–6, taken action against the Order for its support of Alexander. Henry complained to its general council, which met at Cîteaux on 14 September 1166, and threatened that unless Thomas was expelled from Pontigny he would expel the Cistercians from his dominions. After the council Gilbert le Grand abbot of Cîteaux, an Englishman, accompanied by the exiled bishop of Pavia, Peter Toscani, a former monk of the order, and several abbots, visited Pontigny and informed Thomas of the situation and of the council's decision. Thomas was not to be driven out, but was to be invited to consider what should be done in the circumstances. He would not want to harm in any way the Order which he loved so much. Thomas, after consulting his advisers, bowed gracefully to necessity. He would remove himself of his own free will.

The abbot of Pontigny, Guérin de Galardun, and the brethren were greatly distressed. Thomas, and even more his clerks, were not necessarily so much put out. Herbert of Bosham, who still loathed being hidden away between the monks and the stones, reports an interesting conversation with his master on what they should do. When Herbert suggested that Thomas should appeal to Louis for help, Thomas replied that he could see that Herbert was longing for urban delights and all the splendours of courts, but it would be better if they were to remain in a monastery or some other solitude. The other clerks then came to Herbert's aid, and it was agreed that they should seek a refuge in some palace or town, for it was possible to live like a hermit within such a community. Herbert was sent to Louis to negotiate the move, and it was decided to accept the king's offer of a place at St Columba's abbey, a short distance outside the north wall of the royal and archiepiscopal city of Sens, in the pleasant meadows by the River Yonne and facing its chalk cliffs.[25]

Sens was very much to Herbert's taste, and he inserts in his book a panegyric upon *la douce France*. Sens, he declares, was a most beautiful city, well provisioned with corn, wine and oil and inhabited by friendly and civilized people. He could have mentioned that a new, revolutionary, cathedral church was being built and that there was a school. It must indeed have been an agreeable change for the exiles. The archbishop, Hugh de Toucy, formerly precentor of the church, was nearing the end of his long tenure of the see, and the city was going through a quiet period between the departure of the papal curia and the arrival, in the spring of 1168, of a youthful and coming prince of the church, William of the White Hands, brother of Henry I count of Champagne and of Theobald v count of Blois, nephew of Henry bishop of Winchester and of the late king Stephen, brother-in-law of the king of France, who was to have a dazzling career in the church. Bishop-elect of Chartres 1165–7, then archbishop of Sens in plurality and in 1176–7 translated to Rheims, he was made cardinal-priest of St Sabina in 1179. William became not only a powerful political figure, both locally and at the royal court, but also a great patron of scholars. He was to be a valuable patron of the exiled archbishop.[26]

The ancient Benedictine abbey of St Columba, where Thomas was to live, was ruled by Giles I, a former monk of Vézelay. Its new church had been dedicated by Alexander III on 26 April 1164.[27] This time Thomas and his household were not to be a burden on the monks but a charge on the royal revenues derived from the city. Thus Thomas, in reply to Henry's expulsion of him from his retreat, not only reappeared in an important royal and ecclesiastical centre but also put himself directly under the lordship of the French king. In some ways he had benefited from Henry's vindictive action, but he had also been pushed into a more actively hostile role.

Thomas and his household left Pontigny about 11 November 1166, two years after their entry, to the grief of the abbot and convent. His own spirits were low: the parting was painful and he had just had a disturbing dream of his murder by four knights. Nor was the warm welcome he received at Sens capable of cheering him up for long, for the assault he had made on his enemies at Vézelay was being successfully contained by Henry and the English bishops. The earliest description of his life at St Columba's is given by Edward Grim, on the authority of Thomas's chaplain, Robert of Merton, who alone shared the archbishop's bedroom. He paints a picture of active participation in the monastic horarium, daily celebration of Mass, much private prayer and secret austerities. Although Thomas never refused food, he fed sparingly, and the clean and costly bedclothes were only for appearance. He was hardly ever in bed, but passed the night in prayer in his oratory. At least thrice a day, sometimes five times, his chaplain, reluctantly, but compelled by his master, trussed up the archbishop's hair shirt and scourged him on the bare back until the blood flowed. When the chaplain tired, Thomas tore at his flesh with his fingernails. And even when, exhausted, he lay down on the floor with his neck on a stone, the harshness of his shirt infested with lice prevented him from getting much sleep. With these mortifications, Edward Grim thought, Thomas killed all carnal desires.[28]

Guernes, who knew also the testimony of Thomas's servant Brown, who used to wash the hair shirt, adds a little more detail, but whether derived from sound tradition or his imagination it is hard to say. Thomas drank the best wine that money could buy, but always diluted with water, and only in order to warm a congenitally cold stomach and constitution. He also ate handfuls of ginger and cloves for the same purpose. His chamber was furnished with a leather-bound wooden bed, covered with expensive sheets of the whitest and finest linen, and an embroidered quilt strewn with a little straw. His shirt and breeches were of the roughest goat hair – hair of Soissons, according to Benet, *forte et dure*.[29]

Once again we are told of the outward finery and conformity which concealed the extravagant asceticism. And by this time there can be less reason to doubt it. The archbishop's disappointed hopes, the accusations of pride, his secret awareness of faults which he could not bear to acknowledge publicly, the need to subdue strong passions, the example of the Cistercian monks during the last two years, drove him, although not necessarily continuously, to extremes of abasement. He wanted to purify himself in order that he might conquer.

His sentences at Vézelay and his subsequent measures had not been ineffective. Even before Alexander's confirmation of them reached Thomas in November, few of those named, despite the appeals, felt completely at ease. Some men were also susceptible to the blanket anathemas and not a few went in fear of contamination from those manifestly under the ban. Richard of Ilchester got no satisfaction from Ralf of Diss, archdeacon of London, whom he consulted over his excommunication. Ralf thought that, even if the sentence on him was unjust, it could not be disputed at law, and advised him to accept his fate with humility. In a way the problem was even greater for those completely innocent courtiers or visitors to the court who did not want to be infected. John of Salisbury tried to advise his former pupil, Ralf Niger, on how to behave. In October or early November the king at Caen prevented some Templars from embracing

Richard of Ilchester because he was excommunicate; and Thomas's correspondent, possibly the keeper of the seal, Walter de Lisle, who reported this and other happenings at court, thought that Henry was seriously upset by the ecclesiastical censures and threats, indeed he seemed to be going out of his mind. On the day before this incident, when Scottish affairs were under discussion and Richard de Humet, constable of Normandy, had spoken up for William the Lion, the new king, Henry had called Richard a traitor and then behaved like a maniac, hurling his cap to the ground, unfastening his sword-belt and throwing off all his clothes. Finally he had torn the silk coverlet from his bed and, as though 'squatting on a dung hill' (Job 2 : 8), had started to chew the straw.[30]

Also at this time it was rumoured that the excommunicate Richard de Lucy had decided to go on a crusade, and in the winter Alan de Neville, excommunicate *ipso facto* for imprisoning William of Salisbury, decided to do likewise. Gilbert Foliot absolved him on condition that he sought penance from the Holy See en route for Jerusalem; and, although it is likely that the chaplain was released from Corfe early in February, Thomas was furious with Gilbert. At Christ Church, Canterbury, a monk broke from a procession and cried out that they should support Thomas, not the king. The prior had him put in custody.[31]

Even some of the bishops were troubled in mind. Before the year 1166 was out Gilbert Foliot at last managed to resign custody of the benefices of the proscribed archiepiscopal clerks. In November Arnulf of Lisieux, crippled with debt and sickened by the several controversies in which he was involved, wanted to resign his see and retire, temporarily or permanently, to the Cistercian monastery at Mortemer. He approached Henry on this matter at Touques and then at Caen. On the second occasion the king asked him how much money he needed, and when told 200 marks, said that he hadn't so much to hand. But when that evening he managed to find sixty, Arnulf postponed his retirement for a decade.[32] Probably in October Thomas cited the much pestered Robert of Hereford and the king's cousin, Roger of Worcester, to visit him, so as to get their advice. In November Robert informed Henry that he and Roger were about to obey the summons unless Henry could help them avoid it. The king replied angrily that they were on no account to leave England but were to use the expedient of an appeal. If they did cross over, they would not be allowed to return. On 2 February, when attempting secretly to obey the third and final summons, they were discovered by John of Oxford at Southampton, and were ordered back in the name of the pope as well as the king. Robert died three weeks later, on 27 February, of grief at not being allowed to join the archbishop, according to William fitzStephen.[33]

Henry's security measures doubtless contributed to the state of unease and their failure intensified it. John of Salisbury, an indefatigable letter writer, boasted of how easy it was to get his letters through the blockade; but in November there were some losses and scares. In England Scaiman was captured, but escaped to Christ Church Canterbury and then went into hiding no one knew where. In Normandy there was almost a major disaster. One of Thomas's couriers who delivered a papal letter to the king, apparently at Touques, was promptly arrested, and when tortured by having his eyes almost gouged out and hot water poured into his mouth, confessed that he had received the letter from Master Herbert (of Bosham). Herbert had a narrow squeak. It was probably he who delivered a letter from Thomas to Walter de Lisle, who, for not arresting the messenger, was punished by Henry by loss of his office. He may have been replaced by Nigel de Sacquenville (Sackvill), who was excommunicated in April 1169 and at Christmas 1170 because he had been invested with the archiepiscopal church of Harrow. John of Salisbury, in a letter of condolence and congratulation to Walter, refers obscurely to the problems of divided loyalty with which royal clerks were faced. An anonymous correspondent of Thomas's, possibly Walter himself, considered that Herbert had been risked quite unnecessarily in business of little importance. The archbishop of Rouen and Arnulf of Lisieux remonstrated with Henry over the imprisonment of the courier and his treatment of Walter and informed him that they had received papal letters on behalf of Thomas. Henry replied that he cared nothing for the pope's threats. Later the empress ordered her son to release the messenger.[34]

Towards the end of 1166 the archiepiscopal party thought that it was doing particularly well, that the royalists were shaken and on the defensive. The term for the appeals was approaching, and it was rumoured that when it was passed Thomas intended to confirm Henry's excommunication and even put the kingdom under an interdict. John of Salisbury was particularly optimistic, hopeful of peace and again putting out feelers for a personal reconciliation with the king. Henry was driven to renew his pressure on the pope. The political situation was favourable. In the autumn of 1166 the Emperor Frederick was planning his fourth military expedition to Italy and in November entered Lombardy with a large army. Alexander was desperately short of funds. Just after Christmas he even wrote to Thomas begging him to ask the count of Flanders to send him some money.[35]

Henry sent an embassy to Rome consisting of the young and up-coming clerks John of Oxford, John Cumin, the new archdeacon of Bath and future archbishop of Dublin (1181), and Master Ralf of Tamworth, a chancery clerk, later archdeacon of Stafford. This was a low-level and confidential mission, very different from the grand embassy sent twelve months before. Royalist security was strict and Thomas's intelligence service had only moderate success. As a counter measure Thomas sent to Rome an even less impressive messenger, the brother of the imprisoned William of Salisbury, with letters to the pope and, in support, to the cardinals Henry of Pisa, Hyacinth and Conrad of Wittelsbach, the exiled archbishop of Mainz and bishop of Albano. He reminded Alexander of some of the more recent injuries he had suffered from Henry: the expulsion of his kinsmen and servants, some of whom had already died in exile; the violence to William of Salisbury; the threats to the Cistercian order; the ill-treatment of the church abetted by the bishops and the guile of Arnulf of Lisieux. In Thomas's view Henry had wittingly incurred excommunication both by communicating with the imperial schismatics and by laying violent hands on clerks. The royal servant, John of Oxford, who was guilty of apostasy and now of perjury, was on his way to Rome. Finally, Thomas referred to a rumour (in the accompanying letters he says that the cardinal's clerk had told the king) that the pope was about to send William of Pavia as his legate to England to hear the appeals and settle the quarrel; and Thomas expressed his disquiet at the choice. In the other letters he was more outspoken about the cardinal's partiality, and declared that, unless compelled, he would accept no judgment except from the pope himself. In other words, he would appeal against any legatine sentence.[36]

It is not known whether the three royal clerks travelled together to Rome. They had somewhat different assignments, and John of Oxford either left the curia before the others or travelled back at greater speed. He reached Southampton, presumably via the royal court in Normandy or Anjou, on 2 February 1167, whereas the other two had only entered Tours on the previous day. John had his own business to conduct at Rome and seems to have been specially entrusted with obtaining a dispensation for the marriage of Henry's third son, Geoffrey, to the heiress of Brittany – a political marriage displeasing to Louis. Thomas and his friends learnt gradually of the results of the mission mainly from three sources: from Thomas's own nuncio, who seems to have achieved and discovered little; from John Cumin and Ralf of Tamworth, who were close-lipped but let some things slip to a clerk of Saintes, William de Fuerna, who had travelled part of the way with them, and to the dean of St Maurice (-les-Charencey, between Mortagne and Verneuil), where they had lodged; and from the boasting John of Oxford. Early in February John of Poitiers put a report together after intercepting the two royal clerks at Tours and then interrogating their contacts. But it was not until March that a fairly accurate outline account of the mission was constructed, and even then most of the detail was conjectural. There was always more rumour and speculation than hard fact.[37]

One of the few papal documents published by the clerks, on royal authority, was dated 1 December 1166 and addressed to the bishops of England. In reply to the bishops' appeal, and to spare the parties unnecessary expense,

Alexander was sending legates *a latere* with plenitude of power to hear and canonically determine that case and all others they should think it expedient to hear. Meanwhile any one who had been excommunicated by Thomas, and was in danger of death, could be absolved by a suitable person, provided he swore that he would, if he recovered, submit to a papal decision. In all the surviving written notifications of the appointment of these legates there is the crucial and no doubt intentional ambiguity that, although the legates are to have plenitude of power, there is no mention of exclusion of appeal. On the other hand, royalist and archiepiscopal supporters alike unanimously believed that no appeal from the legates' judgment was to be allowed. This may have been one of the secret conditions, or merely, perhaps, a story put about by John of Oxford. It was, and is, difficult to get at the truth. A note added to a shorter papal letter to the king concerning the appointment of legates reads, 'Show this transcript to no one except Master Gunter, for I have given my assurances on this to Master Walter.' If these are Thomas's clerk, Gunter of Winchester, and the ex-keeper of the king's seal, Walter de Lisle, we catch a glimpse of how some documents were leaked.[38]

By February it was generally, and correctly, believed that the two legates were to be William of Pavia, for whom Henry had specially asked, and Otto, who was added to correct the balance. Thomas had already encountered William a year before at Sens. Originally a monk of Clairvaux, then archdeacon of Pavia, cardinal-deacon of St Mary in Via Lata, promoted in 1160 cardinal-priest of St Peter-ad-Vincula, and in 1170 to become bishop of Porto, he had been at the imperial council of Pavia (February 1160) and was always well-disposed towards Henry. Since Otto, cardinal-deacon of St Nicholas in Carcere Tulliano, was something of an unknown quantity, the composition of the legation was generally considered a success for the king.

In a most deferential and secret letter to Henry, Alexander said that he had done his best to agree to all his petitions, and, after notification of the appointment of legates, still unnamed, added that he had forbidden Thomas to make any hostile moves until these cases should be settled; moreover, if the archbishop disregarded this, the pope would hold his sentences void. To the clause concerning relaxation of Thomas's existing sentences of excommunication, he added that the legates would on their arrival absolve the royal intimates and counsellors. Finally he told Henry that he would instruct the legates after Christmas and dispatch them in the course of January. Alexander, however, put Thomas's position a little differently in a secret letter he sent to the archbishop. He had exhorted Henry to make peace with Thomas and hoped he would restore him to Canterbury. He therefore advised Thomas not to harm the king in any way until the case was heard.

If Henry would not make peace, Alexander would help Thomas in every way possible, and, in the last resort, would allow him to exercise his office freely (i.e. promulgate sentences). In a secret letter to Louis, the pope asked whether, if the peace negotiations failed, it would be agreeable to him if he were to appoint Thomas his legate in Gaul. Alexander also reassured Thomas about the impartiality of the legates, particularly William of Pavia.[39]

John of Oxford, however, was proclaiming Thomas's suspension in more positive terms. He had clearly had a great personal success at Rome. He had been absolved from any sentence pronounced against him by Thomas – a necessary prelude to his appearance at the papal court – and had been confirmed in the deanery of Salisbury by a gold ring taken by Alexander from his own finger. Moreover he had secured the dispensation for the royal wedding. He also spoke of a number of personal privileges he had obtained for himself and the king and of the total supersession of the archbishop. On landing in England he acted as a papal legate, possibly using as authority Alexander's ring, immediately ordered the bishop of Hereford, whom he found at Southampton, back to his diocese, and claimed that Thomas's jurisdiction and legation were completely suspended until the arrival of the cardinal legates. He himself, he claimed, had been exempted by the pope from all episcopal jurisdiction and the king was subject to no one but the pope. He was supposed to have shown written papal authority for these statements to the bishop of London and the bishop of Hereford's clerk at Winchester, whereupon Gilbert Foliot had exclaimed 'From now on Thomas is no longer my archbishop.' John was thought to have assembled the English bishops so as to inform them of Thomas's suspension and to have allowed those whom Thomas had excommunicated to be absolved unconditionally by the bishop of St Asaph's on the frivolous grounds that they were in danger of death because they had been summoned to cross the Channel or go to Wales.

On 7 May 1167 Alexander informed his legates William and Otto that he had heard the serious news that his beloved son, the dean of Salisbury, had publicly announced that the pope had deprived Thomas of all jurisdiction and authority over all persons, both ecclesiastical and lay, in the kingdom of England, and that, to please the king, he was sending the legates specifically in order to condemn and depose him. This and another story had confounded the archbishop and had greatly disturbed the king and princes of France. It was probably true, the pope continued, that John of Oxford on his return to England had worked hard for the honour and profit of the church of Canterbury and its archbishop and for the liberty of the church. He had not only secured the liberty of those clerks who had been imprisoned by the king, he had also, as he had reported to the pope, got Henry to declare in public that he wanted the clergy in his kingdom to retain the liberty which they had enjoyed since the reign of Henry I. But, Alexander complained, the disclosures had done his (Alexander's) reputation much harm. It should be noticed that the pope did not claim that John had been telling lies or exceeding his authority, only that he had let the cat out of the bag. And his reference to John's, so far successful, efforts with the king, shows that, as the archiepiscopal party believed, a bargain had indeed been struck and that John had undertaken to make some kind of settlement.[40]

Since some of the secret trading had not been put in writing, and the more inconvenient documents obtained by John of Oxford were destroyed, the depth of the papal 'treachery' cannot be measured. Alexander had not, however, even when most hard pressed, granted a general amnesty. Even Jocelin of Salisbury, who had been punished by Thomas for maintaining John of Oxford in his deanery, was not pardoned when the dean was reinstated. Presumably Alexander wanted an example to be made of one contumacious prelate. There seems to have been a fairly general feeling that this was unfair. Both Jocelin's son, Reginald archdeacon of Salisbury, and his brother, Richard de Bohun, bishop of Coutances, appealed to John of Salisbury to mediate with Thomas. John tried and failed, and wrote apologetically to all three to explain why. Thomas was still enraged with Jocelin for his disobedience, his support for Gilbert Foliot and his frivolous appeal, which he had not withdrawn. Only if Jocelin were to withdraw the appeal, publicly confess his fault and ask for mercy could he be absolved. John's only crumb of hope was that if the bargains that John of Oxford had made at Rome were to be carried out, they would soon all be at peace.[41]

A further success for the royal clerks, according to the dean of St Maurice as reported by John of Poitiers, was their having obtained at Rome copies of all Thomas's petitions to the pope, all letters he had written to the curia against the king and all letters written on his behalf. They possessed, for example, Thomas's report of his actions at Vézelay. They had been surprised to find letters from the archbishop of Bourges – the king would be most interested in this – and they had letters from English bishops, but they were giving no names. Alexander in his letter to his legates on 7 May 1167 also referred to a massive security leak. John Cumin, it was said, had obtained from William and Otto copies of all the papal letters they were carrying – presumably their instructions and a selection of useful instruments – and had shown them to Guy of Crema (the Anti-pope Paschal III). If this was true, the legates were to punish him severely so as to deter others. But even if we disregard this almost incredible story, the royalists' haul more than compensated for John of Salisbury's acquisition from Cologne earlier in 1166 of copies of some letters from the archbishop's archives, including Henry's indiscreet letter to Rainald of Dassel.[42]

As these various items of news filtered out, the archbishop's party was at first little disturbed. Indeed, John of Salisbury was originally quite elated. He informed his correspondents, but in cryptic words, for, he said, he was under a bond of secrecy, that the royalists had had to pay a crippling price for illusory concessions. John of Oxford had agreed to renounce the Constitutions of Clarendon and Henry had promised to make peace with full restitution to the exiles. Everything would be settled soon. Early in February John of Poitiers declared that he believed nothing of this. His information was that the clerk had undertaken to make peace between the king and Thomas and had assured the pope that he could do this; but his reckless undertaking had vexed the other royal clerks for they knew that it was impossible, since it was completely unacceptable to the king. Within a short time all Thomas's hopes had collapsed. After the return of the king's nuncios his authority had simply disappeared. No one would obey him any longer. He knew that Alexander had been two-faced. Defiantly he proclaimed that he would accept no judgment except the pope's. He and his clerks and friends bombarded the pope and curia with protests at his treatment. John of Oxford's 'perjury' was never forgotten. But although hope of a settlement still flickered here and there, realists could not imagine how, as things stood, it could be achieved except at Thomas's expense. And Thomas did not intend to surrender.[43]

CHAPTER NINE

THE PATH OF TRUTH AND JUSTICE, 1167–1169

In each of the remaining four years of Thomas's exile the pope dispatched a legation to Henry's dominions. In 1167 it was the Cardinals William and Otto, in 1168–9 the devout monks Simon of Mont-Dieu, Bernard de la Coudre and Engelbert of Val-St-Pierre, in 1169 the curial officials Gratian and Vivian and in 1170 the archbishop of Rouen and the bishop of Nevers, reinforced, especially as regards Aquitaine, by the archbishop of Sens. Originally the avowed purpose was legal – to hear and determine the several appeals and counter-appeals made to the papal court. But from the start this proved impossible, and the business of the missions became conciliation, the settlement of the quarrels by compromise. As each side had taken up an entrenched position and Henry's gradual retreat was considered by Thomas merely a deceitful ruse, progress towards peace was slow before 22 July 1170.

Thomas's view that Henry was from beginning to end determined to preserve those rights and dignities in the kingdom which he had inherited from his ancestor, Henry I, must be accepted as correct. As regards the church, they were the ancient customs which a series of archbishops of Canterbury, some of them saints, had observed; and he required Thomas's absolute and unreserved acceptance of them. Between 1163 and 1170 he modified his position only in order to make it more defensible and less offensive to churchmen. Among the formulas he offered were: that he was willing to abandon any bad customs introduced by him or since 1135, to insist only on those which had been acceptable to Thomas's holy predecessors, even to have all of them scrutinized by learned churchmen. On the face of it these were reasonable concessions and were recognized as such by moderate opinion. He also, in imitation of Thomas, designed saving-clauses which in appearance were reasonable but could be given a sinister interpretation. Thomas, who knew his man, steadfastly refused to give unqualified assent to the Customs, however defined. Alexander, however, for a variety of reasons, was ready to take the concessions at their face value. Ambiguities and velleities were by no means worthless in long-term diplomacy. Thomas's ruthless destruction of attractive falsehoods was not admired in the curia.

Even the archbishop's staunchest supporters sometimes thought him unreasonable and stubborn. Thomas defended his line by referring to the pope's condemnation of the Customs at Sens and to the opposition to them by his saintly predecessors, for which they likewise had suffered exile. But neither of these arguments completely justified his refusal of some of the royal formulations. In truth, Thomas did not intend to surrender: he was, as Herbert of Bosham wrote admiringly, a house built upon a rock; and the best justification of his inflexible attitude is that he did not believe that Henry was sincere – the king was setting cunning traps. He was convinced, rightly or wrongly, that once peace was patched up and he put himself in Henry's power, the marginal concessions would be revoked, the 'evil' customs would remain in full force and he himself would be persecuted as those out of royal favour always were. It cannot be said that Thomas had no grounds for these beliefs.

None of the parties was under compelling pressure to yield. Thomas, although never reconciled to exile, became accustomed to it. He had become, in his and John of Salisbury's letters, 'the wretched and pitiable exile' and, with his fellow sufferers, 'Christ's outlaws', concerned now not with expediency but with principles, with truth and justice. If he had wanted to compromise he could have settled for a comfortable life three years earlier. Henry found his inability to get his eldest son crowned and the gradual thinning of the episcopal bench inconvenient. Bangor remained vacant throughout. Robert of Bath died in August 1166, Robert of Lincoln in December, Robert of Hereford in February 1167, Nigel of Ely in May 1169 and Hilary of Chichester in July of that year. Roger of Worcester lived abroad from November 1167. Moreover, the bishops of London and Salisbury were for most of the time under at least the threat of suspension or excommunication.

All this, however, could be borne. Alexander was much more anxious than Henry to make peace. It would have suited him well to have both Thomas back at Canterbury and Henry firmly behind the papal throne. But as Henry's support was of paramount importance, Alexander had to keep him moderately happy while preventing the several missions from becoming the tools of Henry's vengeance. His standard practice was to appoint two legates, one favourable to each side, which, although fair enough, pleased neither party. He also had recourse to a deviousness that both sides considered unprincipled, but which he could justify by necessity. The ploy of making concessions and then defaulting on them was typical of his tactics. Like any concern on the brink of failure he lived on borrowed time and promises which were not quite what they seemed. In this stalemate everyone waited for something to turn up. Secrecy was used to cloak deception. The waiting was wearisome only for Thomas. Pope and king had much else, and matters they thought far more important, to keep them occupied. Alexander's biographer, Cardinal Boso, who may have been an Englishman, does not introduce Thomas into his story before the martyrdom: attention is directed almost exclusively to the struggle with the emperor and his supporters.[1]

In 1167 the legates travelled leisurely and by a round-about route to Normandy. Enemy territory had to be avoided, but clearly Alexander was dragging his feet. When Cardinal Otto reached St Gilles in the Languedoc, he reported to Thomas that he had travelled from Venice across Lombardy to Turin and the abbey of Chiusa, and then over the Alps into Provence. It seems he had a rendezvous with William of Pavia, who may have left Rome in March, at Montpellier, 60 kilometres to the west. John of Oxford's indiscretions, which must have been sanctioned by Henry, backfired. Secret papal concessions were, of course, by their nature useless; but their revelation raised such a storm of protest from Thomas's friends that Alexander had to take notice. He would have been in the picture by April, and on 7 May, in a letter to the two legates which has already been discussed in part, he gave them new instructions. In view of John of Oxford's disclosures, they were to continue to comfort Thomas and try to remove all suspicion and bitterness from his mind. They were also to attempt to reconcile the archbishop and the king and get the ancient rights and liberties of the English church fully observed. But then follows a drastic curtailment of their commission: on no account were they to enter the kingdom before the two parties were reconciled. Above all, they were to behave circumspectly and carefully protect the pope's reputation. There may also have been some restrictions. Certainly by the time they arrived in the north the 'full authority' they had started with had been drained away. Crucially, they were without the power to compel the parties to litigate before them and accept their judgments. This, however, was unknown to the parties before November.[2]

Thomas sent a flattering and conciliatory reply to Otto. But William's parallel overture infuriated him, for it included 'a dose of poison', a request that he should avoid aggravating Henry further while negotiations proceeded. This was all the more unwelcome because he was considering announcing that Gilbert Foliot and Geoffrey Ridel had incurred sentences of excommunication. He drafted two hostile answers to William, which caused alarm and distress to John of Salisbury and others of the archbishop's friends, who were ardently hoping for peace and considered Thomas's naked hostility to the legate most unwise. Thomas, however, sent a rebuff to

William and also dispatched bitter letters to Rome rejecting him as a judge on the grounds *inter alia* that he was partial to the king. Moreover, he asked Cardinal Hyacinth to get the pope to instruct all clergy on both sides of the Channel to observe the sentences he was about to promulgate against the king and his land. Another cause for the archbishop's belligerence was Henry's suggestion that the legates might consecrate bishops to the vacant English sees. Perhaps connected with this was Thomas's desire that Alexander should again confirm Canterbury's primacy.[3]

In the summer and autumn of 1167 Thomas's friends were at a loss as to what to do. John of Salisbury, terrified that the archbishop might wreck the negotiations before they started, wrote round frantically for advice. He even consulted astrologers, although he reported it as a joke. In October, when the legates reached Poitiers, and took there one of the masters, Laurence, into their service, John tried to recruit him as a spy. This was the closest he came to dishonourable conduct – and he knew it. A complication for all involved was the fluctuating political situation. Henry and Louis had been desultorily at war since April and the French king had been flirting with the victorious emperor. Frederick had entered Rome, and on 1 August, with his queen, was crowned in St Peter's by the anti-pope. Alexander was forced to flee to Benevento and put himself under the protection of the Normans, with whom Henry was on excellent terms. No less pertinent, the king of Sicily enjoyed by papal authority all those ecclesiastical rights – and more – that Henry was claiming in England. All this was hurtful to Thomas's cause. But shortly afterwards the imperial army was struck down by fever and among the victims was Rainald of Cologne. Frederick had to abandon Rome, and in the spring of 1168 made an ignominious escape from Italy. The anti-pope, however, was able to remain in the city. On 22 August 1167, when the legates were in Aquitaine, Alexander instructed them to strive to make peace between Louis and Henry and forbade them to enter England, particularly in order to consecrate bishops, before Thomas was completely reconciled to the king. And the two monarchs did in fact of their own accord make a truce in that month to last until the following Easter (31 March 1168).[4]

A true accord between the two kings was not necessarily in Thomas's interests, and these political setbacks may have helped him to accept his friends' advice. By the autumn he was interceding with Louis on the legates' behalf and writing pleasant letters to both in anticipation of their meeting. They called in at Sens on their way to Normandy and the meeting seems to have been friendly. But Thomas's attempt to get them to reimpose his sentences of excommunication on those royal servants who had been absolved by the bishop of St Asaph, yet retained possession of the exiles' goods and estates, was politely frustrated.[5]

Henry prepared for the legates' arrival in Normandy by summoning some English bishops and abbots to join him. The bishops were York, London, Chichester and Worcester (the last, according to Thomas, to give the caucus respectability). Salisbury, too, was there, but on his own account. Of the Norman bishops Henry relied especially on Rouen, Lisieux and Bayeux. The legates met Henry at Caen early in November.[6] They reported to the pope that they found him even more enraged against Thomas than they had expected, and that he complained additionally that the archbishop had incited the king of France and the count of Flanders to make war on him. They presented the papal letters, presumably counterparts to those of 7 May and 22 August; and when the royal counsellors discovered that they were discrepant with Alexander's letters sent to the king during the previous winter and suspected that the legates had no power to compel Thomas to stand to their judgment, there was a great row. All the same it appears that both the king and the bishops agreed to accept the legates as judges in their cases against Thomas and that Henry made one concession. After complaining that Thomas had misrepresented to the pope the English customs – a charge with which the bishops concurred – he offered that if during his own reign he had introduced any novelty which was contrary to canon law, he would accept the judgment of the legates and revoke it. This limited, but not negligible, concession, probably already secured by John of Oxford, was taken up by the legates. John of Salisbury believed that Henry had renounced *inter alia* his prohibition of appeals to the pope and his attempt to 'drag clerks before secular courts'. But in the general council of king and clergy which then ensued, all that the legates could offer in return was to beg Henry not to close the door on a negotiated settlement. Conciliation was, in fact, as everyone began to realize, their only function.

The legates then invited Thomas to a meeting, and were probably not surprised, but still displeased, when he proved difficult over both time and place. He would not be hurried and he would not enter Henry's lands, even under a safe-conduct. Thomas's excuses were his shortage of horses, his poverty and the need to reassemble his scattered clerks. This became one of his standing complaints and probably was a real difficulty. The legates gave way and a meeting was arranged for 18 November, the legates to go into France from Gisors and meet Thomas coming towards them from Trie.[7] William and Otto, so as to give no cause for offence, took with them, besides their clerks and advisers, only the archbishop of Rouen, an experienced prelate who remained throughout a true intermediary, trusted by most. Thomas was accompanied by his clerks John of Salisbury, Herbert of Bosham, Lombard, Alexander, John the Cantor and Henry (of Houghton), his chaplains Robert (of Merton) and Gilbert (of Chicksands) and some others. The legates' report to Alexander on this colloquy and the report drawn up by the archbishop's clerks are in general agreement, indeed, extremely close.

Even if there was a hamlet between Gisors and Trie, the colloquy would probably have had to be held in the open air, and from the saddle. Mid-November conditions would have contributed little to the warmth of this encounter; and that is how Thomas wanted it. The legates opened the meeting with general remarks on Henry's power and the difficulties which faced the church, mentioned some of Henry's grievances against Thomas, including that of war-mongering, advised Thomas that peace could only be made if he, remembering the benefits he had received from the king, behaved with humility and moderation, and (tactfully, it would seem) asked Thomas's advice on what could be done. The archbishop conferred apart and then answered some of the king's charges and declared that he would humiliate himself only saving the honour of God, the liberty of the church (or the Apostolic See), his own good name and the possessions of the confiscated churches, and saving in all things the just rights of him and his men.

The legates then proposed that they should get down to detail. And when Thomas made no concrete proposals they asked some practical questions. Would Thomas, in their presence, agree to observe the customs which kings had followed in the times of his predecessors to whom, William of Pavia remarked, Thomas was in no way superior, and, in return, receive back the royal favour, his see and office and peace for him and his men? The reference was to Henry's offer to content himself with the position as it had existed before 1135, the death of Henry I. Thomas replied that it was out of the question for him to agree to such evil practices. Would he, then, at least tolerate them, or make peace without their being mentioned? Thomas quoted in reply the proverb 'silence implies consent' and said that he preferred to remain an exile and outlaw, even, if God should so dispose, die in defence of justice, rather than make peace on those terms. The schedule of the clauses he had condemned at Vézelay was then recited, and he asked the legates whether any Christian could lawfully obey such abominations.

When the legates had established that there was no hope of a negotiated settlement they explored the possibilities of litigation. Would Thomas, in the same way as the king and bishops, submit to their judgment in either or both cases? Thomas answered that he had received no papal order to that effect; but, if he were to be put back into possession of everything of which he had been deprived, he would be willing to proceed according to papal instructions. The archbishop's words, the legates correctly judged, opened the way neither to a trial nor to an agreement. He did not intend either to litigate or to bargain. They therefore paid a visit to Louis, who exonerated Thomas of inciting him to wage war on Henry, and then took their leave of Thomas. In Herbert of Bosham's view, a dream which his master had had the night before the conference – that he was offered poison in a golden chalice – was fulfilled.[8] Rightly or wrongly, Thomas and some of his clerks, advised by their spies in the royal court, believed that Henry had no intention of meeting their minimum conditions and was simply laying a trap for 'the outlaws'.

After the legates had rejoined Henry, who at the end of November had moved south to Argentan, there were some stormy meetings with the king, the magnates and higher clergy. The clergy inquired specifically whether the legates had the authority either by the terms of a special mandate or by virtue of their legation to force the archbishop to stand trial. And when the answer was 'no', nothing remained but to draw what profit they could from the futile exercise. King and bishops renewed in turn their undertaking to submit everything that was at issue between them and the archbishop to the legates' jurisdiction and sentence. Then Henry declared that, as Thomas had refused to stand to judgment, victory was his, and he asked the legates to report to the pope the concession he had offered, his willingness to litigate and his humility and sincerity. The bishops, orchestrated once more by Gilbert Foliot, renewed their appeal to the pope, put the whole clergy and kingdom under papal protection, and fixed 11 November 1168 as the term. In the appeal they protested against Alexander's breaking the compact he had made with the king by sending legates without the agreed powers. The bishop of London also renewed the appeal made at Northampton in his own name, and a clerk of the archdeacon of Canterbury appealed on behalf of his master.

When the meeting broke up on 5 December, Henry begged tearfully that the legates would persuade the pope to rid him entirely of the traitorous archbishop. William of Pavia wept with him, but Otto could hardly keep a straight face. The several appeals were served on Thomas by nuncios of the legates and of the bishops on 14 December 1167. Thomas refused to receive the latter on the grounds that they had incurred the excommunication which infected Gilbert Foliot. To the legates he replied evasively that he would submit to the appeals to the extent of the powers they enjoyed. The legates reported much of this to Alexander and said that it was up to him to deal with the situation and prevent it from going from bad to worse. No doubt various schemes were canvassed. A suggestion that Thomas might be translated to another see, presumably in France, was apparently received coldly by Louis and vehemently rejected by Thomas. Henry, however, kept it very much in mind.[9]

With no trial and no negotiations, the one outstanding problem for the legates was the sentences passed at Vézelay and their consequences. Thomas believed that these, despite some fraudulent absolutions, all remained in force and that the number of excommunicates had been greatly increased by contagion and violations of his orders. He believed, particularly, that Gilbert Foliot and Geoffrey Ridel were under the ban, for reasons which John of Salisbury always describes as impossible to explain in a few words. The legates, however, even Otto, who was a great disappointment to the archiepiscopal party, were by this time quite unsympathetic to Thomas and made up their minds to allow all penitent excommunicates to be absolved, despite the archbishop's claim that their action was *ultra vires*. And to his plea that the royal officials, as long as they retained custody of the estates and churches of him and his men, were obviously impenitent and could in no way escape the ban, the legates replied that those men were custodians simply by order of the king and that the legates were in no position to punish him. William and Otto also each wrote to the pope on behalf of Gilbert Foliot, when he sent nuncios to the curia, and described him as a good influence on the king. It seems that, on legatine authority, everyone who professed penitence and accepted a suitable penance was in fact absolved in due course. But Thomas did not shift from his publicized belief that most of the absolutions were invalid.[10]

In the end everyone concerned complained to the pope. The legates had been scapegoats and had been given a rough ride. The king, archbishop and bishops were all, for different reasons, disappointed. The king of France and the French magnates were outraged. They all wrote letters of protest to Alexander, and John of Salisbury circulated his friends with the news. Thomas's first report (after the meeting of 19 November) was moderate in tone. The English bishops were royalist time-servers and he was suspicious of William of Pavia. But he had no special cause for complaint. After the appeals of 14 December, however, he wrote a very bitter letter. The legates had behaved irregularly and presumptuously towards him. They had suspended him, as far as they could, from all the authority he had over the churches and clergy of England – something the pope had never done and had promised never to do. Alexander was, after God, his only hope and refuge, and he begged him to keep his promises. The legates had only made things worse.[11]

On 30 January 1168 Alexander sent from Benevento an extremely cool reply to one of Thomas's earlier letters. 'Blessed are they which are persecuted for righteousness' sake', observed His Holiness. Thomas must continue his struggle. He was not to make peace with Henry at the expense of the church. But he should, as far as he could saving the honour of his office and the liberty of the church, humiliate himself before him and strive in every way to recover his grace and love. He should not suspect him more than was just or require from him more assurances than was proper. For, Alexander thought, once they had been reconciled the king would treat him well. Finally, the pope assured him of his great love and continued efforts on behalf of his honour, liberty and dignity – insofar as divine grace would allow.[12]

Alexander's advice, with which most of Thomas's more responsible friends would have agreed, was not necessarily mistaken, although it could only be tested by experiment and involved a high degree of risk for the archbishop. The success of all political agreements depends on trust, and irreconcilables can be reconciled only by the generous avoidance of precision. Alexander was obviously right in giving priority to a personal reconciliation. John of Salisbury was saying exactly the same thing at this time.[13] No legal formula could be devised which could bring the mutually hostile king and archbishop together; but given the will to settle, a way could be found. For the time being, however, it was useless for Alexander to recommend his own subtle, or devious, ways to the archbishop. Thomas had become incorruptible. He was prepared to stand *contra mundum*.

The archbishop's fortunes were at a low ebb in 1168. After the renewed appeals by the English bishops, Thomas and his clerks gave anxious thought to the line they should take. Although they recognized that the law of the church was in favour of the appeals being respected, they felt that exceptions could be made and so advised their master. But they also urged him to leave the king's person untouched. Herbert believed, although his memory may have been at fault, that Thomas cited a good number of his oppressors in England to appear before him on pain of excommunication and that, as these summonses were disobeyed, the royal clerks were under anathema.[14] But by July 1168 Thomas had been neutralized. With Alexander at Benevento, even more distant than Rome, diplomacy became even slower.

Towards the end of 1167, after the failure of the cardinal legates, Thomas and Henry had each sent a mission to the pope. The archbishop's envoys were Alexander of Wales and John the Cantor; the king's were Clarembald, abbot-elect of St Augustine's Canterbury, Reginald fitzJocelin, archdeacon of Salisbury, Simon de Prisun and Master Henry of Northampton. Reginald and Henry were to remain active in the diplomacy of this affair during the following four years. The royal envoys were supposed to have conferred en route with the marquess of Montferrat and the emperor, and later to have been in touch with the king of Sicily. Both parties may have reached Benevento before the third week in April 1168, and they remained there for most of May. Many of the papal letters they obtained are dated 19 or 20 May. It was known that on at least one occasion Alexander saw all seven nuncios together and that it had been an acrimonious meeting. The missions could not have got back before the end of June, and in the six or seven months they were away the great quarrel merely simmered.[15]

One vexation for Thomas was the conduct of his monks at Canterbury after the death of Prior Wibert on 27 September 1167. They allowed Ranulf de Broc, the royal custodian of the see, to intrude even more, and 'traitors' within the convent regularly disclosed to him, and so to the king, anything said or done in Thomas's favour in the secret meetings of the chapter. John of Salisbury was given by Thomas the task of disciplining the monks, and he wrote some unusually scathing letters. On 16 May the mission at Benevento secured a mandate ordering the convent to accept Thomas's nomination to the priory. But at some date unknown during the summer the monks elected, by royal licence and without reference to the archbishop, their subprior Odo. Thomas, who had vehemently supported capitular election to the deanery of Salisbury against episcopal nomination, in the case of his own chapter naturally took the opposite line. Legally it was a moot point.[16]

In the early months of 1168 John of Salisbury went on a pilgrimage to St-Gilles and collected, and later reported, all the news coming out of Italy. It was on the whole encouraging. On the way back he called in at Sens and got the impression that the exiles were in good health and engaged in devotional exercises. Thomas, however, was still suffering disappointments. Roger bishop of Worcester, the king's cousin and Thomas's only active supporter among the English bishops, had abandoned his see, despite papal and archiepiscopal letters begging him to remain and work for Thomas within the kingdom. Less important, but a sign of the times, was the conduct of Gerard la Pucelle. Perhaps through John of Salisbury's influence, Thomas's former clerk decided to leave Cologne and renounce the 'schismatics'. But when he returned in May he avoided calling on Louis and Thomas alike, to the indignation of both and the distress of John, and went directly to Henry, did him fealty, accepted all conditions, and joined his court. Also at this time Lombard of Piacenza transferred from Thomas's to Alexander's household. The archbishop sent him to the curia in July to complain about the pope's concessions to Henry, and it is possible that Alexander retained him as a gesture to the exile. It does not seem that Thomas and his friends showed any resentment and Lombard continued to play a part in the archbishop's affairs. Nevertheless, the clerk had started a new and distinguished career. By 1170 he was a cardinal and archbishop of Benevento.[17]

Thomas may in addition have been in financial difficulties this year. John Cumin boasted that he had persuaded Louis and the French nobles to cut off their subventions to the exiles; and John of Salisbury wrote round indefatigably to those whom he thought favoured the archbishop's cause, rallying support and begging for money – but never for himself. He had more than enough for his modest life as a scholar and writer. An undercurrent of criticism of the archbishop's extravagance surfaces now and then. Thomas must have found it hard to economize and was probably always in debt. But if he was to wage a campaign for his restoration, it required funding.

In 1170 he made settlement of his debts by Henry one of his conditions for making peace. It would have been in character if he were to regard most of the subventions he had received from churchmen as loans to be repaid with interest when his fortunes were restored. And Henry's failure to come up with the money seems to have been a weight on his mind.[18]

Thomas's instructions to his envoys to the pope at the end of 1167 had included the importance of securing the recall of the cardinal legates from France and a reminder that the clerks were to do what he had ordered concerning the bishops of London and Salisbury – presumably obtain papal recognition that they were still under Thomas's sentences. On the other side, Henry's ambassadors made 'hard demands under terrible threats'. According to William fitzStephen, they were to ask Alexander either to translate Thomas to another archbishopric or to depose him; failing which, to deprive him, either permanently or temporarily, of the power to harm the king. The royal clerks returned at the beginning of July 1168, when Henry and Louis were due to meet at La Ferté-Bernard, on the River Huisne on the border between Maine and Perche, in order to make peace. There were rumours that Henry was considering going with Louis on a crusade. Henry had also agreed that the count of Flanders could bring Thomas to the conference. With Henry was William of Pavia and with Louis the Cardinal John of Naples. In the royal orchard near Orleans, Louis, in company with the count, had presented Thomas to the cardinal and begged him to take the exile under his protection. And the cardinal, as Thomas was to remind him some sixteen months later, had promised to favour him against all men save the pope. It may also have been about this time that Thomas, when staying in the Benedictine monastery at Fleury, some 35 kilometres upstream from Orleans, received a visit from his former clerk, William fitzStephen, who was on his way to the pope, and reminded the back-slider of the comfort he had been to him during his trial at Northampton. The proposed meeting between the kings and their clients at La Ferté-Bernard seems, however, not to have taken place, prevented by the multiplicity of issues and mutual recriminations. And the news from Benevento destroyed Henry's interest in an interview with Thomas.[19]

The rival missions to the curia had not succeeded where the cardinal legates had failed. Alexander had refused Henry's two main (unstated) petitions, but had granted his minimum request. He suspended Thomas from the power to inflict any sort of harm on Henry and the bishops and dignitaries of England until king and archbishop should be reconciled or, at the latest, 5 March 1169. In his warm and conciliatory letter to Henry, Alexander unblushingly defended himself against the charge of inconsistency by pointing to St Paul. In his apologetic letter of suspension to Thomas, he explained that he had had to bow to Henry's threats, but, if the king did not make peace with Thomas within the appointed term, the archbishop would recover his full authority, and no appeal against his sentences would be allowed. Alexander was to regret this categorical statement when Thomas took full advantage of it.

In an earlier letter to the bishops of England (24 April), Alexander chided them for their negligence towards the rights of Canterbury, but, at Henry's petition, released them from the need to prosecute their appeal against the archbishop. Also Reginald fitzJocelin obtained a letter asking Thomas to relax the sentence of suspension on Reginald's father; and John of Salisbury, who knew that the legates had in the meantime absolved Jocelin, once again intervened with Thomas on the bishop's behalf. John considered that, in general, Alexander had made a disgraceful surrender to Henry. Indeed, Thomas's nuncios had obtained very little: a papal denunciation of lay patronage and investiture in England (aimed at Henry's nominations to vacant benefices in Thomas's patronage) and an order to the royal clerk, John Cumin, to relinquish the archdeaconry of Bath.[20]

Thomas's friends claimed that, when the papal letter announcing the archbishop's suspension was delivered to the king at La Ferté-Bernard, Henry, bursting with joy and claiming a great victory over Rome and Thomas, had this 'licence to sin' read out to his bishops and barons and then sent it to be published in England. It is possible that the royal clerks had promised that it should be kept secret; but the triumph could not be contained. Thomas and his supporters were outraged by this wounding tactical defeat. He sent one of his most remarkable letters to Alexander, pessimistic, indignant, bitter, ironical, disingenuous, sometimes misleading, and full of contemptuous references to recent royal and princely injustices to the church which had been tolerated by an indifferent or powerless pope in the days of their immediate predecessors. He asked also, but in vain, that his primacy should be redefined so as to give him authority over the archbishop of York. And he forwarded letters of protest from the king and queen of France and several French prelates.[21]

Increasingly Thomas's cause was becoming, for better or for worse, involved in Angevin–Capetian rivalry and coloured by nationalistic feeling. The letter of William of the White Hands, soon to be consecrated archbishop of Sens and become one of Thomas's staunchest supporters, sets the tone: Henry was not only a tyrant and an oppressor of the church but also an enemy of France. 'It is being said that the violence and threats of the English are far more effective than the sincere faith, fervent devotion and constant obedience of the French.' Herbert of Bosham describes their party as being almost members of the French court, for they fed at the royal table. Their Englishness, like that of John of Salisbury's, was beginning to wear thin.

At the martyrdom, St Denis was, after God and the Virgin, the saint to whom Thomas commended his soul.[22]

In July the cardinal legates took their leave of Henry. Otto pressed him to make it up with his archbishop, and was not rebuffed. They then visited Louis to make their peace with him. Although there is no suggestion that they called in on Thomas, in the following year the archbishop regarded William of Pavia as a friend and appealed to him for help at least twice; after peace had at last been made at Fréteval in July 1170, he sent him a letter of thanks.[23] Alexander had decided to replace the cardinals, although not urgently, with a mission of another kind. Since litigation or punitive sentences were for the time being out of the question and Henry had given some signs that he desired a settlement with Thomas, Alexander resolved to send monks of the orders particularly favoured by the king – Carthusians and Grandimontines – to put moral pressure on him. In a letter to Henry dated 26 April 1168 he announced the appointment of the bishop of Belley and the prior of the Grande-Chartreuse as his commissioners; but a month later he named as substitutes, in case these could not act, Simon, prior of the Carthusian house of Mont-Dieu in the Ardennes, near Sedan, and brother Bernard de La Coudre or Du Coudray, prior of Grandmont in La Marche, a convent within Henry's own dominions. They were ordered to make their way to Henry within two months of the receipt of their commission, if he was on the Continent. And they were to present first an admonitory letter, but, if that failed, another threatening that, unless there was a reconciliation before the beginning of Lent (5 March 1169), Thomas would be unleashed.

Alexander confirmed to the archbishop on 9 October that, if the truce ran out, he would be at complete liberty to exercise his jurisdiction without the hindrance of appeal, and begged him to be patient in the meantime. He also wrote to Henry on the same day to indicate that he would be delighted to meet the king in person (presumably *en route* for the Holy Land) but also to reprove him for keeping three English and two Welsh bishoprics vacant. Henry was to allow free and canonical elections to them. The problem of how bishops-elect could be consecrated, he passed discreetly by.

In the event it was Simon and Bernard, reinforced by Engelbert, prior of the Carthusian house of Val-St-Pierre in Picardy, who at the end of the year 1168 took up the task of reconciliation. And there seems to have been a slight difference in attitude between the Grandimontine, whose convent was subject to Henry's power, and the two Carthusians, who were friends of the exiles, and in Engelbert's case a former pupil of John of Salisbury.[24]

The commissioners are first noticed at the peace conference held by Henry and Louis near Montmirail, a hill-top town crowned with its castle in the county of Chartres, 15 kilometres south-east of La Ferté-Bernard, on 6–7

January 1169; and they had Thomas with them.[25] As it was known that the two kings were going to make a comprehensive settlement of their differences, it was logical to deal with Thomas's case at the same time. Alexander's monitory letter was served on Henry, who seems to have promised that he would restore Thomas to Canterbury if the archbishop would make a public and adequate show of humility and submission to him. And this the commissioners and peacemakers on the French side made strenuous efforts to procure. What everyone had come to realize was that only by keeping to the bare essentials – a public reconciliation and a formal reinstatement to Canterbury – could all the snags be avoided. Great pressure was therefore put on Thomas by the commissioners and by the French king and his counsellors to submit himself without reservation to Henry. Thomas wanted to include, 'saving the honour of God', and the archbishop had an anguished discussion with his advisers (the *eruditi*) on whether he should yield on this point. As soon as the intermediaries thought that they had persuaded him to renounce this saving clause, they took him to the open field beneath Montmirail, where the two kings were still in conference; but, as they pushed through the throng, Herbert of Bosham whispered in his master's ear that he should hold firm to his principles. When they reached the royal group, Thomas fell on his knees and was raised to his feet by Henry. There is, however, no mention of a kiss.

This was the first time they had met since Northampton, more than four years ago, and each must have found the other much changed. Henry, now in his thirty-sixth year, was in the full insolence of his manhood, an experienced and masterful king. Thomas, just past his forty-eighth birthday, was no longer the gay cavalier of happier days, but a sombre, ravaged and bitter failure. Each may have felt some sparks of the old love. But they were almost immediately fanned into flames of anger. Thomas spoke the proposed words of submission, which are variously reported, and seems to have concluded with the agreed formula, 'I now submit the whole case between us to your clemency and judgment'. But he then added, to the horror of all the principal actors, 'saving the honour of God'.

Whether this was an uncontrollable slip or fully intended, it was Thomas's original condition, and once it had been uttered he stood by it, at least implicitly, until the end. All the same, he had broken his undertaking and destroyed the terms on which a reconciliation had been negotiated. Moreover, he had, as many must have perceived at the time, rejected the best chance that he would ever have of making a true peace. In 1171, after Thomas's death, Bernard de la Coudre wrote to Henry that in 1169 the archbishop had fulfilled the conditions he had laid down a hundredfold. But that is not how it looked at the time either to him and his fellows or to the two kings and their courts. Henry was furious: the reservation

implied that only Thomas, and not he, honoured God! His pent-up grievances against the archbishop poured out, and he used such intemperate
language that, according to John of Salisbury, the French considered him
not only a deceiver but also ill-bred. All the same, Herbert of Bosham
admits that Louis was quite as shocked as Henry and joined in the attempts
to get Thomas to submit without reservation.

Henry then raised, among other matters, the ancient customs of the realm.
He required Thomas to swear, as a priest and bishop, on his true word
and without any reservation, that he would observe those customs which
his predecessors at Canterbury, some of them saints, had observed in their
relations with their royal lords, and which Thomas himself on an earlier
occasion had promised to observe. This formula embodied the concession
that Henry had already made, and also envisaged a review of the English
customs in the light of current canon law. Thomas refused. He said he
had done fealty to Henry, saving his order, and was prepared most faithfully
to carry out his obligations on its terms. None of his predecessors had
been required to undertake additional oaths or obligations.

Henry's formula, however, appeared reasonable to Louis and the commissioners, and they persuaded Thomas to make a conciliatory reply. The archbishop offered that, in order to get peace for the church and the king's
favour for himself, he would observe those customs which his holy predecessors had observed, as far as he could in accordance with God's law (*secundum
deum*) and saving his order. Thomas probably believed that Anselm had
accepted the English customs with such reservations in 1095.[26] But Henry's
advisers thought this no good omen for the future. So Henry refused the
offer and brought the interview to an end.

In the closing stages, as the winter night closed in, Thomas stood alone
with his clerks in the field, abandoned and reviled by all the notables.[27]
They rode back to their lodgings in Montmirail, where they were cold-
shouldered by Louis and the courtiers. At dawn they left for Sens. Herbert
of Bosham paints a picture of a very demoralized party. The clerks were
divided. William fitzStephen believed that some who were anxious to get
back to England, and he names Henry de Houghton, were angered by
Thomas's stubbornness and insistence on minutiae. Herbert ingeniously both
defends his master wholeheartedly (after all, he took responsibility for the
débâcle) and also describes the general hostility and abuse. It was widely
said that Thomas had been proud, wilful and obstinate, and had put his
private judgment against the collective advice of some very distinguished
and religious men. On the road to Montmirail Herbert had congratulated
Thomas on his modest bearing at the conference in the face of aggression.
On the way to Chartres Thomas tried to raise the spirits of his companions.
They were, he explained, fighting for the cause of God and of his bride,

the church; and he was simply leading them along the path of truth and justice, which was a lonely and dangerous road. But they must press on, regardless of every threat or inducement to leave the straight and narrow. The way would get even rougher after the peace between the kings. They might now be expelled from the kingdom, even from the world. Herbert thought that some who had doubted the wisdom of what Thomas had done were comforted by this speech. The archbishop was like a house built upon a rock, a Christian knight at bay in the amphitheatre.

The party received a sympathetic welcome from the citizens of Chartres, but at Sens were ostracized, and waited disconsolately for their expected expulsion. After a few days Louis appeared and, apparently after some hesitation, eagerly made it up. He had begun to quarrel with Henry again and realized that Thomas could still be of use. There was no need for Thomas to migrate to the more generous and safer regions of Burgundy or Provence, as he was threatening to do. He apologized to his guest for having given him the wrong advice at the conference. A man like Henry was clearly not to be trusted. Once more Thomas and Louis were on the best of terms.[28]

At the same time a number of men, believing that peace had been missed only by an unlucky accident, tried hard to repair the damage. The commissioners, according to their instructions, exhorted Henry to make peace with Thomas and restore him to Canterbury. Henry replied that he might sometime allow Thomas to return to his see, but never to his favour, for that would put an end to the archbishop's suspension. Thomas refused to return in disgrace. He did, however, write a most conciliatory letter to the king asking that an agreeable formula might be found. To the pope he wrote that Henry's threats to go over to the schismatics were no longer to be feared since he had bound himself hand and foot to the loyal king of France. Henry also offered to submit the English customs to a council of religious men, and represented himself to the commissioners as a reformer of the corrupt English church. More realistically, he sent messengers to the pope, first Reginald, archdeacon of Salisbury, and then Ralf, archdeacon of Llandaff, to give his own version of the events and seek to prolong Thomas's incapacity. Thomas likewise sent a mission to Benevento.[29]

The last serious attempt at a settlement in this round of talks was made in connection with a second meeting of the two kings on 7 February 1169 in the French Vexin south of the Seine at St Léger-en-Yvelines, halfway between Montfort l'Amaury and Rambouillet.[30] The papal commissioners and Thomas were in attendance and there were many other intermediaries, including William, archbishop of Sens, and two English Victorines, Richard, prior of St Victor at Paris, the mystic and theologian, and Richard of Warwick, formerly abbot of St Augustine's, Bristol. But after futile exchanges between the king and archbishop – Henry's advisers trying out new formulations of his basic demand and Thomas insisting on his basic reservations – the commissioners at last served the papal ultimatum on the king. The full text of this document has not been preserved; but we know that Henry was given the peremptory choice between a complete reconciliation with Thomas and the other exiles and liability to ecclesiastical sentences, possibly of unrestricted ambit. Henry told the commissioners that he would consult the English bishops about the reply he should make. But, when they demanded an unequivocal answer in writing, Henry detached Bernard de la Coudre and offered to go to Grandmont and submit himself to the judgment of the master of that house. He would also summon the bishops to a conference. Whereupon the patient commissioners advised Thomas not to take any hostile action before these events took place, and Thomas agreed to be represented at the meetings by Master Lombard, who was staying for some business (perhaps the transmission of the pallium) with the new archbishop of Sens.

More immediately, Henry sent John of Poitiers in pursuit of Thomas, and at Etampes, some 50 kilometres south-east, the bishop arranged to get talks started again. It was proposed that king and archbishop should meet near Tours on 22 February. But it seems that John had reported Thomas's concessions (possibly Henry's as well) far too optimistically, and received a strong letter of rebuke from the archbishop. The meeting did not take place. Nevertheless, everyone put pressure on Thomas not to promulgate sentences against his enemies either before or after 5 March, the deadline. Mediators were becoming desperate, and discouraged. No letter of John of Salisbury concerned with the archbishop's affairs is extant for the period February to late August 1169. In one of his last letters before the gap, addressed to his namesake at Poitiers, he included a most generous and perceptive appreciation of Henry's greatness as king, shadowed only by his treatment of the church. The same lacuna appears also in Herbert of Bosham's biography. It was an awkward period for everyone.[31]

If Henry sent one messenger to Alexander after Montmirail and the other after St-Léger, the pope did nothing until Ralf of Llandaff reported total failure. He then, in a letter dated 28 February 1169, politely and regretfully but firmly refused all the king's requests and announced the dispatch of a new mission. He had chosen the papal notary and subdeacon Gratian, who was a nephew of a former pope, Eugenius III, and Master Vivian, archdeacon of Orvieto and an advocate in the curia. Both were experienced canon lawyers and administrators. Clearly Alexander was refusing to continue Thomas's suspension; but how much rope he was allowing the archbishop is obscured by the significant omission from the letter-collections of the papal letters obtained by Thomas's nuncios and by Herbert of Bosham's no less significant reticence. On 10 May Alexander, when informing Thomas of the dispatch of the new peace mission, requested, advised and desired the archbishop not to inflict any sentences on the king, the prelates of the realm or the kingdom itself before the end of the mission. And he added that, if by any chance such sentences had already been launched (which he could hardly believe), he would like them suspended until that same term. On 19 June, when he had heard of Thomas's first sentences, he censured Thomas for acting before the return of his messengers, who carried the papal orders and wishes in this matter. It is obvious that Thomas, relying on the papal letters of May and October 1168, supplemented by the papal ultimatum presented to Henry at St-Léger on 7 February 1169, considered that his suspension had terminated on 5 March and decided to act before he could be restrained. But why he postponed action until Palm Sunday is not clear. He may have seen some significance in the festival which marked the beginning of Holy Week.[32]

Thomas proceeded in two stages. Assuming the style, 'archbishop and legate of the apostolic see', and once more making use of the Cistercian order, he travelled from Sens to St Bernard's foundation at Clairvaux, near Bar-sur-Aube, some 120 kilometres to the east, and on 13 April, in the absence of Abbot Pons, who was on a mission to the Emperor Frederick, excommunicated ten persons whose offences he considered notorious. These were Hugh, earl of Norfolk (for the Pentney business), the bishops of London and Salisbury, Ranulf de Broc and his nephew Robert, Thomas fitzBernard, Hugh of St Clair, Nigel de Sacquenville (keeper of the seal) and two smaller fry who were in possession of archiepiscopal property. Ranulf, Thomas and Hugh had been excommunicated at Vézelay in 1166, and Salisbury suspended soon after. None of these ten seems to have been specially warned or cited, which enraged Gilbert Foliot and his friends and seriously disturbed other distinguished canon lawyers like Baldwin, archdeacon of Totnes. But the two bishops had expected the attack and had made preventive appeals to the pope at the beginning of Lent, giving 9 February 1170 as term.[33]

Thomas also intimated in many of his letters announcing these sentences that he had cited other transgressors, some of whom he named, and that, unless they offered suitable satisfaction, he would pass sentence on them on Ascension Day (29 May). This he did, but where and in what circumstances is unknown.[34] At least sixteen names are on the second list. Of those condemned at Vézelay, Richard de Lucy and Richard of Ilchester reappear. The most important newcomers are Geoffrey Ridel, archdeacon of Canterbury and acting chancellor, and his kinsman and deputy-archdeacon, Robert. In Thomas's letter of notification to the last two, he declared them suspended from their offices and revoked all grants of churches made by them during his absence. Two other royal clerks, John Cumin, archdeacon of Bath, and Guy Rufus, dean of Waltham, are included. But Thomas did not dare sentence John of Oxford again and was firmly rebuffed by the pope when in April he tried to reopen the matter. The other named delinquents were, as on Palm Sunday, occupiers or custodians of the property of the exiles. And, perhaps on both occasions, just as at Vézelay, whole classes of sinners were put under the ban: those who, as royal agents, had occupied Thomas's or his servants' possessions, those who had violated the liberty of the church and those who had impeded papal or archiepiscopal messengers. He had deferred to the pope's wishes only in 'postponing' sentences against the king and the kingdom at large.[35]

Thomas's formal notice of the excommunication of Gilbert, 'that wolf in sheep's clothing', did not get through the blockade until Ascension Day (29 May). A volunteer for this dangerous mission, one Berengar, a layman, emerged from the congregation in St Paul's at the Offertory during Mass, thrust letters addressed to the bishop and the dean into the celebrant's hands, forbade the ceremony to proceed and announced to the people that the bishop, who was at Stepney, had been excommunicated. In the resulting tumult the brave fellow was smuggled out of the cathedral under the cloak of his accomplice. Thomas claimed that the sentence was then published in their dioceses by the bishops of Norwich, Chester, Winchester and Chichester; and he asked the absent Worcester to do likewise.[36]

It was no less important to obtain Alexander's approval and confirmation of his actions. He reported what he had done and got William of Sens and the king of France to write on his behalf. And he persuaded the bishops of Auxerre, Thérouanne, Noyon and Paris to canvas those cardinals whom he considered favourable to his cause. News of the excommunications (most likely only the first set) reached the royal envoys on their return journey from Benevento, and Ralf of Llandaff went back to see if he could persuade Alexander to abrogate them. But the pope, on 19 June, before he could have heard of the second batch of sentences on 29 May, after complaining of the excommunications, told Thomas that, although he did not want to revoke the sentences by his own authority, he would like the archbishop himself to suspend them in order to give the present peace negotiations a chance. If he were to agree to this course, and the negotiations failed because of the king's obstinacy, he could reimpose the sentences if he wished, and the pope would approve his measures.[37]

Activity was probably even greater on the other side. Henry wrote in protest to Alexander and asked him to annul the sentences. In order to threaten him, he intrigued with the Italian cities and the king of Sicily. He pursued the plan to get Thomas translated to another see. He sent the bishop of Sées and Geoffrey Ridel to Louis to require him, under the terms of their recent treaty, to expel the archbishop from his lands.[38] And he encouraged Gilbert Foliot to resist. The bishop of London relied not only on the series of preventive appeals he had made, but also on the lack of a citation before sentence had been delivered. Moreover, and possibly mistakenly – for it was not popular with the other bishops – he revived the largely theoretical claim of London to be a metropolitan church and therefore independent of Canterbury.

At the beginning of Lent in London and on 15 May at Northampton, Gilbert attempted to get the whole bench of bishops to join in his appeal. At the first of these meetings, where Bartholomew of Exeter, despite a warning, gave Gilbert the kiss of peace, Jocelin of Salisbury is reported to have said, 'If my idiot of an archbishop (*buisnart*) should order me to do something I should not do, should I do it? Of course not!' But, according to Henry of Winchester's report to the exiles, the bishops as a whole were far from enthusiastic. The Northampton meeting may possibly also be the one described as a general council of the church assembled by royal officials, including Richard of Ilchester, in support of the two excommunicated bishops and in restraint of Thomas, whom the prelates were urged to abjure. As part of the propaganda war, Gilbert composed, or commissioned, an elaborate literary exercise in the form of a debate, 'The case between the archbishop of Canterbury and the bishop of London'. Even if the claim to metropolitan status was primarily a debating point, it was one which caused horror and alarm. Herbert of Bosham waxed almost hysterical.[39]

Nevertheless, Gilbert, as a good monk, bowed to authority and accepted the ban. He was, as he wrote despairingly to Alexander, being crushed between the archbishop and the king. He retained Master David of London, a clerk educated at Clermont and Paris and in the law at Bologna, who was to acquire a fashionable practice, as his advocate at the curia, and also obtained Henry's permission to prosecute his appeal in person. Thomas, however, declared that, in view of the dangers of the journey, he would on no account travel to Benevento. Gilbert, in April and June, secured testimonials from Rotrou of Rouen, Arnulf of Lisieux, the abbots of Westminster, Chertsey, Reading, Ramsey, Llanthony Prima and Stratford Langthorne (Cistercian) and the priors of Holy Trinity Aldgate and St Osyth. It will be noticed that his main support came from English monastic circles; and his friends defended him particularly against the charges that he had been the fomenter of discord between the archbishop and king and that he was a personal enemy of Thomas's.[40]

Late in June or early in July Gilbert, in company or in concert with the bishops of Salisbury and Chichester, crossed to Normandy; but on this occasion he travelled no farther than to meet the king who was returning from Gascony. Rumours of the imminent approach of the latest set of papal commissioners were current, and it was about this time that Jocelin's son,

Reginald, returned from the curia claiming that he had obtained everything that the king had desired. The archdeacon, as he passed through Sens, boasted that he would soon be releasing all those who had been excommunicated by Thomas without the condition of their making restitution to the exiles. And he had with him merchants to whom Henry was to acquit papal debts – an obvious bribe. The royalists were also becoming aware that Alexander was not entirely pleased with Thomas's actions. On 10 May the pope had not only requested the archbishop to suspend any sentence he might have imposed on his enemies; he also wrote a special letter on behalf of Jocelin. He informed Thomas that he loved the bishop dearly and ordered him to treat him with mercy. He was not to hold Jocelin's grant of the deanery to John of Oxford against him, since he had been coerced by the king. In any case Alexander himself had regranted it to the clerk. In the other letter the pope remarked, with a welcome touch of humour, that he believed that some of his own predecessors were saints.[41]

John of Salisbury, however, after a meeting with the papal commissioners, Gratian and Vivian, at Vézelay on 22 July, viewed everything quite differently. Alexander, he gathered, was entirely favourable to Thomas and had no intention of muzzling him (although all the archbishop's wiser friends were advising a temporary restraint); and Reginald of Salisbury spoke without knowledge of the pope's reaction to Thomas's sentences. Hopes rose even higher when the nuncios, after meeting and consulting Louis, chose to await Henry's return to Normandy from Gascony at Sens, where, presumably, they informed Thomas of Alexander's 'form of peace' and the deadline of Michaelmas (29 September) 1169 for a settlement. They carried, as Thomas was often to remark, 'a sort of peremptory proposition'. They also discussed with him, in the presence of Matthew, bishop of Troyes, and probably the archbishop of Sens, the terms on which those whom he had excommunicated in April and May could be absolved in order to allow the negotiations to proceed. Thomas and his household had, and retained, complete confidence in the favour and incorruptibility of Gratian, that 'son of grace'. He was the best papal legate ever. They had less trust in Vivian.[42]

The papal letter to Henry setting out his terms for a settlement has not been preserved; but the substance, which must have been supplied by Thomas, corresponds no doubt to the formula which was repeated many times in the following four months. Henry, for the love of God and of the pope, the honour of holy church and the salvation of himself and his sons, must restore Thomas to full favour and grant him, and all those who were with him and had left the kingdom for his sake, his peace and complete security, which he was also to guarantee as regards the royal servants and intend in all sincerity. He must also restore to Thomas the church of Canterbury, undiminished in any way, together with all other possessions which he had held as archbishop and all the churches and prebends pertaining to the archbishopric which had fallen vacant since his departure; and Thomas was to have power to deal with these benefices as he pleased. Full restoration of property was likewise to be made to Thomas's men. In return, Thomas would do for Henry whatever an archbishop should perform for his king and prince, saving the honour of God and his order. If there was a concession here it was that Henry was not required specifically to renounce the 'evil customs'; but this was only because Thomas regarded them as abolished, abandoned and no longer in debate.[43]

Henry was in two minds. Since Montmirail in January he was committed to settle, but could never quite bring himself to the point. Shrewd and experienced, charismatic but prestigious, pious but grudging, he knew well that it was in his best interests to make peace with Thomas, but was always hindered by the flood of grievances and self-pity which welled up whenever it was necessary to take the last hurdle. A certain meanness of spirit, an aversion from the great and noble gesture, crippled his approach. Nevertheless, the passage of time helped to loosen him up. It was obvious that neither Thomas nor Alexander was likely to die or be at his mercy in the immediate future. The conflict was damaging to his prestige and the excommunication of his bishops and servants was oppressive. The emptying of the bench of English bishops and the inability to get the young Henry crowned hampered his plans. Moreover, he had already made so many piecemeal concessions that nothing remained beyond drafting them into a short legal document and guaranteeing the terms by some acceptable ceremonial, most likely the kiss of peace. But after the four months spent in Aquitaine, away from it all, he found the business particularly tiresome and the unresponsiveness of the legates outrageous. From 15 August at Argentan, where he received the nuncios' letters of credence, through meetings on the 23rd and 24th at Domfront and the 31st at Bayeux, until the close of the session on the following day in the nearby park at Bur-le-Roi, like Woodstock and Clarendon one of his favourite hunting lodges, he let off steam in order to bring himself to accept the papal terms, although with one proviso he thought necessary for safeguarding his position.

For Thomas, however, it was the kiss of peace which was about to take the position in the negotiations previously held by the provisos. The origin of this ceremonial greeting is in the liturgy of the Mass, where, after the priest has consecrated the Host and said, 'Pax Domini sit semper vobiscum', the celebrant, the other participating clergy and the members of the congregation kiss each other in turn. It was omitted only from Masses for the Dead and on some other rare occasions. In a secular context it became an important ingredient in the ceremony of homage and served widely as a guarantee of all kinds of contracts, including truces and marriages. In the twelfth century it was still a physical kiss, and probably on the lips.[44]

By the end of August Henry had assembled a most impressive ecclesiastical council to advise him. It included the archbishops of Rouen and Bordeaux, all the Norman bishops (with Lisieux and Sées especially prominent), the bishops of Le Mans, Redon and Worcester, and the abbots of Fécamp, Bec, St-Wandrille, Caen, Troarn and Cérisy (Benedictine), Tiron, and Rievaulx, Mortemer and Bellet in Brittany (Cistercian). The distinguished but controversial Cistercian, Geoffrey of Auxerre, a Paris scholar, formerly St Bernard's secretary and ex-abbot of Clairvaux, was present at Henry's special invitation. The royal clerks most active were Geoffrey Ridel, John of Oxford, Reginald of Salisbury, Ralf of Llandaff and Richard Barre. The most significant absentee was John, bishop of Poitiers, who pleaded that he was holding a synod. Clearly he was tired of the business. John of Salisbury's voice too was silenced. And there was one there who, although working for peace, could not show his face – Gilbert Foliot, who was hoping that a successful outcome would spare him a journey to Benevento, which he was due to complete before 9 February 1170. He was still hanging about at the beginning of that year.[45]

That Henry should have gathered such a body together shows that he intended to settle and believed that anything acceptable to such prelates should be acceptable to Alexander and Thomas. Even Louis of France might see it that way. The counsellors themselves were determined to secure a settlement. And most of them thought at the end of the long and stormy session at Bur on 1 September that an agreement had been reached. The trouble was that, as each party inched closer to peace, each, especially Thomas, became concerned with practical details. Henry dropped his demand for the accounts of Thomas's chancellorship and for the repayment of debts from that period. But he raised the possibly new matter of Thomas's indebtedness to him as archbishop. This was doubtless because Thomas became increasingly insistent that Henry ought to make recompense for everything that the royal officials had taken from the estates during the exile (that is to say, repay the profits of the confiscated archbishopric). Henry said, correctly, that this had never been done by his predecessors in similar circumstances. Thomas answered that it was a matter of principle: no one could be pardoned unless he restored his ill-gotten gains (and this was an important issue in the matter of the absolution from excommunication of those involved in the administration of the escheated honour). Thomas maintained that he would be condoning sin if he abandoned this requirement. The presence of royal nominees in churches in the gift of the archbishop was a long-standing grievance. There was also the matter of the actual form of the reconciliation. Henry had once told Vivian that a trifle like a kiss of peace would not stand in the way of a settlement. But the exiles would have to return into the king's allegiance, and Thomas believed that Henry's advisers had invented a novel and pernicious form of the oath of fealty which he would require from clerks.

The peacemakers tried to steer clear of subsidiary complications and matters of detail; and in the end, at Bur, Henry accepted the papal terms, except that he wanted a minor and unimportant change in the wording (his 'heirs' for 'sons') and a much more disturbing insertion, 'saving the dignity of his kingdom'. Nevertheless, in return for Henry's permission that the bishops should reduce these proposals to writing, the nuncios agreed that those courtiers under Thomas's ban of excommunication who were present should be absolved immediately and that Vivian should go to England to absolve the rest while Gratian went to Thomas to secure his adherence to the terms. Three royal servants, Geoffrey Ridel, Nigel of Sacquenville and Thomas fitzBernard were then absolved by the archbishop of Rouen, after they had sworn on the Gospels that they would carry out whatever the nuncios should require them to do (Thomas had asked that the penances should be at his discretion). The nuncios had also protected their bargaining position by stressing that all such absolutions would lapse should the peace negotiations fail.[46]

It is possible that Henry had inserted the saving-clause unexpectedly. However that may be, on the following day (2 September) the nuncios, to the general consternation and Henry's fury, backed out. The condition was unacceptable and Vivian would not go to England. Thomas became firmly of the opinion that the 'dignities of the kingdom' were the 'customs' under a new name, and clearly they were. The crucial matter was which dignities or customs Henry was reserving; and, if it was Geoffrey Ridel who advised the king to insist on the clause, he was imitating the sabotage committed by Herbert of Bosham at Montmirail.[47]

After this unexpected disaster, Henry adjourned the meeting to Caen on 8 September and put the nuncios under the tutelage of the archbishop of Rouen. The negotiations he entrusted to the bishops of Lisieux, Sées, Bayeux, Redon and Worcester, and Geoffrey Ridel and Reginald of Salisbury. At some point Thomas wrote to the English bishops instructing them to suspend denunciation of those he had excommunicated while the negotiations were in progress. But the problem of the saving-clauses remained intractable. After the nuncios had proposed balancing Henry's with 'saving the liberty of the church', it was agreed that both should be omitted. But Henry in a meeting at Rouen refused the compromise. Thomas, consulted by the nuncios, wanted 'the dignity of the king's realm' balanced by 'saving his own order and his fealty to the church of Rome'. Proof of Henry's mounting anger is the rough treatment inflicted on the nuncios' messengers to the royal court, Peter, archdeacon of Pavia, and his companions. Proof of the commissioners' disillusionment is the departure of Gratian from the scene. At Domfront he had replied to the furious king, 'Don't threaten us, lord. We are the emissaries of a court which is accustomed to giving orders to emperors and kings, and we fear no man's threats.' He was accompanied to Benevento by William, archbishop of Sens, another implacable enemy, whom John of Salisbury regarded as the main architect of this last attack on the king. Henry sent Reginald of Salisbury, Richard Barre and Ralf of Llandaff to Alexander to protest against the nuncios' behaviour. The archbishop of Rouen, the bishops and clergy of Normandy and Bernard, bishop of Nevers, wrote to the pope in Henry's support. Thomas denounced the king's evasiveness and deceit in letters to the pope and cardinals.[48]

Henry took elaborate security measures. There was little he could do, beyond diplomacy, to protect his Continental lands against ecclesiastical censures, but he could turn England into a fortress and set up his eldest son there as nominal ruler. Perhaps even before the deadline of 29 September he sent to the kingdom the priest Wimar, a servant of the earl of Norfolk and involved in the Pentney affair, and Walter of Grimsby with a series of ordinances which the royal justiciars were to enforce; and he ordered Geoffrey Ridel and Richard of Ilchester to obtain the adherence of the English church to the measures. The blockade was to be strengthened. Bearers of Thomas's and Alexander's letters, especially of notifications of an interdict, were to be arrested and punished as traitors to the king and kingdom. All English beneficed clerks who were living abroad were to return home. All Welsh clerks were to be expelled. No one in Holy Orders was to leave or enter the kingdom without a royal passport. Some clauses of the Constitutions of Clarendon which forbade recourse to the papal curia were also revived. And every freeman over the age of fourteen was to take an oath to observe and help to enforce these regulations, which were to be effective from 9 October. Also about this time Henry ordered his justiciars to seek out and punish those prelates who had sent money to the exiles. They did not dare accuse Henry of Winchester, Thomas's consecrator, who had frequently furnished him with gold and silver in order to keep the wolf from the door, but they forced others to purchase immunity from prosecution.[49]

As soon as the deadline passed, Thomas, with the help of the legates, reactivated the sentences on Geoffrey Ridel, Nigel de Sacquenville and Thomas fitzBernard, together with the 'English' contingent, Robert the deputy-archdeacon of Canterbury, Richard of Ilchester, William Giffard, John Cumin, Richard de Lucy and Adam of Charing. He also gave notice that, unless five other clerks submitted to the church and him before 18 November, he would pronounce sentence on them. They were John of

Oxford, Guy of Waltham, John Cumin (perhaps a mistaken repetition), Ralf of Llandaff and the priest Wimar, all, except the last, important royal justices or ambassadors. He added general sentences against those who had accepted ecclesiastical offices or benefices from the laity (aimed at royal interference with his patronage, especially at Geoffrey Ridel who held the church of Otford), those who compelled ecclesiastical persons to celebrate divine services against the orders of their prelates (aimed at attempts to nullify his sentences) and those who impeded papal or his own messengers.[50]

The inclusion of John of Oxford, whom he called in a letter to the pope, 'nominally and gainfully' dean of Salisbury, was particularly provocative. But Thomas believed that John and Geoffrey Ridel, whom he called 'his arch-devil', had prevented the king from concluding the peace, and that Reginald of Salisbury and Richard Barre, Henry's ambassadors to Alexander, were *ipso facto* excommunicate for having communicated knowingly with royal clerks under the ban. For the moment Thomas was once more free to punish his enemies, and the release of his passions led to some intemperate language. In a letter of instruction to his own nuncios to the curia, he referred to Reginald as 'that bastard, fornicator, enemy of peace in the church and son of a priest'. Reginald, he said, always called him a traitor, alleging that the archbishop had assured him that he would never harm his father (Jocelin of Salisbury). 'I would no more do that for him', Thomas remarked, 'than I would for a dog.'[51] He informed those whom he thought favourable to his cause at the curia that, as always, it was Henry, not he, who had stood in the way of peace.

The intermediaries, with the exception of Gratian, believed that they had been within an ace of a settlement. Herbert of Bosham, although long after the event, thought that Henry had repented of his obstinacy. Thomas was convinced that Alexander would appoint William of Sens as his legate over Henry's Continental lands and that the king was terrified of this. The deadline of 18 November he had set for the publication of the excommunication of Henry's servants was also at hand. On 29 October Vivian, who had reached Tours on his way back to the curia, received through the prior of Bec letters from Henry, the archbishop of Rouen and Geoffrey Ridel urging him to return and make a final effort. Vivian, who seems to have had Master Lombard with him and recruited the aid of John of Salisbury, agreed and begged Thomas to co-operate. The consequent negotiations at St-Denis and Montmartre are particularly well reported and were given extensive coverage by Herbert of Bosham, who, of course, was present. It was undoubtedly at the back of the clerk's mind that, if peace had been made at this time -- and many of Thomas's clerks thought it should have been -- the ultimate tragedy might have been avoided.[52]

Vivian wrote again to Thomas, this time enthusiastically, inviting him to a meeting of Henry and Louis at the abbey at St-Denis, north of Paris, due to be held on 16 November (two days before the deadline for Thomas's sentences). He was convinced that the king would settle. Thomas made a most grudging answer. He feared that the nuncio had gone over to the other side and pointed out that he was no longer in any way subject to him since his commission had expired. He was amazed at the summons. But to show his generosity he would meet Vivian at Corbeil on the 14th to hear more about it. He also restated in writing the papal form of peace from which he did not intend to budge. What is more, and this is perhaps an indication that he was giving serious thought to a settlement, he listed additional conditions in great detail. The elaboration of terms could, and can, of course, be interpreted otherwise.[53]

Henry travelled to St-Denis to meet Louis, carrying, Thomas believed, letters patent, already sealed, restoring the archbishop to Canterbury. At the shrine he offered a fine pall and eighty pieces of gold; and it was agreed that he would meet Thomas, who had stayed in Paris, at Montmartre, the halfway mark, on 18 November. On the appointed day Thomas and his suite took up position in the chapel of the Holy Martyrs at the foot of the hill. The two kings, the count of Flanders, Vivian, the archbishop of Rouen, the bishop of Sées and the rest remained outside.[54]

The papal and archiepiscopal terms were again presented to Henry and this time it was only the details which were in dispute. Thomas did not like the formula for the restoration of his property; and when, in return, he was asked for a schedule of the estates he expected, naturally he could not produce one, but professed special anxiety about the fiefs of Henry of Essex and William of Ros and the land at Mundham which had been in dispute with John the Marshal. He declared that he would prefer perpetual exile to making peace at the cost of giving up those three estates which the king had stolen from him. The intermediaries were sure that Henry would concede. The matter of financial compensation for the moveables proved more difficult. Henry objected to paying financial reparations on principle (there was also the underlying dispute over whether Thomas had been expelled or had cut and run), but offered to put it to the judgment of the French royal court, the Gallican church or the scholars of Paris. Thomas said he preferred an amicable settlement to litigation. Henry offered an *ex gratia* payment of 1,000 marks. Thomas reckoned his losses at 30,000 marks (£20,000), which would not seem an understatement.[55] He offered, however, to be content with half on the nail so that he could pay off his creditors and re-equip his estates when they were released from the royal officials who had ravaged them. The other half could be left to the judgment of the pope or some other religious person. It is revealing that, after the failure of the negotiations, he should have informed his nuncios to the pope that he was not unduly bothered about the second instalment, 'for it is useful for both the Roman and the English church to keep some claims in reserve which can come in handy on a later occasion against a recalcitrant king'. In other words he would settle for 15,000 marks. Alexander, however, accepted Henry's figure, and by March 1170 Thomas was doing his best to collect just that.

Herbert of Bosham, and apparently most others present, believed that by the end of the day the intermediaries had settled everything satisfactorily. Henry had renounced, in general, all evil customs which harmed the English church; the aggressive saving-clauses had been dropped by both sides; it was agreed that both Henry and Thomas would respect the other's rights after the archbishop had returned to England; and Henry covenanted to make full and proper restitution to the archbishop. Under pressure, both sides had suppressed detailed claims and expressions obnoxious to the other. Finally Thomas asked for the kiss of peace. He did not doubt the sincerity of the king but he did doubt the goodwill of his advisers. He had expressly consulted the pope on what security to require, and Alexander had replied that a kiss of peace would suffice. Henry replied, however, that he would gladly oblige if he had not once in anger sworn in public that he would never give Thomas the kiss of peace. That was his sole reason for refusing; no trace of anger or rancour remained in his heart. His son and heir could give the kiss on his behalf. But Thomas was not to be moved and Louis expressed his doubts. The case of Robert of Sillé, a rebel against Henry in Poitou, who had been punished in some way despite Henry's kiss and an oath to Louis, was bandied about.[56]

The negotiations were broken off without Thomas meeting Henry face to face. It was nightfall, and the king, tired out and exasperated beyond measure, had to ride with Louis in the darkness to Mantes, where their lodgings had been prepared. On the way he met, as planned, the French queen and the belated heir, Philip Augustus. His inspection of the four-year-old boy seems to have been thought significant. He was considering handing over his own twelve-year-old son, Richard, for education in Louis's household. Family matters were very much on his mind.[57]

Thomas and his clerks returned to the Temple, outside the walls of Paris. According to Herbert, and William fitzStephen was of the same opinion, there was general agreement that it was the kiss alone which had prevented the peace treaty, and there was a division of opinion on the wisdom of their master's stand. After Nocturns (about 4 a.m.) most of the *eruditi* asked for an audience with Thomas. They expressed the view that a careful appreciation ought to be made of the situation. For six years they had followed Thomas on the road of truth and justice, always seeking peace, but never finding it. There had been conference after conference and one disappointment after another. Now, it seemed, the only obstacle was a kiss of peace. Everything else had been agreed. Now the cause of the exile was no longer whether customs were good or evil, or whether 'the honour of God' should be expressly mentioned, but simply a kiss of peace. As a result of the exile many episcopal sees were vacant with disastrous results on the religion of the people. The shepherd was absent (Lam. 1: 6). And after yesterday's conference the absence had become criminal. It was Thomas's duty to return on the terms offered by the king, and they would go with him. They did not believe that Henry was laying a trap for him or had designs on his life or liberty. He had given Thomas his peace and security in public and had condemned all the bad customs. Herbert in this reportage is probably dissociating himself from these views and, with hindsight, writing ironically. When he had reported the events at Montmartre at the time to William of Sens he had expressed the view that it was by God's will that Henry had wrecked the peace by refusing the kiss of peace, for there could be no real accommodation between the king's peace and their justice. It would have helped if Herbert in his Biography had given a few names. John of Salisbury could easily have led the group of protesters. The monk Stephen of Rouen, a hostile reporter, closed his *Draco Normannicus* with Thomas's refusal of Henry's offer: 'The archbishop remained silent, pondering the matter. I don't know what he wanted; but he fears to return.'[58]

Thomas, however, justified his intransigence vigorously to his clerks. He had refused the king's offer of peace for one reason alone: because Alexander had instructed him to require the warranty of the kiss. But, if they thought it right, he would make a full report of the conference to the pope and take his advice. He then repeated the words he had spoken after Montmirail in similar circumstances. The path of truth and justice was hard, and those who followed it were bound to suffer. The *eruditi* were moved and not unsympathetic. They knew that they were no match for their inflexible leader. So they went from Paris to Sens and prepared to send an embassy to the papal curia.

They also announced, in a series of letters to all the ecclesiastical authorities in England, except York, a new set of sentences which Thomas felt free to impose or threaten. All those excommunicated in April and May were once more placed under the ban. The five who had been warned to submit by 18 November had the term extended to Christmas. The general sentences were reimposed. And the archbishop and legate announced that, unless Henry made peace with him and the other exiles by 2 February 1170, there was to be a general interdict over England: that is to say, all church services were to cease, except for infant baptism and the confession and unction of the dying, which, however, had to be performed in private. In some notifications Thomas also threatened that, unless Henry corrected the excesses of his servants, he too would be excommunicated. Privately, however, he believed that the mere threat of action would bring the king to submit.[59]

All the same, he posted to his mission, already *en route* for Benevento and once more led by Alexander of Wales and John the Cantor, very full instructions in preparation for the final assault. They were to impetrate from the pope a series of letters. Those addressed to Thomas should include a prohibition to him to offer the king any newfangled security (a reference to the supposed revision of the oath of fealty), an order to stick to the form of peace he had given in writing to the king, and instructions to absolve no one who would not take an oath, according to the custom of the church, that he would stand to the judgment of the church – although this, Thomas recognized, was contrary to the Constitutions of Clarendon (5). Henry should be ordered to restore to Thomas half his losses, threatened with an interdict and urged to give Thomas the kiss of peace. In another letter Alexander should order Henry to restore the three named estates – otherwise there would be no peace. The pope should also write to Louis urging him to support Thomas's claim to the restoration of his losses. The archbishop's continued concern with detail shows that, on one level at least, he was still negotiating seriously.[60]

Thomas also reported to his messengers that the ecclesiastical council summoned to London by Geoffrey Ridel and Richard of Ilchester had been a fiasco. The bishops of Winchester, Exeter, Norwich and Chester were recalcitrant and the last three were taking evasive action. Only Clarembald, the abbot-elect of St Augustine's, was enthusiastic. The earl of Norfolk (in connection with the long-standing Pentney affair) had been excommunicated. The pope was triumphing in England. William fitzStephen names the archbishop of York and the daughter of Baldwin de Reviers (I), earl of Devon, no doubt acting for her infant grandson, as the principal recusants. Nevertheless, some men, both clerical and lay, had been forced to take the oath; and Thomas empowered bishops or (failing whom) priests to absolve from their oaths those who had thus abjured their fathers in God, but had acted under compulsion and were penitent.[61]

Henry, without waiting for his next scheduled meeting with Louis at Tours on 13 January, when the case of Thomas could have been raised again, sent a second mission to Alexander consisting of John of Oxford, Giles, archdeacon of Rouen (the nephew of the archbishop), and John, archdeacon of Sées. They took back the papal–archiepiscopal form of peace in a revised version which the king could tolerate. It incorporated changes made on the advice of the archbishop of Rouen and the king's barons and seems to have been what Henry offered at Montmartre. Although this was to prove acceptable to both Alexander and Thomas and provide the terms on which peace was made in 1170, its text has not been preserved *in extenso*, presumably because in some respects it represented a defeat for Thomas's complete demands.[62]

Henry spent the Christmas feast at Nantes in south Brittany, Thomas his sixth in exile at Sens. Both, and many others too, were awaiting the results of the several missions to the papal curia. Gratian and William of Sens had been the first to set off; the king had two parties *en route*, Thomas probably only one; and Gilbert Foliot was about to go – with Geoffrey Ridel, Thomas believed. The earliest news of the papal reaction to these embassies could not reach Normandy before the end of February 1170 and Alexander's measures would not be known in detail before the second week in March. Meanwhile the archbishop's threat to lay an interdict on England on 2 February, although unlikely to be implemented before his nuncios returned with papal approval, had not been revoked by Thomas and could not be vetoed by any other ecclesiastical authority.

CHAPTER TEN

THE ROAD TO GLORY, 1170

By February 1170 the pressure on Henry to settle had become intense. He had conceded all the substantial points at issue; his lands and his person were threatened by ecclesiastical sentences; and there was a feeling in many church circles that he was now straining only at gnats. He was toying with the idea of going on a crusade and it would also be of advantage to him in all his worldly activities if he could enlist an unembarrassed church on his behalf. But in his unsurmountable enmity for Thomas he was not without zealous and respectable supporters. The royal clerks, the next generation of bishops, were obviously enjoying the fight. Bishops of the stature of Gilbert Foliot and Arnulf of Lisieux were completely staunch. Rouen and York were loyal. No bishop within Henry's dominions was by this time an active supporter of the exile, few were secret admirers. A sigh of relief as well as of sorrow would have swept through the Angevin's lands if Thomas had died.

Thomas, as can be seen from his unwillingness to be rushed into returning without precise royal undertakings and cast-iron guarantees, scented victory. He had acquired an important champion in the archbishop of Sens and his influence at Benevento had improved since the return of Gratian. In the spring of 1170 a friend at the curia, perhaps Lombard, reported that he and Master Walter were beavering away to get papal letters for Thomas written and sealed, and transcripts made, and hoped that they would reap their reward at Thomas's restoration. It was, however, extremely difficult now to get secret messages through to the archbishop, and Thomas, he complained, 'as was his custom', confided his secrets to anyone who passed by. This led to confusion at the curia: he would do better to rely more on the justice of his cause than on the number of his advocates. However that may be, it is evident that, the longer Thomas persisted, the more his moral stature increased. He was becoming not only the conscience of the church but also an institution. In the autumn of 1170 Alexander, in a rescript for him, referred to the constant goodness and faith and the strength and resolution he had shown in preserving the liberty of his church.[1]

Moreover, in the course of that year, Alexander's own fortunes were on the mend. The alliance between the Queen-Mother Margaret, ruling for the youthful William II of Sicily, the league of the Lombard cities and the Eastern Emperor, Manuel I Comnenus, against the Emperor Frederick and his anti-popes began to make Alexander's recovery of the Patrimony of St Peter a possibility. In February–March 1170, at the invitation of the Lombard League, he returned to the Roman Compagna, and in October he moved to Frascati (Tusculum), where he remained for more than two years engaged in war against the Romans and the imperial faction. But Henry, too, was an associate member of this confederation. In 1168 he had married his daughter to Henry the Lion, duke of Saxony and a possible rival of Frederick's. He maintained friendly diplomatic relations with the Lombard League and his plans for a crusade drew him even closer to Benevento, Palermo and Byzantium.[2]

For at least a year Thomas had known that he could recover his archbishopric on terms which a majority of those involved would consider reasonable and honourable. But he feared that in victory might lie defeat. In exile it was not too difficult to follow the path of truth and justice. In office, under an unfriendly king and court, amid hostile or difficult bishops and an alienated nobility, in a church with a rebellious chapter and a diabolical archdeacon, the road would become rougher. Friendless and without power, he would still have to punish all those who had harmed the church and him. The prospect was such as to daunt even the bravest zealot. As everyone knew, and Thomas knew particularly well, everything depended on Henry. Only if he would forgive and forget and try sincerely to work in amity could a peace treaty be anything for the exiles but the opening of a prison door. That is why Thomas put such emphasis on the kiss of peace. In his heart of hearts he knew that Henry never forgave his enemies. And so, with both king and archbishop reluctant to take the irretrievable step, the outcome depended on chance.

While the parties waited for news from the curia, Henry discussed with the French king and Frederick, archbishop of Tyre, the possibility of his going on a crusade.[3] He thought that he would be able to leave by Easter 1171, and all concerned realized that a necessary preliminary was a settlement with Thomas. Froger, bishop of Sées, had little success as an intermediary, and Gerard la Pucelle, invoking the help of John of Salisbury, tried in vain to get Thomas to meet him and Geoffrey Ridel. Whereupon Henry assembled a great council of archbishops (including Tyre), bishops, other distinguished ecclesiastics and nobles and, after taking its advice, announced that he was inviting Thomas and his followers to return to England in order to recover all their possessions in peace and security, and named the whole assembly, together with his uncle Amaury (Almaric), king of Jerusalem, as pledges that he had banished from his heart all complaints, anger and rancour against the archbishop and his men. All he required in return was that Thomas should perform every service that an archbishop should render a king. He then sent the bishop of Sées, Alexander of Cologne, abbot of Cîteaux, Geoffrey of Auxerre and Geoffrey Foulquia, the Master of the Temple, to Sens to invite Thomas to a meeting in Normandy. But when Thomas reached Pontoise and was about to go on to Chaumont (both in the French Vexin), in order to have a preliminary talk with the archbishop of Rouen, he was instructed by Rotrou to proceed no farther, as Henry was about to leave for England.

Much of this, and more besides, was reported by John of Salisbury, taking up his pen again after a long silence, in a letter to Exeter. He attributed the fiasco to the arrival from Benevento of Richard Barre and Ralf of Llandaff with a letter from Alexander and views on the pope's mood and intentions. It was rumoured that they had secured the absolution of Gilbert Foliot and of all others under Thomas's ban and that once again the archbishop had been deprived of authority over the king, his land and his men. But John doubted the truth of this, for Gilbert had immediately departed for the curia. All the same, the clerks had conspired with Geoffrey Ridel to prevent Henry's meeting with Thomas. It was said that Geoffrey had persuaded Henry to return to England to persecute those bishops and priests who had refused to take the oath against the pope and the archbishop. For, John thought, Henry had been warned by the nuncios and others that, unless he carried out the terms of the form of peace by 1 May, all the censures of the church would be unleashed. Herbert of Bosham, who had accompanied Thomas to Pontoise, blamed Gilbert Foliot for the rupture. In a tirade he composed for Thomas against 'Ahithophel', he hoped that the spirit of wisdom and knowledge would instruct Alexander how to treat the wicked bishop of London when he arrived at the curia. Thomas, in a letter more likely to have been sent, reported mournfully to the pope the latest disaster; and he complained to some of the intermediaries, including the bishop of Sées and Geoffrey of Auxerre, of his treatment by the king.

Although Richard Barre and Ralf of Llandaff represented what was really a royal defeat as a triumph for the king, they and their colleagues had secured terms on which they expected the quarrel to be settled. The papal letter they brought back, dated 19 January, rehearsed Henry's concessions at Montmartre and accepted them as the agreed 'form of peace'. They were, with minor modifications, the archiepiscopal–papal demands recast as a royal grant.[4] And Alexander, to enable Henry to implement them fully, absolved him from his oath never to give Thomas the kiss of peace. Henry was enjoined to put the whole business through as quickly as possible and was informed that Alexander had empowered Rotrou of Rouen and Bernard of Nevers to see that he did so. In return, these new commissioners, as soon as they were convinced that peace would be established, could absolve, where it was proper, those whom Thomas had excommunicated. Alexander also granted these sinners a most generous, and in the eyes of the exiles an outrageous, indulgence: they were not to incur any loss of honour, office, benefice or reputation because of the length of time they had been under the ban. If peace was not made, however, the absolutions would lapse. Any appeals had to be prosecuted at the curia before October 1170. Alexander did not state here, as he did to the commissioners, the basic condition that those wishing to be absolved would have to take an oath that they would acept a penance to be imposed by him, because that was repugnant to the Constitutions of Clarendon and therefore a subject to be avoided. But the terms he offered to Thomas's enemies were generous enough to induce them to press Henry to settle.

In fact Alexander was even more indulgent. Reginald of Salisbury, Thomas's former clerk, had at last obtained authority for his father, the bishop and the one whom Thomas hated most after Gilbert, to be absolved. Reginald had been joined by a former pupil of John of Salisbury, Peter of Blois, that rising star in the literary firmament, who had been acting as tutor to the boy king of Sicily, and had travelled from Benevento to Bologna in the early months of 1170 in the company of some papal nuncios. Peter answered complaints about his behaviour from Thomas's clerks by professing that he was completely unaware that Reginald was an enemy of the archbishop. In any case the archdeacon was anxious to make it up and Peter was urging him to do so. Reginald was a wise and diligent man, and a gesture from Thomas would do the trick. No gesture was made. Even worse, on 12 February Master David obtained papal authority for Gilbert Foliot to be absolved by Rotrou of Rouen or another bishop, probably Exeter, with the indulgence but also with the proviso that he would accept penance from the pope. Thomas was to be instructed to keep the absolution secret until it could be published without danger to Gilbert (presumably from the king). Gilbert intercepted this letter at Milan, turned back and was absolved by Rotrou on Easter Day (5 April) at Rouen and reinstated in his see on 1 May. Thomas and his clerks wrote bitterly about this disgraceful betrayal of their cause to Rotrou, Alexander and all whom they thought sympathetic. William of Sens complained to the pope that he had done it behind his back. And Alexander even tried to countermand the permission.[5]

The offence was great, for it was to William that Alexander had in January entrusted his most important instructions. The archbishop, who was also papal legate in France and was given an auxiliary role in the English affair, was expected to be back by Easter. The principal instruments he carried were commissions to Rotrou of Rouen and Bernard of Nevers, dated 19 January, to make peace between the parties. They were to go to Henry within a month of receiving these instructions and tell him to give Thomas the kiss of peace and restore him and his followers to their positions and possessions in England on the terms which had already been agreed. They were also to exhort Thomas immediately to submit humbly to the king, provided it would entail no threat to the liberty of the church or danger to himself or his men. The requirement that Henry should pay 1,000 marks as compensation could be waived, and Henry could substitute his son in giving the kiss of peace if Thomas was agreeable. But, if Henry would not complete the major requirements (including a kiss of peace) within forty days of being warned so to do, the commissioners were to subject all his Continental lands to an interdict, without the hindrance of appeals, although they could allow him a little more time if they thought fit.

After peace had been made, they were, after a suitable interval, to warn Henry to abolish all evil customs, especially those which he had recently introduced against the liberty of the church, and were to absolve all bishops and other dignitaries of the kingdom from the oaths they had taken to observe them. They were also to exhort Henry to repay to Thomas and his men all the revenues he had collected from their properties. Henry's response to these additional requirements should be reported to the pope. If the commissioners were convinced that peace was going to be made, they could absolve all those under sentence of excommunication on the terms which have already emerged. The pope added two afterthoughts. If Henry refused to give the kiss of peace, the commissioners were to press Thomas to accept it from the son, if he knew he could do so without danger to himself or his men. And they were to punish those royal servants who had ill-treated Peter, archdeacon of Pavia, and take Henry to task for that outrage.[6]

The papal mandates secured by Thomas's own nuncios between 12 and 26 February were mostly notifications to ecclesiastical provinces of the interdict which would be laid by the pope on Henry's lands in the kingdom of France or by Thomas in the province of Canterbury if the commissioners were unable to induce the king to complete the peace. Among the addressees was Roger of York, described as legate of the Holy See. In further instructions to the commissioners, the conditions on which they could absolve the excommunicate, particularly Geoffrey Ridel in illegal possession of Otford, were tightened up. And two letters concerned the possible coronation of the young Henry. In the first (24 February), Alexander ordered Thomas and all the English bishops on no account to crown and anoint the prince unless he took the traditional coronation oath, including the promise of liberty to the church, particularly the church of Canterbury, and also released everyone from observing those customs, and from the oaths extorted in support of them, which had been recently introduced into the kingdom. No bishop was to take part in the coronation unless those conditions were respected. In the second (26 February), the pope forbade Roger of York and all bishops to crown Henry's son while Thomas was in exile, for everyone knew that the coronation and unction of the kings of England was a dignity which pertained to Canterbury by ancient custom. Anyone disobeying this command was in danger of losing his office and orders.[7]

It was Richard Barre's report to Henry about the probable content of the papal mandates which William of Sens and Thomas's clerks would bring that caused the king to panic. Herbert of Bosham sent an urgent message to William of Sens in which he claimed that Richard was spreading a pack of lies about William and his instructions, but also blamed the long-absent archbishop for contributing to this by keeping all his friends in the dark. The bishops of Noyon and Paris informed Alexander that they had heard that the nuncios were boasting that they had obtained permission for the archbishop of York or some other bishop to crown the king's son and that Henry had gone to England for that purpose. As usual on these occasions some false information was put out or invented by trouble-makers and scandal-mongers.

What the royal nuncios probably told the king was that all his earlier demands had been either withdrawn as hopeless or refused. As far as diplomacy was concerned, they had reached the end of the road. Henry would have to carry out the form of peace. But they had a respite of at least two months before the new commissioners could be instructed and get into action; and even that period could easily be prolonged. So Henry abruptly cancelled the elaborately planned reconciliation with Thomas and crossed with forty ships to England. He landed at Portsmouth on 3 March after an extremely hazardous passage and celebrated Easter (5 April) at Windsor. In order to keep in with the archbishop of Rouen, he wrote from Westminster to inform him that he had received a letter of thanks from the pope for having sent him the form of peace that had been drawn up on the advice of Rouen and his other barons, and that he intended, with the help of Rotrou and the bishop of Nevers, to carry it out in its entirety in accordance with the pope's wishes. But naturally he did not disclose that he was making preparations to have his eldest son crowned and anointed king of England.[8]

To secure this guarantee of his lineage had, of course, been a long-standing wish of the king; but why he had to carry it out at this moment is not entirely clear. William fitzStephen, who was at court at the time, expresses the general bewilderment. Henry, he says, decided unexpectedly to have his son crowned in order to prevent any possible harmful consequences of the imminent settlement with Thomas. He reasoned that it would be improper for the archbishop to punish the kingdom for actions for which the new king was in no way responsible. This, fitzStephen adds, was Henry's secret motive, a thing quite inexplicable. 'God, who "trieth the hearts and reins" (Ps. 7: 9), alone knows, not I. But those who before, during and after the event gave credence to deeds, believed this of him.' This is *obscurum per obscurius*.[9]

Henry had in fact embarked on a policy of devolution, possibly with regard more to his crusade than to a settlement with the exile. In May, apparently at the insistence of his wife, the duchess of Aquitaine, he yielded that duchy to their second son, Richard, then in his thirteenth year; but, probably as a result of the events in England, Richard's investiture was delayed until June 1172, when there were ecclesiastical ceremonies at Poitiers and Limoges. The easiest way for Henry to obtain the coronation of his eldest son was to make peace with Thomas and use the ceremony as a symbol of their complete reconciliation. That he chose to do the opposite does not prove that he had no intention of settling: he probably wished to inflict a final wound before bowing to the inevitable. He and York still had the papal privilege of 17 June 1161,[10] and he decided to use it before it could be irresistibly nullified. It is even possible that Richard Barre had in January extorted from Alexander some sort of verbal assent to a coronation, a lapse which the royalists knew would be remedied by the archbishop's nuncios and friends behind their backs. Henry put an embargo on all cross-Channel traffic and made careful arrangements. He managed to recruit York and a few of the remaining English bishops, although it was rumoured at one time that the bishop of Sées was prepared to substitute for York. He had left his wife and the constable of Normandy, Richard de Humet, in charge of the duchy, and they had with them at Caen the young Henry and his wife, Margaret, the daughter of King Louis, ready to cross to England, but only at the very last moment, in order to deceive objectors.

Alexander would have heard of Henry's crossing by the end of April, and in a mandate to his commissioners, which could not have reached them before the end of June, instructed them to follow him within twenty days of the receipt of the letter, unless they had done so already. They were to require him, as before, to carry out the peace terms within forty days; and, even if they were physically prevented from issuing the ultimatum, an interdict was to be placed on Henry's Continental lands at the expiry of the term. Any bishop who did not observe it was to be suspended and then, if necessary, excommunicated. Henry was to be informed that Alexander would not be as merciful to him as he had been to the 'so-called' Emperor Frederick, but would excommunicate him in person. It would seem that at this time Alexander really meant business; and Thomas regarded this letter as the instrument of his victory. The blow should have been struck four or five years before.[11]

John of Salisbury later berated Thomas for the danger and misfortune he had caused by his delay first in handing over the form of peace to the commissioners, then in serving the English bishops with prohibitions of the coronation. The archbishop had foolishly trusted in auguries, 'prophecies not inspired by the Holy Ghost', 'delusions', 'vain fantasies', instead of following good advice. As Herbert of Bosham called Richard Barre the main prophet who filled the whole land with windy words, it would seem that John believed that the archbishop had paid far too much attention to the misleading stories spread by the royal nuncios and too little to John's own scepticism and good sense.[12]

However that may be, Thomas, in anticipation of the legates' crossing, provided them with elaborate and shrewd instructions and advice on how to deal with a slippery customer. He required fulfilment of all the terms, including the 1,000 marks and the kiss of peace, to the letter. A schedule of his possessions that he was providing must be expressly accepted by the king. He showed great and repeated concern about guarantees. He would like some of the barons and bishops to act as sureties. Royal letters patent, signifying Henry's adherence to the terms, must be produced in triplicate, with copies addressed to the archbishop, the pope and the commissioners. Only transcripts of the papal letters authorizing the interdict must be taken to England, lest they be confiscated at the port of entry. The originals should be left with the archbishop of Sens, who would see that they were executed in case of failure. Remember, Thomas concluded, how all your predecessors have been bamboozled by the king. There can be no doubt that at this point the archbishop, although deeply suspicious of Henry's good faith and intentions, was ready to settle if every clause of the form of peace was met.[13]

It will be noticed that the requirements were concerned only with the restoration of the archbishop and his followers to their offices and possessions and with the terms on which those men who had been excommunicated by Thomas would be absolved. This narrowing of the objectives was clearly a tactical move and can be justified as a necessary deviation from the path of truth and justice. It was part of the strategy which the pope himself had devised. It was the way of the realist, not of the fanatic. As the goal came into sight, Thomas began to keep his feet more firmly on the ground. At the same time the exiles were swept by moods of impatience and despair. Money was short. Delays were endless. Friends and allies could not be depended on. Enemies triumphed. The pope and cardinals were broken reeds. God was their only help and refuge.

As rumours grew more insistent that the coronation was being planned, Thomas prepared counter-measures. He issued a prohibition, both general and individualized, against taking part in a coronation, and appealed against such a ceremony, setting 2 February 1171 as the term. He complained comprehensively to the pope and wrote to some bishops, including York, Winchester and Exeter, individually, urging them to support the papal prohibition and defend Canterbury's privileges. His letter to Roger of York, however, is noticeably moderate and respectful. Given his title of 'legate of the Holy See', he was reminded of his indebtedness to Canterbury, their common mother, and Thomas protested that it was his earnest endeavour, 'to keep' with Roger 'the unity of the Spirit in the bond of peace' (Ephes. 4: 3). Means of getting the prohibitions and letters through the blockade were also explored. Perhaps Roger of Worcester, if he returned to England, would carry the dangerous contraband. Later he was forbidden to go, by both sides, and never went. A nun, Idonea ('a suitable vessel'), fortified by the example of biblical heroines, was instructed to seek out Roger of York. At one point John of Salisbury believed that the papal letter of prohibition had reached the kingdom and asked the monastic chapter of Canterbury to get a copy and disseminate it. But some bishops – perhaps those who took part in the ceremony – evaded its delivery. John of Salisbury was not the only one to blame Thomas for the failure to stop the ceremony.[14]

Thomas was outgunned. Henry sent Knights Templar to him in order to keep him quiet, and the new archdeacon of Bath, Thomas, to the archbishop of Rouen to keep the commissioners out of England until after 14 June. He announced repeatedly that he was about to return to Normandy to deal with the case, and it was even reported that the archbishop of Sens wanted to make his peace with him.[15]

Henry pushed the coronation through. He summoned a great council of the magnates to meet in London on 14 June and sent Richard of Ilchester to Caen to bring the young Henry over. The bishops of Bayeux and Sées returned with him, but, to everyone's amazement, Margaret was left behind, although ceremonial outfits had been prepared for her both at Caen and at London. As Richard left with the prince and bishops on the same day as he arrived, 5 June or later, there may simply not have been enough time to get the girl ready. Urgency or some undisclosed indisposition or difficulty is the likeliest explanation, although it is quite possible that this insult to the French royal family was the settling of another score. Henry would wound as many birds as he could with the same stone. Hence on the 14th the prince alone was crowned in Westminster Abbey by Roger of York, assisted probably by the bishops of London, Salisbury, Chester, Rochester, St Asaph, Llandaff, Durham, Bayeux, Evreux and Sées. Probably absent were the bishops of Winchester, Norwich and Worcester.

Bartholomew of Exeter, although reported to have been present, was later exculpated by Thomas. The other English sees were vacant.[16]

The coronation dealt Thomas a shattering blow. One of Canterbury's principal and most prized privileges had been violated, and Henry had been supported by the English episcopate, *nemine contradicente*, for Winchester and Norwich were very old, and apparently excused themselves on the grounds of sickness, while Worcester had been detained in Normandy. Besides, he had much loved, it was said, the young Henry, whom he had once had in his household and certainly expected to crown. Peter of Blois wrote solicitously to John of Salisbury that he had heard that Thomas was prostrated by the event; and John wrote to Thomas urging him to stop being irresolute and issue immediately to the archbishops of Rouen and Tours the papal letter ordering action if the king did not make peace – this would also terrify 'their guest' (presumably the bishop of Nevers). Moreover, the archbishop of Sens wanted to send his own mandates to this effect to the archbishops of Auch and Bordeaux, thereby completing the coverage of Henry's Continental lands. But we are still, it should be noticed, concerned only with threats, not with action. Thomas's chancery did produce, but probably before the coronation, for it is not specifically mentioned, a sheaf of letters addressed to all ecclesiastical authorities in the kingdom. These were instructed, because of the accumulation of injuries perpetrated by the king on the holy church of Canterbury and the expiry of the church's patience, to order, within fifteen days of receipt of the letter, either by papal authority or Thomas's own as legate, the cessation of all church services, except the two allowed. But there is no evidence that an interdict was in fact laid at this time on either Henry's Continental lands or on the kingdom. Thomas, unexpectedly, decided to make peace with him so that he could more easily wage war on his other enemies.[17]

He had, however, made a careless and impetuous mistake which he seems never to have properly rectified, and which was to have disastrous consequences. His letters to the curia about the coronation have not been preserved, presumably because they included the untrue allegation that the young Henry, far from taking the complete and traditional coronation oath which included an undertaking to protect the holy church of God, its liberties and servants, had instead confirmed by oath that he would observe the ancestral customs of the kingdom, that is to say, the Constitutions of Clarendon. The truth of this was later expressly denied by Arnulf of Lisieux and others, and it is obvious that by the time of the peace negotiations at Fréteval Thomas no longer held to it, for he never raised the matter with the king. Unfortunately he forgot to cancel this charge at the curia, and Alexander, as we shall see, not unnaturally took it most seriously. It was an important factor in the causes of the archbishop's death.[18]

About ten days after the coronation, Henry crossed from Portsmouth to Barfleur. The papal commissioners, Rouen and Nevers, presented the papal ultimatum, and the king agreed to all the pope's terms (as expressed in the form of peace) except the giving of the kiss of peace, because this he had sworn, in the previous November at Montmartre, never to give. They then visited Thomas at Sens on 16 July to get his reactions and persuade him to attend a conference between Henry and Louis planned for Tuesday, 21 July on the frontier, in the rather featureless countryside between the border towns of La Ferté-Villeneuil (*Firmitas*) in La Beauce and Fréteval in Touraine. The archbishop expressed some reluctance to set off without a formal royal invitation; but William of Sens persuaded him to go in company with himself and the two commissioners. Meanwhile, as Henry travelled towards the frontier, he was met 5 kilometres from Falaise by his cousin, Roger, bishop of Worcester. Henry called him a traitor for not attending the coronation of his kinsman; Roger explained that the queen and the constable had detained him, but in any case he would not have taken part in the illegal ceremony; and they had a blazing 'family' row in public, the bishop giving at least as much as he received. When both had exhausted their complaints and taunts, they made friends again and discussed how to make peace with Thomas.[19]

We have three accounts of the conference at 'Fréteval' and its antecedents which can be attributed to Herbert of Bosham, the lengthy report of the archbishop to the pope in some 3,000 words, a less formal report to Rheims in the form of 'a friend to Master Ralf of Sarre', and the relatively short account in his *Vita*. William fitzStephen seems likewise to have been an eye-witness, from the other side, and his quite long narrative serves as a check on his former colleague's story.[20] The two kings met on the appointed day and, after settling their differences, particularly the insult to Margaret, parted without summoning Thomas to them. But, since there were present, as well as the papal commissioners, the archbishops of Rheims (Louis's brother), Sens and Tyre and almost all the Norman bishops, together with John of Poitiers and Roger of Worcester, the business had not been forgotten. William fitzStephen says that Henry quipped in public to Louis, 'Tomorrow your thief shall have his peace, and have it good.' 'What thief, for Heaven's sake?', Louis asked. 'Your archbishop of Canterbury,' Henry replied. To which Louis answered, 'I only wish he was ours. And if you really are going to grant him a good peace, I thank you.' The two kings then conferred in private. Louis had decided not to attend or be directly involved in the settlement. The royal clerk's explanation is that Louis had worked so energetically for Thomas in the past that he now wanted Henry to be seen to be acting entirely of his own free will.

The intermediaries then moved in and managed to get rid of the one obstacle that had wrecked an agreement at Montmartre. Henry swore that, in refusing to give a kiss of peace, he was laying no trap for Thomas and named the archbishop of Sens as security for his good faith. According to fitzStephen, who, however, supported by Guernes, puts the discussion after the reconciliation at the conference, Henry said, 'In my own land I will kiss his mouth, his hands and his feet a hundred times, and a hundred times I will hear his Mass. But not now. This is not in order to deceive him. But I ought to be granted just one indulgence. And in England (according to Guernes, at Tours) I will give of my own free will what here would only be done under compulsion.' Thomas accepted the refusal, perhaps on the assurance that it was only temporary. It was his one major concession and the price he had to pay for the agreement. Opinions differed on the cost of the surrender. He also agreed not to press at this time for the payment of damages to himself and the other exiles. For his part Henry consented to grant the exiles the full peace and entire restitution of property as defined in the form of peace.[21]

At dawn on Wednesday, 22 July, Henry and a large suite set off for the rendezvous between the towns of Fréteval and Viévy-le-Rayé, in the wooded country on the east bank of the Loir, a little to the south of Tuesday's meeting-place. They waited for the archbishop in a meadow, which at the time Herbert thought a most beautiful spot, but which much later he discovered was known to the locals as 'Traitors' Meadow'. When Thomas approached, with a party which included the archbishop of Sens and Theobald, count of Blois, Henry rode out to receive him, removed his hat, shook hands, embraced and greeted him warmly. At first the two had William of Sens with them, and in this phase Thomas complained 'mildly and modestly' or 'emotionally and strongly' of all the injuries done to him and his church, and Henry, without striking back, promised to make amends. They then dismissed the French archbishop and conferred together in private for most of the day, apparently sitting on their horses (Thomas, because of his hair breeches, shifting from one haunch to the other in great pain),[22] while their bored followers waited impatiently.

Among the details discussed, the most important was the coronation. In the report to the pope it is the major item. Henry was at first unrepentant and quoted historical precedents – York consecrating William I and Hereford (a mistake for London) Henry I. Thomas explained the special circumstances in each case. And when the king produced, and appealed to, the papal privilege he had obtained in June 1161,[23] the archbishop demolished that in turn. Thomas then said some words which caused more uneasiness later than, it seems, at the time: a coronation obtained by such means lacked validity; it was an execration rather than a coronation; Thomas did not want to degrade the young Henry or reduce his position in any way, for he always worked for his success and glory. But, if father and son wanted to be spared from the vengeance of the Canterbury saints, condign satisfaction would have to be made to the injured church.

In the end, Henry, quite lightly and perhaps slightly evasively, agreed to everything the archbishop demanded and said that he would treat those who had betrayed him and Thomas as traitors, and offered that Thomas could recrown the youth together with his wife. Guernes believed that he offered to put the young Henry and the kingdom in Thomas's charge when he went on a crusade, and that Thomas replied that he should rather entrust them to that faithful knight, Hugh of Beauchamp. Although this is a strange story to invent, the archbishop's interest in Hugh, lord of Eaton Socon in Bedfordshire and castellan of Rhuddlan, an illegitimate scion of a great baronial family, who actually died on crusade in 1187,[24] seems unlikely; and Thomas did not make jokes. William fitzStephen describes Henry's concession as agreeing to do whatever the pope should require from him on account of the coronation and to allow Thomas to make his complaints against York and the Canterbury bishops for the wrongs they had done him and his church. Herbert in his *Vita* claims that Thomas was granted permission to punish York and his own suffragan bishops for the coronation. Whatever was said, it was enough to satisfy Thomas. Overcome by a flood of relief and gratitude, he got off his horse and threw himself at Henry's feet. The king then dismounted in turn, and, holding the right stirrup, forced Thomas to get back into the saddle.

Thomas after his return to England in November repeatedly invoked this concession, and an hour or two before his death called on the leader of his murderers, Reginald fitzUrse, 'and the two hundred other knights who had been present' on 22 July, to testify to the truth of his claim. But Reginald denied that he and his companions were witnesses. After the murder, Theobald of Blois testified to the pope that he had been there when Henry had agreed to do justice to the archbishop in the matter of the coronation and allow him to punish the bishops for their part in it.[25]

Whatever ambiguities there may have been at Fréteval, this was the breakthrough. Henry, no less affected than Thomas, restored his old friendship, renounced all ill-will and, taking the archbishop over to the royalist bivouac, declared that they were reconciled and that he intended to be a most generous and kind lord. Thomas then returned to his party, so that the bishops could negotiate the settlement of all outstanding matters. Thomas was pressed to put all his demands, including those concerned with the evil customs, the losses of the church of Canterbury, of ecclesiastical liberty and of his own honour, as well as the usurped coronation, to the king's judgment. But, on the advice of the archbishop of Sens and his fellow-exiles, he refused. Instead, he asked through the archbishop that Henry should accept the terms of the often rehearsed form of peace, including the restoration of all Canterbury's possessions as described in the list furnished by Thomas, and also correct the injury done to Canterbury and him through the coronation of his son. In return, Thomas would render his love and honour and all the services which an archbishop could do to a king and ruler in the Lord. He also raised the highly controversial matter of the damages which Henry ought to pay him and his men for their loss of revenue (*ablata*). When Henry refused this last demand, on the grounds that Alexander had not ordered him to do so, Thomas agreed to defer, but not abandon, the claim. The rest Henry accepted; and on those terms firm peace was made and publicly declared.[26]

After Thomas had been restored to royal favour and his archbishopric, the other exiles (unfortunately not named, but certainly including Herbert of Bosham and John of Salisbury) went forward one by one, humbled themselves at Henry's feet and likewise were restored to the king's peace and their possessions. Herbert boasted, in his report to the pope, that from none of them had Henry required any kind of oath (as at Angers in April 1166).[27] Henry urged Thomas and his clerks to rejoin his court and travel with him for a time, both for the sake of recreation and to proclaim their renewed friendship, and promised to pay all their expenses. But Thomas said that he must first go back to France and Sens and make his grateful adieus to all those who had helped him. King and archbishop then conversed in private until Vespers (mid-afternoon). As they were about to disperse, Arnulf of Lisieux, on behalf of Geoffrey Ridel, asked Thomas to reciprocate by granting his pardon and favour to all those who had stood by the king. Thomas replied that it was not on a par. He had to distinguish various categories among the king's supporters. Those who had been excommunicated by papal authority could not be absolved without Alexander's assent. It would be contrary to law and justice to treat all his opponents in the same way. He would, however, do what he could. When Geoffrey Ridel replied angrily and scornfully to this – according to Guernes he exclaimed, 'If he hates me, I'll hate him; but if he chooses to love me, I'll love him' – Henry calmed it down, told Thomas to take no notice and asked for his blessing.[28] The meeting then broke up.

As Herbert's report to the pope triumphantly proclaimed, they had won a glorious victory. Henry had not so much as mumbled the customs that he used to claim so eagerly. The oaths they had so feared had not been demanded from any of them. All Canterbury's possessions, according to their own schedule, had been restored. It was a settlement which did honour to God and would also be, they hoped, of great advantage to the church. If only – and it was with this that Herbert opened the letter – if only they had been listened to at the very start of the quarrel, all the abuses of the tyrants against the liberty of the church would have been extirpated at once. They had known, and Alexander had only just now learnt the lesson, that stern measures alone were effective. Henry had bowed to the real threat of excommunication and interdict. Towards the end of the report some residuary worries were mentioned. There was still the matter of the damages which Henry ought to pay. If Alexander was to order him, with the sort of vigour he had used in his recent decisive letter, doubtless Henry would give way on this too – and it would be an excellent precedent to establish.[29]

The exiles were also taking precautions. They informed the pope that they were going to wait in France until the nuncios they were sending to England reported that all their confiscated possessions had been restored. They would not go back if even a single yard of the stolen land was retained. This would be a test of the king's sincerity. They did not doubt his good intentions, but feared his counsellors. They had just heard that the papal commissioners had empowered the bishop of Sées to go to England and absolve all those excommunicated by Thomas, but on what terms they did not know. If they had exceeded their powers, or Sées acted irregularly, it was imperative that Alexander should order that the sentences must stand until all the conditions imposed by the pope had been fulfilled. Thomas asked for this not in a mood of vengeance but because the law ought to be observed and the guilty punished. This matter is treated at some length. Finally, the archbishop begged Alexander to listen carefully to his courier and take vengeance on all those who had injured Canterbury through the coronation. Letters which went at the same time to Thomas's friends at the curia reiterate some of the archbishop's suspicions both of the king and of the pope. The messenger who carried this large batch of letters to the curia was Gunter of Winchester.[30]

It will be apparent from the contents of these letters that the chances of a real peace were slim. Both Thomas's best and worst qualities worked in the same direction. His refusal to rejoin the king's court, although the reasons did him credit, was a great mistake, for it encouraged the rapid dissipation of all the emotions and goodwill aroused at Fréteval. And, if there was some insincerity on Henry's part, on Thomas's there was to be no magnanimity in victory. No claim was abandoned. He would fight to the death for each and every right that the church and archbishop of Canterbury had ever possessed or claimed. The demand for revenge was loud and clear. In retrospect, Herbert of Bosham regarded the famous victory as a sham. Thomas had deliberately, with his eyes fully open, dispensed with the kiss of peace because he wanted peace and had conquered his fear of death. He had known what sort of peace he was buying. The clerk, even if he exaggerates, indicates another factor which contributed to its failure.[31]

After Fréteval Thomas had two main immediate interests: the recovery of his and his men's possessions in England and the results of his missions to the pope. The former could be pursued while waiting for the latter, for Alexander's reaction to the coronation could not be expected to reach northern France before late in September and to the peace and Thomas's renewed declaration of war on the bishops before early in November. (In fact both sets took about a month longer.) Thomas had, therefore, at least two or three months in which to clear up all problems concerned with his return to Canterbury. And, *pace* Herbert of Bosham, he was by no means uninterested in securing guarantees of his personal safety once he had left his haven in France.

Henry, from Cloyes-sur-le-Loir, 12 kilometres north of Fréteval, issued writs to his justiciars and bishops in England announcing the peace and restoration of property and ordering both to be implemented. But on the strength of these the proctors of the exiles obtained only a temporary recovery of part of their property, and at the end of the financial year (Michaelmas, 29 September) royal officials collected all the archiepiscopal revenues. This was considered in England a sign that peace was still a long way off.[32] Meanwhile Thomas attempted to monitor progress through John of Salisbury and Herbert of Bosham. The two clerks were to go first to the king in Normandy, spy out who were the archbishop's enemies, open or covert, and who his friends at court, and see to the restoration of his possessions, especially those which had been in dispute, namely the fee of William of Ros, Saltwood (formerly held by Henry of Essex of the archbishop) and the custody of Rochester castle. If Henry was prepared to carry out his promise in respect of these, they were to continue their journey to Kent, otherwise return immediately to Sens.

The mission started badly, for about the middle of August they found Henry near Domfront so ill with fever that, in expectation of death, he had divided up his lands between his three eldest sons and put his youngest, John, in the custody of the eldest. He also expressed the wish to be buried at Grandmont, near St Léonard in La Marche, and said that he had a charter from the monks promising this. His barons, however, strongly objected to the idea – it was contrary to the dignity of the kingdom – and the acrimonious dispute was resolved only by the king's recovery. Thomas's business was delayed first by the king's incapacity then by his 'usual' procrastination; and in the end Henry dismissed the clerks empty-handed, saying to John, 'I won't give you a single town, my dear John, until I find that you are behaving somewhat better towards me than you have done in the past.' So they returned to Sens, and Thomas was most upset. Henry then went on a pilgrimage to the famous and spectacular shrine of St Mary at Rocamadour in Quercy in the duchy of Aquitaine to give thanks for his recovery.

As a result, after the one-day meeting on 22 July Thomas did not see Henry again for two or three months. Instead, as he had announced, he visited the French king. On 4 September he was received at the abbey of St Victor at Paris and preached to the brethren in the chapter house on the text, 'His place is made in peace' (Ps. 75: 3, Vulgate text). But what he had to say on this theme was not recorded.[33]

It was probably towards the end of September that he rejoined the king, possibly uninvited, in the Loire valley, where Henry had gone in order to confer with Theobald, count of Blois.[34] For Thomas this was a move of some importance. It was the first time he had ventured into Angevin territory, and he may have thought that a kiss of peace from the ruler was obligatory and had perhaps been promised. But their first meeting at Tours was decidedly cool. Henry did not visit Thomas in his lodgings that evening, and, although William fitzStephen says that a kiss was neither requested nor bestowed, there can be no doubt that the next morning Henry, on the advice of the hated Nigel de Sacquenville, the keeper of his seal, avoided exchanging a kiss at the customary early Mass by ordering that it should be the office for the Dead (Requiem).

Henry then left abruptly for the meeting with Theobald at Amboise, 25 kilometres upstream from Tours and 35 kilometres from Blois. Thomas caught him up at Montlouis and they had a fierce quarrel, each taunting the other with ingratitude. After the conference, which had been delayed by the bickering, Thomas complained of Henry's broken promises over the restoration of his property and demanded 'bitterly and peremptorily' that everything should be released to him. He referred to the king's speciousness and deceit. The count of Blois intervened and Henry, either on the spot or at Chaumont a little later, once again made many promises and urged Thomas to return to his see. They would meet again at Rouen, when the king would satisfy all his creditors and settle all his other financial claims, give him the kiss of peace and either conduct him in person to England or substitute the archbishop of Rouen. He or Rotrou would then complete the restoration of property to Thomas and his men, should anything remain to be done.

A few days later Thomas visited Henry at Chaumont-sur-Loire, halfway between Amboise and Blois, simply as a friendly gesture, and Henry responded eagerly. They had an amicable meeting, and, according to John of Salisbury, it was agreed that Thomas should leave Sens on 1 November. But on the way back the archbishop told Herbert of Bosham that Henry had said, 'Why don't you do what I want you to do, for, if you would, I'd entrust everything to you.' Then he added the ominous comment, 'And I was reminded of the words of the Gospel, "All these things will I give thee, if thou wilt fall down and worship me."' (Matt. 4: 9). According to William fitzStephen the last words the two men exchanged were: Henry, 'Go in peace. I will follow and meet you as soon as I can either at Rouen or in England.' Thomas, 'Something tells me, my lord, as I leave you on these terms, that I shall never see you again in this life.' Henry, 'Do you take me for a traitor?' Thomas, 'Heaven forbid, my lord.'

When Henry reached his great fortress of Chinon, on the Vienne, a tributary of the Loire, he wrote to his royal son, announcing that, since Thomas had made peace with him on satisfactory terms, the archbishop and his men were to have the royal peace and were to be restored to all the possessions they had had three months before Thomas had left England. As regards Saltwood (which Thomas had not held at that date), he was to recover that part of the honour which a jury of the better and more senior knights should declare had formerly pertained to the archiepiscopal fief. The writ was attested by Rotrou of Rouen and marked the conclusion of the peace negotiations conducted by the papal commissioners. John of Salisbury announced this new settlement and the probable date of Thomas's return to Canterbury (after 1 November) to the monks of Christ Church. They should begin to make preparations to welcome him and in the meantime send a belated gift of money.[35] In many ways it was at Amboise and Chaumont, rather than Fréteval, that firm peace was made.

Thomas's agents reported back after their meeting with the young king at Westminster on 5 October.[36] Their news was most discouraging. They had failed to recruit any helpers *en route* except for Robert, sacrist of Canterbury, and two others, and were generally shunned. One whom they had found unco-operative was Thomas's steward, William fitzNeal, who was to play an equivocal role at the martyrdom. The new king had received them in the presence of his great-uncle, Reginald, earl of Cornwall, Geoffrey Ridel, Richard of Ilchester and others of his council, and had replied through Geoffrey that his father's mandate of restitution could not be implemented on the spot because the archbishopric was in the hands of Ranulf de Broc and his servants. They were to return to court on 15 October, when it was hoped the business could proceed. The agents thought that the young king himself was not unfriendly, but his advisers were hostile. They had discovered some secret friends and believed that many would welcome the archbishop back. But there was general pessimism about the implementation of the peace. Some of their contacts advised the archbishop to go most carefully with the senior king until he had re-established real confidence and completely regained his favour. There also were some most sinister developments. The young king had immediately made a report to his father, who had sent Walter de Lisle to England to summon to the royal court in Normandy the archbishop of York and the bishops of London and

Salisbury, together with four or six representatives of each of the vacant bishoprics, in order to make elections to those sees. And the bishops-elect were to be sent to the pope for consecration, to the detriment of the church of Canterbury. Gilbert Foliot, however, had been staying for some time at Beverley Minster in Yorkshire on pretext of a pilgrimage. Other 'abominations' the messenger would impart verbally. On no account was Thomas to return to England unless he was confident that he was genuinely restored to Henry's favour.

One of the 'abominations' was that Ranulf de Broc was using the delay to strip the archiepiscopal estates of all their stores and stockpile them in Saltwood castle. The weather remained very warm and the harvest had presumably been good. Thomas wrote to Henry to complain of the spoliation and urged him to intervene and expedite the restoration. He feared he would have nothing to live on if there was much more delay. 'But,' he concluded, 'whether we live or die, we are and shall always be yours in the Lord; and, whatever may befall us and ours, may God bless you and your children.' It is clear that Thomas had decided to return, come what may.[37]

It was rather later, perhaps towards the end of October, that the papal letters concerning the coronation eventually arrived in northern France.[38] In mandates dated 16 September, one addressed to the bishops of London, Salisbury, Exeter, Chester, Rochester, St Asaph and Llandaff, and the other to the archbishop of York and the bishop of Durham, the prelates were blamed for a whole series of offences against Thomas and his church. Particularly they had sworn to observe, and indeed had observed, the wicked Constitutions of Clarendon, refused the archbishop help in his struggle against them, taken part in the coronation and substituted in the ceremony an oath to observe the evil customs. As punishment all were suspended from their episcopal dignities and London and Salisbury were to relapse into excommunication. The bishop of Rochester and the archdeacon of Canterbury (Geoffrey Ridel), since they were Thomas's vicars, were in addition to be punished by him, *appellatione remota*. Certain clerks of Earl Hugh of Norfolk also were to be anathematized. In the letter to York and Durham Alexander wrote that it was the cowardice of the bench of bishops which upset him even more than the king's violence.

These punitive measures were dispatched to the archbishop of Rouen, the papal commissioner, for service on the culprits. He was also to investigate whether the bishops of Bayeux and Sées had attended the coronation – if so, Alexander would punish them too. Thomas was informed of the papal sentences and given additional authority not only in respect of Rochester and the archdeacon (whose excommunication Alexander confirmed) but also in the cases of Geoffrey Ridel's vicar, Robert, Godfrey, bishop of St

Asaph, and his archdeacon David. In a separate rescript Alexander declared that the irregular coronation by York should in no way prejudice Canterbury's privileges by creating a precedent. Cardinal Humbald, in an accompanying letter, informed Thomas that, when the pope had consulted the cardinals, he found more for the archbishop than against. Humbald had advised that York should be deposed and his accomplices (the suffragan bishops) excommunicated. No less welcome to Thomas was the news that the cardinal had sent, via the archbishop of Bourges, a present of 7 marks of silver and 45 maravedis (Spanish gold coins).

In June, when Thomas had impetrated these letters, he had asked the papal notary Gratian, the commissioner in 1169, to make sure that all the more important letters sent to the king were entered in the papal register, for they would be important legal precedents. By the time the papal letters arrived the political situation had completely changed. Thomas was committed to return to England and was engaged in delicate negotiations whose success depended on his maintaining and, if possible, strengthening royal favour. He knew that the charge he had made that the coronation oath had been perverted was untrue. And the general tenor of the letters, harping as they did on the Constitutions of Clarendon, which Henry had renounced, was not only misguided and inappropriate, but also provocative, indeed explosive. He could not possibly use such letters, and wrote to Alexander begging for another set.[39]

He explained to the pope that the struggle to get the peace, as promised at Fréteval, fulfilled to the last jot and tittle was proving difficult. Henry had promised that, if he were patient and earned it by his devotion, he would get everything. Thomas doubted this and enclosed the report from his proctors in England. But, as advised by the pope and cardinals, he was being as patient and tolerant as he could during this period of 'shadowy concord'. Moreover, the letters of censure on the bishops that he had just received, with their references to the royal enormities (*excessus*), although justified, when they came to the king's ears would certainly destroy any chance of peace. He therefore required a new set which omitted all references to royal abuses, the enormity of the oath to observe the customs, the wicked customs themselves, and the imperfect coronation oath. They should inflict the same sentences, but simply on the grounds that the archbishop of York had presumed, while Thomas was in exile for the sake of the justice and liberty of the church, to carry out the coronation within Thomas's province, when it was common knowledge that the church of Canterbury had possessed the right for many years and should not be deprived of it without the judgment of a court.

He would also like Alexander to write affectionately to Henry, explaining why the sentences were necessary, and, while sparing the king as much as possible, stress the enormities (*excessus*) of the priests (i.e. the suffragan bishops). The excommunication or suspension of the bishops would certainly upset the peace and he would like the pope to leave everything he possibly could to his judgment, only excepting, if he should so wish, the archbishop of York, who was the ringleader. And he would like to be able to show mercy to the bishop of London, although he was the standard-bearer of the whole sedition, not to say schism, and also to the bishop of Salisbury, if they could not be punished without provoking a renewal of the schism.

On the advice of King Louis, whom the pope had asked him to consult, he would like the papal chancery to issue three separate letters: the first suspending York, without including any matter offensive to the king; the second excommunicating the bishops of London and Salisbury; and the third suspending all the bishops. This would allow him the maximum flexibility and discretion: he could serve or withhold any of them according to the circumstances. He would also like Alexander to send a mandate to the bishop of Meaux and the abbot of St Crispin at Soissons, authorizing them to order the king to restore all the possessions of the church of Canterbury and repay all Thomas's losses under threat of anathema on him and his land. And should this be ineffective, he would like for himself as much, or even greater, power and authority as was granted to the archbishop of Rouen and the bishop of Nevers to enforce the peace treaty. He would also like the pope to increase York's punishment for his disobedience by reintegrating the English church and ordering him to submit to Thomas's primacy. All these measures, Thomas explained, were not for his personal glory but in order to secure firm and lasting peace in the English church. He believed that he would in fact return to England, but whether it would be to peace or to punishment he could not say. His fate was in the hands of God. He thanked the pope (rather perfunctorily) for the help he had given him. And he added, clearly as an afterthought, that the bishop of Exeter was completely innocent as regards the coronation.

This is an exceptionally realistic letter. Thomas was re-entering the world of practical politics. His draft of the papal letter to Henry, in which clerical enormities were to be stressed, seems almost unprincipled. The moderate terms in which he stated Canterbury's right to crown the kings is noticeable. There is no reason to think that he was abandoning his intention to punish the bishops, and as severely as he could – he even tried again for an effective primacy over York – but he did not intend to jeopardize his return to Canterbury. As the new papal letters would not be available before the end of December at the earliest (they were in fact issued at Frascati on 24 November), he would have to bide his time.

He had also to prepare for his return to England. He took leave of the many friends he had made in the kingdom of France and thanked them for their support. And by some of the nobles he was re-equipped, particularly with clothes and horses, so that his party could make an honourable show. Herbert of Bosham thought that the archbishop returned with a retinue of over a hundred horsemen. Although they had sometimes been poor, Thomas, Herbert exclaimed admiringly, was always magnificent (*magnus*): magnificent in the palace, magnificent at the altar, magnificent in hall, magnificent in church, magnificent in exile, magnificent in his return and especially magnificent at journey's end. Herbert, looking back from afar, saw more than a sense of theatre in his actor; he was conscious of an innate and constant greatness.[40]

Thomas had need to keep his spirits up in October and November 1170, for nothing was going particularly well: indeed, as he moved towards his restoration, the peace collapsed around him. The archbishopric was still in the king's hands, and it was believed that the custodian, Ranulf de Broc, and his officials were still plundering it by selling off the stock, woods and corn. Towards the end of October Thomas finally left Sens to rejoin Henry at Rouen, as they had agreed. He said grimly to Louis, possibly early in September, 'We are going to England to "play at heads".' 'So it seems,' Louis answered. 'And if you were to take my advice, you wouldn't entrust yourself to Henry before you got his kiss of peace. You can stay with us, and as long as I'm alive you shall not lack wine and food and French abundance.' But Thomas only said, 'Let God's will be done.' He also told the bishop of Paris that he was returning to England to die. Although only his gloomier remarks were remembered after the event, it is likely that he was becoming increasingly apprehensive.[41]

At Rouen he was met by John of Oxford, whom he particularly disliked and considered excommunicate, carrying a letter from the king. Henry, writing from Loches in Touraine, excused himself for not having kept the appointment. He had to meet Louis's military threat to Auvergne. The dean of Salisbury would conduct him to England and inform the young king that he was to have the full restoration of his property. Henry and his son had heard that Thomas was dragging his feet. He trusted the rumours were untrue and that Thomas would cross to England without delay. This was bad news indeed. There was to be no kiss of peace and no money for the archbishop's creditors who had accompanied him to Rouen; the archbishop of Rouen had not been ordered to take him to the kingdom. Rotrou tried to allay Thomas's fears and gave him £300 of his own money. But most of his debts were never paid. Louis was proving difficult in the Berry-Auvergne area and Henry did travel to confront him; but the situation was not serious, and he could have gone to Rouen had he wished. He obviously had no intention of conducting Thomas to Canterbury (it was simply another of his rash promises), and Rotrou may not have particularly wanted to go in his place. The choice of John of Oxford was probably deliberately insulting. Thomas is supposed to have exclaimed, 'How things change! Once upon a time it would have been for the archbishop of Canterbury to provide you with a safe conduct to England – and one a little safer than you can offer him.'[42]

Rouen was effectively the point of no return, and Thomas lingered there or thereabouts perhaps for a fortnight. It had been agreed – John of Oxford may have carried the news – that the archbishopric would be handed over to his agents at Martinmas (11 November), and Thomas wanted to hear that it had actually happened.[43] He had also to decide what he was going to do about those whom he had excommunicated in the course of 1169, those who had communicated with men under the ban and the bishops whom he intended to punish. The papal commissioners had been empowered by Alexander on 19 January to absolve on certain conditions all those anathematized, should a peace treaty be made. But after Fréteval Thomas had declined to annul his sentences, and, although, according to Anonymous II, the commissioners had absolved all royal courtiers present at the conference, and Thomas had heard a rumour that they had sent the bishop of Sées to England to absolve all the repentant delinquents there, the situation in November was by no means cut and dried. Certainly the bishops of London and Salisbury had been absolved by papal authority; but few of those involved in the administration of the escheated archbishopric had surrendered their 'illegal' possessions, made amends or paid damages, and therefore, as notoriously unrepentant sinners, were undoubtedly still under the ban or had forfeited their absolution. On 9 October Alexander from Anagni informed the commissioners that this was so, unless the culprits made complete amends within twenty days of being warned by Thomas so to do.[44]

On 15 November Thomas sent John of Salisbury to England. He was to represent him at a synod to be held at Canterbury on the 18th at which those laymen and clergy who had incurred excommunication by contagion would be absolved. John delegated to a senior monk, Thomas of Maidstone, the absolution of his contaminated brethren. By thus cleansing all those who had been forced to do business with Ranulf de Broc and Geoffrey Ridel and their subordinates, Thomas's return was made socially possible. But John discovered that the lands had been stripped of their moveables and the farms of their buildings, that the churches were still occupied by intruders (the most important being Geoffrey Ridel at Otford and Nigel de Sacquenville at Harrow), that rents due at Christmas had been collected in advance and that nothing had been done about Saltwood. Even worse, three days before his arrival, that is to say a day or two after Martinmas, Ranulf de Broc's men had expelled Thomas's proctors and taken the estates back into royal custody. There was, John reported, general confusion and despondency. He had gone to visit the young king, possibly to protest, and was, as he put it, received tolerably well. He then went off, either to Salisbury or Exeter, to see his old mother who had been ill for some time.[45]

The Exchequer accounts tell a rather different story. At Michaelmas 1170 Ranulf de Broc accounted for the farm for the whole year, £1560 5s. 5d. And at Michaelmas 1171 two new custodians, John Mauduit and Thurstin fitzSimon, accounted for three-quarters of the year, £1172 1s. 7d. In other words, the Exchequer affected to believe that Ranulf had handed over to the archbishop's agents at Michaelmas 1170 and that Thomas then enjoyed the revenues, assessed at some £400, until his death three months later, when the fief reverted to royal custody. The official figures simply ignore how difficult it had been in October to prise the estates out of Ranulf's hands.[46]

Although Thomas had been warned, and was to receive many more warnings, it is doubtful whether he fully realized how fierce and widespread was the opposition to his return to England. His restoration would upset long-standing arrangements in Kent. There would be a new territorial revolution and a new set of losers. The monks of Christ Church, under their 'illegal' prior, had been disobedient and were aware that they would be punished. There were numerous collaborators with the 'unlawful' régime who would be discarded by the in-comers. The archbishop of York and the bishops involved in the coronation had learned by this time of the papal letters of censure, and York, London and Salisbury were especially bitter and dangerous. According to John of Salisbury, they had petitioned Henry not to allow Thomas to return unless he renounced his papal legation, surrendered all the papal letters he carried and swore to observe the laws of the realm. Otherwise he would inflict damage and shame on the kingdom. It was remarked in London circles that Thomas was employing the title and dignity of Legate of the Holy See without the king's consent, contrary to English custom.[47]

The young king and his advisers had, therefore, some cause to fear disorder; and they also suspected that Thomas might invalidate the coronation and bring the lawfulness of the government into question. The senior king was in Berry, keeping clear of the whole business, seemingly indifferent to its course and outcome. John of Salisbury and other archiepiscopal agents had found some well-wishers in Kent. But on the whole they were the smaller men who had suffered from the depredations of Ranulf de Broc. For the moment they could do little for the archbishop. Their time would come.

What probably decided Thomas to return was the arrival of his clerk Gunter with a batch of letters from the curia in reply to his announcement of the peace at Fréteval. The papal letters were dated at Anagni and Segni, not far from Rome, 8–13 October, and were accompanied by letters from at least five cardinals to whom Thomas had also written.[48] The principal letter, conveying Alexander's rejoicing at the settlement and his instructions to proceed to England and Canterbury, was not preserved, presumably because of features which, after the tragedy, were best forgotten. He probably declined to grant all of Thomas's requests, he may have advised doing without the kiss of peace, and undoubtedly, like the cardinals, he would have counselled mercy and patience. Thomas would destroy the hard-won peace if he did not act with restraint. The pope's letter to Henry was characteristically moderate and conciliatory in tone. All he asked was that the king, for the remission of his sins, should make full reparations to Thomas, leave to him and other prelates control over churches, in future pay no attention to advisers who had been hostile to the archbishop and correct the irregularities in the coronation oath of the young king.[49]

At the same time Alexander provided his local subordinates, Rouen and Nevers with respect to Normandy, Sens and Rouen with respect to the rest of Henry's Continental lands, and Thomas, whose legation in England was confirmed, with everything necessary to safeguard the terms which had been agreed at Fréteval. Any short measure could lead to interdicts covering the whole of his empire and the excommunication of all delinquents except for the royal family. Clergy who disregarded the interdict should be arrested and imprisoned for life in a monastery. Alexander also gave notice, and named Geoffrey Ridel, that all detainers of archiepiscopal property had lapsed into excommunication.

Thomas must have felt that his position was fully protected. The confirmation of his legatine powers must have given him the greatest pleasure. His enemies could be punished severely. There were, however, two complications. His well-wishers at the papal court had begged him not to revenge but to pardon. He should be merciful in victory. And the only papal letters he possessed which passed sentence on York, London, Salisbury and the other participants in the coronation were provocative in the extreme. A month ago he had considered their use impossible. Unless he was prepared to offer the other cheek – and with Thomas this was unthinkable – he had his difficulties. But, he may have thought, the circumstances had changed; for once the pope seemed resolute; and his influence in the curia was undoubtedly increasing. Cardinal Theodwin had just sent him a length of green samite which the bearer, presumably Gunter, had personally chosen out of several pieces of silk. Green, which signifies *fides*, was, as we know, also Herbert of Bosham's favourite colour. Thomas probably brushed all difficulties aside. He would take things as they came.

Accordingly, fortified by two portfolios of papal letters, or, more likely, copies, he travelled north with John of Oxford into the county of Boulogne. From St Bertin's abbey at St-Omer he was conducted to Guines by Peter, abbot of Ardres, representing Baldwin, the new count of Guines, whom Thomas, when chancellor, had knighted. And the count now repaid the debt by entertaining the archbishop and his military retinue in the castle. Thomas could not spare the time to visit Peter's abbey, but next morning took the advice of the count's chaplain before hastening to complete the 15-kilometre journey to the port of Wissant.

While he and his household waited there for ships and a favourable wind, they received the latest news and rumours out of England. It was all bad. Moreover, the count of Boulogne, Matthew, whose marriage to the heiress, the abbess of Romsey, Thomas had once opposed, sent a messenger to warn him that all the English ports were guarded and that he would be in danger if he crossed. The archbishop answered that he was determined to press on; and William of Canterbury records his remark that he was not returning empty-handed: indeed, owing to the uncertainties, he was forced to take with him the *Bibliotheca* which he had intended leaving for the time being on the Continent. And with this in his baggage, his return, in order to be buried at Canterbury, should be far more welcome than in the past, when his merits had done little to recommend him. *Bibliotheca*, although normally to be understood as a full edition of the Bible, in this context probably means the whole library he had collected while in exile. He must have meant that the monks would at last recognize that he was now a changed man, a scholar and a 'master of the sacred page'.[50]

The most alarming feature of the intelligence reports was that opposition to Thomas's return was being organized by the archbishop of York and the bishops of London and Salisbury in alliance with the sheriff of Kent, Gervase of Cornhill, Ranulf de Broc and a royal justiciar, Reginald of Warenne, the younger brother of the earl of Surrey. Thomas knew that these would certainly arrest him and search for papal letters. He told the pope that they had intended to cut off his head. Robert, sacrist of Christ Church, who had joined Thomas at Wissant, was, on the way back, arrested at Dover and, because he did not hold a royal passport, expelled. This may have sparked the explosion. But the main reason why the archbishop imposed the papal sentences on the three prelates, to the fierce resentment of the victims and the dismay of moderate opinion, was probably the news that the bishops had with them at Dover the electors to the vacant bishoprics, whom they were to convey to the royal court.[51] If, as was indeed the case in 1173, Henry intended that promotion to the bench was to be the reward to his main clerical agents against Thomas, John of Oxford, Richard of Ilchester, Geoffrey Ridel and Reginald of Salisbury, Thomas's action is understandable and was hardly preventable. But it added even more fuel to the fire, for the frustrated clerks hated him all the more.

Towards the end of November, probably on the 29th, Advent Sunday, Thomas sent his baggage over, presumably as a diversion, while he dispatched separately, by a servant named Osbern, the papal letters imposing sentences on York and the two bishops. The youth eluded the watch, served the letters personally on the three in the church of St Peter at Dover, and disappeared before he could be taken and killed. When news arrived of this success, probably on the next day, Thomas, Herbert of Bosham says, rejoiced mightily, for 'the righteous shall rejoice when he seeth the vengeance' (Ps. 58: 10). The verse concludes: 'He shall wash his feet in the blood of the wicked.' But, as it happened, the archbishop had sealed his own death warrant.[52]

Thomas and some of his clerks (the cautious John of Salisbury was still in England) had, with their eyes wide open, exposed themselves to great danger. Herbert of Bosham was informed privately, by the pilot of the ship who had brought the news, of the consternation which had been caused by the serving of the letters, of the outrage provoked by such a hostile action at the beginning of Advent (29 November) and of the likelihood that they would be seized at Dover, where their enemies were assembled. Herbert informed Thomas; and Gunter, when he joined them, advised their master to wait until the storm of protest had subsided. Thomas then asked Herbert for his opinion. This fiery clerk thought that they had a straight choice between a shameful return into exile and advancing boldly and acting with courage. They should not repeat their ignominious flight from the enemy at Northampton. That might have been excusable; this could never be. They were now soldiers hardened in battle, proven like gold in the furnace (Wisd. 3: 6). They should accept the dangers, enter the kingdom, fight and conquer. Thomas agreed, and told Gunter so.[53]

Perhaps that same Monday night, 30 November, they embarked and set sail for Sandwich, an episcopal manor where they might escape the guards and the indignant bishops and find friends. After a calm passage they landed unopposed. The archbishop's cross had been raised in the prow as the ship came into harbour, and a crowd of poor people acclaimed his coming and prostrated themselves for his blessing. It was probably Tuesday, 1 December.[54] Thomas had been in exile for six years and one month. He was three weeks away from his fiftieth birthday and four weeks from his death.

CHAPTER ELEVEN

THE END OF THE ROAD

Hardly had Thomas and his company disembarked at Sandwich when the three principal royal officers in Kent, alerted at dawn, rode up in command of troops who were mailed and armed under their cloaks and tunics. John of Oxford confronted them bravely (Thomas generously informed the pope of his services), and only when they disarmed would he allow Gervase of Cornhill, the sheriff, Ranulf de Broc, the custodian of the archbishopric, and Reginald of Warenne to have an interview with his charge. Thomas did not rise to greet them, an offensive but understandable gesture, and firmly resisted their demand to investigate his company. His refusal, on principle, to allow one alien in his suite, Simon archdeacon of Sens (another not mentioned here was Henry of Auxerre), to take an oath of fealty to the king, as required under the blockade regulations, provoked angry words from the officials about his conduct in general. Gervase complained that, instead of peace, he had brought fire and sword into the kingdom, that he wanted to un-crown the new king and had punished all the bishops only for doing their duty to the monarch. Unless he was more careful, something would happen that had better not. Thomas answered that he was not cancelling the illegal coronation but simply punishing the bishops for having performed it contrary to God and the dignity of Canterbury. And when he added that the senior king had authorized the punishment, they quietened down a little, although they continued to demand that he should absolve the prelates. He explained that the sentences were the pope's, not his, and that he had no authority in the case. When pressed further, he offered to consider the matter and give an answer on the following day at Canterbury.[1]

It seems that the party, exhausted by the night crossing and the frightening encounter with the royal officials, spent the rest of the day and the night at Sandwich. This would also allow the news to be carried to Canterbury and preparations for the archbishop's reception to be made. The 12-mile ride on the following morning must have raised the spirits of the returning exiles, for in each village they were met with a festive procession led by the priest and were given an enthusiastic welcome. After the new-fangled angel on the steeple and the gilt cockerel weather-vanes on the new towers came into sight, they passed the ancient suburban church of St Martin and St Augustine's abbey and were greeted at Burgate by a procession of chanting Christ Church monks. Thomas took off his boots and finished the journey on foot while the bells pealed joyfully and the cathedral organ sounded in triumph. On entering the monastery he prostrated himself and then saluted each monk in turn with a kiss of peace. Finally, in the chapter house, he preached on the text, 'For here we have no abiding city, but we seek one to come' (Heb. 13: 14). Herbert of Bosham remembered that the arch-bishop's face lit up and took on a rosy hue as he re-entered his see. It was, the clerk thought – and he told Thomas so – a day of triumph for the church and for Jesus Christ, thanks to him.[2]

But Thomas had agreed to answer the royal officials that day at Canter-bury; and they arrived, presumably in the afternoon, accompanied by clerks instructed by the archbishop of York and the bishops of London and Salis-bury. Master David of London represented Gilbert Foliot. The meeting is well reported. The clerks notified the archbishop that the three bishops had appealed to the pope against the sentences recently imposed upon them. Thomas replied that the appeals, since precluded by the pope, were ineffec-tive. They then asked that he should withdraw the sentences as they were contrary to the peace made at Fréteval. The royal officials added that they were also contrary to the customs of the realm (the Constitutions of Claren-don) and in contempt of the king. All promised that, if the prelates under sentence were absolved, the whole bench of bishops of the province would come to the archbishop and freely submit to his authority, saving the honour of the kingdom (the new royalist catch-phrase). Thomas replied, as at Sand-wich, that the sentences were the pope's and he had no power to intervene. William fitzStephen, in his account of the proceedings, comments that the archbishop was put in a quandary, because, if he confessed that he had no power of release, his papal legation would be seen to be worthless; but, if he admitted that he had the power of absolution, he exposed himself to secular pressure and violence. The episcopal clerks put the further points that the initiative had come not from the pope but from the archbishop and that surely he could withdraw what he had instigated; also that the sentences had been obtained by misrepresentation, and no doubt they meant, although the reporters do not spell it out, by the false charge that the bishops had made the new king swear at his coronation to observe the Constitutions of Clarendon. Thomas seems to have parried both these points by indicating that Alexander was simply punishing sinners and avenging insults to the church and archbishop of Canterbury. He also reiterated that at Fréteval Henry had agreed that the bishops could be punished for their usurpation.

At some point he so blamed Master David for having accepted from the king a benefice worth £20 in the vacant diocese of Lincoln that the clerk, on reaching the royal court with his master, persuaded Henry to substitute a fief on the royal demesne.

The episcopal clerks had skilfully probed such weaknesses as there were in the archbishop's position; and when the royal officials weighed in with predictions of what enormities the king might commit if no relief were offered and what disturbances and hostilities there might be in the kingdom, Thomas gave way a little. He would consider giving conditional absolution to those censured. If they would show repentance and promise satisfaction and take the necessary oath that they would stand to the pope's judgment in the case and obey his commands, he would consider being merciful and risking the pope's displeasure. He would consult Henry of Winchester and other blameless bishops on the matter. When the offer was transmitted to the three petitioners, Roger of York replied that it was contrary to the dignity of the king and the customs of the kingdom for bishops to take such an oath without the king's consent (Constitutions of Clarendon, clause 5). But when Thomas stood firm and pointed out that two of them had accepted the condition at the beginning of the year in respect of his earlier sentences, it was rumoured that those two were inclined to submit on the terms offered. They were, however, it was said, dissuaded by York. He had £8,000 in his treasury to finance their fight and he had the king and the pope in his pocket. They should all stand together and go to the senior king, who had always protected them in the past, and complain about Thomas. They should also inform the young king that Thomas intended to depose him.[3]

This rumour, current in Canterbury circles and intended to defame the archbishop of York, is not to be trusted. The two bishops believed passionately that the new sentences were both unjust and inhumane, besides being unwise, and that they should be absolved unconditionally. Sympathy for them was widespread. Even a few of the biographers, particularly the Anonymous 'of Lambeth' (II), report the divided opinions in the country. Some men said that Thomas was a just man of great courage and judgment, while others said, 'No! He deceives himself and acts rashly.' Moreover, the attempt to put all the blame on York hides the probability that Gilbert Foliot remained the leader of the opposition. The diplomatic offensive at the curia was again entrusted to Master David of London.[4]

Before the three prelates made their way to Normandy they had a meeting in Kent with the two archdeacons, Geoffrey Ridel and Richard of Ilchester, who were in transit between the two royal courts and who decided, or were persuaded, to return to the new king in order to give him all the latest news and then cross from Southampton. Their failure to visit Thomas was considered sinister by the archbishop's household. Thomas remained for about a week at Canterbury, engaged, we are told, in devotional exercises and dispensing justice. Either in October, or at this time, he brought the long-running and most vexatious case of the earl of Norfolk and the canons of Pentney to an end. He congratulated the earl on his submission and made provision for the conditional absolution of his chaplains. And in this week he wrote to the pope the last of his letters to have been preserved, in which he recounted some of the events since Fréteval, denounced his opponents and justified his recent behaviour. It was Gunter of Winchester whom he sent off once more to Frascati, by way of Sens, where the clerk was overtaken by news of his master's death.[5]

Thomas also decided to pay his respects to the new king and use the occasion for a visitation of his diocese. He sent ahead to announce his arrival and explain his behaviour an old friend from the days in Theobald's household, Richard, prior of Dover, who was to be his successor as archbishop. Richard, although *persona grata* for having entertained both Henry's mother and sister in his priory, had a cool reception at Winchester. The new king's guardians, officials and courtiers were mostly fiercely hostile to the archbishop, and, whereas Thomas and his agents were anxious to get the ear of the fifteen-year-old Henry, who had, of course, been in the archbishop's household, the guardians reduced access to the minimum. Also assembled there were the electors to the vacant bishoprics, perhaps about to be conducted to Normandy by the two archdeacons. Richard answered the guardians' charges and reproaches as best he could; but when he was finally allowed an audience with the king, although the boy's great-uncle, Reginald of Cornwall, thought that Thomas's visit should be allowed, Geoffrey Ridel said, 'I know the king's wishes: he would never want his son to receive the man who is undoubtedly trying to disinherit him.' In the end Richard was dismissed and told that a reply would be sent by a royal servant.[6]

Meanwhile, probably on 8 or 9 December, Thomas set off for Winchester, by way of London, and took with him, as 'first-fruits for his new lord', three magnificent warhorses wonderfully caparisoned, which fitzStephen, who rejoined the archbishop's household about this time, describes in loving detail. On the second day of his expedition he was received at Rochester by the bishop and clergy; but it is not stated how Walter, his old colleague at Theobald's court, greeted him. Circumspectly, it may be thought. On the third day he was welcomed in Southwark, the suburb at the south end of the old wooden London bridge in the diocese of Winchester, by enormous crowds, which fitzStephen, who was probably an eye-witness, estimated at 3,000. A procession from the Augustinian priory of St Mary Overy, now Southwark cathedral, went to meet him. Contingents of poor scholars and London clerks struck up *Te Deum laudamus* on his approach, and were rewarded with generous alms. A silly woman named Matilda, who always made a spectacle of herself at courts and public meetings, kept on shouting out, 'Archbishop, beware of the knife!' But rejoicing prevailed. Thomas was conducted by the canons to the palace of the bishop of Winchester, later known as Winchester House or the Clink, where he was to spend the night. The St Albans chronicler thought that he spent some days feasting after the austerities of his exile.

Here, on the following day, he received the messengers of the young king, Jocelin of Louvain, the brother of Adela formerly Henry I's queen, Thomas de Tournebu, Hugh de Gundeville and possibly William of St John. They told him that Henry did not wish to see him. He was to stop visiting royal cities and manors, return to Canterbury and stay there. Thomas asked if this meant that the king was putting him outside his peace and protection. 'Not at all,' they replied. 'But how can I conduct my ministry under those conditions?' he rejoindered. 'We have come here simply to give the king's orders, not to discuss them.' 'Will you then carry my instructions to the king?' 'No, you have plenty of clerks for that purpose.' 'Will you at least conduct them to the king and give them help?' But at this the knights jumped up, and, after rebuking a rich citizen, whom they found in attendance on the archbishop, for consorting with an enemy of the king, they went away.

It is clear that it was believed at court, with some justification, that Thomas was intending to make changes in his diocese, particularly to remedy the effects of his exile, by force if needs be. Herbert of Bosham remarks, with this charge in mind, that they had taken only a smallish escort of knights with them and simply for their protection. FitzStephen says that Thomas returned from London with an escort of five knights, and it was immediately reported to the king across the sea that the archbishop was perambulating the kingdom with a large army in full armour in order to capture towns and drive his son out of the kingdom. Although both Thomas and Herbert of Bosham were militants and were attracted to military measures, it can hardly be doubted that the archbishop was only taking precautions in dangerous times. And, while he was still in London, he received a message from Canterbury urging him to return. One or more of his ships, laden with wine, a present from the senior king, on arriving at Pevensey in east Sussex had been destroyed by Ranulf de Broc, the sailors either killed or imprisoned in the castle and the cargo seized. Thomas's love of fine wines occasionally escapes the censorship that his reputation for austerity imposed.[7]

He did not, however, return immediately to Canterbury, as his biographers imply. He continued in a westerly direction to visit the Deanery of Croydon in Surrey and Middlesex, one of the 'peculiars' under his immediate jurisdiction. Two notorious usurpations existed in this deanery, Charlwood in the possession of Robert, vice-archdeacon of Canterbury, and Harrow occupied by Nigel de Sacquenville. According to St Albans tradition, Thomas arrived at his manor of Harrow about St Lucy's day (13 December) and was still there to celebrate the seventh day before Christmas (*O Sapientia*). Simon, abbot of St Albans, some 20 miles to the north, apparently an old friend and clearly a strong supporter, sent him a magnificent present of food and drink and arrived in person on the heels of his servant. The archbishop's courtly pun (in French), that he was grateful for *sun present* but would enjoy even more *sa presence*, was sedulously preserved. Simon offered to go to the royal court to intercede for Thomas, and left with Richard of Dover and an unnamed 'London clerk', just possibly William fitzStephen. Thomas also dispatched a reluctant William of Canterbury, who describes both missions at great length, as a spy to Reginald of Cornwall, his only friend at court.[8]

Neither operation was successful. Simon was denied an audience with the king, whom he found at Fordingbridge, in the purlieus of the New Forest, and was forced to present his message to the royal courtiers and servants. He made five protests in the archbishop's name. Clerks were not being allowed benefit of clergy. The restoration of the archbishopric, as it had been held by Thomas three months before his departure, and of the honour of Saltwood, both of which had been promised at the peace, had not been implemented – also the archbishop's houses had been vandalized, the hays emptied of game, the trees felled, the peasants ruined by tallages, the estates pillaged and the heirs disinherited. Ranulf de Broc had destroyed the archbishop's ships and seized his wine. The archbishop's churches were still occupied by the intruders. And, finally, clerks were being prevented from both leaving and entering the kingdom. To this list of complaints Reginald of Warenne answered, 'Both sides are stretching their bows,' and the earl of Cornwall added his usual prediction of doom. In the end the legates were informed that, although much did seem to be amiss, the archbishop's petitions would not be heard while he persisted in his opposition to the king and the magnates. William fitzStephen, however, believed that the king ordered the return of a ship to Thomas and that this was done.[9]

According to the St Albans story, Thomas waited at Harrow for the return of the embassy, which would have taken at least four days. Simon had ordered his cellarer to attend on the archbishop daily and see to his needs, and, after reporting the failure of his mission, begged Thomas to spend Christmas with him. But Thomas declined with great regret and left for Canterbury. This could have been no later than 17–18 December. Thomas's disappointment at being debarred from the Christmas celebrations at the royal court, and also at being denied access to the aged bishop Henry of Winchester, must have been acute. Things were going from bad to worse. His 'roaming round the country' in defiance of the royal prohibition must further have alarmed and enraged the government. Signs of its hostility were mounting. Ranulf de Broc and Gervase of Cornhill cited the senior clergy and leading citizens of London to a meeting in order to discover who had welcomed Thomas to the city. But, apparently, it came to nothing because the clergy did not attend and those citizens who put in an appearance declared that as royal burgesses they obeyed only royal writs.

William of Canterbury also had had no success with his spying mission. He had found Reginald of Cornwall at Breamore, not far from the royal court at Fordingbridge, and was received grudgingly. The earl said before his domestics, 'The archbishop has greatly disturbed the kingdom and, unless the Lord God intervenes, will drag it down to everlasting ignominy. So far but a few, soon all of us, will be sent to Hell because of him.' By mischance William was recognized the very next day by a royal servant delivering a gift of venison from the king to the earl; and, although the servant was told that he was mistaken – it was the earl's doctor – the earl insisted that his unwelcome visitor should take an oath of secrecy and leave that very day under cover of darkness. He was to warn Thomas that not only he, but also John of Salisbury, John the Cantor, Gunter and Alexander of Wales were in great danger. They should take the utmost care, for wherever they were found they would be slain. When William reached Canterbury, probably about the same time as the archbishop and not later than Saturday, 19 December, Thomas called in only John of Salisbury to listen to his report. John burst into tears. But Thomas stretched out his neck, tapped it lightly with the palm of his hand and said, 'This is where the varlets will get me.'[10]

Despite all the hindrances, Thomas was doing his best to carry out his spiritual duties. He distributed alms generously. As he travelled to and from London he confirmed children and revealed his exceptional piety by dismounting for the ceremonies. On the way back, at Wrotham in the deanery of Shoreham, an archiepiscopal peculiar in the diocese of Rochester, he had a strange encounter. He was approached by William, the lowly and penurious curate of Chiddingstone, who offered him relics of St Laurence, St Vincent and St Cecilia, at the command, he claimed, of St Laurence himself. The saint had made the order and identified the relics during a dream; and when William had asked how he could convince the archbishop of the truth of these things, the saint told him to remind Thomas that recently he had put his hand in his bosom and discovered that his hair shirt had split, but, after wondering whether to have it repaired or change it for another, had found it made whole again. At this, the archbishop told the priest to keep the whole matter secret until after his death. And when William drew attention to his poverty and lack of a benefice, Thomas asked him to come to Canterbury before the fifth day after Christmas when he would make provision for him. When the priest failed to reappear and could not be found, Thomas had a charter drawn up, which was entrusted to an acquaintance of William's, granting him the chapel of Penshurst, likewise in the deanery of Shoreham. This grant, we are told, was honoured by the young king after the martyrdom.

The archbishop also carried out pastoral duties in the cathedral. On Sunday, 20 December, in the Ember Days, he held an ordination ceremony for monks and clerks of his diocese. But he slighted his own convent. He regarded the entry of all those who had taken the habit since his departure, except in one case, as irregular, and deferred their ordinations. Until he decided their fate, they were to be excluded from chapter. The one exception was his future biographer, William, whom he ordained deacon, possibly as a reward for his recent services. But, as Christmas Day approached, Thomas relented and allowed the others to re-enter the chapter house and petition him for admission to the community. And this he granted in an emotional scene of reconciliation. Meanwhile, on his name-day, 21 December, he celebrated what was probably his fiftieth birthday.[11]

On returning to Canterbury Thomas had dismissed the five knights, although the de Broc family, the *Brokeis*, based, to Thomas's indignation, on Saltwood castle, kept up the blockade of the city with troops stationed at bridges and crossroads. They hoped to catch him outside, thereby breaking the royal edict, and they monitored all visitors. They hunted in his deerpark and caught a stag, and they captured his hounds hunting in his own woods. On Christmas Eve Ranulf's nephew, Robert de Broc, encountered on the king's highway a sumpter beast carrying provisions from an archiepiscopal manor to Canterbury, and got his nephew John to cut off its tail. The mutilated animal was taken for Thomas to see. When the archbishop warned Robert that, unless he made amends, he would be excommunicated, he received a defiant answer. Although the biographers do their best to produce precognitions of the martyrdom and interpret remarks in a sense which was not intended, they supply no good evidence that Thomas was seriously expecting his end, or was resigned to it. Herbert of Bosham believed that his master considered himself the ram of the Lord's flock which was under attack by wolves.[12] He thought only of fight, never of flight. We may be sure that Thomas was aware of the dangers involved in such a course and realized that he could suffer injury, but may think it most unlikely that he envisaged, still less courted, disaster. As always he wanted to win.

On Christmas Eve Thomas celebrated the night Mass and read the lesson from the first chapter of St Matthew's Gospel. On the Nativity itself he preached to the people assembled in the nave of the cathedral on the text,

'Glory to God in the highest, and on earth peace to men of good will' (Luke 2: 14, Vulgate text), which was one of the Lessons for the day. Unfortunately we are not told whether he used French or English. And, to prepare for the anathemas he was to pronounce, he spoke of the archbishops who were saints, particularly of the confessors and especially of St Ælfheah, the one martyr. St Alphege's church was across the road from the palace, a constant reminder to the archbishops. 'Soon there will be another martyr,' he is believed to have said. Then, after the customary prayers for the pope and the peace and prosperity of the people, he excommunicated all violators of the rights of his church and the fomentors of discord in general, and named Robert and Ranulf de Broc and the vicars intruded into Charlwood and Harrow by the vice-archdeacon Robert and Nigel de Sacquenville, all previously excommunicated in April–May 1169. He also announced the sentences which had been imposed on the prelates involved in the illegal coronation. 'May they all be damned by Jesus Christ,' he intoned as he hurled the flaming candles to the floor. Just as he had sentenced the bishops on Advent Sunday, so he completed the process on Christmas Day. He was not one to mask his intentions.

After the subsequent High Mass, which he celebrated, he dined happily and well. Herbert of Bosham reveals that, although it was a Friday, Thomas (quite correctly) ate meat, saying that on such a day it was more seemly to feast than to fast. The archbishop celebrated High Mass again on St Stephen's (Boxing) Day and prepared his clerks for a series of missions. Herbert of Bosham and Alexander of Wales were to go to the king of France, the archbishop of Sens and other French magnates; Gilbert de Glanville to the pope; and the chaplain Richard and John Planeta to the bishop of Norwich in order to absolve priests involved in the Pentney affair. Herbert left on the Sunday at dead of night.[13]

The purpose of the foreign missions was to inform the pope, the papal commissioner, William of Sens, and other sympathizers that the peace promised at Fréteval had not been implemented in England. Although it is not certain what action was requested, for none of the letters has been preserved, the only possible response would seem to be the laying of the interdict on the Continent, a reinforcement of the measures he himself had taken. Herbert, who left reluctantly, believed that his master was anxious to place him out of danger. It has also been suggested that Thomas deliberately disembarrassed himself of the hotheads among his clerks, retaining of the old guard only the temperate John of Salisbury. But Thomas had little choice in the matter. To breach the blockade and conduct business of the utmost secrecy and importance it was necessary to use his most experienced and resourceful men. It would not be easy to work the archbishop's backers up to the same pitch again when they thought that they had at last got him off their hands. But although the dispersal of the *eruditi*, the disciples, was born of danger and actually increased it, the move suggests that Thomas did not see an immediate crisis ahead. Louis, William of Sens and Alexander could give him no immediate relief. He was still planning for the future, planning a new campaign. The biographers were, either unconsciously or consciously, drawing what parallels they could with the last days of their Redeemer, from the triumphant entry into Jerusalem onwards. Thomas himself, although he had the sufferings of Jesus and of Christian martyrs very much on his mind, was, however, in a rather different situation: he trod a road which led he knew not where.

Roger of York, Gilbert of London and Jocelin of Salisbury, all elderly men, had left England shortly after their negotiations with Thomas had failed and reached the senior king's court at Bur-le-Roi, near Bayeux, a few days before Christmas. Richard of Ilchester arrived from Winchester and Southampton at about the same time, but Geoffrey Ridel was prevented by bad weather from crossing. The prelates were full of their grievances, complaining to everyone they met, including the archbishop of Tyre, who was still a frequenter of Henry's household. The court discussed frantically what counter-measures should be taken. Unfortunately no firsthand account of the proceedings exists and the biographers' reconstructions inspire little confidence. Certainly a diplomatic offensive was organized and mounted in order to contain Thomas's own efforts. Master David carried at least six letters to the pope, and other unrecorded letters may have been sent on behalf of York.

Henry contributed a most bitter outcry. Arnulf of Lisieux wrote three eloquent epistles, one in support of the king, the others for each of the bishops; and the archbishop of Rouen and the new bishop of Evreux, the former archdeacon of Rouen, added their entreaties. They all censured Thomas's rash and unexpected declaration of war; they all affirmed that the coronation had been entirely regular and that allegations to the contrary were misrepresentations. Arnulf, who had not been present at the ceremony, even believed that it had been authorized by Alexander. By fraudulent deception bishops, never warned, not cited, unheard, had been shot down to their own humiliation and to the great sorrow of both kings. Jocelin, he thought, was being punished for the alleged crimes of his son Reginald. All asked that Alexander should restrain the aggressor, and Henry asked that, if anyone wished to lay charges against the bishops, the cases should be judged by the pope or remitted to judges delegate. Arnulf also found time to write a letter of recommendation to Thomas on behalf of a clerk, Master 'Errard', who had been deprived during the troubles of the church of Saltwood, to which he had been presented by the abbey of Bec and admitted before the archbishop had gone into exile. Arnulf hoped that the clerk might participate in the solaces of the archbishop's restoration. It was probably in this way that Master Edward Grim came to have his arm almost hacked off at the martyrdom.[14]

At the same time there were discussions on what steps should be taken in the short run to restrain Thomas. It is likely that almost everyone at court was of the opinion that the archbishop had violated the peace, particularly by suspending nearly the whole bench of bishops (anything that Henry had said at Fréteval was by now 'forgotten'), that he was ignoring the ancient customs of the realm and that, by insulting both kings, he was guilty of lèse-majesté, that is to say, treason. Henry objected to Thomas's papal legation and to what he thought was an attempt to deprive him and the nobility of their ecclesiastical patronage. Above all, he felt again all the bitterness of a benefactor who had been treated with the cruellest ingratitude. No doubt he said many contemptuous things about his former friend; no doubt some quite untrue and reckless charges were made, especially that Thomas was leading an army through the kingdom with the intent of dethroning the new king. York is again regarded by the biographers as an instigator of violence, and the hostile opinions of some of the king's most faithful baronial counsellors, the new earl of Leicester, the old Enjuger de Bohun, paternal uncle of the bishop of Salisbury, and William Malvoisin, nephew of Eudo, count of Brittany, are mentioned. Enjuger thought that Henry should have Thomas executed. William Malvoisin said that he had heard once in Rome, while returning from Jerusalem, that some pope had been killed because of his intolerable insolence. They seem to have been not the only ones to think that, as long as Thomas lived, the king and the kingdom would enjoy no peace or quiet. At some point, probably on Christmas Day itself, Henry, maudlin with anger at Thomas's ingratitude and railing at the cowardice of his vassals, uttered the fatal words reported by Edward Grim, 'What miserable drones and traitors have I nourished and promoted in my household, who let their lord be treated with such shameful contempt by a low-born clerk!'[15]

This was the signal for a secret plot to be hatched by four of his knights, William de Tracy, Reginald fitzUrse, Hugh de Morville and Richard le Bret. All four had their roots in England and the first three were substantial barons, who, according to fitzStephen, had been Thomas's vassals when he was chancellor. William (II) de Tracy was probably the oldest and noblest, although Benedict of Peterborough asserts, and Thomas probably held the view, that Hugh de Morville was the highest ranking of the four. William, the second son of John de Sudeley, a descendant of Ralf of Mantes, count of the French Vexin, and Godgifu, the sister of King Edward the Confessor, chose to take his name from the family of his mother, Grace, daughter and heir of William (I) de Tracy, lord of Bradninch in Devon and illegitimate son of King Henry I. He held, besides the barony of Bradninch, lands in Gloucestershire and Somerset, and in 1166 had answered for thirty knight's fees. By 1170 he was a brave and experienced soldier, married, and with a son who eventually inherited.

Reginald fitzUrse, who emerged as the leader of the band, also could claim royal descent, and in 1170 was married with a daughter. His father, Richard, one of Henry I's 'new men', lord of Bulwick in Northamptonshire, had married the daughter of Baldwin de Boullers and Sibyl de Falaise, described as niece, but perhaps a bastard, of Henry I. Reginald also had an interest in Somerset and Montgomery. It seems that on the 29th in the cathedral Thomas charged him with ingratitude, for it was through him that he had obtained his position in the royal court.

Hugh de Morville was a younger man – Benet calls him a bachelor – who had inherited from his father Simon only in 1167 and did not marry until much later. His mother had been the heir to the barony of Burgh-by-Sands in Cumbria. About her William of Canterbury tells a scandalous story which shows that the family spoke English at home. As we have seen, Hugh remained in Thomas's service after his promotion to Canterbury. He was, however, a witness to the Constitutions of Clarendon and in 1170 was farming the royal town and honour of Knaresborough in Yorkshire, which had a part to play in the plot.

Richard le Bret was the younger son of Simon, a military tenant of the Mohuns, lords of Dunster in north Somerset. Simon's fief, Sampford-Brett, was close to the fitzUrse manor of Williton. It may be that Richard, besides being socially inferior to the others, was the youngest of the gang, for William of Canterbury writes that, while he battled in the cathedral, he changed from a beginner into a Thraso, the swashbuckling knight of Terence's *Eunuchus*. But, as he struck the archbishop, he claimed to be avenging his lord, William, the king's brother, who had died six years before.[16]

These four secret conspirators seem to have acted within, or on the fringe of, an official mission sent to confront and restrain the archbishop. Henry ordered William de Mandeville, earl of Essex, who had come over, perhaps with Richard of Ilchester, only recently from the young king's court, Saher de Quincy, lord of Bourn in Cambridgeshire, and the constable, Richard de Humet, to go to England, present an ultimatum to Thomas, and, it would seem, if he refused the terms, arrest him. Up to that point both parties had the same programme, and it is quite possible that the outcome would have been the same even if the earl and his associates or agents had reached Canterbury first. In both cases there was a lack of control, caused largely by the division of authority between the two kings. When William de Mandeville eventually reached Canterbury, the archbishop was already dead. He told the monks that he had intended, if he had caught Thomas, to make certain demands on matters which pertained to the king's dignity; and, if the archbishop had agreed to them with goodwill, he would have left him in peace. But, if he had presumed to refuse, he would no doubt have compelled him to yield. Others in the earl's company said that, if the monks had hidden the archbishop, they would have set the monastery on fire so as to smoke out the traitor who deserved to be executed. Thus, although even at the time few, if any, believed that Henry had given orders to anyone for the killing, he had set in motion operations which could easily produce that result.[17]

The situation was further confused by the fact that both parties split up before or after reaching the French coast. Guernes believed that various ports (he mentions Barfleur, Dieppe and Wissant) were occupied by royal forces in order to prevent news of the expedition reaching England, but that unfavourable weather made it difficult to cross. The four conspirators, however, whom he thought had been provided by Roger of York with 60s. apiece for their expenses, with the luck of the devil had a miraculously fortunate journey, two of them landing at Winchelsea in East Sussex, the others at Dover (more exactly, at 'the port of dogs'), at precisely the same time, and reaching their rendezvous at Saltwood again simultaneously. As they arrived at the castle, about a mile from Hythe, on the evening of 28 December, they must have left Bur during the night of the 25th at the latest; and the ride to Dieppe and Wissant would have been hard going. If the official party was destined for Southampton and the young king, it is likely that they planned to cross from Barfleur. However that may be, William and Saher were, owing to adverse winds, unable to set sail, although Richard managed to embark at another port. On arriving in England the constable instructed the new king's guardians, Hugh de Gundeville and William fitzJohn, that, without informing their young master, they should take a squadron of household knights to Canterbury and arrest the archbishop. He himself would remain on the English coast to block any attempt to escape, while the earl and Saher would keep watch on the Continent.[18]

When the four barons arrived at Saltwood castle on the evening of Monday, 28 December, they found only the castellan's wife at home, for Ranulf de Broc, warned of their crossing, had gone out to meet them and also to put his forces on the alert. The five then spent the night making plans. The scheme they devised was to surround the cathedral complex in order to prevent Thomas's escape and apply pressure on him to absolve the bishops, give pledges of good behaviour and, perhaps, prepare to stand trial. At some point Ranulf called out the garrisons of Dover, Rochester ('Rophe') and Bletchingley (a Clare castle in Surrey), presumably ordering them to join him at Canterbury. On the Tuesday morning, no doubt at dawn, 8 o'clock, leaving only two boys behind at Saltwood, they set off for the city, an easy ride of some two-and-a-half hours up the old Roman road, Stone Street. They mobilized other knights *en route*, and, before entering the city, called in on the abbot of St Augustine's in order to take his advice. Since Clarembald was no friend of Thomas's, he may well have blessed the project, short of recourse to physical violence. Indeed, he provided a knight, Simon de Criol, to whom fitzUrse was to assign a special task.

Somewhere, perhaps in the abbey, the royalists must have had a meal and a drink. All the leaders, and especially the visitors, who had been travelling almost non-stop for at least three days and nights, must have been extremely tired, so fatigued that they appeared to be drunk. And the rashness of their behaviour may be attributed in part to this. When they entered the city with their small army, they first ordered the citizens to take up arms and converge on the archiepiscopal palace. But when these showed reluctance, they were ordered to stay quiet and keep out of the way of the soldiers. It would seem that Ranulf de Broc retained overall command of the besieging force, while the four barons, led by Reginald fitzUrse, with about a dozen knights and some other helpers, including Robert de Broc and a subdeacon, Hugh of Horsea, nicknamed Mauclerk (Bad-clerk), went on to deal with the archbishop.[19]

Among those who described Thomas's last day were five eye-witnesses: his clerks John of Salisbury and William fitzStephen, the monks Benedict of Peterborough and William of Canterbury and the visiting clerk, Edward Grim.[20] All these, except John, who tells us little about what happened before the final scene (which he missed), describe the events of the afternoon in some detail. Benedict, of whose narrative we have only fragments, provides the fullest account of Thomas's interview with the king's barons, William fitzStephen of what happened outside the chamber; but each of the four remembered something that others had forgotten or chosen to omit. In general it seems safe to conflate the several accounts. But, although there are few direct contradictions, memories were inevitably confused: for example, the exact course that the interview took is far from clear. There was also some editing, if little censorship, so as to provide a suitable introduction to the martyrdom. Besides these four accounts, little of value is contributed by those writers who were not present, apart from Guernes, who carried out an investigation. They were in much the same position as we.

It is Guernes, possibly filling out the indications of those present when the archbishop's corpse was undressed, who provides the most detailed inventory of what Thomas was wearing on that day. As it was mid-winter, he wore, in the usual twelfth-century fashion, ample layers of clothing, probably exaggerated in his case not only by his notorious susceptibility to cold and liability to stitch in the side but also possibly for symbolical reasons. Next to his skin was his long hair shirt, the unusual breeches hidden by white underpants. Herbert of Bosham, who of course was not there, in his description reduces the ferocity and squalor of the penitential garment: it was a *poderis* (the ankle-length robe worn by priests in the ancient world), Joseph's coat of many colours. (He managed to stop short of referring to Tamar's robe.) Thomas had put this garment on shortly after he was ordained priest and retained it all his life.

On top of this, in Guernes's list, came the allegedly monastic garb, a linen shirt followed by a cowl, with the skirts and sleeves of both so shortened that they would not be seen. Herbert, however, no great lover of monks, states that it was a black tunic without a hood (*colobium sine caputio*), which was mistaken at the inspection of the body for a cowl. And it would be in keeping with Thomas's habits if this should have been the garment which the pope had sent him in 1165, an article from the beginning of doubtful identity. However that may be, above it came two ample but short soft pelisses, both of lambskins. Finally he wore the supposed habit of a canon regular: another pelisse of lambskins, a fine white surplice or tunic (sometimes called a rochet), and, to cover all, a black mantle without a fringe, lined with white lambskins, and with a black tassel for fastening it up. Guernes says that he wore nothing of samite or silk or of the expensive furs vair or gris, and that no garment was padded. We learn elsewhere that Thomas had a cap (*pileum*) on his head and on his feet heavy shoes (*caligae*).[21]

Some of his actions on this last morning of his life are recorded. After attending Mass, he made his usual circuit of the altars in the cathedral, starting with the high altar, and called on the various saints for their aid. Next, according to William of Canterbury, he made his confession to a senior monk, Thomas of Maidstone, presumably in the chapter house; but why he should not have confessed, as usual, to Robert of Merton, who was certainly in attendance, is unclear. It is also said that he was scourged three times that day, presumably by Robert. At about 2 o'clock he dined in hall, the one main meal of the monastic winter horarium. According to Gerald of Wales, he enjoyed a dish of pheasants. And it was soon after this, when he had withdrawn to his chamber and sat in conference with his council, that the arrival of messengers from the king overseas was announced.[22]

The archiepiscopal palace had been built by Archbishop Lanfranc to the north-west of the monastery and church, to which it was connected by way of the cloister, on a site from which twenty-seven households had been cleared. The main gateway was in the west wall, in Palace Street, north of St Alphege church and lane. The head porter in 1170 was either

William de Porta or his son James, both rich and important citizens, who lived across the road. The visitor entered a vast courtyard, some 200 yards long and over 80 yards wide. To his left, some 80 yards to the north, were the archbishop's extensive stables in Stablegate. To his right, about 120 yards to the south, was the great hall, running from the north-west angle of the present cathedral in a westerly direction. It had a projecting porch and at the west end its kitchens. Within the palace, the chamber and other private rooms were at the east end of the hall, which communicated with the south cloister passage. To the south of the hall was a private garden or orchard, which could be reached by skirting the kitchens.[23]

Reginald fitzUrse left his escort of twelve or so knights, probably under the command of Robert de Broc, in the house of a certain Gilbert, opposite the gateway to the palace, while he and his companions, with apparently only a single archer in attendance, a de Broc's man, entered the courtyard and dismounted and disarmed under a great mulberry tree. They then went through the porch into the hall, where they found the servants, who had just served Thomas and his company, taking their own meal. The chief officer of the hall, the steward, William fitzNeal, greeted the visitors with every honour and, when he learnt that they came from the king, offered them refreshments, which they declined, before going, as they required, to announce their arrival to his master.[24]

Thomas was with his closest advisers in the inner chamber, his actual bedroom, sitting on his bed and talking to a monk, perhaps William. Others of his household were in the larger outer chamber. It was probably, by modern reckoning, about 3 o'clock when the four barons, conducted by the steward, were introduced. Thomas continued his conversation and did not deign to notice them for a while. They too, without speaking, sat down at his feet, the archer sitting behind them. The archbishop's failure to rise and greet the barons, most, if not all, of whom he knew well, was a studied discourtesy similar to that at Sandwich, two months earlier. When finally he greeted them – and apparently only Hugh de Morville by name – he got nothing much in reply, except possibly a 'God help you' from Reginald fitzUrse. It should be noticed that the barons presented no letter or other credentials. Their known familiarity with the king seems to have been accepted, from beginning to end, as sufficient authorization for their actions.

It was Reginald who conducted the business, and this could have aggravated Thomas's displeasure, for he knew Hugh best and seems to have regarded him as the most distinguished of the four and the obvious spokesman. Reginald announced that they came from the king overseas with an important message and asked whether the archbishop wanted to hear it in public or in private. Thomas first chose the latter and dismissed everyone except the usher, who kept the communicating door open. But as soon as he realized the importance of the matter and the hostility of his visitors, he called his inner circle back, monks and clerks, but no laymen. If we follow Benedict of Peterborough's order of events, and it seems marginally the most likely, Reginald required in the name of the king that Thomas should go to his royal son at Winchester and make satisfaction to him. The archbishop asked what this meant, and a rambling dispute developed concerning his barony and his feudal duties, and in what ways he had transgressed. He maintained that, although he was anxious to greet his new lord – indeed, had failed to do so only because prevented by his guardians – he would not go to Winchester to be put on trial, for he was completely innocent of any crime.

The barons then made the stock royalist charges against the archbishop: his breaking the peace after his return to England by suspending and excommunicating the prelates, excommunicating royal servants and threatening to un-crown and disinherit the new king. To which Thomas made his stock replies: they were papal sentences and the pope was punishing the wrongs done to the church of Canterbury and its archbishop; and no one was intending to invalidate the coronation. As for the bishops, he had already offered them merciful terms, which they had refused, and the offer was still open. In any case, what he had done was with the king's permission, as Reginald, and all others who had been at Fréteval, knew full well. Reginald, however, denied either that he had been there or that Henry had given permission.

When the barons, tiring of the arguments, exclaimed that by God's wounds they had borne the archbishop long enough, Thomas counterattacked with bitter complaints of his own sufferings in England, of his treatment by the *Brokeis*, of the retention of his churches and of the restriction on his movements. He reminded the barons that three of them had been his vassals and done him homage when he was chancellor. Tempers rose, voices were raised. More and more of the archiepiscopal household, attracted by the shouting, crowded into the two chambers. Among them were his steward, William fitzNeal, and another knight, Ralf Morin. In the end both Thomas and Reginald were making threats, the archbishop of drawing the sword of his priestly office to avenge the crimes committed against him, the baron of driving the archbishop into renewed exile or of something much worse. Benedict describes the barons twisting their gloves into knots and throwing their arms about. Thomas too stood up. Reginald declared that the archbishop was no longer under the king's peace and protection. He ordered all present to leave the rooms (perhaps intending to arrest the archbishop then and there), but, when no one made a move, he substituted the order that the monks present should guard their lord and prevent his escape until the king should execute full justice on his body. He then arrested the two archiepiscopal knights and carried them off. William fitzNeal, who had collaborated with the royal guardians during the exile, was thought to have been a willing captive and deserter. Thomas, enraged, followed them to the door, shouting, 'Do you think I'm going to sneak off? I haven't returned to Canterbury in order to run away. You'll find me here. And in the Lord's battle I will fight hand to hand, toe to toe.' He also appealed to Hugh de Morville to come back and talk it over.

So far the encounter differed from Thomas's earlier disputes on the same matters with royal officials only in two respects: the heat of the exchanges and his having been arrested and put in ward. Logically, the next step was for the barons to conduct him to prison or the royal court, either at Winchester or in Normandy. But unarmed, and with only one archer, they probably felt that this would be difficult in the face of a hostile household and citizenry. So they removed the two knights from the archbishop's company and went out to get armed assistance. After they had gone, Thomas and his household sat discussing the surprising and frightening events. Benedict reports that John of Salisbury said to his master, 'It's quite amazing that you should take no advice in this matter. And why should you exacerbate them further by getting up and following them to the door? Surely it would have been better to consult with us, who are here, and make a more conciliatory answer to men who were deliberately and evilly working you up and provoking you to anger so that they could catch you out in something.' To this, Thomas replied with a sigh, 'My mind is made up. I know exactly what I have to do.' 'Please God, you have chosen well!' John rejoindered.

William fitzStephen claims that John had much earlier interrupted the interview with, 'My lord, discuss the matter in private with your council,' to which the archbishop had replied, 'What's the use? They are demanding things that I neither can nor should perform.' And it is, indeed, likely that the diplomatic clerk had tried several times to prevent the encounter developing into a slanging match. FitzStephen also tells us that in the discussion after the barons had left opinions differed. Some thought that there was no cause for alarm. The barons were obviously drunk: only men who had dined could have said such things. In any case it was Christmas and Thomas and his clerks had also been granted the king's peace. Others, however, thought the opposite: there were clear signs of danger. But fitzStephen, always discreet when fellow-clerks were concerned, gives no names.

The four barons, after breaking off their interview with Thomas, had retraced their steps through the hall and the porch into the courtyard and activated the second phase of a well-planned military operation.[25] They had to work fast, for soon it would be dark. Robert de Broc had already, by following the barons through the street gate, taken possession of the gatehouse, replaced the archbishop's porter with his own man, stationed some troops on its inside and closed the gate, thus isolating the palace from the city. He had also, probably, done a little reconnoitring. The barons themselves, as they came out of the hall, secured their return, as they thought, by posting William fitzNeal and the St Augustine's abbey knight, Simon de Criol, both on horseback, within the porch. These kept the outer gate closed, except for the postern, and the inner door open, thus giving them a view of what went on in both directions. Reginald fitzUrse then, either in the porch or with his companions under the mulberry tree, put on his hauberk with the requisitioned help of Robert Pipe (*Tibia*), one of the scullions from the kitchen. When all was ready, the signal was given, the street gate was opened, and the rest of the soldiers rushed in, shouting, '*Reaus!*, royal knights, king's men, king's men!' The gate was then shut behind them.

The royalists, however, suffered an immediate check. Distracted, perhaps, by the charge of the soldiers across the courtyard, the two knights failed to keep the door between the porch and the hall open. Two palace servants, Osbert and Algar, alarmed by the noise, promptly shut it in their faces and secured it with a bar or bolt. It could not be broken open, and the uproar caused almost all within the palace, except the archbishop and his council, to flee from or through the hall into the church. Robert de Broc then led some of the troops past the kitchen and through the orchard to a private entrance, a postern door, to the chamber, on the southern side of the palace. It is described as within an oriel, that is to say, an upper porch or gallery, at the head of some stairs. The steps were broken in the middle and under repair by workmen, who had gone to dinner. But Robert, with the aid of a ladder and the tools they had left behind, climbed up and broke through a window. Possibly he had also to smash through a partition. He then opened the postern door to let the others in, and went on into the hall, where he struck and wounded the servants who had shut its door and opened that too. The palace was now wide open.[26]

Thomas and his advisers had still been discussing the events when they heard the blows on the hall door, the shouts and cries and the noise of men running through the building. In their fear those in attendance wanted to run away with the rest and urged the archbishop to take refuge in the church. But he remained calm and scornful of cowards, jibing at monks for their timidity; and his men found his reckless bravery no less alarming than the threat from the soldiers. No one doubted that he had plenty of physical as well as spiritual courage: the trouble was that he had far too much. Even in the absence of Herbert of Bosham it was going to be difficult to keep him under control. All the same, it would seem unfortunate that, at this juncture, he was deprived of the company of Herbert, Alexander, Gunter and John Planeta, his loyal companions in exile. In comparison with these, John of Salisbury, William fitzStephen, Simon, archdeacon of

Sens, Henry of Auxerre, William of Canterbury and Edward Grim were either more peripheral or newcomers. Had his faithful clerks been present, events might well have taken a different course. In later years Herbert was bitterly resentful that he had not been allowed to participate.

It was the noise of Robert de Broc breaking into a nearby room that drove the archbishop's council to desperate action. Combining pleas to escape with entreaties that he should attend Vespers in the cathedral, and using physical force, they managed to get him moving. As they could see that the palace was beset by armed men on both sides, in the courtyard and the orchard, some other route to the church had to be found; and by forcing a door and traversing a disused passage to the cloisters through the cellarer's range, where two cellarers, Richard and William, unbarred the way, they managed to get ahead of the intruders. Unless they had had to follow a very roundabout route they would have found themselves in the south cloister, with some 60 yards still to go.

Thomas was determined that he should not seem to be in flight or seen to behave indecorously. His cross had to be carried before him, and, in the absence of Alexander, it was entrusted to Henry of Auxerre. Edward Grim and Guernes thought that Thomas was dragged and shoved, half-carried, all the way to the cathedral. William of Canterbury, Benedict of Peterborough and William fitzStephen preferred to remember that he walked slowly and calmly, in all his dignity, behind his little flock. Guernes, with Anonymous I, harmonized the views by making Thomas twice break free from his escorts in the cloister, and once dart into the chapter house, on the east side, in order to halt this unseemly rout. The truth may be that once Thomas found himself securely ahead of the soldiers, he managed to calm his companions, reassert his authority and succeed in entering the church with dignity.

At Canterbury cathedral there were, as both Guernes and the Saga pointed out, two daily evensong services, the first for the monks in the choir, followed by another in the nave for clerks and townsfolk. The monastic Vespers were already in progress when they were halted by the mounting distractions. It must have been about 4 o'clock, at sunset, when Thomas entered the north transept of the church. The monks, some of whom had already come down from the choir, greeted him with relief, for they feared that something had happened to him. They urged him upwards towards the high altar and began to bar the door. But Thomas ordered that it be reopened – exclaiming that a church was not a castle – and even perhaps helped to pull some of the stragglers in. There was, naturally, an altercation with the monks over this apparent act of folly; but he had his way. He then started to mount the staircase in the north aisle which led eastwards to the choir. But he had not got very far before the first of his pursuers, perhaps Reginald fitzUrse, entered the north transept by the same door.[27]

The royalists had had first to search the palace for Thomas and then discover where he had gone. This would have taken, say, ten minutes. Robert de Broc and the main force had then remained to guard the palace and, no doubt, have a good look round, while the four barons, accompanied by the clerk, Hugh of Horsea, went in further pursuit. Any soldiers they took with them were left in the cloisters in order to secure their line of retreat. The barons were in mail, with their heads covered, and had naked swords in their right hands and axes, for breaking doors open, in their left. On entering the church, they shouted, 'Where is the traitor? Where is the archbishop?' and, according to Grim, 'Where is Thomas Becketh, a traitor to the king and kingdom?' Thomas started back down the steps and turned right to stand by a pillar in the centre of the opening to the transept, between the wall of the eastern apse with its altar of St Benedict, where four English and two Norman archbishops lay buried, and the Lady chapel, which closed the north aisle of the nave. He called out to the barons, 'Here I am. No traitor to the king, but a priest of God. What do you want?'

It was either when Thomas went to get the church door reopened or when he returned to face the royalists that, according to William fitzStephen, he was abandoned by John of Salisbury and all his clerks except Robert, canon of Merton (his chaplain and constant companion, whom, as usual, no one else mentions), Edward Grim and himself. FitzStephen also points out how easy it would have been for their master to escape. Nearby were the steps to the crypt, full of hiding-places, and also the door to a spiral staircase leading to the upper regions of the church. The long night approached; Thomas would not be easily discovered; and, given time, anything could happen. But this choice the archbishop deliberately refused.

Although the general course of the subsequent events is not in doubt, there is much disagreement, even among the eye-witnesses, over detail. This is not surprising. Daylight was fading; the even darker church was illuminated possibly only in the choir and at the altars by lamps or candles; Thomas was in a black mantle amid black-robed monks; the heads and faces of the assailants were covered by their mailed coifs; there was general confusion; and the eye-witnesses were such only up to a point. John of Salisbury had already hidden himself away. William of Canterbury admitted that he left Thomas's side when the first blow was struck and went to his brethren in the choir. It was that blow or the next which almost severed Edward Grim's arm, and, although he remained at the scene, by one of the altars, he was thereafter in no fit state to take exact notice of what was happening. William fitzStephen and Benedict of Peterborough do not say exactly where they were in the church during these events. As they make no claims, it can be assumed that they were among the groups who watched from a safe distance. No one mentions what happened to Robert of Merton, Simon of Sens and Henry of Auxerre. In any case, it is doubtful if anyone present, except Thomas, knew the barons, and only his immediate circle had had the opportunity of observing them closely that afternoon. Edward Grim, a complete stranger, could have seen them only in passing, Benedict of Peterborough not at all. The recorders constructed a story out of confused recollections of imperfectly observed events and from what the participants are alleged to have said later. These factors make a completely certain reconstruction of the happenings in every detail impossible.

No more certain is the state of Thomas's mind. The memorialists believed unanimously, although with varied insistence and consistency, that he was prepared, even anxious, for martyrdom. In such a case he should not flee from city to city, but give an example to his flock. He wished to follow the royal road, that trodden by his Lord Jesus Christ and the Apostles.[28] However that may be, he was undoubtedly not prepared either to go tamely into captivity or to be pushed around and arrested by soldiers who were of only middling baronial rank. Henry himself had, more realistically, entrusted the task to an earl, William de Mandeville. It was sacrilege to touch God's anointed; and there was Thomas's pride and dignity. This being so, only the utmost restraint on the part of the barons could spare him from injury or death. And that patience and forbearance were not forthcoming – in the circumstances were out of the question.

Yet it does seem that their original intention, as they are supposed to have confessed later, was to capture Thomas and use greater force only if he resisted arrest, and that their immediate aim was merely to remove him from the church. According to Edward Grim, and he should have known, the barons, when they caught up with the archbishop, demanded once more that he abrogate his sentences on the prelates, and, when he refused on the grounds that they had given no satisfaction, threatened him with death. Thomas replied that he himself was willing to die, but forbade them to harm any of his men, whether clerks or laymen. They then tried to arrest him. Benedict and fitzStephen believed that one of the assailants, identified by Guernes as Reginald fitzUrse, shouted, 'Run away: you are a dead man!' And, when Thomas refused, menaced him with his sword and, with the point, dislodged his cap from his head. Then one of them, this time almost certainly Reginald, grabbed him by the border of his cloak and with the help of the others, pushing and tugging, tried to hoist him on to William de Tracy's back. Thomas was outraged. Not only did he lash Reginald with bitter charges of ingratitude and shameful conduct, he even called him, according to Grim, a pimp (*leno*). He also resisted physically, shaking him off so fiercely that Reginald almost fell to the ground. With Edward Grim holding on tightly, Thomas could not be moved. Herbert of Bosham rhapsodizes over this feat of strength. Thomas was a second Samson, Paul, Jesus Christ in the temple, boy David!

In Grim's view the barons wanted to get the archbishop out of the church either to kill him in a less sacred place or to carry him off as a prisoner. But the plan had failed. Thomas's resistance and the increasing number of onlookers, including townsfolk coming to evensong, made his rescue possible. The situation had got out of hand. While Hugh de Morville kept the watchers at a distance, the others struck in turn. When Thomas realized that he was close to death, he adopted a submissive pose, his head bent forward, his arms stretched out and his hands joined as in prayer. 'I commend myself to God, the Blessed Mary, St Denis and the patron saints of this church,' he said. Perhaps he also named St Ælfheah, the martyred archbishop.

Grim believed that it was the baron whom Thomas had addressed as Reginald who struck the first blow. And he was most likely right. FitzUrse had been the leader all along, had clashed physically with the archbishop and had been called foul names. Grim thrust out his arm to ward off the blow. But the swung sword sliced off the top of the archbishop's head and cut through the clerk's arm to the bone. Later that night at Saltwood William de Tracy is supposed to have claimed that he had cut off John of Salisbury's arm. If he did say this, it would seem that he was doubly deceived. In the heat of the affray the barons could see no more than the onlookers. He was, however, probably the one who felled the archbishop to the ground, either, as fitzStephen and Benedict thought, at his first attempt, or, as Grim, followed by Guernes and Anonymous I, believed, with his second blow. Thomas subsided to his knees and then his hands, and finished flat on his face, with his head to the north and the altar of St Benedict to his right. Grim alone reports that, as he collapsed, he murmured, 'For the name of Jesus and the protection of the church I am ready to embrace death.' While he lay there, a third knight, identified by fitzStephen and Guernes as Richard le Bret, delivered the *coup de grâce*. He struck the archbishop such a fierce blow to the head that he completed the severance of the crown and also broke his sword in two on the pavement. As he struck, he shouted, 'Take this for love of my lord William, the king's brother!' Finally, the subdeacon, Hugh of Horsea, put his foot on the victim's neck, thrust the point of his sword into the open skull and scattered blood and brains on the floor. 'Let's be off, knights,' he cried. 'This fellow won't get up again!' Some of the biographers note, and it was a disturbing feature, that the only one who had tried to help and protect the victim was a complete stranger to them all.[29]

The murder occurred about half past four. The date, 29 December 1170, is undisputed, but was usually given as 1171, as in the famous couplet of

William Turbe, bishop of Norwich, quoted by William fitzStephen, because at Canterbury, as in many monasteries, the new year was reckoned to begin at Christmas. It was, as they almost all say, the fifth day of that festival, the day after the feast of the Holy Innocents. It was also the last of the memorable Tuesdays.[30]

The four barons left the church immediately, again shouting, as they cleared a way with the flat of their swords, '*Reus!*, royal knights, king's men, king's men!' A monk was stunned, a French servant of the archdeacon of Sens wounded. The barons rejoined Robert de Broc in the palace and completed its pillage. Their primary aim was to search for papal letters and privileges – evidence of treason – and all books and documents they found they handed over to Ranulf de Broc for transmission to the king overseas. But they also beat the servants and took everything of value, including horses, which they removed while retreating through the stables, and these spoils they divided among themselves. William fitzStephen estimated the damage at more than 2,000 marks. Eventually they retired for the night to Saltwood castle.[31]

Once they had gone, the monks cleared the church of all visitors and secured the doors. They were at a loss over what to do. As well as being dazed by the extraordinary events, they did not know how to regard them. Thomas's death was not recognized immediately by all as a martyrdom. The 'illegal' prior of Christ Church, Odo, whom the archbishop had been about to replace, was hostile; at least some of the monks remembered Thomas as the proud royal chancellor and fiscal agent, a potential plunderer of their possessions. They were, too, as Thomas had observed, timid, and therefore unlikely to resist the king. Royal servants had proclaimed that the dead man was a traitor to the king and the kingdom; and the city was under military occupation. The murderers were English nobles and the archbishop had become an alien. Thomas's clerks, no doubt unpopular with the community, were in disarray, leaderless and dispirited. Edward Grim, Benedict of Peterborough and Anonymous II report various unfavourable opinions of the archbishop expressed by onlookers and those who heard the news. Some said, 'He wanted to be a king: he wanted to be more than a king. Let him be a king now.' A clerk said that it had been his stubbornness which had caused his death. Anonymous II, probably reporting London opinion, mentions accusations of vindictiveness, pride and vainglory. In the monastery there was for a time paralysis and disorder.[32]

At first the body was left almost unattended and without a light. Gradually the clerks, monks and servants reassembled in the church and townsfolk crowded in. While the body still lay where it had fallen, several people put fingers or rags in the gory mess; some collected blood in small receptacles or applied it to the rims of their eyes. The archbishop's chamberlain, Osbert, cut a strip from his own shirt and tied the severed crown to the head. The body was then lifted on to a bier. Beneath it was found an iron hammer and a double-headed axe. Richard le Bret's broken sword was also preserved as a trophy at the shrine. Benedict describes the face of the murdered man as almost unbloodied except for a graceful line running from the right temple across the nose to the left cheek. The body was carried on the bier through the choir and placed before the high altar. The head was freshly bandaged with a clean cloth and a small cap, perhaps his own, pulled on over the top.[33]

The exact order in which some of the subsequent events occurred is doubtful, partly because John of Salisbury's influential account makes no pretence to be a circumstantial report, partly because of the disorder in William fitzStephen's narrative, or the manuscript, and mostly because of the influence of later events. It may be that it was when the body was placed before the altar that the outer garments, because soiled, were removed and given away as valueless rags to the poor, that Robert of Merton, by disarranging other garments, revealed the hair shirt and breeches, and that, as a consequence, the blood spilled on the pavement was carefully collected in a basin. But, all things considered, some, if not most, of these events would seem to be better associated with the preparation of the body for burial, which undoubtedly took place the following morning.

After the grieving monks had kept watch over the body all night they received a probably not unexpected visit from Robert de Broc, who had returned with a troop of soldiers. He justified the killing of a traitor and threatened that, unless the monks buried the archbishop immediately in some obscure place, he would seize the corpse and subject it to every possible indignity – drag it through the city at a horse's tail and then hang what remained on a gibbet or throw it on to a dunghill. There also arrived Richard, prior of Dover, and Walter, abbot of the Cistercian abbey of Boxley, south of Rochester, both of whom Thomas had summoned in connection with the deposition of Prior Odo: he had intended to look for a replacement outside Christ Church, an act which would have been most unpopular and reminded the community of the 'tyranny' of Theobald. The undoubted tensions which still existed between Thomas and the monks were inevitably forgotten by the hagiographers.[34]

Richard of Dover, Thomas's friend and recent associate, took over control. It was decided to bury the archbishop immediately in the Trinity chapel at the eastern end of the crypt, by a pillar between, on the left, the altar of St John the Baptist and, on the right, the altar of St Augustine. Thomas's outer garments down to the 'cowl', if not already removed, were cut away with knives, and, because they were bloodstained and dirty, distributed as worthless alms.[35] But there were some in attendance, probably both clerks and monks, who were already beginning to push Thomas's claims to martyr-dom. The discovery of the supposed monastic cowl and shirt, we are told, surprised and deeply impressed the monks. They realized for the first time that, contrary to all appearances, he had secretly been one of them. 'Look, he's a true monk!' they exclaimed. These garments were not removed; but it was probably now that Robert of Merton, by opening up and exploring the underclothes, drew attention to the hair shirt and breeches. This caused a sensation, for, we are assured, none of these proofs of austerity had been known before, except to a few of his most intimate circle. Even more remarkable, the penitential garment was still alive with lice and worms. It would seem that it was these revelations which converted an important section of the monks to Thomas's cause. Had his furs been of gris and vair and his underclothes of samite and silk there might easily have been no martyr. And it was probably because of the changed atmosphere that some monks, led by Arnold the Goldsmith, went to collect in a basin what remained of the archbishop's blood, either from the floor or from earlier collectors and cleaners.

Owing to the haste and possibly other factors, the body was not washed or embalmed, as was normal Canterbury custom – at least with monks. It was, however, as men reflected later, washed in his own blood. In all other respects it was properly decked out for burial. They dressed him, on top of the 'cowl' and existing underwear, in the vestments which he had specially put aside to be used on this occasion: the alb in which he had been consecrated priest, a simple superhumeral or amice, a stole and maniple and, on his head, the chrismal cloth from his baptism and a mitre. Finally they put on his archiepiscopal vestments, his tunic, dalmatic, chasuble and pallium with its pins, and provided him with a chalice, gloves, ring, sandals and pastoral staff. He was to be kept in his tomb even warmer than in life itself. The body thus arrayed was put in a marble sarcophagus with a coped lid, already prepared for another burial, and sunk into the floor of the crypt. It was far from the company of his recent predecessors in office; and there was no funeral Mass or any other public religious service because of the pollution of the church.[36]

Thomas was buried as though in the lull of a battle by demoralized troops who had become more concerned with their own safety and future than with the lost cause of their dead commander. He would need all the interces-sion with God they could offer: but that could, would have to, wait. For the time being they had become a rabble, completely at the mercy of the tyrants of this world. Although God was their strength and refuge, there was little hope of immediate comfort.

CHAPTER TWELVE

FROM DEATH UNTO LIFE

The murder created a void which no one hastened to rebuild. The shock was great and the ten to twelve weeks it took at the quickest to make the return trip to Frascati, not to count the delays at the curia, prevented precipitate action. Nonetheless, once the legal process had been set in motion by the archbishop of Sens on 25 January 1171, it advanced, despite some hindrances and unexpected turns of events, to a whole series of definitive results. All the guilty, including some who considered themselves blameless, were punished and the martyr was officially recognized. If some of the deserving were overlooked when it came to the rewards, and some of the convicted were able, after purging their crimes, to prosper exceedingly, that is the way of the world. And by the summer of 1174, when the last loose ends had been tied up, little bitterness remained, except in those of Thomas's clerks, like Herbert of Bosham, who had gone down, but not risen again, with their master.

The young king must soon have heard of the crime. He is reported to have expressed great sorrow and also relief that none of his own men had been involved. The senior king was informed three days after the event at Argentan and was grief-stricken. News reached the papal court about a month later and Alexander went into deep mourning for a week. John of Salisbury's description of the scene at Canterbury, with the innocent champion of the liberty of the church murdered 'in the mother church of the kingdom, before Christ's altar, among his fellow priests and troops of monks' – addressed primarily to John of Poitiers, but repeated to Rheims and Sens and widely circulated – was written almost immediately after the event.[1]

The question on all men's lips, asked anxiously by some, gloatingly by others, was what part had the king played in the murder? John of Salisbury had named no one. The assassins were anonymous knights and he reported the belief that (as with Jesus) the killing had been procured by treacherous disciples and directed by the chief priests, men who in their evil doings outstripped Annas, Caiaphas, Pilate and Herod. The chief priests would have been understood as York, London and Salisbury. But it is not obvious who represented Judas, perhaps Geoffrey Ridel, possibly Reginald fitzJocelin. The silence as regards the king is deafening, although the casual mention of Herod provided a pointer. The letter which Herbert of Bosham wrote for the archbishop of Sens to convey the news to the pope, which is probably based on John's, puts names to the knights and the three bishops, but again omits any clear reference to the king.[2]

The French church, however, was not going to join in a conspiracy of silence, and its support for Thomas and animosity towards Henry are striking. William of Sens sent a Carthusian monk to Henry to investigate the matter and, according to William, the king admitted to the monk that he had provided the cause of Thomas's death and had in effect killed him. The Grandimontine Bernard de la Coudre, one of the papal commissioners in 1168–9 and now *corrector* of Vincennes, was agonized by the report spread by the archbishops of Sens and Rheims (the French king's brother) and the bishops of Poitiers and Nevers that Henry was the murderer. He felt that the failure of his mission made him in some way responsible. His prior-general, William de Trahinac, absolved him of all blame, but wrote to Henry to inform him that, as soon as he had heard news of the crime, he had dismissed the work-force which the king had provided for the building of the church at Grandmont, lest the monks be partners with the king in anything. Bernard, however, in an exceptionally long letter to Henry, professed himself unable to believe in the guilt of one who was such a benefactor to their order and urged him to punish the murderers with death.[3]

Henry himself seems to have made little immediate effort at exoneration. It is likely that he did at first have strong feelings of guilt and remorse. In any case, he had a mission already on its way to the pope, and this could maintain his interests at the curia until he knew what was going to happen in France and could decide what line to take. This was the mission sent to protest against Thomas's sentences on the bishops. It had left Normandy immediately after Christmas and seems to have kept completely ahead of news of the murder. It consisted of John Cumin, a royal clerk, and the professional advocate Master David of London, together with nuncios of the archbishop of York and of the bishops of Durham, London and Salisbury. London was represented, as well as by Master David, by two canons of St Paul's, Master Hugh of London and Henry of Northampton, the schoolmaster. The mission broke up *en route*. John Cumin with the clerks of York and Durham arrived a fortnight before Master David and the rest. By aggressive methods and promising 500 marks (perhaps Roger of York's money) Cumin was on the point of securing the mission's purpose, when news of the archbishop's death halted all business and ruined its hopes. The party stayed on to do what they could for the king until reinforcements should arrive.[4]

In pursuit of vengeance for the murdered archbishop were Alexander of Wales and Gunter of Winchester, who, in company with Herbert of Bosham, had been with the archbishop of Sens when the news arrived. The two were sent on to Frascati with letters from Archbishop William, King Louis and Theobald of Blois, perhaps among others. These writings presented the case for the prosecution. The archbishop's letter, as we have seen, improves on John of Salisbury's by naming the knights and bishops and also by describing Thomas as standing before the altar, holding his cross in his hands and asking the murderers not to harm anyone but himself. It also mentions visions men had had of the still living martyr, showing scars instead of wounds. All the letters demanded the severe punishment of those responsible. And the nuncios were to tell more. Alexander and Gunter arrived at Frascati after John Cumin and before 20 March. It is possible that they were the first to bring the news of the murder to the papal court.[5]

Meanwhile the archbishop of Sens had begun to wreak the vengeance demanded of him. He and the other papal commissioner, Rotrou of Rouen, had in their possession the papal mandates dated 9 October authorizing the imposition of an interdict should the terms of the peace of Fréteval be disregarded; and these may have been reinforced later by others ordering similar action if Thomas was arrested or imprisoned. Accordingly, William of Sens summoned a provincial council to meet on 25 January with a view to implementing the threat, and required his co-commissioner to take part. Henry organized a large legation which was to go first to Sens to try to prevent the laying of the interdict and, if it failed, to appeal against the action and proceed to Frascati to prosecute the appeal. This party consisted of Rotrou of Rouen, Arnulf of Lisieux, Giles of Evreux and Roger of Worcester (once Thomas's champion), Robert de Neufbourg, dean of Evreux, Richard de Blosseville, abbot of the Cistercian house of Le Valasse, near Lillebonne, a friend of Arnulf's, Robert of Arden, archdeacon of Lisieux, an unnamed Knight Templar and the royal clerks Reginald fitzJocelin, archdeacon of Salisbury, Richard Barre and Master Henry Pinchun.

At the council Rotrou objected to the laying of the interdict on several captious technical grounds, which were brushed aside, and then, arguing that Henry should not be exacerbated further, appealed against its imposition. But William of Sens, with the unanimous support of the French bishops and abbots, laid an interdict on all Henry's Continental lands and ordered the archbishop of Rouen and the Norman bishops to observe it. Rotrou, however, wrote to Henry's Continental bishops and abbots to explain what had happened and why he would disregard the sentence. One of his reasons was that, as the king had offered to make full satisfaction to the church, the sentence, even if it had been imposed, should be relaxed.[6]

After the Council of Sens, Archbishop William sent another batch of letters to the pope, informing him what he had done and asking him to confirm the sentences. These letters are stronger than the earlier set, indeed almost hysterical. The archbishop describes Henry as another Herod, of the seed of Canaan not of Judaea, the offspring of vipers, who, having dispatched his executioners, had not feared to plough deep wounds in the symbol of the Lord's passion. Stephen, bishop of Meaux, in a supporting letter, referred to the new martyr and claimed that he had been killed by the servants of Herodian cruelty by the order of the king.[7]

The rival Anglo-Norman mission to Frascati was furnished with letters which told a quite different story. Henry's own letter is both defiant and remarkably laconic. It would seem to have been written by a chancery clerk, perhaps Geoffrey Ridel. He accused Thomas of having broken the generous peace Henry had granted him by carrying fire and sword into England and raising the question of the coronation and the kingdom. He had also, without any justification, excommunicated royal servants; and it was these, together with Englishmen who had been unable to tolerate such insolence any longer, who had attacked him and, he regretted to say, killed him. Since Henry feared that the anger he had conceived against the archbishop in times past had served as a cause of this wicked deed, he was, as God could witness, greatly upset. And as in this affair he feared even more for his reputation than for his conscience, he asked the pope to favour him with the medicine of his salubrious counsel: in other words, how best could he clear his name? This coolness was offset by a brilliant letter contributed by Arnulf of Lisieux, now in his mid-sixties and unable to go with the others to Frascati. He repeated the view that Thomas had been murdered by some enemies whom he had exacerbated so often that they had been driven to anger and madness. And he painted a touching picture of the king so prostrated by grief that they had begun to fear for his very life. Henry, Arnulf averred, feared that he might be suspected of having engineered the crime or being privy to it; but he called Almighty God to witness that he had neither willed, nor been cognizant of, nor instigated that terrible deed. He had sinned, perhaps, only in this: that he was thought still to dislike the archbishop. And on this (limited) matter he was prepared to submit himself unreservedly to the judgment of the church and humbly accept any penance imposed. Arnulf begged the pope both to punish severely the perpetrators of the abominable crime and also to preserve unsullied the innocence of the king. Later, Arnulf became so ashamed of this plea in defence of a tyrant that he omitted it from his collected correspondence.

Henry's distress on hearing of the murder is a well-attested fact. Henry de Beaumont, bishop of Bayeux, an eye-witness, described it to Herbert of Bosham, and the clerk completely accepted that Henry's sorrow had been genuine. The degree of the king's complicity, however, was, and remains, a problem for casuists. Some time after September 1174 Herbert had a private talk with Henry on the subject in circumstances unexplained. He said to the king that Thomas had been killed for Henry's sake (*pro*) and also through his agency (*per*). To this, Henry, quite unmoved as far as the clerk could see, replied – and Herbert claims to be quoting (although presumably in translation) the king's own words – 'I have sadly to grant you your *pro*, but I strenuously deny your *per*.' Herbert comments, 'Only God and the king know whether this is so.' Henry had then admitted that he was partly responsible for the death since in his anger he had uttered some callous and unlucky words in the presence of his courtiers and domestic knights which had been the occasion for the act. Herbert, writing in the late 1180s, was still agonizing over the matter.[8]

In February 1171 the royal legation, less Arnulf, and later abandoned by Rotrou of Rouen, struggled through the wintry Alps to Siena, where it was detained by political or military troubles. It was essential that some of them should reach Frascati before Maundy Thursday (25 March), when it was the custom for the pope to punish enemies of the church; and Richard Barre left the main party and made a dash for the papal court. But he found that he had been beaten to it by Alexander of Wales and Gunter, and was refused an audience. Indeed, even the cardinals would hardly speak to him. On 20 March, just in time, his fellows, the abbot of Le Valasse, Reginald fitzJocelin, Robert of Arden and Master Henry Pinchun, arrived. Their principal business seems to have been the exculpation of the king. At first they too were repulsed, but eventually Alexander agreed to see the abbot and the archdeacon of Lisieux, whom he considered the least contaminated by the murder. They did their best against the case made by Thomas's clerks; but afterwards they learnt from the more friendly cardinals that, despite their pleas, the pope intended on the Thursday to pronounce an interdict on Henry by name and on all his lands on both sides of the Channel, as well as confirm Thomas's sentences on the bishops.

In this desperate situation they took the only possible way out, a way which could have offended their masters: they informed Alexander through the friendly cardinals that they were authorized by the king to swear in the pope's presence that he would stand to the pope's judgment and would, when required, swear this oath in person. As a result, on the Thursday, about noon, when Alexander was about to celebrate Mass in the presence of all the cardinals and people of many nations, the five royal legates, as well as all the clerks representing the English bishops, were summoned into the general consistory, and were allowed to take an oath that they were empowered by their principals to swear that these would submit to the pope's judgment and mandate and confirm their submission in person. The only one not required to swear was Master William, representing the bishop of Durham, apparently as a special papal favour to the noble Hugh of Le Puiset. This total submission made with the utmost publicity allowed the pope not to name the king or the bishops when, after Mass, he excommunicated generally the killers of the archbishop and all those who had given them counsel, aid or approval, as well as those who had received them on to their land or shown them favour. One of the party, perhaps Richard Barre, immediately drafted an interim report to the king, the messenger leaving Frascati on Easter Day (28 March).

After Easter the two bishops and the dean of Evreux arrived. Their main commission seems to have been the appeal against the sentence imposed by the archbishop of Sens on 25 January, and they were not required to take the oath proffered by the others. After a fortnight or more they were called in to receive the answer to their petition, and, instead of the favourable reply they had expected, were mortified to hear Alexander confirm the interdict laid by the archbishop of Sens on Henry's Continental lands and also the sentences of excommunication and suspension imposed by Thomas on the English bishops. The pope also enjoined that Henry should not enter any church – a personal interdict. He would, however, in due course send legates to Normandy to investigate Henry's humility.

There was little satisfaction for the royal legates in any of this, except that they had prevented the laying of an interdict on England. But in the end, after a good deal of persuasion and, it was believed, the passing of a fair sum of money, they obtained letters addressed to the archbishop of Bourges and the bishop of Nevers, dated 24 April, authorizing them, provided they had not heard within a month of the return of the royal nuncios to Normandy that papal legates had crossed the Alps, to absolve conditionally the bishops of London and Salisbury from excommunication, but not from suspension, which was to remain in force. Alexander also agreed, although not readily, to write to the king. The only letter to have survived, however, is his testimonial to the services of Reginald fitzJocelin, Richard Barre and Master David, who had not been named in the other letter, because they had arrived separately at the curia. Alexander confirmed that they had negotiated most wisely and should be rewarded quite as much as the others. It seems that the royal embassy had not been one big happy family. Finally, in this series of events, on 14 May the pope ordered the archbishop of Tours to observe the interdict imposed by the archbishop of Sens in January until he or his legates should order otherwise.[9]

News of the papal actions would have reached the king in Normandy from early in May onwards, as the members of the legations straggled back.[10] By the middle of June the only matter still in doubt was when

Alexander would send legates to investigate the crime and reconcile the king, and who they would be. It might well have been conjectured that he would be in no great hurry. He clearly intended that the punishment for the murder should be exemplary. The position in the summer of 1171 was, then, that all Henry's Continental lands, from Eu and Aumale in the north to the Pyrenees and Mediterranean in the south, were under an interdict. The British Isles, however, were not included in the ban, probably because England was suffering in other ways. In addition, the murderers and all their accessories, supporters and harbourers were excommunicate. This general sentence was extremely wide-ranging and undoubtedly embraced the royal court and many of the royal servants. Moreover, none of Thomas's sentences had been relaxed, and some, particularly the excommunication of the bishops of London and Salisbury and the suspension of the archbishop of York, had been expressly confirmed. The pope had not sentenced anyone else by name, apart from declaring that the interdict extended to Henry's person.

At the beginning of August Henry went to England and, after spending some weeks in south Wales preparing for a military expedition, crossed to Ireland. He had obtained in 1154, ironically with the help of John of Salisbury, then at the papal court, the bull *Laudabiliter* from Pope Adrian IV, which sanctioned and blessed the king's intention to go to Ireland and reform the scandals in the church and Christianity to be found there, and invested him with the country. In 1171 the time had at last come. The political and military situation in the island required his personal attention, and an expedition aimed at establishing orderly government and reforming the church would not only keep him incommunicado but also earn him merit. There is some evidence that one of his ambassadors to the curia in the spring had been instructed to air this matter again. A conquest of Ireland was one of the few cards Henry could play to prevent his excommunication by name.[11] And in Ireland, where he did much to pacify the land and even held a reforming ecclesiastical synod at Cashel, he remained until May 1172 when, this time dragging his feet, he returned to meet the papal legates, Albert and Theodwin, who had arrived in Normandy some five months earlier. The casualties of the Irish expedition are a conspicuous feature of William of Canterbury's collection of St Thomas's miracles. Many of the knights who took part in it must have felt that they were in some way involved in the tragedy for which four of their members were responsible.

The murderers themselves are noticed at South Malling on the second or third day after the crime as they made their way, avoiding Rochester, to London. Eventually they took refuge at the royal castle of Knaresborough, in the West Riding of Yorkshire, south of Ripon, which was held in custody by Hugh de Morville. From there they could retreat, if necessary, by way of Hugh's lands in Cumbria to Scotland. Although they seem, at some point, to have gone temporarily to the northern kingdom, they remained at Knaresborough unmolested for about a year. William of Canterbury tells how Hugh pressingly invited an old friend, a rich man named Robert, whom he accused of neglect, to go and visit him, and how Robert declined in horror. But everyone may not have felt like this. Henry's failure to impose any constraint or punishment on the four provoked little comment and no explanation from the memorialists. Evidently Henry accepted responsibility for their misguided actions: they were his men and had acted in good faith. In 1172 he was maintaining that he had been unable to arrest them.[12]

The murderers are supposed to have asked him for advice, presumably in August 1171, when he crossed England on the way to Ireland, and were told that they had now to fend for themselves. William de Tracy had consulted his diocesan bishop, Bartholomew of Exeter, who in turn consulted the pope on the appropriate punishment for all those involved in the murder. And the four were instructed that they must go in person to the pope and accept his judgment. Hugh de Morville and Richard le Bret were with Reginald fitzUrse on his estate at Williton in north Somerset, when, in preparation for his journey, he divided that manor between his half-brother Robert and the Knights Templar. William de Tracy, with a band of retainers, seems to have followed later, but had reached Rome by the spring of 1172. Perhaps all visited the papal legates, Albert and Theodwin, *en route*. One of the penances imposed on them by the legates or the pope was to crusade in the Holy Land, possibly for fourteen years. The term would certainly have been more than the three years to which the king was sentenced later that year. William de Tracy reached Cosenza in Calabria at the toe of Italy, where he fell seriously ill and was thought by Herbert of Bosham to have died. There he granted 100 librates of land at Doccombe in Moretonhampstead in Devon to the Canterbury monks for his own soul and that of his forebears and for love of the blessed Thomas. The king confirmed the grant at Westminster in 1173–4, probably shortly after 12 July 1174 when he himself did penance at the martyr's tomb. It was believed that all four died soon, in, or on the way to, the Holy Land. But this may be wishful thinking. The William de Tracy who died about 1194 may, or may not, have been the murderer's son and namesake. But the Hugh de Morville who after 1184 married Heloise, daughter of Robert de Stuteville of Cottingham and widow of William (II) de Lancaster, and lived until 1202, when his lands went to his daughters Ada and Joan, may well have been the murderer himself. And it may be that Richard le Bret's daughter and heir, Matilda, was born after 1171. She, with her second husband, was a benefactor of the Augustinian priory of Woodspring, north of Weston-super-Mare, founded in honour of St Thomas by William de Courtenay, Reginald fitzUrse's grandson and a relative of William de Tracy.[13]

Some months after the murder Henry replaced the *Brokeis* at Canterbury by new custodians, John Mauduit and Thurstin fitzSimon; but the displaced servants were not, of course, in royal disgrace and continued to prosper elsewhere. In October 1173 Ranulf was holding Haughley castle in Suffolk (unsuccessfully) for the senior king against the rebels, and he witnessed a royal charter in 1176. He built up his estates in the Godalming–Guildford area, and these with his two serjeanties went at his death through Edelina, the eldest of his five daughters and co-heirs, to her husband, Stephen of Thornham. Ranulf's nephew, Robert, is noticed serving as a royal forest justice in 1186–7. It is not known whether the *Brokeis* blamed St Thomas for the shortage of sons in the family. One of the clan, probably Ranulf, founded a chapel in honour of the martyr in the castle of Vernay at Airvault in Poitou.[14]

By the summer of 1171 not only the king and the four murderers and many other laymen but also the archbishop of York and most of the English bishops knew that they were under ecclesiastical censure. Those whom the pope called the Gilbertian trinity, London, York and Salisbury, were in the gravest danger, for they were accused both of spurning the papal prohibition of the coronation and of advising and planning Thomas's murder. Master David of London had reported most pessimistically to his lord after Easter; but in the end wiser counsels prevailed at the curia and on 24 April Alexander sanctioned the absolution of the two bishops from their excommunication, although not from their suspension from office, provided they met his requirements. In the summer Arnulf of Lisieux wrote to the pope on behalf of Roger of York, and on 23 October Alexander authorized his release from suspension if he could rebut the accusations. Accordingly, Gilbert Foliot was absolved from excommunication on 1 August at Chaumont in the French Vexin and Roger had his suspension lifted at Aumale on 13 December. Among his oath-helpers was Master Vacarius, the Roman lawyer and canonist whom he had taken with him from Theobald's household to York. Roger in his letter of thanks to the pope interceded for the still suspended London; Gilbert dispatched a legation which included his archdeacon, Ralf of Diss, and on 27 February 1172 Alexander authorized his restoration to office if he could legally clear himself of complicity in the martyrdom. This he did at Aumale on 1 May. On 30 March Alexander had informed Jocelin of Salisbury that, because of the intercession of 'our beloved son', Jocelin's son, Reginald, and also of Robert, dean of Evreux, and the king and queen-mother of Sicily, he could be absolved on stated terms without having to travel to the curia. The exact dates, however, on which he and the rest of the delinquent English bishops were freed from their sentences are not known. But as Exeter and Chester, the latter certainly once under suspension, could reconcile the church of Canterbury in December 1171, it looks as though the papal legates on their arrival in Normandy had quickly dealt with at least the less serious cases.[15]

The papal mercy to the unholy trinity, especially the indulgence to Roger of York, caused great offence to the martyr's supporters, especially since both Roger and Gilbert were completely unrepentant in 1171–2 and regarded their plight as the work of unscrupulous enemies. In return, Herbert of Bosham raved almost unintelligibly, and John of Salisbury, in a letter to Archbishop William of Sens, resurrected the sexual scandal in which Roger had been involved when archdeacon of Canterbury. Nor was this the last outrage that Thomas's followers had to suffer. Indeed, it was the beginning of a hateful series. Roger had the prohibition of having his cross carried before him throughout the whole of England, imposed by Alexander in January 1164, once more removed – until the case should be definitively settled. And once the king had been absolved, he and the pope, able at last to become again the dearest of friends, started to promote each other's interests with enthusiasm. Only the degradation of Thomas's old enemy, Clarembald, abbot-elect of St Augustine's, by the bishops of Exeter and Worcester, acting on papal authority, in 1173, because of his dissipation of the abbey's property, gave them a little satisfaction.[16]

The legates whom Alexander sent to clear up all the consequences of Thomas's exile and death were the cardinal priests, Albert of San Lorenzo, the future Pope Gregory VIII, and Theodwin of San Vitale.[17] They were both of excellent repute and carried out their mission successfully, although, inevitably, not to the satisfaction of all. When they arrived in north France towards the end of 1171, they sent Henry, bishop of Bayeux, Richard, abbot of Le Valasse, and others to summon Henry to return from Ireland. The messengers also carried letters from Louis and several French bishops and magnates to the same end. In April Henry began to move. While crossing England he visited the dying Henry of Winchester, his kinsman, and received some salutary advice; and in the middle of May he landed at Barfleur. On 16 May he met the legates at the royal castle at Gorron in Maine and exchanged kisses of peace. Next day they moved the short distance north to the abbey of Savigny, where some Norman bishops and barons had assembled. But here Henry refused the legates' conditions because they required him to take an oath of submission before he knew what penalties they intended to impose; and he threatened to return to Ireland. But through the mediation of Rotrou of Rouen, Arnulf of Lisieux, Richard of Ilchester and Reginald fitzJocelin, who no doubt were busy negotiating the terms, he agreed to a further meeting at Avranches on the following Friday, 19 May. There everything was arranged satisfactorily, and it was settled that the ceremony of reconciliation should take place on the Sunday, when the young king would have arrived from England. On the 21st Henry publicly admitted that he was the effective cause of the archbishop's death, but swore, touching the Gospels, that he had neither ordered nor desired the killing and that he was very sorry when he heard the news. He also swore that he would accept any penance which the legates should impose.

The legates then recited from a written schedule seven requirements. Henry was not to withdraw his obedience from Alexander or his successors as long as they treated him as a catholic and christian king. He was for the period of one year, starting at the coming Whitsun (4 June), to pay the Knights Templar sufficient to maintain 200 knights in the defence of Jerusalem. He was himself to take the cross at Christmas for three years and set off in the following summer, unless he was excused by the pope. He could also count any time spent fighting the Saracens in Spain against the other. He was not to impede lawful appeals to the pope in ecclesiastical cases, but could take security from the appellants that they would not seek his or his kingdom's harm. He was to abolish all customs introduced in his time injurious to the churches of his land and not require bishops to observe them in the future. He should restore to the church of Canterbury all its possessions as they had stood one year before the archbishop had left England. Finally, he was to restore his peace and grace and their possessions to all clerks and the laity of both sexes who had been despoiled because of the archbishop. It was thought that the legates also imposed private penance on Henry, fasts and alms-giving.

After Henry had agreed to the conditions, the young king made his oath to carry them out, except those applicable to his father alone. Then the legates conducted Henry to the door of the church, where he knelt down, and, after absolving him, they took him inside the church. It was remarked that the king had neither removed any of his clothes nor been scourged before being granted absolution. Finally it was agreed that, in order to publicize the settlement, it should be confirmed in a larger assembly to be held at Caen on Tuesday, 30 May, when the archbishop of Tours and his suffragans also should attend. There Henry not only repeated his pledges but also may have released the bishops from the promise he had extorted from them to observe the Customs and renounced such a demand in future. He may also have given the legates some private assurances. Alexander confirmed the terms on 2 September.[18]

There was a feeling among Thomas's supporters that the king, like the bishops and all their enemies, had got off lightly; and clearly he, like them, was still unrepentant at heart. With Thomas out of the way, he had been able to circumscribe the concessions he had been forced to offer in the course of 1170. Although in some unofficial versions of 'the compromise of Avranches' Henry's undertakings with regard to the Customs are amplified, possibly in the light of the events at Caen or of Henry's unofficial remarks, Henry himself privately reserved his position. In a joyful letter sent immediately after Avranches and before Caen to the English bishops (only the one to Bartholomew of Exeter has survived) he remarked that he reckoned that in his time he had introduced few, if any, bad practices. In other words, his offer was illusory. Even though some rigorists might believe that promises he had made in 1170 were still binding, Henry maintained that it was Thomas who had broken the peace and abrogated the settlement. After 21 May 1172 he was bound only by the new and freely negotiated terms.[19]

The requirement that Henry should make amends to all Thomas's co-exiles and other victims of his cause, probably owed much to the repeated appeals of Herbert of Bosham to the pope and his legates. All Thomas's sisters benefited by the amnesty. Agnes Beket and her family recovered their land and position in London. In 1173 Henry, at the request of Odo, prior of Canterbury, made Mary abbess of Barking. And when he did penance at Canterbury, he asked Roheise's pardon and gave her an endowment in that city. She had with her at least two sons. After Alan 'of Tewkesbury' became prior in 1179 he and the convent presented John, son of Agnes, to the perpetual vicarage of Halstow in East Kent, in return for a pension of 1 mark of silver, and John, son of Roheise, similarly to St Mary Bothaw in the City of London, near the Beket house, for 5s. a year, a strange reversal of their apparent geographical situations. It would seem that all Thomas's relations who wanted to return were able to do so and get some compensation from the king.[20]

Thomas's ecclesiastical family did not fare so well. After the murder, deprived of a master, it dispersed, for it was not until 5 October 1174 that Richard, prior of Dover, was at last enthroned as archbishop of Canterbury. He was joined by John Planeta, perhaps from Exeter. William fitzStephen seems to have re-entered royal service without difficulty. John of Salisbury, although remaining in touch with Christ Church, probably soon took refuge at Exeter, and, under Bishop Bartholomew's patronage, made a respectable administrative and judicial career in the English church before he was elected bishop of Chartres in 1176. He died in 1180. Henry of Houghton also seems to have obtained another post, for he reported amicably two miracle stories to the Canterbury monks.

Thomas's foreign clerks must have returned to their foreign bases. Those of English domicile who had been abroad at the time of the murder did worst. Herbert of Bosham's career, the best recorded, is a sad story. In the course of 1172 he wrote letters to the legates and the pope so strange in language that it looks as though he was almost demented. To the legates he indicated that both he and 'his dear companion, Gunter' had been told that they could not return to England even if they wished. To the pope he complained of the oath of allegiance to the two kings of England being demanded, apparently by Robert de Broc. He objected particularly to a clause promising the kings no loss of their regalities, which he understood as a reference to the customs. Some clerks, including John of Salisbury and Gunter, he told the pope, had taken the oath. He himself had escaped it earlier since he and Alexander had been sent abroad; and he had no intention of taking it now.

On 24 June the pope thanked Herbert for his letter and for his services to the martyr. He condoled with him. He had instructed the legates to look after the interests of Thomas's clerks and lay servants and make sure that they could return to England and live there in safety. If they failed to secure this, Herbert was to let him know and he would do what he could for him. Alexander continued to write on his behalf. But it was a hopeless case. The clerk was an unwelcome reminder of everything that the post-martyrdom world wanted to forget. Thomas had been disarmed, purified, mythified, transformed. Herbert, bitter, dissatisfied and irreconcilable, attracted all the odium and none of the solaces of the affair. He had become, in every sense, an exile. In the late 1180s he returned to England to write his History of Thomas, which he dedicated to Archbishop Baldwin (1184–90) and his successors. Although he recovered some of his property, he claimed that nearly all involved in his story were dead and that he himself was a pilgrim wandering through a trackless desert. He had been entirely rejected by the English prelates who had started to worship the dead but would do nothing for the living.

On Henry's death Herbert entered the household of King Richard's vice-regent, William of Longchamps, bishop of Ely, possibly through the influence of Benedict of Peterborough, but soon returned to France and took refuge in the Cistercian abbey of Ourscamp in the diocese of Arras. He did not, however, become a monk. A clerk and scholar to the end, he earned his keep by writing a commentary on Jerome's 'Hebrew Psalter'. He seems to have died in 1194.[21]

The last we hear of Alexander of Wales is in a dream which a Burgundian abbot had in 1174 on the night before Guérin, abbot of Pontigny, was to be consecrated archbishop of Bourges. He saw the clerk approaching the sleeping archbishop-elect with quick steps, as though on a mission, and telling him that St Thomas intended to be present at the consecration and supply the place of the necessary fourth bishop. Clearly he was remembered with the greatest respect in those circles and as Thomas's messenger *par excellence*. But what happened to him, the faithful Gunter of Winchester and the lesser fry is unknown. One of Thomas's lay servants, his marshal, William de Capes, was provided for by Christ Church, Canterbury. He was appointed Keeper of the Back Gate, gave the monks faithful service and was still alive in 1189.[22]

Meanwhile extraordinary events had been taking place at Canterbury. While the *Brokeis* remained there as royal agents, they acted vigorously to prevent the murder having vexatious consequences, and at least until Whitsun hampered pilgrims and threatened the monks. Shortly after Whit, Robert de Broc's brother, William, was cured at the tomb; and this must have changed their tune. The cathedral church, although reopened to the public in Easter week 1171, remained out of liturgical use until the festival of St Thomas the Apostle (21 December), the martyr's secular birthday, when, with the permission of the pope and the legates, it was reconciled by Bishops Bartholomew of Exeter and Richard Peche of Chester. In the course of that year, while the monks murmured the offices in the chapter house, the cathedral went through a series of transformations. At first it had been desolate and deserted, with the crosses veiled and the altars bare, the bells silent; and then, no doubt to the discomfiture and consternation of the monks and the amazement of all authorities, it was changed into a kind of field-dressing-station, the goal for all sorts of sick and indigent, the seat of new trades and occupations.[23]

John of Salisbury, in his letter describing the Passion, had proclaimed Thomas to be a martyr and had asked his correspondents whether, in anticipation of papal authority, it would be in order to honour and treat him as such. In due course he got a reply from his old friend, Peter of Celle, abbot of St Rémi at Rheims, agreeing with his implied wish: where there are manifest signs of the judgment of God it is unnecessary to await the judgment of men. John and his allies in the French church relied primarily on a favourite text from the writings of St Augustine: it is the cause, not the punishment, which makes the martyr. And this was quite enough for some fastidious theologians, like Herbert of Bosham, who despised or suspected the more popular signs of sanctity, miraculous cures and other vulgar marvels.[24]

Nevertheless, John had, again possibly in anticipation, quoted and slightly expanded the equally popular texts from St Matthew's Gospel referring to the blind receiving their sight, the lame walking, lepers being cleansed, the deaf hearing, the raising of the dead and the casting out of devils, at the martyr's tomb. And his opinion was not misplaced, for these signs were, after a slow start, to appear in great numbers. Thomas was to become one of the great thaumaturgical saints. Cures through his intervention, either at Canterbury or elsewhere, became not only numerous but also comprehensive in range. Some saints, or their clientèle, specialized, but not Thomas or his. William of Canterbury faced the question, which some people must have been raising: why did Thomas, who, it might be supposed, was now stripped of all covetousness, pay so much attention to men's vows and promises that it looked as though he delighted in their gifts? It was, William thought, because during his lifetime he had received so much money on loan for the maintenance of his fellow-exiles and household, which he had been unable to repay, that, in death, in order to avoid the reputation of a debtor and give further cause for complaint, he wanted to repay every creditor in full. William also thought that young saints should relieve their elders of the burden of providing miraculous signs and allow those to retire with the title of *emeriti*.[25]

The Canterbury monks themselves were, however, for a variety of reasons, originally fearful of or hostile to the cult. The royal officials in control of the city issued a proclamation that the dead archbishop should not be venerated as a martyr and arrested any pilgrim or well-wisher they found, either punishing him on the spot or conveying him in fetters to prison. Prudently the monks kept the church closed to the general public and only admitted, and then secretly, persistent or influential visitors. One of their members, a certain Ralf, was exiled to Colchester Abbey for his championship of Thomas.[26] The cult seems to have started spontaneously, and at Canterbury among the poor and sick. Elsewhere, the impact of the news of the murder caused a number of individual sufferers to call on the martyr for help, and, if their health improved, to travel to Canterbury in order to return thanks and tell the tale.

At the heart of the cult was the blood of the martyr. And this added to the monks' difficulties. There were the practical problems, such as shortage of supply, its deterioration and their dislike of some of its applications, even fear that the smell and taste might cause nausea rather than relief in the patient. There was also the theological difficulty that hitherto the only blood drunk in Christian ceremonies was that of the Saviour. The drinking of a martyr's blood, and of one still unconfirmed in that rank, was not only revolutionary but could be regarded as wrong. The answer to the first problem was, of course, dilution; and from the start this was practised by all holders of the precious commodity. The appeal at first was to the widow's cruse; but the practice of mixing wine and water in the sacrament of the Eucharist together with the general belief in contagion obviously rendered any subterfuge or excuse unnecessary. However, reluctance on the part of the monks to administer the potion lingered for some time.[27]

On Monday, 4 January, six days after the murder, a poor woman named Britheva recovered her sight through a neighbour's application of one of the blood-stained rags obtained on the previous Tuesday. On the following day arrived William, a London priest, suffering from paralysis of the tongue. He had been instructed by a clerk of his acquaintance, who in his turn had received the order during a dream, to go to the new martyr at Canterbury: he would be cured if a drop of the martyr's blood was put on his tongue. William was allowed to spend a night at the tomb, have the application of blood and also have a drink of water tinctured with blood. But this second case may have imposed a check, for, although William showed a small improvement at Canterbury, he did not recover his speech until after he had returned to London. Benedict records only three more cures at Canterbury before Easter, that is to say for most of the three months of January, February and March. Audrey, a fever patient, after receiving a drink of water and blood, changed colour to a rosy pink. The dying son of a local citizen, whom it took three days to persuade the monks to provide a draught, recovered on 25 March. And Godiva, wife of Matthew of Canterbury, was cured of swollen legs.[28]

Blood was also released sparingly for use elsewhere. Ulviva, matron of a hostel for the poor and vagrant, acquired as much as could be contained in a filbert nut. Later, the monk Ralf sent a very small portion in an ampoule sealed with wax as a thanksgiving to Colchester Abbey. Also important in the beginnings of the cult were the operations of William, priest of either Patrixbourne or, more likely, Bishopsbourne, both 4 or 5 miles south-east of the city. He foresaw the value of Thomas's relics should he be recognized as a saint and set about collecting what he could. He bought at little cost the martyr's cloak, stained with blood, from the pauper to whom it had been given and also acquired an ampoule of liquid blood which proved to be inexhaustible. When, however, he gave some of it in a little wooden box, sealed with wax, to an itinerant preacher, it mysteriously disappeared. When the daughter of a local knight lying in a coma was wrapped in the cloak she recovered her senses.[29]

The breakthrough occurred on Easter Sunday (28 March), ironically through a miraculous cure in which few of the monks had much faith and about which Benedict himself had serious doubts. The apparent cure of Samson, a supposed dumb man from Oxfordshire, but probably an impostor, after being given a draught of water and blood in the church, caused a mob to burst in and a lame woman named Emmeline to throw away her crutch. On the same day Godefrid, the monastic baker, acquired a small piece of cloth stained with blood and cured his son of fever by giving him an infusion of it to drink. Later he equally successfully attached pieces of the cloth to the necks of two other febrile children.[30]

Perhaps even more influential were the reports which began to come in of miracles performed by St Thomas elsewhere, in Kent, Sussex, Surrey, Essex, Berkshire and Gloucestershire, and even as far away as West Yorkshire. It was decided to reopen the church, and on 2 April access to the tomb was allowed to pilgrims. It was probably at this time that Benedict was assigned to be in attendance. His duties were to distribute the healing water, to collect the oblations and investigate and record the cures and miracles. These developments provoked the de Brocs to make plans to snatch the body. The monks, forewarned, transferred it from the sarcophagus to a wooden coffin, which they hid behind the altar of St Mary, presumably the one also in the crypt, not far away. And their precautions, aided by a terrible thunderstorm, foiled the attempt. By Whitsun (16 May), it seems, persecution had stopped. The church had been full of sick persons on 3 May, and up to ten cures on a single day were recorded.[31]

Once the scare was over, the monks boxed in the sarcophagus with massive reinforced stone walls surmounted by a heavy marble slab. In both the side walls were two windows which allowed the worshipper to insert his head and kiss the tomb. The miraculous water, which began to be called 'the water of St Thomas' or 'Canterbury water', was at first distributed in anything handy, but increasingly in little wooden boxes, perhaps turned out of boxwood, which naturally tended to split or dry up. After experiments, the *ampulla* or phial cast in tin or lead was devised; and this, hanging from the neck, became the badge of a Canterbury pilgrim as familiar as the scallop-shell of those who had travelled to St James at Compostella in Spain and the palm of the visitors to Jerusalem. The phials seem to have cost a farthing and were taken by the pilgrim from an altar near the tomb and filled by the attendant monk from some sort of jug. Herbert of Bosham averred that even the Welsh respected pilgrims who carried them.[32]

Innumerable cults sprang up in the Middle Ages, some spontaneous, some contrived; some soundly based, others clearly spurious. Each newcomer was in competition with those already in existence, and most were short-lived. Almost all had their ups and downs. The cult of St Thomas, after recovering from a shaky start, was one of the most successful of all times. The murder in his cathedral of an archbishop who was fighting for a cause could not fail to be regarded by some people as a martyrdom; and the vast army of poor and sick would seek any possible remedy. No doubt also, as is often said, Thomas was regarded as the victim of a harsh government, as a popular hero. Angevin rule pressed heavily on most sections of the population, and Kent during the archbishop's exile had probably suffered more than most. But this protest would not have carried the cult very far, even though the Christ Church monks soon realized that they had acquired a most valuable financial asset. The movement acquired amazing momentum. The scepticism of enemies and the fastidiousness of some friends were both drowned in the torrent. After seventeen months, at the end of July 1172, William of Canterbury was appointed to help the existing custodian, Benedict, who was finding the job too much for him.[33] The inexhaustibility of the water and the simplicity of the procedures were important factors. There were enough reputable cures to arouse general hope, and failures, were, as usual, explained by sin, lack of faith or some other insufficiency on the part of the petitioner. There was also a rapid and extensive distribution of the water and other relics, particularly shreds of the hair shirt, for this had been in direct contact with the body. But if miracles occurred at Pontigny, none was reported from Sens or Rheims.

What was decisive in the end was the public acceptance of the martyr in a relatively short time by most of his enemies as well as his friends. If the cause had remained in the hands of Louis VII of France and French bishops, the triumph of the cult might not have been so overwhelming. When the students at the University of Paris organized themselves into nations in the early thirteenth century and the host nation opted for St Thomas as its patron saint, the English had to make do with St Edmund. Henry II, however, was shrewd enough to heal the rift with his old servant posthumously and make renewed use of him, thus depriving Louis of his former spiritual advantage. England lacked a really popular national shrine, like St Denis in France. St Edmund was only of limited interest, the cult of St Edward at Westminster always precarious. Neither had contributions to make like the water of St Thomas. The proliferation of miraculous cures and other 'signs' confounded the doubters. Papal canonization made the cult official.

The process was, however, even by the unformalized standards of the period, remarkably casual. It is most unlikely that any official dossier of evidence and testimonials was compiled; and few preliminary documents appear in the several letter collections. It may be that William of Canterbury had been made an additional custodian of the shrine in July 1172 in order to compile a Book of Miracles suitable for transmission to Rome; but that project was overtaken by events. It is certain that no petition for Thomas's canonization went to the pope from the English king and church, as in the case of King Edward the Confessor twelve years before, and as would normally be expected. The involvement of the monastery of Christ Church was, in view of Henry's hostility, probably both late and clandestine. William of Canterbury states that the convent sent a clerk, William of Monkton, to Rome to get the martyr's festival recognized, but at a time when, unknown to them, the bull of canonization had already been issued. The main thrust seems to have come from Thomas's clerks, especially John of Salisbury and Herbert of Bosham, who were not only active as individuals but also organized influential support in the French kingdom and church. Alexander and his court needed convincing; and the Anonymous 'of Lambeth' (II) claims that the first petition was turned down.[34]

Thomas's advocates, as exemplified by John and Herbert, rested their case on three planks: the *poena*, the punishment or martyrdom; the *causa*, the issues the martyr had died for; and the *signa*, the miracles. Herbert naturally emphasized the first two, which were controversial. Alexander naturally, and with typical prudence, preferred the third, which was open to investigation and bypassed the most contentious matters. It is likely, again sensibly, that he took no action before Henry's submission to the church in May 1172. He then instructed his legates, Albert and Theodwin, to inquire into the miracles. And, on receipt of their favourable testimony (based, it seems, on hearsay), he canonized the martyr on Ash Wednesday, 21 February 1173, at Segni. According to his biographer, the Cardinal Boso, Thomas was canonized at the request of the clergy and people of France, because of the miracles. In the letters announcing the event, dated 10–12 March, the papal chancery varied the grounds for the act according to the destination. There is, for example, much more emphasis on the justice of the martyr's cause in the letter to the bishop of Aversa in Italy than in those to the English church. In the notification to Christ Church, the monks were ordered, as was customary, to translate the body to a more honourable tomb. But, because of the fire of 5 September 1174, the rebuilding of the church, the death of Archbishop Richard in 1184, and the bitter quarrel between the monks and his two successors, Baldwin and Hubert Walter, and the interdict in John's reign, this was not done until 1220 by Archbishop Stephen Langton in order to celebrate the martyr's jubilee.[35]

It was, therefore, to the fortress-like tomb in the crypt with its four portholes that the pilgrims continued to flock. In the autumn of 1172 the young king joined them. And the success of the cult was both confirmed and assured when, in July 1174, the senior king made a much more spectacular visit. A rebellion against his rule had started in April 1173, instigated by his wife and elder sons, aided by all his external enemies, including the kings of France and Scots, and supported by disaffected barons in all parts of his empire. The murder of the archbishop and Henry's submission at Avranches may well have reduced respect for his authority. He had become a king of ill-repute. But the young Henry's attempt to exploit his father's offences against the church and thwart his plans to fill the vacant bishoprics with Thomas's enemies failed completely. The pope and the entire Norman and English churches, with the possible exception of Arnulf of Lisieux, who later was accused of harbouring relatives of the rebels, rallied whole-heartedly to the senior king. But by the summer of 1174 it looked as though the Angevin empire was about to collapse. In June Henry left Anjou, the fatherland and strategic centre, passed through Normandy, crossed from Barfleur to Southampton, taking with him some of his most important political prisoners, including his own queen and the young Queen Margaret, and, after putting them in safe custody, travelled direct to Canterbury. He had come in order to make his peace with the martyr and entreat his support.

On Friday, 12 July, as he approached Canterbury down the London road, he dismounted at Harbledown, where the cathedral came into sight, and walked the rest, about a mile, wearing a raincoat. Half way, at St Dunstan's, outside the West Gate, he removed his boots. On reaching the tomb, he prostrated himself and, in the presence of his own men, all the monks and some abbots and bishops, publicly confessed his sins, including his being the unwitting cause of the martyrdom. He asked that he should be punished and that the brethren should pray for him. He removed his cloak but retained his underwear, described by Guernes as a green smock over a hair shirt. The prelates in attendance, led by Gilbert Foliot, administered five strokes of the rod apiece, each of the eighty monks three strokes. As Henry survived the flagellation, it must have been largely symbolic. After the punishment he offered at the shrine 4 marks of pure gold (£24) and a silk pall, assigned the convent 40 librates of land and promised to restore to them every right that the martyr had claimed. Finally he undertook to build a monastery in honour of the saint. The rest of the day and the whole night he spent fasting and without leaving for any call of nature, lying on the bare ground by the tomb, in public humiliation, for he ordered that no other pilgrim should be kept out. Next morning, after attending Mass and visiting each altar in the main church, he was given the water to drink, hung a phial of it round his neck, pulled his boots on to his dirty and probably blood-stained feet and rode off to London, which he reached the next day, 14 July. There he fell sick and continued his acts of piety, granting a charter to the hospital at Harbledown. In return, Thomas had pity on his old master. The fortune of war changed decisively in Henry's favour. By September all enemies and rebels had either been defeated or were ready to submit.[36]

Herbert of Bosham recalls that at the meeting he had with Henry some time after September 1174, he told him of a dream Thomas had had of the rebellion. He had seen the king attacked by a great flock of birds who were tearing him to bits, and, mindful of their old friendship, had intervened and driven them off. One man, however, had helped the birds, an old courtier, now dead, whom Thomas had named. But when Henry asked Herbert eagerly who it was, the clerk refused to tell. For his part, Henry informed Herbert that it was on the very day he had left Canterbury, Saturday, 13 July, and at the very hour at which he had attended Mass, that William, king of Scots, had been captured by royal troops at Alnwick.[37]

In many ways Henry's pilgrimage to Canterbury ends the story of Thomas's life and death. It remains to consider his achievements. Most obvious is his extraordinarily successful career. For a London merchant's son to have become royal chancellor, archbishop of Canterbury and a saint can hardly be matched. He climbed adroitly the ladders of opportunity. The main shadow over his career, until the final illumination, was the sin of pride, one of the deadliest of the cardinal sins, with which he was charged venomously by his enemies. Although admitted ruefully by some of his friends, it could be transmuted into grandeur and magnificence. It also, paradoxically, saved him from remaining a worldly archbishop and carried him to victory, against all the odds, over the rulers of the world.

He certainly left his mark on history, and, characteristic of many great men, the totality of his achievement appears to be greater than the sum of the parts. He was a glorious royal chancellor, but, it seems, in no way a creative or even an assiduous administrator. Although his influence on Henry's policy cannot be gauged, his supposed measures earned him more odium than praise in church circles. His rule as archbishop can be viewed as disastrous for all concerned. From beginning to end Christ Church, Canterbury was without proper direction and for more than eight years the see and diocese were in the hands of probably rapacious royal officials. His lasting unpopularity with the monks is undoubted. The English church was gradually denuded of bishops and abbots. The most distinguished member of the bench, Gilbert Foliot, was almost destroyed and few of the other survivors escaped damage. There was every reason for the bitterness of Gilbert and his supporters. The immediate interests of king and pope alike were harmed by Thomas's intransigence. Only Henry's enemies gained. The one benefit which accrued to the papacy from his stand, and in the long term it outweighed the damage, was the proliferation of appeals to the curia. This traffic led to the rapid development of the papal appellate jurisdiction, the reorganization of ecclesiastical courts and the system of judges-delegate. All parties had striven to use or manipulate papal power. And this enhanced Alexander's dignity. Most churchmen admitted that Thomas was fighting for the rights and liberties of his church and of the whole church, as he saw them, although many thought from start to finish that he was an ignorant and incompetent general, with the great weakness of uncompromising obstinacy.

The effect of the martyrdom is no less problematical. During the first flush of the new cult Benedict of Peterborough thought that a great religious revival had occurred at Canterbury, in the country and in Christendom at large. But even in the medium term that was a mistaken view. The monks of Canterbury, already undisciplined, were corrupted by the new wealth brought by the pilgrims and were considered disgraceful by two archbishops as unlike as the Cistercian Baldwin (1184–90) and the royal servant Hubert Walter (1193–1205). It is of interest to note that in September 1172 the monks wanted to elect as archbishop their prior Odo and nominated him again in 1184 when he was abbot of Battle, and that in 1191 they successfully elected Reginald fitzJocelin, by then bishop of Bath. Both these were former enemies of the saint and only sudden death kept Reginald from this triumph. It is of the deepest significance that Benedict, when he was translated to Peterborough in 1177 against his will, took with him the pavement stones on which the martyr had fallen and spilt his blood. From these he had two altars made for his new church. Benedict had also thought that Thomas was a martyr for Alexander's cause and that the martyrdom put the seal of authenticity on that pope, strengthening him against his rival. No doubt Thomas was exploited posthumously by Alexander as by many others.[38]

The key to the effect that the martyrdom had on the lot of the church in England is the form and contents of the Compromise or Concordat of Avranches. It is rightly so called, for it does indeed have the character of a negotiated peace treaty incorporating mutual concessions. Even the penal clauses were from the start understood to be renegotiable. It may be presumed, but cannot be shown, that Henry did contribute to the defence of Jerusalem – according to one commentator to the tune of 300 bizants per knight, that is to say, 60,000 gold pieces in all. But he never went on a crusade. Gerald of Wales, a severe critic, informs us that this part of the penance was commuted by the pope to the building of three monasteries, and that Henry acquitted it fraudulently by changing the secular canons of Holy Cross Waltham in Essex into regulars, by replacing the nuns of Amesbury in Wiltshire with foreign sisters from Fontevraud in Anjou, both in 1177, and by founding a modest Carthusian priory at Witham in Somerset in 1178–9. Henry, however, in reality did rather better than this. Although he was not a deeply pious king like his descendants Henry III and Edward I or Louis IX of France, he had always taken his religious and charitable duties seriously, favouring those religious orders which were fashionable at the time. After the mid-1170s his benefactions to churches, just like his grandfather's after the White Ship disaster, increased considerably. But, characteristically, he usually aimed at the maximum effect at the lowest cost. Generosity went against the grain.[39]

As for the issues for which Thomas had gone into exile and for which his supporters believed he had died, Alexander had reduced his immediate requirements to three: an end to restrictions on appeals to Rome in ecclesiastical cases, the abolition of all evil customs introduced by Henry and the release of bishops, present and future, from the obligation to observe the customs of the realm. No doubt, as with the proposals in 1170, Alexander intended this to be merely the start of a more extended reform of the English church. But equally well, as Henry himself believed, it could lead to little or nothing. In fact papal clemency and patience paid off. Alexander was most helpful to Henry during the rebellion of 1173–4. Disregarding all objections and dispensing with all impediments, he confirmed the elections of Richard of Dover to Canterbury, Reginald fitzJocelin to Bath, Dean John of Greenford to Chichester, Geoffrey Ridel to Ely, Robert Foliot to Hereford, Geoffrey, Henry's bastard, to Lincoln, Richard of Ilchester to Winchester and, in 1175, John of Oxford to Norwich. The inclusion of four of Henry's most active agents in his struggle with Thomas, some of whom were defamed of other grave sins and imperfections, shows Italian diplomacy at its most supple.[40]

In return for this benevolence Henry made some further limited concessions. One effect of the martyrdom had been to change the tune of the Bolognese decretists. The majority accepted the martyr's arguments, asserted a blanket immunity of clerical criminals from the jurisdiction of secular judges and reduced the exceptions to one: incorrigibility. After 1190 English and Norman canonists, who had been more hesitant, fell into line. Henry, affected by feelings of guilt, the change in juristic opinion and political considerations, gave way in some directions. In 1172–3 he conceded 'free elections' to the bishoprics – with the results we have just noticed. In 1175 a papal legate, Hugh of Pierleone, cardinal-deacon of Sant'Angelo, arrived in England, the first to be admitted since 1138. He came to deal with Henry's proposed divorce of Eleanor of Aquitaine, and, instead, negotiated a concordat. Henry agreed to abandon the procedure laid down in chapter 3 of the Constitutions of Clarendon for the trial and punishment of criminous clerks. In return the legate conceded that clerks guilty of forest offences could be tried and punished in the royal court, and, moreover, that all cases concerning the secular lands and services of clerks should be heard in the appropriate feudal court. In 1178 Alexander went further and abandoned to the lay court the hearing of all cases concerning the possession of land, even when held in free-alms. In 1175–6 Henry also promised the legate that royal courts would punish most severely murderers of clerks (he had not punished Thomas's assassins in any way), that he would not force clerks to fight the ordeal by battle and that he would not keep bishoprics and abbeys vacant for more than a year without adequate cause.[41]

Thus within a decade of the martyrdom most of the frictional points between two competing jurisdictions and systems of law were resolved by negotiation. Whether such a settlement could have been made without the murder of an archbishop is a moot point. But the occasion did not greatly affect the result. While Henry abandoned formally most royal customs which were repugnant to canon law as newly interpreted, he still retained the substance of power, control over 'free' elections and the real lever, control over the temporalities of the church.

· Meanwhile, Alexander, cautious as usual, had given no rulings on these controversial matters. But perhaps in the year following the English concordat of 1176 he accepted the new Bolognese line in a decretal (*Licet praeter* or *At si clerici*) addressed to Sicily. However, this late conversion to the repudiation of double punishment tied the church's hands unduly, for there were occasions when it actually wanted the lay authority to add a second penalty. What was it to do with dangerous rebels against ecclesiastical authority, particularly the heretics who were beginning to become a problem? It began to backtrack, and by 1209 (Innocent III's decretal *Novimus*) it had restored its power to ask (in effect, require) the lay authority to add a temporal punishment, such as execution by fire. The procedure had become an option open to the church. Initiative had been transferred from the secular to the ecclesiastical authorities. That made all the difference.[42]

We can see that after Thomas's death things were never quite the same again, whether in the English church or in Latin Christendom at large. He had, through his stand against Henry and his martyrdom, brought the archaic English customs to the notice of the pope and cardinals and all canon lawyers and had succeeded in getting them scrutinized, debated and in part abolished or reformed. That these changes would probably have come about in process of time as the common law of the church developed and expanded into the remotest regions does not diminish Thomas's achievement. He succeeded, with the help of the French king and church, despite the violent opposition of his own king and the discouragement of the pope, in accelerating the process. Also, although himself not much of a jurist, by his martyrdom he had persuaded the cream of the cream, the Bolognese masters, to change the actual law of the church in deference to his opinions. Such an influence on events is given to few. What is more, Thomas's behaviour reanimated the tradition of bellicosity in the church, a truculence which not only protected the church's own rights but also helped to defend the rights of other men against tyrannical rulers. Stephen Langton, Edmund Rich and John Pecham were archbishops of Canterbury in the thirteenth century who were not unmindful of the example set by their awkward and determined predecessor.

Thomas's life contains so many contradictions and controversial features that it has always been of interest. A year or two after his death, Peter of Celle, abbot of St Rémi at Rheims, in a letter to John of Salisbury, then at Exeter, reminded his old friend of how, during the exile, they had often joked together about Thomas and groaned over the impossibility of ever being able to obtain a shrine big enough to contain him. And now God had made of them a laughing-stock, for now everyone in England as in France was flocking to his tomb – and he himself had just returned from a pilgrimage to Canterbury. These two choice souls and exquisite scholars retained, even after the tragedy, a touch of the old affectionate mockery which they had been wont to bestow on that *monstre sacré*, to whose cause they were nonetheless totally committed. But they were also awed by his unexpected triumph through the mysterious working of God, to whom all things were possible. It was something to ponder.[43]

NOTES AND REFERENCES

Method of reference

So as to avoid unnecessary interference with the text, and to save space, references are usually grouped at the end of a paragraph, and within the note are cited in order.

Common abbreviations

A.I	(? Roger of Pontigny), in *Mats.* (q.v.), iv
A.II	(of Lambeth), in *Mats.* iv
Abbott	E.A.Abbott, *St Thomas of Canterbury, his death and miracles* (2 vols., 1898)
A. of T.	Alan of Tewkesbury, in *Mats.* ii
Arnulf, *Letters*	*The Letters of Arnulf of Lisieux*, ed. Frank Barlow, R. Hist. Soc., Camden 3rd ser., lxi (1939)
Barlow, *EC*	F.Barlow, *The English Church, 1066–1154* (1979)
Benet	Benet of St Albans, ed. F.Michel, *Chronique des ducs de Normandie* (Docs. inédits sur l'histoire de France, Paris, 1844), iii. 461–509, 619–25
B. of P.	Benedict of Peterborough, in *Mats.* ii. His miracles are cited by book and chapter
Brooke and Keir, *London*	C.N.L.Brooke, assisted by Gillian Keir, *London, 800–1216* (1975)
Cant. Chron. 1970	*The Canterbury Chronicle 1970*, no. 65, published by the Friends of Canterbury Cathedral
Councils and Synods	*Councils and Synods with other documents relating to the English Church, I, A.D. 871–1204*, eds. D.Whitelock, M.Brett, C.N.L.Brooke, Pt. II, 1066–1204 (1981)
Delisle–Berger	L.Delisle and E.Berger, *Recueil des Actes de Henri II . . . concernant les provinces françaises et les affaires de France* (3 vols., Paris, 1909–20)
Diceto, *Abbrev.Chron.*	*Radulphi de Diceto Opera Historica*, ed. W.Stubbs (Rolls ser., 1876)
—, *Ymagines*	*Radulphi de Diceto Opera Historia*, ed. W.Stubbs (Rolls ser., 1876)
Domesday Monachorum	*The Domesday Monachorum of Christ Church, Canterbury*, ed. D.C.Douglas (1944)

Draco Normannicus   by Etienne de Rouen, in *Chronicles of the reigns of Stephen, Henry II and Richard I*, ed. R. Howlett (Rolls ser., vol. ii, 1885)

Duggan, *TH*   A. Duggan, *Thomas Becket: a Textual History of his Letters* (1980)

E. G.   Edward Grim, in *Mats.* ii

E.H.D.   *English Historical Documents*, ii. 1042–1189, eds. D. C. Douglas and G. W. Greenaway (2nd edn 1981)

E.H.R.   *The English Historical Review*

Eyton   R. W. Eyton, *Court, Household and Itinerary of King Henry II* (1878)

Foreville, *Becket*   R. Foreville, *Thomas Becket dans la Tradition historique et hagiographique* (Variorum Reprints, London, 1981)

—, *ER*   *L'Église et la Royauté en Angleterre sous Henri II Plantagenet* (Paris, n.d., ? 1942)

—, 'Les Origines'   in Foreville, *Becket*

—, 'Lettres "Extravagantes"'   in Foreville, *Becket*

—, *TB* (Sédières)   *Thomas Becket, Actes du Colloque International de Sédières, 19–24 aôut, 1973*, ed. R. Foreville (Paris, 1975)

—, 'Tradition et Comput'   in Foreville, *Becket*

Gervase, *Act. Pontif.*   *Actus Pontificum* in *Historical Works*, ed. W. Stubbs (Rolls ser., 1879–80)

—, *Chron.*   *Chronica* in *Historical Works*, ed. W. Stubbs (Rolls ser., 1879–80)

GFol, *Letters*   *The Letters and Charters of Gilbert Foliot*, eds. A. Morey and C. N. L. Brooke (1967)

Guernes   Guernes de Pont-Sainte-Maxence, ed. E. Walberg (Lund, 1922)

H. of B.   Herbert of Bosham, in *Mats.* iii

Howden, *Benedict*   *Gesta Regis Henrici Secundi Benedicti Abbatis*, ed. W. Stubbs (Rolls ser., 1867)

—, *Chronica*   *Chronica Rogeri de Hovedene*, ed. W. Stubbs (Rolls ser., 1868–71)

J.E.H.   *Journal of Ecclesiastical History*

J.–L.   P. Jaffé, G. Wattenbach, S. Loewenfeld *et al.*, *Regesta Pontificum Romanorum . . . ad a. 1198* (1885–8)

J. of S.   John of Salisbury, in *Mats.* ii

—, *Entheticus*   'The *Entheticus* of John of Salisbury', *Traditio*, 31 (New York, 1975)

—, *Hist. Pont.*   *Historia Pontificalis*, ed. M. Chibnall (1956)

—, *Letters*   *Early Letters*, eds. W. J. Millor, H. E. Butler, C. N. L. Brooke (1955); *Later Letters*, eds. Millor and

	Brooke (1979)
—, *Metalogicon*	ed. C.C.J. Webb (1929)
—, *Policraticus*	ed. C.C.J. Webb (1909)
Knowles, *ATB*	D. Knowles, 'Archbishop Thomas Becket: a character study', in *Proc. of the British Academy*, 35 (1949), 177
—, *Ep. Col.*	*The Episcopal Colleagues of Archbishop Thomas Becket* (1951)
—, *TB*	*Thomas Becket* (1970)
Lansdowne Anonymous	in *Mats.* iv
Mats.	*Materials for the History of Thomas Becket, archbishop of Canterbury*, ed. J.C. Robertson (i–vi), J.B. Sheppard (vii) (Rolls ser., 1875–85)
Morey and Brooke, *GFol*	A. Morey and C.N.L. Brooke, *Gilbert Foliot and his Letters* (1965)
Newburgh, *Historia*	in *Chronicles of the reigns of Stephen, Henry II and Richard I*, ed. R. Howlett (Rolls ser., vol. i, 1884)
Ohnsorge, *Legaten*	W. Ohnsorge, *Die Legaten Alexanders III. im ersten Jahrzehnt seines Pontifikats (1159–1169)* (Berlin, 1928)
PR	Pipe Rolls: 31 Henry I, 2–4 Henry II, ed. J. Hunter (1833, 1844); 5 Hen. IIff., publ. by Pipe Roll Soc.
Quadrilogus	by Elias of Evesham, in *Mats.* iv
Radford	Lewis B. Radford, *Thomas of London before his Consecration*, Cambridge Hist. Essays, VII (1894)
Reuter, 'Papal Schism'	T.A. Reuter, 'The Papal Schism, the Empire and the West, 1159–1169', unpubl. Oxford D.Phil. thesis, 1975
RHF	*Recueil des historiens des Gaules et de la France*, eds. M. Bouquet *et al.* (Paris, 1733ff.)
R. of C.	Robert of Cricklade's *Vita*, as reconstructed by M. Orme, 'A reconstruction of Robert of Cricklade's Vita et Miracula S. Thomae Cantuariensis', *Analecta Bollandiana*, 84 (1966), 379–98
Saltman, *Theobald*	A. Saltman, *Theobald, archbishop of Canterbury* (1956)
Sanders, *Baronies*	I.J. Sanders, *English Baronies . . . 1086–1327* (1960)
Smalley, *Becket Conflict*	B. Smalley, *The Becket Conflict and the Schools* (1973)
SSC	*Select Charters . . . of English Constitutional History*, ed. W. Stubbs, revised by H.W.C. Davis (1921)
Stanley	A.P. Stanley, *Historical Memorials of Canterbury* (2nd edn, 1855)
Summa Causae	*Summa Causae inter Regem et Thomam*, in *Mats.* iv.
Thomas, *Acta*	*English Episcopal Acta II, Canterbury 1162–1190*, eds. C.R. Cheney, B.E.A. Jones (1986)
Thómas Saga	*Thómas Saga Erkibyskups*, ed. E. Magnússon (Rolls

ser., 1875–83)

Torigni, *Chron.*   *The Chronicle of Robert of Torigni*, in *Chronicles of the Reigns of Stephen, Henry II and Richard I*, ed. R. Howlett (Rolls ser., vol. iv, 1889)

Tout, 'Place of St Thomas'   T. F. Tout, 'Place of St Thomas of Canterbury in History', *Bull. of the John Rylands Library, Manchester*, 6 (1921–2), 235–65

Urry, *Canterbury*   W. Urry, *Canterbury under the Angevin Kings* (1967)

W. fS.   William fitzStephen, in *Mats.* iii

Winton Domesday   F. Barlow, M. Biddle, O. Von Feilitzen, D. J. Keene, *Winchester in the Early Middle Ages* (1976)

W. of C.   William of Canterbury, in *Mats.* i. His miracles are cited by book and chapter.

World of J. of S.   *The World of John of Salisbury*, ed. M. Wilks, Studies in Church History, subsidia 3 (1984)

Introduction

General

Most of the early Lives are printed, in an arbitrary order, in *Mats.* i–iv. The relationship between them has been much discussed. Radford, pp. 244ff., gives a summary of the views generally held at the time of writing (1894), primarily those of J. C. Robertson, who had written a life of the saint (1859) and, with J. B. Sheppard, had edited *Mats.* (1875–85). Cf. also Abbott in 1898. Since then important work has been done by E. Walberg. See the introduction to Guernes (1922), pp. xiiiff., and his several articles collected in *La Tradition hagiographique de Saint Thomas Becket avant la fin du XIIe siècle* (Paris, 1929). Knowles, *TB*, pp. 172ff., summarized the orthodoxy of 1970. The date of John of Salisbury's *Vita* is the most controversial. Duggan, *TH*, p. 97, suggests that his *Vita et Passio* were prefaced to his own collection of Becket correspondence, which in 1174–6 was incorporated into A. of T.'s great collection. This would account for the brevity of the *Vita*. I have also benefited from discussions with Dr Timothy Reuter on this matter. For William fitzStephen, M. Cheney, 'William fitzStephen and his Life of Archbishop Thomas', in *Church and Government in the Middle Ages*, ed. C. N. L. Brooke *et al.* (1976), pp. 139ff. For Herbert of Bosham, Smalley, *Becket Conflict*, pp. 59ff. For *Quadrilogus*, Duggan, *TH*, pp. 205ff. For the use made by the biographers of the Becket correspondence, *ibid.*, pp. 175ff.

    The general letter collections are printed in *Mats.* v–vii, and are treated magisterially by Duggan, *TH*. She is now preparing an edition and translation of Thomas's letters for the series, Oxford Medieval Texts. Good editions exist of the letters of Arnulf of Lisieux, Gilbert Foliot and John of Salisbury (see abbreviations).

    Translations of extracts from the Lives and letters, with commentaries, by G. W. Greenaway are to be found in *E.H.D.* ii. 749ff., and *The Life and Death of Thomas Becket* (The Folio Soc., 1961).

A very full bibliography up to 1942 is in Foreville, *ER*, pp. 565ff. See further J.W.Alexander, 'The Becket Controversy in Recent Historiography', *The Journal of British Studies*, IX, no. 2 (May 1970), 1–26; Duggan, *TH*, pp. xiv–xxii; and cf. D.Luscombe, 'John of Salisbury in Recent Scholarship', *World of J. of S.* (1984), 21–37.

W.H.Hutton's *Thomas Becket* (1910) is still, in my opinion, the most readable and sympathetic short account.

1. *Mats.* iii. 539–40. 'Montanism', a second-century apocalyptic movement which forbade *inter alia* flight from persecution, had been condemned as unorthodox.

2. Reference is to *Bibliotheca Hagiographica Latina*, ed. Socii Bollandiani: Subsid. hagiograph., 6 (Brussels, 1898–1901).

3. Barlow, Arnulf, *Letters*, no. 57 and nn. He would have been ejected after April 1163, when the king confiscated the honour of Saltwood as part of Henry of Essex's forfeiture: see p. 89.

4. According to the prologue, *Mats.* iv. 80. This, however, has been generally disbelieved: cf. Robertson, ibid., p. xiv; Radford, p. 253; Abbott, i. 21.

5. William is sometimes incorrectly described as 'remembrancer' or 'recorder'. A *dictator* was the clerk who drafted letters, charters, laws, etc., according to the rules of *dictamen*. Cf. C.R.Cheney, *English Bishops' Chanceries, 1100–1250* (1950), p. 23, where he translates *patronus causarum* as 'judge in law-suits'.

6. B. of P., ii. 96–101. For Robert, Smalley, *Becket Conflict*, pp. 196–200. A.B. Emden, *A Biographical Register of the University of Oxford to A.D. 1500* (1957), i. 513–14; P.G.Foote, 'On the fragmentary text concerning St Thomas Becket in Stock. Perg. Fol. Nr. 2.', *Saga Book of the Viking Society*, xv (1957–61), 403.

7. His notice of Thomas at Pontigny includes, iv. 64, 'We will not pursue the subject of the archbishop's religious behaviour there lest we impute a reproach to our brethren and also exceed the bounds of brevity.' Whoever the brethren may be, they are unlikely to be the Cistercian monks of Pontigny.

8. M.A.Harris, 'Alan of Tewkesbury and his Letters', *Studia Monastica* (Abadia de Montserrat, Barcelona), xviii (1976), 77–108, 299–351. Duggan, *TH*, pp. 84ff., 144–5.

9. Foote, 'Fragmentary Text', especially pp. 442–6.

10. Torigni, *Chron.* See further E.M.C.Houts, 'The *Gesta Normannorum Ducum*: a history without an end', *Proc. of the Battle Conference on Anglo-Norman Studies, III, 1980*, ed. R.Allen Brown (1981).

11. Howden, *Benedict*, and *Chronica*. Barlow, 'Roger of Howden', with an additional note, *The Norman Conquest and Beyond* (1983), p. 303. Fullest treatment now in D.Corner, 'The *Gesta Henrici Secundi* and *Chronica* of Roger parson of Howden', *Bull. of the Inst. of Hist. Research*, lvi (1983), 126.

12. Diceto, *Abbrev. Chron.* and *Ymagines*. See also Smalley, *Becket Conflict*, pp. 230–4; C. and A. Duggan, 'Ralf de Diceto, Henry II and Becket', in C.Duggan, *Canon Law in Medieval England* (Variorum, 1982), no. xiv.

13. Newburgh, *Historia*.

14. Gervase, *Chron.* The common belief that the Canterbury monk, Thomas of Maidstone, was his blood brother is due to a misunderstanding of *Chron.*, i. 173.

1 The London merchant's son: background and youth, 1120–1143

General

The fullest treatment of Thomas's youth is in W. fS. and Radford. For London see Brooke and Keir, *London*. For English schools and schooling at this time see Barlow, *EC*, pp. 217ff.

One of the most difficult problems is the year in which Thomas was born. Cf. Foreville, 'Tradition et Comput'. There is a conflict between the widely discordant historical writers and the unanimous liturgical tradition. The *Thómas Saga*, i. 46–7 (? from R. of C.), makes Thomas thirty-eight in 1155, i.e. born in 1116, but adds, incorrectly, that he had spent fifteen winters at Theobald's court. B. of P., as transmitted by *Quadrilogus*, ii. 19, thought that he was murdered in his fifty-third year; accordingly, he was born in 1118. H. of B., iii. 185, 189, says twice that he was about forty-four when made archbishop. If born in 1117, he would have been four or five months over forty-four, if in 1118, seven or eight months under. Although 1118 has often been favoured by modern historians, Herbert, writing late in life, long after the events and guilty of at least one important chronological error, cannot be relied on. In Gerald of Wales's works, *Opera Omnia* (Rolls ser.), v. 262, vii. 56, viii. 162, n. 3, the martyrdom is placed in either the forty-eighth or fifty-fourth year, which give birthdays in 1123 or 1117.

In contrast, the quite independent liturgical tradition supports 1120. It was believed at Canterbury by 1172 (Guernes, vv. 5871–5; cf. A.I, iv. 78; H. of B., iii. 326 – but birthday omitted) that Thomas was born and died on a Tuesday and that three other important events in his life occurred on that day. The accuracy of this for the martyrdom is undoubted, but for some of the other dates is by no means so certain. If Thomas was indeed born on a Tuesday, the year would be 1115, 1120, or 1126; and by the Jubilee of 1420 it was believed that Thomas was born in 1120. The weaknesses here are the wish to put all important events on a Tuesday (to agree with the martyrdom) and the attraction of the jubilee period of fifty years. For the Tuesdays see also A. Duggan, 'The cult of St Thomas Becket in the thirteenth century', in *St Thomas Cantilupe bishop of Hereford*, ed. M. Jancey (Hereford, 1982), pp. 39–40 and n.

Although 1120 may be erroneous, it cannot be far out and it has no persuasive rival since the biographers and other historical writers were obviously guessing. For convenience sake, 1120 has been adopted here.

1. For the year of birth, see under General. Birthday and baptism in Guernes, vv. 5856–9; cf. A.I, iv. 4. Baptism in the font by the great conduit in St Mary Colechurch, *Cal. of Patent Rolls, 1446–52*, p. 70, 19 June. For the preservation of the 'chrism cloths', see p. 250, and for how they should be treated, *Councils and Synods*, index, s.v. For the house, see p. 13.
2. W. fS., iii. 15; cf. W. of C., i. 408. Foreville, 'Les Origines', pp. 442ff. Michelin map 54, pli 19. Knightly status in the eleventh century is a controversial subject. For some views, see P. Van Luyn, 'Les Milites dans la France du XIe siècle', *Le Moyen Age*, lxxvii (1971), 5, 193; J. Flori, 'Chevaliers et chevalerie au XIe siècle en France et dans l'Empire germanique', ibid., lxxxii (1976), 125; *idem*, 'Les Origines

de l'adoubement chevaleresque', *Traditio*, xxxv (1979), 232–3.

3. In *PR 31 Hen. I* (1129–30), p. 146, under London, is an entry recording the offer of ½ mark of gold (£3) made by Gilbert fitzWilliam for the enforcement of a debt. Clearly this Gilbert is a London merchant banker and the only Gilbert to appear in the London section; indeed, only one other of the name occurs in the whole record. Shortly after the Gilbert fitzWilliam entry is one featuring Osbert Huitdeniers, Gilbert Beket's kinsman: see pp. 26–7.

4. H. of B., iii. 309–10.

5. For the places, Michelin map 54, plis 9, 20. Foreville, 'Les Origines', p. 448. For 'Beaky', Knowles, *TB*, p. 4n. For 'Brooky', Radford, p. 2n., citing Robertson. For personal names at Winchester, O. von Feilitzen, *Winton Domesday*, pp. 145ff.

6. Matilda: E.G., ii. 356; H. of B., iii. 161; Gervase, *Chron.*, p. 150; Machildis: A.I, iv. 3; Mahalt: W. fS., iii. 14; Guernes, v. 170; Maild: *Thómas Saga* i. 12; Roesa: A.II, iv. 81. It was not uncommon for women, then as today, to have a pet name. But Roheise, which was given to one of her daughters, is not well represented by Rose or Rosy, for it was borne by ladies of rank and wealth, including Roheise de Vere, countess of Essex, and the wife of the London banker, Osbert Huitdeniers. For ducal Caen, M. Gibson, *Lanfranc of Bec* (1978), pp. 98ff.; D. Bates, *Normandy before 1066* (1982), pp. 130–2. For the London house, *Historical Gazetteer of London before the Great Fire*, ed. D.J. Keene, i, *Cheapside*, ed. Keene and V. Harding (1986), 105/18. For the vision, below, n. 10.

7. A.J. Forey, 'The Military order of St Thomas of Acre', *E.H.R.* xcii (1977), 484ff., demolished the late tradition that Theobald of Helles was Agnes's husband; but it was left to D.J. Keene (as in n. 6) to reintegrate him into the Beket family. I have greatly benefited from information supplied by Dr Keene and from discussing it with him. We remain, however, unsure which of Gilbert's daughters produced Theobald. Despite the obvious difficulties, I incline towards Agnes. For Hills-Court, E. Hasted, *The History and Topographical Survey of the County of Kent* (1800), ix. 203. For Mary, abbess of Barking, Diceto, *Ymagines*, p. 371; Gervase, *Chron.*, p. 242; Guernes, pp. 210–11. For Roheise, Urry, *Canterbury*, p. 182. For Roheise's Ralf and John, ibid., index, s.v. For the other nephews: for Geoffrey, J. of S., *Letters*, no. 136 (p. 14); *Mats.* no. 405; for Geoffrey and Gilbert, *Mats.* no. 449; for one of the two, nos. 138, 146. Cf. also J.C. Robertson, 'On the kindred of Archbishop Becket', *Archaeologia Cantiana*, x (1876), 16ff. See further below, n. 11.

8. W. fS., iii. 14. *Winton Domesday*, pp. 4ff. See also J.H. Round, 'Gervase of Corn-hill', *Geoffrey de Mandeville* (1892), pp. 304ff., on this London money-lender.

9. For Gilbert's social position, *Mats.* no. 224 (p. 515), cf. 205 (p. 410), 223 (p. 499); J. of S., ii. 302; E.G., ii. 356; A.II, iv. 81; W. of C., i. 3; Guernes, vv. 168–70: *barons de la cit*. Although the Bekets were only middling citizens, it must be remembered that citizens were an aristocracy above the urban proletariat. Gilbert witnessed a most important London lawsuit in 1137: J.H. Round, 'London under Stephen', *Commune of London* (1899), p. 101; Brooke and Keir, *London*, pp. 35–7. For Gilbert's shrievalty, W. fS., iii. 14; Brooke and Keir, pp. 208ff., 372. For the fires, E.G., ii. 359; W. of C., i. 3; *Thómas Saga* i. 13; *The Chronicle of John of Worcester 1118–1140*, ed. J.R.H. Weaver (Anecdota Oxoniensia, 1908), pp. 36–7.

10. For Matilda's visions, E.G., ii. 357–8; W. fS., iii. 13–14; Guernes, vv. 171–200; A.I, iv. 4; *Thómas Saga*, i. 13–17. For Thomas's vision, H. of B., iii, 162.

11. J. of S., ii. 202–3; A.I, iv. 7–8; *Thómas Saga* i. 19. A.I says explicitly that

Thomas was entrusted to a nursemaid so that Matilda could give her attention to acts of worship and piety. For the marriages and nephews, see above, n. 7, and pp. 30, 126–7 and 262.

12. Barlow, *EC*, pp. 228ff. For Thomas at Merton, W. fS., iii. 14. For the Order, J. C. Dickinson, *The Origins of the Austin Canons and their Introduction into England* (1950), 'Les Constructions des premiers chanoines réguliers en Angleterre', *Cahiers de Civilisation Médiévale*, x (1967), 179; Barlow, *EC*, pp. 90, 211. A fairly detailed, chronologically signposted and coherent Foundation Narrative, written shortly after the death of the first prior (31 Dec. 1149), together with an even earlier account of Gilbert the Sheriff's death, is printed by M. L. Colker, 'Latin Texts concerning Gilbert founder of Merton Priory', *Studia Monastica* (Abadia de Montserrat, Barcelona), xii (1970), 241–70. There is a useful bibliography in n. 1. See also Round, *Commune of London*, pp. 121–3; Brooke and Keir, *London*, p. 205. The first site of the priory has not been identified and no physical remains of any period survive above ground by the Wandle. For Huntingdon priory and its school, Barlow, *EC*, pp. 224, 232, cf. 202, and for Guy, pp. 232–3. See further J. A. Green, *The Government of England under Henry I* (1986), pp. 197–8.

13. R. L. Poole, 'The Early Lives of Robert Pullen and Nicholas Breakspear', *Essays in Medieval History presented to T. F. Tout* (1925), p. 66. A. II, iv. 82, however, thought that a career in the church was envisaged for Thomas from the start.

14. For the London schools, W. fS., iii. 4ff.; for Thomas's attendance at them, iii. 14. For St Paul's schoolmasters, Barlow, *EC*, p. 235. It is unlikely that Gilbert would have boarded Thomas out while attending a London school, but very little is known about the organization of such schools at this time. Especially obscure are the rules for attendance and the duration of terms. It is possible that, although the working day was long, lessons were not available or compulsory every day.

15. For Richer, Sanders, *Baronies*, p. 136; genealogical table in F. Barlow, *William Rufus* (1983), p. 467, no. 4. For Richer's adventures under Henry I and Stephen, *The Ecclesiastical History of Orderic Vitalis*, ed. and trans. M. Chibnall, vi. 298–30 and *passim*. He witnessed a charter of Henry, duke of Normandy, in 1150–1, Delisle–Berger, no. 14. For him at Clarendon, *SSC*, p. 164; *Mats.* no. 45.

16. E. G., ii. 359–61; Guernes, vv. 206–30; A. I, iv. 6–7; *Thómas Saga*, here attributed to Robert of Cricklade, i. 30–5. Cf. Abbott, pp. 216–19. In E.G.'s story, but not followed by Guernes, the hawk was in pursuit of a duck (*ana*). The *Thómas Saga* puts the episode after Paris; but by making Thomas into Richer's *notarius*, clearly confuses the baron with Osbert Huitdeniers. The Saga also conflates the two versions of the incident.

17. When *adolescens* (i.e. between the ages of fifteen and twenty-eight), W. fS., iii. 14; *Thómas Saga* i. 20–5. For the schools at Paris at this time, J. of S., *Metalogicon*, II, 10, pp. 77–83; Barlow, *EC*, pp. 251–3. For Robert, bishop of Hereford, 1163–7, D. E. Luscombe, *The School of Peter Abelard* (1970), p. 281; Smalley, *Becket Conflict*, pp. 51ff.; Barlow, *EC*, pp. 114, 251–3. By 1166 J. of S. did not think so highly of him: *Letters*, no. 175 (pp. 156, 162). That he was Thomas's teacher at Paris is inferred from his recall to England and promotion to the bench through the chancellor's influence: W. fS., iii. 24; H. of B., iii. 260. Cf. Radford, p. 21.

18. Foote, 'Fragmentary text', pp. 407–10. The Saga gives some other unsupported and incredible information about Thomas's pious and scholarly activities at Paris. For the interest of Paris masters in the martyr, cf. F. M. Powicke, *Stephen Langton*

(1928), pp. 58ff.; P. B. Roberts, 'Langton on Becket: a new look at a new text', *Medieval Studies*, xxxv (1973), 38ff. *Historia Insignis Monasterii S. Laurentii Leodiensis*, in E. Martène and U. Durand, *Veterum Scriptorum et Monumentorum Amplissima Collectio* (Paris, 1724–33), iv. 1090; *Mats*. iv. 260–1.

19. E.G., ii. 359; Guernes, vv. 231–40; A.I, iv. 8; H. of B., iii. 165; minimal information: J. of S., ii. 303; A.II, iv. 82; W. of C., i. 3; W. fS., iii. 14.

20. *The Chronicle of Jocelin of Brakelond*, ed. and trans. H. E. Butler (1949), p. 36.

21. For the curriculum, Barlow, *EC*, pp. 237–8. H. of B., iii. 461.

22. J. of S., ii. 302; cf. A.I, iv. 5–6. For his clerks and secretaries, see pp. 77ff. and 131ff. For him at Tours, *Draco Normannicus*, p. 744, lines 997–8. Stephen expressly contrasts Thomas, who was insufficiently educated to speak Latin ('ut minus edoctus verba Latina loqui'), with his rival, Roger of York, who had been educated from childhood and was a legal expert ('a puero doctus studiis legisque peritus'), line 1009. For Thomas speaking at Gisors-Trie, J. of S., *Letters*, no. 231 (p. 418). For the vision, B. of P., ii. 27. For a view of Thomas's education, Smalley, *Becket Conflict*, pp. 109–11.

23. For London, Barlow, *EC*, pp. 86–7, 96. For Theobald, ibid., pp. 93ff.; Saltman, *Theobald*.

24. W. of C., i. 3.

2 The lower rungs of the ladders, 1143–1154

General

For the political background, J. H. Round, *Geoffrey de Mandeville* (1892); R. H. C. Davis, 'Geoffrey de Mandeville reconsidered', *E.H.R.* lxxix (1964), 299; *idem, King Stephen* (1967); H. A. Cronne, *The Reign of Stephen 1135–54* (1970). For London, see also Round, *The Commune of London* (1899); S. Reynolds, 'The rulers of London in the twelfth century', *History*, lvii (1972), 337. For Theobald, Saltman, *Theobald*. Cf. Tout, 'Place of St Thomas', pp. 237–40.

1. E.G., ii. 359–60; W. of C., i. 3; W. fS., iii. 17; R. of C., p. 368; *Thómas Saga* i. 28–9, 248; Foote, 'Fragmentary text', p. 444.

2. A. of T., ii. 330; W. of C., miracles, ii. 35; cf. B. of P., miracles, iv. 65; W. of C., miracles, vi. 36. For Meymac, Michelin map 73, pli 11. For the illness at Northampton (? renal colic), cf. Knowles, *Ep. Col.*, pp. 167–8.

3. J. of S., ii. 303; E.G., ii. 359–61; A.II, iv. 82–3; W. of C., i. 3–6; W. fS., iii. 17; A.I, iv. 8; H. of B., iii. 167; *Thómas Saga* i. 30–1. 'aura popularis' is a phrase familiar probably from Horace, *Odes*, 3. 2. 20; cf. also Cicero, *Harusp. Resp.*, 20 *ad fin.* Knowles, *ATB*, pp. 6, 8, stresses Thomas's lovelessness. For Thomas's clerks, see pp. 140–2.

4. Cf. J. of S., *Letters*, nos. 150 (p. 48), 167 (p. 98), 187 (pp. 236, 244).

5. E.G., ii. 361; W. of C., i. 3; W. fS., iii. 14–15; Guernes, vv. 241–5; A.I, iv. 8. *Thómas Saga* i. 31, turns Osbert into Richer. For Osbert and his position, Round, *Geoffrey de Mandeville*, app. Q; *idem, Commune of London*, pp. 114–16; Davis, 'Geoffrey de Mandeville', pp. 301–2, 306; Reynolds, 'The rulers of London'; Brooke and Keir, *London*, pp. 222ff., 332–3.

6. *The Complete Peerage* (by G.E.C.), x. 198; Davis,. 'Geoffrey de Mandeville', pp. 305–6, *King Stephen*, pp. 140–1; Reynolds, 'The rulers of London', pp. 342, 354.

7. *Mats.* no. 648. For leading citizens in Stephen's reign, Round, *Geoffrey de Mandeville*, app. K, *Commune of London*, pp. 105ff.

8. J. of S., ii. 303; H. of B., iii. 167; cf. *Thómas Saga* i. 34–5.

9. Canterbury version: E.G., ii. 361; Guernes, vv. 246–59; A.I, iv. 9–10. London version: W. fS., iii. 15. R. of C., p. 385, attributes the entry to Gilbert Beket's initiative: cf. Benet, vv. 85–7.

10. Saltman, *Theobald*, no. 255, p. 482. Brooke, J. of S., *Letters*, i, p. xxiv, thinks, however, that John was at Rome for most of the years 1150–3.

11. W. fS., iii. 15. For Baldwin, Foreville, *Becket*, p. 235; J. of S., *Letters*, nos. 46 and n., 240. According to the chronology based on the chosen year of Thomas's birth, he would have entered Theobald's household in 1145 (see p. 27). He witnesses five documents which can be dated 1143–8: Saltman, *Theobald*, nos. 55, 86, 146, 252, suppl. F; but the crucial charter is suppl. B, p. 538, dated 1146, apparently after 19 August. Gervase, *Act. Pontif.*, p. 384, says that Thomas advised Theobald to go to Rome in 1144, and some modern historians have claimed that the clerk went with his master on the six-month journey: cf. Saltman, *Theobald*, p. 20; F. A. Batisse, in *Cant. Chron. 1970*, pp. 40, 46. Neither part of the story seems likely.

12. For the sisters, see ch. 1, n. 7.

13. W. fS., iii. 16. Saltman, *Theobald*, p. 165. For John of Canterbury, C. Duggan, 'Bishop John and Archdeacon Richard of Poitiers: their roles in the Becket dispute and its aftermath', Foreville, *TB* (Sédières), pp. 71ff. For John of Tilbury, Brooke, J. of S., *Letters*, no. 256n.

14. For Bartholomew, A. Morey, *Bartholomew of Exeter, bishop and canonist* (1937). For J. of S., Saltman, *Theobald*, pp. 169ff.; Brooke, J. of S., *Letters*, i, full bibliography and *corrigenda*, ii, pp. ixff.; Smalley, *Becket Conflict*, pp. 87ff.; *World of J. of S.*; Arnulf, *Letters*, no. 26 and n.

15. For Jordan, Saltman, *Theobald*, p. 538; J. of S., *Letters*, i. 95 and n. For Ralf, Saltman, p. 546 and index, *s.v.*; Barlow, *William Rufus*, pp. 200–1. For Vacarius, Barlow, *EC*, pp. 255–6, with bibliography.

16. J. of S., *Letters*, no. 256. For the library, D. Luscombe, in *World of J. of S.*, p. 28. For John's scholarship, see also R. Thomson, G. Evans, J. Martin, G. Micza and others, ibid.

17. Gervase, *Chron.*, pp. 142ff., 160; *Act. Pontif.*, p. 385; J. of S., *Letters*, no. 244 (p. 486). M. A. Harris, 'Alan of Tewkesbury and his letters', *Studia Monastica* (Abadia de Montserrat, Barcelona), xviii (1976), 77–8. Alan cites Theobald's treatment of Walter Little as a tyrannical injustice similar to his own banishment from Canterbury to Tewkesbury in 1186. In 1148 Queen Matilda lodged in St Augustine's while she supervised the building of Faversham abbey, 8 miles west on the London road: Gervase, *Chron.*, p. 139. Cf. R. Eales, 'Kent in Stephen's Reign', *Anglo-Norman Studies VIII* (1986), 105–6.

18. Saltman, *Theobald*, pp. 6ff.; Barlow, *EC*, pp. 36, 93ff.

19. J. of S., *Letters*, no. 307. Brooke, ii, p. xliv, is more courageous than most of his predecessors. For a bibliography, Barlow, *EC*, p. 94, n. 175.

20 W. of C., i. 4; *Thómas Saga* i. 38–41. Radford, pp. 32–3, makes Roger of Neustria into a separate person; but there is no trace of a second Roger in the witness lists.

21. J. of S., *Hist. Pont.*, pp. 6ff.; *Mats.* no. 250; J. of S., ii. 303; W. fS., iii. 16; Guernes, vv. 261–5; A.I, iv. 10; H. of B., iii. 356 (reporting Thomas's speech to the cardinals at Sens in Nov.–Dec. 1164); *Thómas Saga* i. 38–9. N. M. Haring, 'Notes on the Council and the Consistory of Rheims (1148)', *Medieval Studies*, xxviii (1966), 39; Barlow, *EC*, pp. 99–100; *Councils and Synods*, no. 148.

22 For Gilbert, Knowles, *Ep. Col.*, pp. 37ff.; Morey and Brooke, *GFol*, GFol, *Letters*; Saltman, *Theobald*, pp. 19–21, 23ff., 107–10. J. of S., *Hist. Pont.*, pp. 47ff., gives a probably biased account of Foliot's election. See also Barlow, *EC*, p. 100. A.II, iv. 98–9.

23. For the legation, Gervase, *Act. Pontif.*, p. 384, in a very confused context; Radford, pp. 40–2; Saltman, *Theobald*, pp. 30ff.; Barlow, *EC*, p. 102; C. R. Cheney, 'The deaths of popes and the expiry of legations in twelfth-century England', *Revue de Droit Canonique*, xxviii (1978), 90–2. For the Eustace affair, J. of S., *Hist. Pont.*, pp. 83ff.; Gervase, *Chron.*, p. 150; *Mats.* nos. 250 (p. 58), 643 (p. 242), the last to be dated June–July 1168, not 1169 or 1170.

24. *Thómas Saga* i. 35–7.

25. *Chronica Mon. S. Albani*, ed. H. T. Riley (Rolls ser.), i (1867), 187–8; cf. Matthew Paris, *Historia Minor*, ed. F. Madden (Rolls ser.), i (1866), 361. W. fS., iii. 17; cf. Guernes, vv. 271–2; A.I, iv. 10. Brooke and Keir, *London*, p. 140 and n. If Otford was indeed a reward for his services at Rheims, as A.I thought, it would have antedated John of Pagham's gift. For Philip, see p. 93; for Richard, see p. 46.

26. J. of S., ii. 304; W. fS., iii. 17; A.I, iv. 10. R.-H. Bautier, 'Les Premières Relations entre le monastère de Pontigny et la royauté anglaise', Foreville, *TB* (Sédières), p. 41, casts doubt on the visit to Auxerre on the grounds that its schools had lost their former distinction. H. of B., iii. 528–9; cf. J. of S., *Letters*, no. 289. Barlow, *EC*, p. 256.

27. J. of S., ii. 304; *idem, Letters*, no. 261; E.G., ii. 362–3; A.II, iv. 83; W. of C., i. 4; W. fS., iii. 17; Guernes, vv. 266–75; A.I, iv. 10–11; H. of B., iii. 168ff.; *Thómas Saga* i. 38–9; R. of C., p. 391; Benet, p. 623a; *Thómas Saga* i. 402. For the letters, see pp. 149ff.; *Mats.* nos. 224 (p. 515), cf. 203 (p. 410), 223 (p. 499); Diceto, *Ymagines*, p. 300. Barlow, *EC*, pp. 96ff.

28. A.I, iv. 11; H. of B., iii. 173. Pope Alexander III laid down the rules of clerical celibacy definitively in a decretal to Roger, bishop of Worcester, dated 26 Nov. 1164: M. G. Cheney, 'Pope Alexander III and Roger bishop of Worcester', *Proc. of the 4th Internat. Congress of Med. Canon Law, Toronto, 21–25 Aug. 1972: Mon. Iuris Canonici*, ser. C, Subsidia, vol. 5 (Vatican City, 1976), pp. 211–13. For the archdeacon's official residence in Canterbury, Urry, *Canterbury*, p. 201. For the aids, J. of S., *Letters*, no. 28 (p. 46); *Mats.* no. 7. Perhaps second aids were when both the archbishop and the archdeacon took an aid from the same church. *The Life of St Hugh of Lincoln*, eds. D. L. Douie and H. Farmer (1961), ii. 38.

29. Saltman, *Theobald*, pp. 538–9. For Thomas's seal, used as a counter-seal or *secretum*, J. H. Round, *Calendar of Docs. preserved in France* (1899), nos. 1337–8, dated there 1162–4; Foreville, 'Lettres "Extravagantes"', p. 235; C. R. Cheney, *English Bishops' Chanceries*, pp. 50–1, Thomas, *Acta*, p. xlix. Cf. E. M. A. Richter, *Engraved Gems of the Romans* (1971), no. 314.

30. For Henry's grief and remorse, Lansdowne Anonymous, iv. 156–7. W. of C., miracles, II. 48, V. 19–22, VI. 66, 109–10, 147; *Thómas Saga* (? from R. of C.), ii. 140–6. In 1286 Edward I sought the martyr's help to cure one of his gerfalcons:

A. J. Taylor, 'Edward I and the shrine of St Thomas of Canterbury', *Journ. of the British Arch. Assoc.*, cxxxii (1979), 26, n. 22.

3 Royal chancellor, 1155–1162

General

For Henry II's government and actions, W.L.Warren, *Henry II* (1973); J.E.A. Jolliffe, *Angevin Kingship* (1955); J. Boussard, *Le Gouvernement d'Henri II Plantagenêt* (1956); F.J.West, *The Justiciarship in England, 1066–1232* (1966). For Henry's ecclesiastical policy, 1154–63, Foreville, *ER*, pp. 79–101. For the royal itinerary, Eyton and Delisle–Berger. For Thomas as chancellor, Radford, pp. 57–190; Tout, 'Place of St Thomas', pp. 240–2.

1. W. of C., i. 122. R. of C., pp. 385–6, seems to have thought that Thomas started as a royal chamberlain.

2. Foreville, 'Tradition et Comput', p. 9. J. of S., ii. 304; E.G., ii. 363; W. of C., i. 4; W. fS., iii. 17–18; Guernes, vv. 281ff.; A.I, iv. 11–12; R. of C., p. 385; Benet, vv. 109–17; *Thómas Saga* i. 44–7; Gervase, *Chron.*, p. 160. *Constitutio Domus Regis*, in *Dialogus de Scaccario*, ed. and trans. C.Johnson (1950); Barlow, *William Rufus*, pp. 136–7, 145–8.

3. GFol, *Letters*, no. 170 (p. 230); W. fS., iii. 18; Ralf Niger, *De Re Militari*, III. 15: Ludwig Schmugge, 'Thomas Becket und König Heinrich II. in der Sicht des Radulfus Niger', *Deutsches Archiv*, xxxii (1976), 577, n. 30. Barlow, *William Rufus*, pp. 257–8. W.H. Hutton, *Thomas Becket* (1910), p. 20, Morey and Brooke, *GFol*, p. 171, and Knowles, *ATB*, p. 8, are prepared to believe that Thomas did buy the office. Cf. Radford, pp. 62–3.

4. J. of S., ii. 304–5; A.I, iv. 12; H. of B., iii. 177; *Thómas Saga* i. 58–9.

5. For zoos, Barlow, *EC*, p. 265. For Thomas's monkeys, see p. 56; for the wolves, one of which escaped to rejoin his wild brethren, A. of T., in Oxford CCC MS 32, fo. 96, quoted by B.Ross, 'Audi Thoma … Henriciani Nota: a French scholar appeals to Thomas Becket', *E.H.R.* lxxxix (1974), 337. For Thomas's magnificence, J. of S., ii. 305: minimal, but cf. *Policraticus*, viii. 25, pp. 424–5; E.G., ii. 363–5; A.II, iv. 83–4; W. of C., i. 5; W. fS., iii. 20ff.; Guernes, vv. 336ff., 416ff.; A.I, iv. 12–13; H. of B., iii. 173–7; R. of C., p. 386, *Thómas Saga* i. 48–9. *Lamberti Ardensis Historia Comitum Ghisnensium*, ed. J.Heller, *M.G.H. Script.*, xxiv (1879), 602; *Willelmi Chronica Andrensis*, ibid., 708. John of Salisbury was welcomed by Count Arnoul in 1164, *Letters*, no. 136, and Thomas, when returning to England in 1170, by Baldwin, *Willelmi Chronica Andrensis*, 709. W. fS., iii. 135.

6. In the financial year 1157/8 the sheriff of Surrey accounted for the royal grant of an estate in Ewell worth £17 17s. p.a.: *PR 2–4 Hen. II*, p. 162. For William Anglicus and his appointment to Ramsey, Torigni, *Chron.*, p. 210.

7. J. of S., *Entheticus*, vv. 1435ff.; H. of B., iii. 173–4; E.G., ii. 365: 'licet aliter aliqui aestimaverint.'

8. *Thómas Saga* i. 50–3; W. fS., iii. 21–2; A.I, iv. 13–14. For Thomas of St Martin's,

Urry, *Canterbury*, p. 181. For Richard, *PR 2–4 Hen. II*, pp. 10, 17–18, 76, 133 *bis*, 135; *5 Hen. II*, 5, 7, 17; *6 Hen. II* (Amery), 38; *7 Hen. II* (Ambl'), 68; *8 Hen. II* (Ameri), 41–2; J. of S., *Letters*, nos. 73–5; GFol, *Letters*, no. 113. For the canon of Lincoln, *English Episcopal Acta. I. Lincoln 1067–1185*, ed. D. M. Smith (1980), s.v. Almaria; Barlow, Arnulf, *Letters*, p. 64n.; J. of S., *Letters*, no. 48; GFol, *Letters*, no. 173, p. 535. For the Oxfordshire family of Amory or Damory, *John le Neve: Fasti Ecclesiae Anglicanae, 1066–1300, III (Lincoln)*, compiled by D. E. Greenway (1977), pp. 12, 45. There was, however, a family d'Amblie in the Essex–Suffolk area: *Sir Christopher Hatton's Book of Seals*, ed. L. C. Loyd and D. M. Stenton (1950), nos. 109, 291, 405. See further Thomas, *Acta*, no. 30.

9. W. of C., i. 6; *Thómas Saga* i. 52–5; Guernes, vv. 301–30. The Canterbury monk places the event at Stafford, but gives no personal names; Guernes identifies the woman as Avice of Stafford, but puts Thomas at Stoke (one MS gives Woodstock), and names his host. The chancellor was unlikely to have been in Staffordshire on his own: Henry was there in February 1155 and possibly in August 1157 and January 1158. For the barons of Stafford, Sanders, *Baronies*, p. 81; for Robert as sheriff, 1155–8, *PR 2–4 Hen. II*, pp. 29, 97, 160.

10. H. of B., iii. 173–4.

11. Barlow, *E.C.*, pp. 268ff., 275–6, 'The King's Evil', *E.H.R.* xcv (1980), 19. J. of S., *Policraticus*, VIII. 25, pp. 418ff.; cf. Brooke, *World of J. of S.*, pp. 3–4.

12. See ch. 2, n. 4. E.G., ii. 365.

13. Thomas's movements are based on charter evidence: see Eyton and Delisle–Berger. For the king's 'family', Jolliffe, *Angevin Kingship*, pp. 143–4; for Manasser Bisset, ibid., pp. 217–18; for Richard de Lucy, West, *Justiciarship*, pp. 37ff. For Thomas and the Norwegian embassy to England, W. fS., iii. 26; *PR 2–4 Hen. II*, p. 15, cf. 4.

14. See pp. 51ff. West, *Justiciarship*, pp. 34–5, claims that Thomas, alone of the officials, could authorize payments from the royal treasury by his own writ. But the few cases cited (two with the joint authority of the justiciar, the earl of Leicester) hardly support this. Throughout Thomas's chancellorship, authority for pardons, disbursements, etc., except on very few occasions, is regularly cited on the Pipe Rolls as *per breve regis* – on the authority of a royal writ. For Thomas's importance, cf. Guernes, vv. 371ff.; *Thómas Saga* i. 46–9. Arnulf, *Letters*, no. 10.

15. J. of S., *Letters*, nos. 27–31. G. Constable, 'The alleged disgrace of John of Salisbury in 1159', *E.H.R.* lxix (1954), 67.

16. *The Chronicle of Battle Abbey*, ed. and trans. E. Searle (1980), pp. 21–3, 154–60; and see pp. 50–1.

17. In 1156/6 £6 12s. was paid for the overthrowing of the bishop's castle at Winchester: *PR 2–4 Hen. II*, p. 54. For Westminster Hall, W. fS., iii. 18–20; see also p. 52. The few references to 'assizes' held by the chancellor alone, or with another official, are in Essex, Lincolnshire and Kent in the period Michaelmas 1155 to January 1156, and in Middlesex and Huntingdonshire in the period Michaelmas 1157 to August 1158: *PR 2–4 Hēn. II*, pp. 17, 26, 65, 114, 164.

18. *Chronicle of Battle*, pp. 176ff.; Foreville, *ER*, pp. 91–2. For Theobald, see pp. 32–3. It is worth noting that he, despite Hilary's failure, succeeded in 1157, with the help of a bull of Adrian IV, to force Silvester, abbot of St Augustine's, to submit to him: Gervase, *Chron.*, p. 163; Foreville, *ER*, pp. 88–90, 93. For Thomas's letter of 1168, *Mats.* no. 643 (pp. 242–3): dated wrongly there 1170 and by Duggan, June–

July 1169.

19. For the instructions to Ernulf, see p. 51. For the pardons, *PR*, indexes, s.v. *cancellarius*.

20. W. fS., iii. 20, 53; H. of B., iii. 275.

21. Cf. Barlow, *William Rufus*, pp. 221ff.

22. *PR 2–4 Hen. II*, pp. 21, 152; *5 Hen. II*, p. 7; *6 Hen. II*, p. 12; *7 Hen. II*, p. 68; *8 Hen. II*, p. 49; *9 Hen. II*, pp. 24, 34; W. fS., iii. 18, 29; H. of B., iii. 299; J. of S., *Letters*, no. 128. *PR 8 Hen. II*, p. 57.

23. H. of B., iii. 180: apparently immediately after the death of Theobald; cf. W. fS., iii. 34, who believed that Thomas was custodian by the summer of 1161: see p. 63. *PR 7 Hen. II*, pp. 62–3; *8 Hen. II*, p. 55. For Pain, see Saltman, *Theobald*, pp. 378, 398; for Philip, ibid., p. 536. Both men seem to have been Thomas's stewards or bailiffs during his archiepiscopate, for they appear regularly in the sheriff's accounts from Michaelmas 1165, after the confiscation of the archbishopric. Both men had been fined £200: *PR 11 Hen. II*, p. 104, and subsequent rolls. Philip was dead before Mich. 1169: *PR 15 Hen. II*, p. 165.

24. *Mats.* nos. 10, 15. *PR 8 Hen. II*, p. 73; cf. also p. 19 (Lincs), 72 (Herts); *9 Hen. II*, p. 23. Stubbs, Diceto, *Ymagines*, p. xli, was prepared to believe that Thomas had held the prebend of Reculverland.

25. W. of C., i. 38; A.I, iv. 49. For the case, see pp. 109ff. The sum of £30,000 is supported by E.G., ii. 392, 396. H. of B., iii. 299, thought it was about 30,000 marks; and Gilbert Foliot is alleged to have claimed in 1167 that Henry had demanded 44,000 marks (£29,332): *Mats.* no. 339 (p. 271).

26. W. fS., iii. 29–33; cf. H. of B., iii. 175. For the circumstances, Torigni, *Chron.*, p. 196; Diceto, *Ymagines*, p. 302. The Temple at Paris was just outside the walls. Thomas lodged there again in November 1169 for the conference at Montmartre. It seems that Henry also visited Paris later in 1158: Diceto, ibid.

27. If Guy was a descendant of the daughter of Robert, count of Mortain, the Conqueror's half-brother, who married a Guy of Laval (Torigni, *Chron.*, p. 201), the rebel would have been related to both Henry II and his queen, Eleanor of Aquitaine. For Guy V (*c.*1130–*c.*1185), see Bertrand de Broussillon, *La Maison de Laval* (Paris, 1895), i. 89–129.

28. Torigni, *Chron.*, pp. 196–8; Gervase, *Chron.*, p. 166. Louis again acknowledged Henry's office at Orleans in 1158: Delisle–Berger, no. 87.

29. For Toulouse, Barlow, *William Rufus*, pp. 416–18. W. fS., iii. 33–4; H. of B., iii. 175–6; Guernes, vv. 346ff.; cf. J. of S., *Policraticus*, viii. 25, p. 424. Torigni, *Chron.*, pp. 201–3; Gervase, *Chron.*, p. 167. Torigni, *Chron.*, p. 205, mentions Thomas's custody of Cahors, and notes that Henry was relying on the help of Raymond-Berengar (IV), count of Barcelona, and other local allies. For the constable's alleged cowardice, J. E. Lloyd, *A History of Wales* (3rd edn, 1939), ii. 498. W. fS., iii. 53–4, lists two royal loans 'at Toulouse', both of £500, the second as surety for the chancellor's loan from a Jew; H. of B., iii. 298–9, mentions only one loan of £500 which he does not locate.

30. Torigni, *Chron.*, pp. 205–7. Treaty printed *RHF*, xvi. 21, corrected by A. Saltman, 'Two early collections of the Becket correspondence . . .', *Bull. of the Inst. of Hist. Research*, xxii (1949), 157; Delisle–Berger, no. 141. Cf. J. of S., *Letters*, no. 9; H. of B., iii. 175; *Thómas Saga* i. 56–7.

31. W. fS., iii. 142; H. of B., iii. 328; *Thómas Saga* i. 253–5; Torigni, *Chron.*, pp. 206–7;

Diceto, *Ymagines*, p. 303; *Heads of Religious Houses*, eds. D. Knowles, C. N. L. Brooke and V. London, p. 219. It should also be noticed that Louis's marriage to Adela of Blois in Nov. 1160 was considered incestuous by the archbishop of Rheims: Diceto, *Ymagines*, p. 303. For the Isabel of Warenne marriage, see p. 106.

32. For the scutages of 1156, 1161 and 1162, see *PR 2, 7, 8 Hen. II, passim*. For the scutage 'of Toulouse', *PR 5 Hen. II, passim* under *Nova Placita et Nove Conventiones*. Gervase, *Chron.*, p. 167, puts the yield of the English scutage at £180,000, a reference to all the constituent parts of the *donum*, and says that there was a similar tax on all Henry's other lands. Torigni, *Chron.*, p. 202, claims that Henry took 60s. (angevin) from each knight's fee in Normandy.

33. Malmesbury and Cerne were vacant; Glastonbury was held by the bishop of Winchester and paid only on its knights – as did Sherborne, for reason unknown. Other possible beneficiaries were Shaftesbury and Muchelney.

34. J. of S., *Letters*, nos. 13, 168 (pp. 104–6); cf. GFol, *Letters*, no. 170 (p. 231). B. of P., ii. 162–3. Richard de Lucy was to found an Augustinian canonry at Lessness in Erith in Kent in honour of St Mary and St Thomas, saint and martyr.

35. Barlow, 'The English, Norman and French councils called to deal with the papal schism of 1159', reprinted in *The Norman Conquest and Beyond* (1983), with bibliographical note, p. 311; Reuter, 'Papal Schism', pp. 9ff., 36ff.; *Councils and Synods*, no. 154. For J. of S.'s friendship with the pope, *Policraticus*, vi. 24, p. 67, *Letters*, no. 235 (pp. 432–4). For Henry's insistence on neutrality, Saltman, 'Two early collections', pp. 154–5. For Henry's victims, W. fS., iii. 27–8. Thomas's protection of Nicholas, archdeacon of London, ibid., p. 26, may have been in the same context. Henry wrote from Rouen to congratulate Alexander on his election and promise him reverence, a letter witnessed by Thomas: Delisle–Berger, no. 139.

36. Torigni, *Chron.*, p. 208; Diceto, *Ymagines*, pp. 303–4. The dispensation for youth, addressed to Archbishop Hugh of Rouen and his suffragans, is printed, *RHF* xv. 700, no. 14. See also Reuter, 'Papal Schism', pp. 39–41, 219–20. Henry had been very generous to the Templars, granting them, apparently immediately after his accession, 1 or 2 marks of silver annually from each English county. He also made some grants of land: *PR 2–4 Hen. II, passim*. The Templars who surrendered the castles were Richard of Hastings and Hostes of St Omer; they made an important reappearance in Thomas's life: see p. 98. For Edward's canonization, F. Barlow, *Edward the Confessor* (2nd edn, 1979), pp. 277ff.

37. J. of S., *Letters*, nos. 120–3, 125, 127–9, especially 128–9; *Metalogicon, ad fin.* For the will, *Letters*, no. 134; Saltman, *Theobald*, no. 28. For John's affection, *Letters*, nos. 256–7.

38. Torigni, *Chron.*, pp. 208–11; Diceto, *Ymagines*, p. 303, dates Louis's marriage 13 November. Eyton, pp. 51–4; Reuter, 'Papal Schism', pp. 39–41.

39. W. fS., iii. 34–5; E.G., ii. 365. For the war, Torigni, *Chron.*, pp. 210–11. For the Lactantius notes, Ross, 'Audi Thoma'.

40. W. fS., iii. 25–6. The church, whose site was considered most salubrious, is where the Conqueror had spent his last days. For the papal privileges, see p. 68. It is difficult to believe that there was anything serious behind Thomas's words, for the scholars he admired were clerks, not priests.

41. *Mats.* no. 2 (before 1162, when Peter became abbot of St Rémi at Rheims). No. 240, cf. 280 (p. 141). For Gerbuin, Brooke, J. of S., *Letters*, no. 31 (p. 51n.); Smalley, *Becket Conflict*, pp. 114–15.

4 Archbishop of Canterbury, 1162

General

Radford, pp. 191ff.; Foreville, *ER*, pp. 101–6.

1. Gervase, *Chron.*, pp. 168–9. Ralf of Diss, however, writing from the London standpoint, claims that Rochester consecrated Bartholomew only because Richard, bishop of London (the dean of the province) was paralysed and his deputy, Henry of Winchester, was at Cluny: Diceto, *Ymagines*, p. 304. For the temporalities, see p. 53.

2. R. of C., p. 387; Benet, vv. 271–82; *Thómas Saga* i. 76. Hilary held this royal office from Mich. 1160 until Mich. 1162, when his archdeacon took over: *PR 7, 8, 9 Hen. II*, pp. 13, 30, 13.

3. J. of S., *Entheticus*, vv. 1293–1300; cf. *Metalogicon, ad fin.*

4. See diagram in Barlow, *EC*, p. 318. Stigand (1052–70) was the exception. Cf. A.II, iv. 84–5, 87; H. of B., iii. 183. For the satirical and farcical justification of the election of a completely unworthy candidate, J. of S., *Policraticus*, vii, 19, pp. 175–8.

5. Cf. E.G., ii. 366; H. of B., iii. 182–3. Barlow, *EC*, pp. 82, 118–19.

6. Ohnsorge, *Legaten*, pp. 22ff. Delisle–Berger, no. 223; Torigni, *Chron.*, pp. 212–13.

7. Cf. J. of S., ii. 305; A.II, iv. 84; W. fS., iii. 35–6; A.I, iv. 14; Smalley, *Becket Conflict*, pp. 118, 145–6; Diceto, *Ymagines*, p. 308; see also p. 69.

8. Torigni, *Chron.*, pp. 184, 208; Diceto, *Ymagines*, p. 306; *Mats.* nos. 684 (p. 331), 310, to be dated 1161, not 1167: for both see A. Heslin (now Duggan), 'The coronation of the young king in 1170', *Studies in Church History* (Eccles. Hist. Soc.), ii (1965), 165. *PR 8 Hen. II*, pp. 43, 67 (under London). For the education of princes, Barlow, *William Rufus*, pp. 14ff.

9. J. of S., ii. 305; E.G., ii. 366; W. of C., i. 6; H. of B., iii. 182.

10. Barlow, *EC*, pp. 300–2.

11. *PR 7 Hen. II*, pp. 56–9.

12. E.G., ii. 366; W. of C., i. 6; H. of B., iii. 181; cf. *Thómas Saga* i. 62–4; Diceto, *Ymagines*, pp. 306–7; Gervase, *Chron.*, p. 169; Eyton, pp. 56–7; J–L, no. 10719; Ohnsorge, *Legaten*, p. 43 and n. For the papal permission, Guernes, vv. 745–7.

13. J. of S., ii. 305–6; A.II, iv. 85–6, 88; W. of C., i. 7–8; A.I, iv. 18.

14. E.G., ii. 366; W. of C., i. 8; Guernes, vv. 426ff.; A.I, iv. 14–16. Gervase, *Chron.*, p. 169, for Walter. For guardianship, W. fS., iii. 22; Guernes, v. 381; A.I, iv. 13; H. of B., iii. 176–7, 185. For homage and fealty, J. of S., ii. 305; E.G., ii. 366; W. of C., i. 9; Guernes, vv. 381ff., 506–10; *Thómas Saga* i. 48–9; Diceto, *Ymagines*, p. 306. For York's privilege, *Mats.* no. 13. For John's letter, J. of S., *Letters*, no. 136.

15. For the election, which exactly followed the procedure used in 1114 and 1138, J. of S., ii. 306; E.G., ii. 366–7; A.II, iv. 86–7; W. of C., i. 8–9; W. fS., iii. 36; Guernes, vv. 436ff.; A.I, iv. 14–17; H. of B., iii. 183–5; R. of C., p. 387, Benet, vv. 247–360, *Thómas Saga* i. 70ff.; *Councils and Synods*, no. 156. The date is given only by Diceto, *Ymagines*, p. 307, who, however, dates Thomas's priesting and consecration a week early (Whit Saturday and Sunday). For reservations and opposition, A.II, iv. 85; W. fS., iii. 36; H. of B., iii. 183, 246–7; *Thómas Saga* i. 73. In 1166 'the English church', led by Gilbert Foliot, publicly expressed these feelings: GFol, *Letters*, no. 167 (p. 224); cf. Thomas's reply, *Mats*. nos. 223 (p. 498), 224 (pp. 516–17), and Foliot's riposte, GFol, *Letters*, no. 170 (pp. 230–2). J. of S., ii. 306.

16. Gervase, *Chron.*, p. 168; cf. Diceto, *Ymagines*, p. 304. *Mats*. nos. 451, 463, cf. 583 (end of Sept. 1169); J. of S., *Letters*, no. 288.

17. J. of S., *Letters*, no. 187 (p. 239); GFol, *Letters*, no. 170 (p. 238), cf. *Mats*. no. 339 (p. 271); A.II, iv. 104–5; W. of C., i. 9; W. fS., iii. 36; Guernes, vv. 514–30; A.I, iv. 17–18; H. of B., iii. 185; cf. *Thómas Saga* i. 80. Lansdowne Anonymous, iv. 154–5, puts the acquittance on the day of Thomas's consecration. Radford, pp. 140ff.

18. Guernes, v. 490; cf. *Thómas Saga* i. 80–2.

19. For the cathedral, modelled on Lanfranc's abbey at Caen, see articles by R. D. H. Gem and H. J. A. Strik in *Medieval Art and Architecture at Canterbury*, Archaeolog. Assoc. Transact., iv. (1982); F. Woodman, *The Architectural History of Canterbury Cathedral* (1981); A. W. Klukas, 'The architectural implications of the *Decreta Lanfranci*', *Anglo-Norman Studies, VI*, ed. R. A. Brown (1984), pp. 136ff.

20. For the ordination and consecration, J. of S., *Letters*, no. 261; W. fS., iii. 36; A.I, iv. 18–19; H. of B., iii. 187–8; Lansdowne Anonymous, iv. 154–6; Diceto, *Ymagines*, p. 307; Gervase, *Chron.*, pp. 170–1, *Act. Pontif. Cant.*, p. 390. For the struggle over the primacy and York's profession, Barlow, *EC*, pp. 39ff. In 1123 William of Corbeil was consecrated by London instead of by York for the same reason. In 1162 the canons of St Paul's asked that Winchester should act for them. Rochester, the archbishop's chaplain, seems never to have advanced a claim before and was 'trying it on'. Diceto reports that a Welsh bishop also claimed as the senior bishop by date of ordination. For the prognostic, GFol, *Letters*, no. 170 (p. 232); Barlow, *EC*, p. 100. For the feast of Holy Trinity, Gervase, *Chron.*, p. 171; *The Oxford Dictionary of the Christian Church* (1961), s.v. Trinity Sunday.

21. A.II, iv. 105; W. of C., i. 9–10; W. fS., iii. 36–7; Guernes, vv. 596ff.; Diceto, *Ymagines*, p. 307; Gervase, *Chron.*, p. 172. According to A.II, Henry included in his letter to the pope requesting the pallium a statement that Thomas had been absolved from secular obligations. According to Guernes, the mission had difficulty in getting the pallium because it refused to pay for it; but *Draco Normannicus*, p. 741, says that Thomas sent 'the white with the red' (silver and gold). For pallium visits, Barlow, *EC*, pp. 37–8.

5 Thomas at Canterbury: the first year, 1162–1163

General

For ecclesiastical government, see Barlow, *EC*; C. R. Cheney, *From Becket to Langton* (1956). For Thomas's Acta, Cheney, 'On the acta of Theobald and Thomas, archbishops of Canterbury', *Journ. of the Soc. of Archivists*, vi (1981), 467, and *English Episcopal Acta. II. Canterbury 1162–1190*, ed. Cheney and B. E. A. Jones (1986). For the papal council of Tours, *Councils and Synods*, no. 157, based on R. Somerville, *Pope Alexander III and the Council of Tours (1163)* (1977).

1. H. of B., iii. 249.

2. Lansdowne Anonymous, iv. 156. F.M.Powicke, 'Maurice of Rievaulx', *E.H.R.*, xxxvi (1921), 21; *idem, Walter Daniel's Life of Ailred* (1950), pp. xlix–li, where he wondered whether the true au.hor of the reply to the archbishop's letter was not Ailred, Maurice's successor as abbot.

3. H. of B., iii. 185–6; 189ff.; 238ff.

4. A.II, iv. 104, realistically ascribes the radical change in Thomas's appearance and habits to his remorse at agreeing to the Constitutions of Clarendon in January 1164; see also W. of C., i. 24. Cf. E.G., ii. 368; A.I, iv. 21 (after a short time); H. of B., iii. 196. For Thomas's dress as archbishop, J. of S., ii. 306–7; A.II, iv. 89 (brief); E.G., ii. 368–9; W. of C., i. 10–11; W. fS., iii. 37; Guernes, vv. 561ff.; A.I, iv. 20–1; H. of B., iii. 193–7. Guernes, vv. 577–8, thought that Thomas consulted the prior of either Kenilworth (Robert) or Alnwick (? Richard) about his dress. For his clothes on 29 December 1170, see pp. 238–9. For his alleged profession as a canon, H. of B., iii. 196–7, probably answering the story of Robert of Cricklade, himself a regular canon, that he made a profession at Merton *en route* for his coronation as archbishop, R. of C., p. 387, Benet, vv. 367–78, *Thómas Saga* i. 84. For the stole, H. of B., iii. 195; cf. W. fS., iii. 37. See also p. 115.

5. H. of B., iii. 226ff.; J. of S., ii. 308; E.G., ii. 370; W. fS., iii. 37, thought that he drank an infusion of fennel; A.I, iv. 20–1. For Thomas's table at Sens and his cold stomach and wine, Guernes, vv. 3916–20. For his household in 1164, see p. 109.

6. Map, *De Nugis Curialium*, I, xxiv (ed. T. Wright, Camden Soc., 1850), pp. 41–2.

7. For his changed behaviour, J. of S., ii. 306–9; A.II, iv. 88–91; W. of C., i. 10–11; Guernes, vv. 536–740; A.I, iv. 19–21; cf. E.G., ii. 368–71; W. fS., iii. 37–41. A.II and W. fS. mention scourging. For the household, H. of B., iii. 206ff., 523ff., cf. 201; for the household in exile, see pp. 130ff.

8. J. of S., *Letters*, no. 27. W. fS., iii. 1, claimed that he served as subdeacon when the archbishop celebrated Mass and had duties when he heard cases. It is possible, however, that Herbert considered some of the clerks he omitted as experts in secular law.

9. For Gervase, see Smalley, *Becket Conflict*, pp. 221–8; D. Sheerin, 'Gervase of Chichester and Thomas Becket', *Medieval Studies*, xxxviii (1976), p. 468. John of Tilbury witnesses charters before 1153 and was often in company with J. of S.: Saltman, *Theobald*, nos. 10, 16, 46, 95, 125, 140, 225, 255. H. of B., describes him as an old man in 1164. See also J. of S., *Letters*, no. 256 and n. For Hugh, Silvester and Gilbert de Glanville, see Arnulf, *Letters*, p. xiii and ff. Arnulf wrote to congratulate Thomas on his election, no. 36. For Gerard, see Brooke, J. of S., *Letters*, ii. 68n. For Reginald and his family, ibid., ii. 360n. For Lombard, ibid., ii. 401n. For J. of Tilbury and Lombard, see also Thomas, *Acta*, nos. 18, 34; 26.

10. For Philip, W. fS., iii. 101, where it is said that he was in bad health. For him, Gilbert de Glanville and Gerard as canonists, S.Kuttner and E.Rathbone in *Traditio*, vii (1949–51), 289ff. See also *Acta*, no. 3.

11. Nicholas of Mont-St-Jacques to Thomas, *Mats*. no. 76 (p. 146). For Robert, *Acta*, nos. 3, 26.

12. H. of B., iii. 199ff. The pre-Conquest Canterbury *horarium* is reconstructed by T.Symons in *Regularis Concordia* (1953), pp. xliii–xliv, and Lanfranc's (without clock times) by D.Knowles, *The Monastic Constitution of Lanfranc* (1951), pp. xxxv–xxxvii. For the canonical hours, Sir Harris Nicolas, *The Chronology of History* (1833), pp. 183–4.

13. J. of S., ii. 306; A.II, iv. 88 (after confession); W. fS., iii. 37; H. of B., iii. 236; cf. W. of C., i. 10. *PR 11 Hen. II*, pp. 108–9 (£180), and subsequent rolls to 18 Hen. II. N. Brooks, *The Early History of the Church of Canterbury* (1984), pp. 29–30, 32.

14. J. of S., ii. 306; cf. W. of C., i. 11.

15. H. of B., iii. 225. Peter, *Verbum Abbreviatum*, caps. 22, 38, in Migne, *PL*, ccv, coll. 81, 132. In a variant reading (col. 404) he refers to charges for sealing (selling an image) and explains that the handle of a knife could contain gold or silver. Thomas, *Acta*, nos. 3, 16, 23, 34 (originals); copies, *passim*; witnessed, nos. 2–3, 5, 13, 18, 34, cf. 26, 39–40 (? St-Omer, Nov. 1164). See no. 8 for a notification to the archdeacon of Gloucester and the rural chapter of Cheltenham of the settlement of a dispute between two clerks 'in audientia nostra'. Jocelin bishop of Salisbury ratified an agreement made between Walter, clerk of the church of Sturminster, and the proctors of the hospital of St Giles at Pont-Audemer in the presence of his lord the archbishop of Canterbury and himself: J. H. Round, *Calendar of Docs. preserved in France*, no. 246, cf. 255.

16. Cf. also W. fS., iii. 38, where he refers to the archiepiscopal 'family', this session and his tutor in theology (i.e. Herbert).

17. Diceto, *Ymagines*, p. 308, cf. ii. 279; W. fS., iii. 120; W. of C., i. 106.

18. W. of C., i. 12; Guernes, vv. 741–50; Diceto, *Ymagines*, pp. 269, 307–8. Ernulf was engaged in the mission for the pallium June–August, and is unlikely to have delivered the seal to Henry *en route*.

19. W. fS., iii. 43; H. of B., iii. 250–2, 467–8. Cf. *Summa Causae*, iv. 209. Diceto, *Ymagines*, p. 311, cf. ii. 279; Gervase, *Chron.*, p. 174, *Act. Pontif.*, p. 391. For the complications re the barony of Ros, see Thomas's own statement, *Mats.* no. 610 (p. 174), and D. C. Douglas, *The Domesday Monachorum of Christ Church Canterbury* (1944), pp. 29–30; Sanders, *Baronies*, pp. 105–6; G. R. Duncombe, 'Feudal Tenure in Eleventh-Century England', unpublished Exeter University M.A. thesis, 1967, p. 120n. Thomas relied on a grant of King Stephen. See further, F. R. H. Du Boulay, *The Lordship of Canterbury* (1966), pp. 198ff., 361; M. Cheney, 'Inalienability in mid-twelfth-century England', *Monumenta Iuris canonici*, ser. C: subsid., vol. 7 (Vatican City, 1985), pp. 467ff. *Idem* in M. Chibnall, *Festschrift* (1985), pp. 183ff. And see pp. 108ff.

20. Cheney, 'On the acta', pp. 467–81. Arnulf, *Letters*, no. 42. An order of restitution and citation to Henry of Winchester, *Mats.* no. 149, may possibly date from 1162–4.

21. H. of B., iii. 252–3. *Diplomatic Documents preserved in the P.R.O.*, i, ed. P. Chaplais (1964), no. 2. Eyton, pp. 58–63. Cheney, *Bishops' Chanceries*, pp. 10, 154 and pl. IV. Diceto, *Ymagines*, p. 308, however, claims that Thomas, although he received the kiss of peace, was not readmitted to the king's full favour.

22. For Tours, see above, *General*. Acta in Mansi, *Sacrorum Conciliorum nova et amplissima Collectio*, xxi. 1175ff. Alexander, in a letter dated Paris 18 March, in return for Henry's promise to send all his archbishops and bishops to Tours, gave him an assurance that this would cause no new custom or precedent: *Mats.* no. 21. For London, *Mats.* nos. 16–20, 93; Diceto, *Ymagines*, p. 309. Ralf of Diss, then archdeacon of London, had carried out the negotiations with the pope. H. of B., iii. 255–60, is particularly partial to Roger because he became a supporter of the archbishop. Robert of Melun was to disappoint. *Mats.* no. 179.

23. See p. 61.

24. H. of B., iii. 253–5. For the attendance, T. Reuter, 'A list of bishops attending the Council of Tours', *Annuarium Historiae Conciliorum* (Augsburg, Freiburg), 8 (1976), p. 116. For the absentees, Diceto, *Ymagines*, p. 310. For Arnulf's sermon, Mansi, xxi. 1167–75; Reuter, 'Papal Schism', pp. 105–6. For London, *Mats.* no. 67. For the dispute with York, *Draco Normannicus*, vv. 1005ff.; for Rheims (1148), J. of S., *Hist. Pont.*, p. 5, Saltman, *Theobald*, pp. 141–2, and other occasions, Barlow, *EC*, pp. 31ff.

25. J. of S., *Vita S. Anselmi*, in Migne, *PL*, cxcix, coll. 1009ff.; papal bull, *Mats.* no. 23. R. W. Southern, *St Anselm and his Biographer* (1963), pp. 336–43, sets out the evidence and is inclined to think that the process was completed in England in 1163–4, but that Anselm's cult was never more than local and that the formal declaration was forgotten. Hence the renewal of the process in the fifteenth century. *Councils and Synods*, p. 850, is more cautious. In fact the negative evidence is unusually weighty. No provincial council in this period is recorded and it is unlikely that the bishops would have been enthusiastic for the measure. Nor does it seem that there is a single reference to the canonization in the 'Becket correspondence'. But see further, D. Luscombe in *World of J. of S.*, pp. 34–5.

6 The quarrel with the king, 1163–1164

General

For 'benefit of clergy', R. Génestal, *Le Privilegium Fori en France du décret de Gratien à la fin du xiv* siècle (Paris, 2 vols., 1921–4). For papal and curial politics, R. Foreville, *Latran I, II, III, IV* (Histoire des Conciles Œcuméniques, 6, Paris, 1965); Reuter, 'Papal Schism'. For a scholarly account written completely from the point of view of the church, Foreville, *ER*, pp. 107ff. For intellectual attitudes, Smalley, *Becket Conflict*.

1. Diceto, *Ymagines*, p. 311. Eyton, p. 63; Lloyd, *History of Wales*, ii. 512–13.

2. E.G., ii. 373–4; W. of C., i. 12; Guernes, vv. 751–70; A.I, iv. 23–4; J. A. Green, 'The last century of Danegeld', *E.H.R.* xcvi (1981), 255–7.

3. H. of B., iii. 262; 237.

4. *Mats.* nos. 116 (p. 222), 610 (p. 174); H. of B., iii. 467–8. This common royal 'injustice' was partly remedied by *Magna Carta*, cap. 32. For the other cases, Diceto, *Ymagines*, p. 311, cf. ii. 279. And see pp. 108ff.

5. Barlow, *EC*, pp. 104ff., 145ff.

6. Ibid., pp. 148ff. For the problem of appeals, M. G. Cheney, 'Pope Alexander III', pp. 214–15.

7. W. fS., iii. 43–5. Cf. Eyton, p. 33, and the York charters cited. Pierre Chaplais, 'Henry II's reissue of the canons of the council of Lillebonne of Whitsun 1080', reprinted in *Essays in Medieval Diplomacy and Administration* (1981), no. XIX. For archidiaconal courts and the procedure, Barlow, *EC*, pp. 155–6. For J. of S.'s views, Smalley, *Becket Conflict*, pp. 99ff. For the Symphorian–Osbert case, Saltman, *Theobald*, pp. 124–5; J. of S., *Letters*, no. 16 and pp. 261–2.

8. Barlow, *EC*, pp. 164–6, 176.

9. W. fS., iii. 45–6 (a section he cut out of the revised edition); H. of B., iii. 264–5; but cf. 269, where he claims that Thomas at the Council of Westminster expressly declared that a clerk could not be branded and that this barbarity was condemned even by secular law.

10. *Mats.* no. 25. Cf. C. Duggan, 'Bishop John and Archdeacon Richard of Poitiers', Foreville, *TB* (Sédières), pp. 75–7. For the Lincoln case, E.G. ii. 374–6; W. of C., i. 12–13; W. fS., iii. 45; Guernes, vv. 770–820; A.I, iv. 24–5 (the best account); H. of B., iii. 265–6; Diceto, *Ymagines*, p. 313, cf. ii. 280. Philip witnesses a deed of Bishop Robert Chesney dated 30 May 1163: *English Episcopal Acta*, i, *Lincoln 1067–85*, ed. D.M. Smith, no. 160. For Thomas as canon of Lincoln, W. fS., iii. 17. Robert de Broi and his son Walter restored land at Husborne Crawley (Beds.) to Ramsey Abbey about 1150: *Ramsey Cartulary*, ed. W.H. Hart and P.A. Lyons (Rolls ser., 1884), i. 257–8; cf. *Lincoln Acta*, no. 225. Simon fitzPeter became sheriff of Northamptonshire at Michaelmas 1163: *PR 10 Hen. II*, p. 31. According to H. of B., iii. 267, Henry maintained that banishment was a royal penalty and should not be used by ecclesiastical courts. Outlawry was certainly a royal prerogative; but the church had always imposed the penance of pilgrimage for a term of years.

11. W. fS., iii. 43; Diceto, *Ymagines*, pp. 311–12, cf. ii. 279. Constitutions of Clarendon, cap. 7. Cf. Barlow, *EC*, pp. 279–80. For the family and the trouble over the church, D. Douglas, *Domesday Monachorum*, pp. 44ff., 108–10; Urry, *Canterbury*, pp. 54–5. There were three generations called William. William III witnesses several of Theobald's deeds, twice as steward (*dapifer*): Saltman, *Theobald*, pp. 269–70, and see index. Thomas was soon reconciled to him: see p. 111.

12. H. of B., iii. 266–7. Barlow, *EC*, pp. 142, 145–7, 253ff.

13. *Mats.* nos. 24, 27–8. In no. 40 he styles himself 'your humble friend'.

14. J. of S., ii. 310; W. of C., i. 13; A.II, iv. 95–7; A.I, iv. 25–7; H. of B., iii. 261, 266–75; Guernes, vv. 826–50; R. of C., p. 388; Benet, vv. 421–98 (ascribed to Clarendon); *Thómas Saga* i. 146–56 (London); *Summa Causae*, iv. 201–5; Richard of Cirencester, *Speculum Historiale de Gestis regum Angliae*, ed. J.E.B. Mayor (Rolls ser., 1869), ii. 325–6. Barlow, *Edward the Confessor*, pp. 283–4. Located at London by A.II and *Summa Causae*, at Westminster by H. of B. Dated only in *Summa Causae*, where 'Kal. Oct.', i.e. 1 October. As, however, the translation of St Edward took place almost certainly on 13 October, and it is difficult to bring the ceremony in after the conclusion of this council, it seems better to shift the council to the later date. There are no obvious difficulties in this. I have changed my mind since *Edward the Confessor*, appendix E, where I date the translation. The earlier date for the council is adopted by *Councils and Synods*, no. 158. Several of the biographers thought that the council was summoned by the king and so, according to the ideas of the time, it was a national rather than an ecclesiastical council: Barlow, *EC*, pp. 120–1. For the tombstone, cf. also E. Mason, 'St Wulfstan's staff: a legend and its uses', *Medium Ævum*, liii (1984), 170.

15. Except Hilary of Chichester, who used the less offensive formula, 'bona fide': H. of B., iii. 274; Gervase, *Chron.* pp. 174–5. But see Thomas on this reservation, p. 113. Cf. also GFol, *Letters*, no. 170 (pp. 232–3).

16. H. of B., iii. 275; A.I, iv. 27–9.

17. E.G., ii. 377–8; W. of C., i. 14; Guernes, vv. 851ff.; A.I, iv. 29–31; H. of B., iii. 276–7; cf. J. of S., ii. 310–11; A.II, iv. 98. Arnulf had been out of royal favour and was recovering his position. The only defectors named are Chichester and York (E.G., A.I), London (E.G.) and Lincoln (A.I; 'L'eveske de Nichole', Guernes, vv. 682–3). There may be confusion between Lincoln and London. H. of B. admits an almost general defection. The seduction of the bishops took place at Gloucester (A.I), at Colchester (Guernes). Papal letters, *Mats.* nos. 26 (4 Sept.), 37 (9 Nov.).

18. Diceto, *Ymagines*, p. 312, cf. ii. 279. *Mats.* nos. 29–38, 46; no. 44 would seem to date from Thomas's exile.

19. Migne, *PL*, cc. 260; *Mats.* no. 35.

20. W. fS., iii. 58; *Mats.* nos. 27–8, 36, 41, 43, 798.

21. *Mats.* no. 34 (although possibly from Oct. 1164). E.G., ii. 378–9; W. of C., i. 14; Guernes, vv. 881ff., 910ff.; A.I, iv. 31–3. Guernes and A.I put the first meeting at Harrow; the meeting with the king is located at Woodstock (Guernes, A.I), at Oxford (H. of B., GFol, *Letters*, no. 170, p. 233). The two places are, of course, close. For the consecration, Gervase, *Chron.*, p. 176. For Henry's Christmas, Eyton, p. 66.

22. The best text is in *Councils and Synods*, no. 159, where there is a valuable commentary. Text also printed *SSC*, pp. 163ff., *EHD*, ii. 766 (in translation). Diceto, *Ymagines*, p. 312, dates the council 25 January; Gervase, *Chron.*, pp. 176–7, 13 January. The chirograph is dated 29 January. For accounts of the council, GFol, *Letters*, no. 170 (pp. 233–4, 239); J. of S., ii. 311–12; E.G., ii. 379–83; A.II, iv. 99–103; W. of C., i. 15–23; W. fS., iii. 46–9; Guernes, vv. 920–1035; H. of B., iii. 278–92; Benet, vv. 421–510; *Thómas Saga* i. 161–77; Diceto, Gervase, *loc. cit.*

23. If there had been a preliminary draft, this could have been in either French or Latin. The findings of the recognitors would have been reported in French for the benefit of most of those present. But for the purpose of legal record, the final declaration had to be in Latin. At Christmas 1164 Nicholas of Mont-St-Jacques, Rouen, at the Empress Matilda's request, read the Constitutions to her in Latin and then expounded them in French: *Mats.* no. 76.

24. 'quarto die ante purificationem BMV', 2 February minus 4 days, makes 29 January. This date is correct even if the fourth day should be translated 'Wednesday', for in 1164 2 February fell on a Sunday. For chirographs, V.H.Galbraith, *Studies in the Public Records* (1948), pp. 9–12. But a Christ Church, Canterbury, chirograph dated 1146, witnessed *inter alios* by John of Salisbury, bears the seals of both Theobald and the prior and chapter: Saltman, *Theobald*, p. 536.

25. Although W. fS., iii. 48–9, differs from the others in stating that all sealed the document, when describing the proceedings at Northampton, p. 66, he makes Hilary of Chichester explain how they had got out of sealing. John of Poitiers, writing to Thomas in July, understood, partly on the testimony of a letter from the archbishop, that Thomas had not agreed unconditionally to observe the Customs and, unlike the others, had not sealed them: *Mats.* no. 60. In October 1167, however, John of Salisbury admitted freely that Thomas had sworn to observe the Constitutions: *Letters*, no. 225 (pp. 390–2). For Thomas's explanation at Northampton, W. fS., iii. 66–7; cf. H. of B., iii. 288. At Avranches in 1172 Henry, in his turn, swore that he would carry out his undertakings *bona fide et absque malo ingenio*: Gervase, *Chron.*, p. 239.

26. W. fS., iii. 46; cf. H. of B., iii. 524, 526, where Robert is said to have had good cause for receiving Thomas's leave and benediction, while Jordan was hindered by his purchase of a manor. For Thomas's penance, see n. 36.

27. W. fS., iii. 63. See p. 113.

28. The procedure is explained and the views of both the king and the archbishop are displayed by E.G., ii. 385–9; cf. W. of C., i. 25–9; Diceto, *Ymagines*, p. 313.

29. H. of B., iii. 280. *Decretum*, I. viii. 5, cf. 3–9. Cf. W. fS., iii. 48.

30. *Decretum*, II. xi. 1, is devoted to *privilegium fori*. My own views and interpretation are closer to those of R. M. Fraher, 'The Becket dispute and two decretist traditions: the Bolognese masters revisited and some new Anglo-Norman texts', *Journ. of Med. Hist.*, iv (1978), 347, than to those of C. Duggan, *Canon Law in Medieval England* (Variorum, 1982), especially no. X, where he attempted to establish Thomas's legal orthodoxy. For Master Roland's views, Fraher, p. 351; cf. Smalley, *Becket Conflict*, pp. 149–51.

31. *Decretum, de Paenitentia*, dist. III, cc. 39–44. In some texts *vindicavit* is the reading instead of *iudicabit*. The Vulgate version is, 'Non consurget duplex tribulatio', also quoted by Gratian, ibid., *c*.42, and rendered by A.V. as, 'affliction shall not rise up the second time'. J. of S. used it in this form in *Policraticus*, viii. 18, p. 364.

32. *Decretum*, XIII. ii. 30. Saltman, *Theobald*, p. 72 and n. See further Foreville, *ER*, pp. 146–51; Smalley, *Becket Conflict*, pp. 125ff.

33. Cf. Council of Toulouse (1119), can. 3; Lateran II (1139), can. 23; Newburgh, *Historia*, pp. 60ff. Barlow, *EC*, p. 166. Although it is possible that those burned in 1148 were laymen, the conciliar decrees do not make a distinction. Cf. also Assize of Clarendon (1166), cap. 21, *SSC*, p. 173, for an English decree on the subject.

34. Nicholas of Mont-St-Jacques to Thomas, *Mats*. no. 76. A.II, iv. 99; H. of B., iii. 278.

35. E.G., ii. 383–4; W. of C., i. 24–5; W. fS., iii. 49; Guernes, vv. 1036–45; A.I, iv. 37–8. For a charter witnessed by the bishop of Evreux at Woodstock and his other movements, Eyton, pp. 70–1. Some biographers believed that the pope was aware that Thomas did not really support this move. Alexander's answer is, perhaps, *Mats*. no. 49 (undated); the matter is elaborated in no. 50 (27 Feb.).

36. The biographers in general place Thomas's self-imposed penance immediately after Clarendon and before the arrival of the bishop of Evreux, and make Thomas at the same time write to the pope to explain the situation: J. of S., ii. 311–12; E.G., ii. 383; W. of C., i. 24; Guernes, vv. 1030–5; A.I, iv. 37; A. of T., ii. 324–5. But W. fS., iii. 49, puts the penance after the pope's 'condemnation' of the Constitutions; and Alexander's first recorded reaction to it is dated Sens, 1 April. He wrote to Thomas informing him that he had heard indirectly of his suspension of himself from the altar, absolved him from any imprudence he had committed, and ordered him to resume his priestly functions: *Mats*. no. 52. It would have taken a messenger only a few days to travel from Sens to Canterbury, and Thomas was certainly conducting public services again by 19 April. H. of B.'s story, iii. 292, that Thomas maintained his penance for forty days, if realigned with the papal letter, would support its commencement towards the end of February.

37. Torigni, *Chron.*, p. 221; *Draco Normannicus*, pp. 676–7. See pp. 58, 247.

38. E.G., ii. 384–5; W. of C., i. 25; Guernes, vv. 1051–100; A.I, iv. 38–9; Diceto, *Ymagines*, p. 308. A copy of the legatine commission to York has not survived. For correspondence concerning it, *Mats*. nos. 47–8, 50–4, 60. For Roger being addressed as legate, cf. *Mats*. nos. 630, 651, 683. On 16 September 1170, no. 701, the pope may have omitted the title; but Roger was using it again in December 1171: no. 766. For the problem of abbatial professions of obedience to bishops, M. Chibnall, 'From Bec to Canterbury: Anselm and Monastic Privilege', *Anselm Studies* (Kraus Internat. Publications, 1983), pp. 23ff.

39. W. of C., i. 25; Guernes, vv. 1101–80; A.I, iv. 39. The biographers admit that Thomas protected priests, deacons and clerks in minor orders, reputed to be homicides, murderers, thieves and robbers, from their fate. E.G., ii. 383, followed by A.I, seems to think that the matter was again debated in a council. For the Assize of Clarendon, *SSC*, pp. 167–73; H. G. Richardson and G. O. Sayles, *The Governance of Mediaeval England*, pp. 197ff.

40. *Annales Radigenses Posteriores*, ed. C. W. Previté-Orton, *EHR* xxxvii (1922) 400; *Ann. Winton.*, in *Ann. Monastici* (Rolls ser.), ii. 57; *Ann. Bermondsey*, ibid., iii. 441–2; Torigni, *Chron.*, p. 221; W. of C., miracles, I. 418. K. J. Leyser, 'Frederick Barbarossa, Henry II and the Hand of St James', reprinted in *Medieval Germany and its Neighbours, 900–1250* (1982), p. 215. Thomas, *Acta*, no. 35. Henry of Essex, Thomas's fellow captain in Toulouse in 1159, had become a monk at Reading after his defeat in the *duellum* in 1163 in connection with his 'cowardice' in Wales: Torigni, *Chron.*, p. 218; *Ann. Winton, loc. cit.*

41. J. of S., *Letters*, no. 136, cf. 137–9. Brooke, ibid., ii, pp. xxii–xxiii.

42. *Mats.* no. 61 (p. 121); Guernes, vv. 2291–320; cf. H. of B., iii. 524–5. *Mats.* nos. 60–1.

43. Consecration: 26 August, Diceto, *Ymagines*, p. 312; after Easter, Gervase, *Chron.*, p. 182; 23 August, *Chron. Theokesberia* in *Ann. Monastici*, i. 49. Rebuff at Woodstock: W. fS., iii. 49. Attempt to escape: GFol, *Letters*, no. 170 (pp. 234–5); E.G., ii. 389–90; A.II, iv. 104; W. of C., i. 29; W. fS., iii. 49; Guernes, vv. 1356–75; A.I, iv. 40; A. of T., ii. 325–6; H. of B., iii. 293–4; Diceto, *Ymagines*, p. 313. Several attempts (A.II), two attempts (H. of B.). E.G. states that the sailors made the excuse that the wind was contrary; and the reluctance of the sailors is stressed by W. of C., Guernes and A.I. GFol asserts that Henry received Thomas on his return graciously and kindly. For Adam of Charing, Guernes, Urry, *Canterbury*, pp. 180–1; F. R. H. Du Boulay, *The Lordship of Canterbury*, pp. 201, 203; for Aldington, A. of T.; for the interview at Woodstock, H. of B.

44. See p. 84. *Mats.* no. 74. E.G., ii. 390–1; W. of C., i. 30–1; W. fS., iii. 50–1, 70; Guernes, vv. 1400–60; A.I, iv. 40–4; H. of B., iii. 296–8; Diceto, *Ymagines*, p. 313, cf. ii. 280; Howden, *Chronica*, i. 224–5. When the pope, probably early in 1165, quashed the sentence in this case pronounced at Northampton, he accepted that Thomas had not answered the first citation in person (*tui copiam non fecisti*): *Mats.* no. 94. All the biographers but W. fS. and H. of B. claim that he sent an essoin of sickness; but the former says that Thomas sent not an essoin but a justification for non-attendance, the latter thought that he sent a proxy; cf. p. 297, 'sufficient answer'. In 1166 GFol asserted that Thomas had sent a messenger to say that he did not intend to obey the summons: *Letters*, no. 170 (p. 235). For Pagham, *DB*, i. 16b. The disputed land was apparently Mundham (*Mats.* nos. 507, 610), which in 1086 (*DB* i. 24) had no connection with the neighbouring Pagham, although in Canterbury's forged Pagham charter it is included: N. Brooks, *The Early History of the Church of Canterbury* (1984), pp. 240–3. John had vassals at Pagham in 1168–9: *PR 15 Hen. II*, p. 166, and his son, the great William the Marshal, held Mundham in 1202: F. R. H. Du Boulay, *The Lordship of Canterbury*, p. 361. For John the Marshal,

Barlow, *William Rufus*, pp. 153–4; *Histoire de Guillaume le Maréchal*, ed. Paul Meyer (Soc. de l'Hist. de France, 1891–1901); S. Painter, 'The Rout of Winchester', *Speculum*, vii (1932), 70.

45. Barlow, *EC*, pp. 281–7, *William Rufus*, pp. 85–9, 339–42. W. fS., iii. 59; Diceto, *Ymagines*, p. 313. *Councils and Synods*, no. 160.

46. For the retinue, A.I, iv. 45. For the preliminaries and trial, E.G., ii. 391–2; W. of C., i. 30–1; W. fS., iii. 49–53; Guernes, vv. 1391ff.; A.I, iv. 42–3; H. of B., iii. 297; *Thómas Saga* i. 184–6. Guernes, vv. 1432–4, followed by A.I, and cf. Howden, *Chronica*, i. 224, believed, probably in error, that Thomas immediately asked for permission to go to the pope, but was ordered to stand trial first. There is confusion over the penalty: fined £500 for contempt (E.G., A.I, cf. Diceto, *Ymagines*, p. 313); £300 (Guernes, vv. 1446–7); £50 (W. of C.).

47. *Mats*. no. 94; GFol, *Letters*, no. 170 (pp. 235–6).

48. E.G., ii. 391–2; W. of C., i. 30–1; A.I, iv. 43. Disorder of the spleen (E.G.); colic, W. of C., i. 32; A. of T., ii. 330; H. of B., iii. 30; kidney trouble, W. fS., iii. 56; pain in the side, A.I, iv. 44. The malady is discussed by Knowles, *Ep. Col.*, pp. 167–8, who infers that it was renal colic.

49. W. fS., iii. 53–4; H. of B., iii. 298–9. The former thought that two sums of 500 marks were demanded. According to *Thómas Saga* five laymen paid the fine for him. On the *PR* from 11 Henry II (1164–5), p. 104, sureties in debt to the king are Geoffrey Ridel, archdeacon of Canterbury (£100) and the earl of Gloucester, William of Eynesford and the count of Eu (each 100 marks). Of these only William of Eynesford was required to pay up; the debts of the others, although carried for many years on the books, were allowed to rest. In the spring of 1166 John of Poitiers pointed out to Thomas that, since his flight, Henry had been extorting money from the sureties and that Jocelin of Salisbury had been forced to sell all the stock on his manors: *Mats*. no. 116 (p. 223). For the sum of £30,000, see p. 54. For the offer, W. fS., iii. 54.

50. According to Gervase, *Chron.*, p. 185, the only absentees were the paralysed Nigel of Ely and William of Norwich. A. of T., ii. 326–8, analyses the attitude of some of the bishops on the Saturday or Sunday; cf. *Mats*. no. 73, a letter from 'Thomas's enemies' to the pope and cardinals, justifying the bishops' behaviour; conversations of Thomas's clerks with their master, reported by W. fS., iii. 58, H. of B., iii. 308 (who does not mention William); *Thómas Saga* i. 190. For Thomas's isolation, W. fS., iii. 53. Roger of York was almost equally isolated: the Canterbury suffragans would have united against him if he had taken undue advantage of their metropolitan's disgrace.

51. Arnulf, *Letters*, no. 42 (pp. 71–2). Although Gilbert seems to have taken personal responsibility for these services and later sent money to the exile, the origin of their friendship is unknown. For Scaiman, see also *Mats*. no. 254; A.I, iv. 57.

52. J. of S., ii. 312; E.G., ii. 393ff.; W. of C., i. 32ff.; W. fS., iii. 56ff.; Guernes, vv. 1551ff.; A.I, iv. 45ff.; A. of T., ii. 330ff.; H. of B., iii. 301ff.; Benet, vv. 517ff.; *Thómas Saga* i. 204ff. For the appeals and counter-appeals, see also H. of B., *Mats*. nos. 221 (pp. 471–3), 537 (p. 18).

53. W. fS., iii. 57; Guernes, vv. 1671–7; A. of T., ii. 330. Howden, *Chronica*, i. 226–7, gives a slightly different version of these events. For GFol's attitude, Smalley, *Becket Conflict*, p. 179.

54. Howden, *Chronica*, i. 228. Cf. Barlow, *William Rufus*, pp. 343, 373–5.

55. J. of S., ii. 312–13; E.G., ii. 398; W. of C., i. 39–40; Guernes, v. 1929; A.I, iv. 52; cf. A. of T., ii. 333. For Thomas's rejoinder, W. of C. Hamelin was cured by St Thomas of cataract of the eyes: W. of C., miracles, VI. 45. Ranulf de Broc obtained the estate of Catteshill in Godalming, Surrey, from either Oin Purcell or Oin's son Geoffrey, who had succeeded his father by 1130: *PR 31 Hen. I*, p. 50; *Rot. Chart.* i. 160b (1205). According to King John's charter, Ranulf was Oin's son. Henry II confirmed or attached to this land the serjeanty of doorkeeper (usher) to his chamber and keeper of his whores. Acquisition of Guildford brought another serjeanty in the marshalsea. These estates and serjeanties descended through Edelina, the eldest of Ranulf's five daughters and co-heirs, and at least two more heiresses to their respective husbands: *Book of Fees*, pp. 66–7, 1377; J.H.Round, *King's Serjeants*, 96ff.; Barlow, *William Rufus*, pp. 153–4. To Robert de Broc, probably Ranulf's younger brother, Henry II gave in marriage Margery, together with the lands of her brother, William Croc, who had been hanged for some unspecified crime. She also transmitted estates from her grandfather, the Cannock huntsman, Richard Cheven. These several lands in Staffordshire and Warwickshire carried forest serjeanties in Cannock Chase, particularly the custody of Teddesley Hay. Ranulf de Broc's nephew and protégé, Robert, since he was educated as a clerk and had been a monk, is unlikely to have been the Robert who married Margery Croc, or even their son Robert, who inherited Huntington in Cannock and the custody of the Hay and passed them to his son Henry. For this branch of the Broc family, *Book of Fees*, pp. 7, 348, 594–5, 1236, 1245–6, particularly 1277; *V.C.H., Staffs*, v. 75–6, 79, 119, 183; *Warwicks*, v. 42. As, in the Becket biographies, it is the nephew Robert who is described as usher of the king's chamber, he must have acquitted Ranulf of the duties: B. of P., ii. 128; Guernes, vv. 5750–1.

56. Cf. *Mats*. nos. 71–6. *Draco Normannicus*, pp. 676–7, 741–2, 744–6, 756–7.

57. For these three manors, *DB* i. 3a, 3d, 9. Higham, a manor held in 1086 by a subtenant of Bishop Odo of Bayeux, earl of Kent, and worth £15 a year, was presumably one of the estates in dispute between Archbishop Lanfranc and Odo. Memories were long at Canterbury. For the escape, E.G., ii. 399–400; Guernes, vv. 1986–2085; A.I, iv. 53–5; A. of T., ii. 335; H. of B., iii. 323–5, 329–30; Diceto, *Ymagines*, p. 314; *Vita S. Gileberti Confessoris*, in *Monasticon Anglicanum* (1817–30), vi, pt. 2, p. xvii*. It is impossible to reconstruct the exact itinerary, which was obviously unknown to the biographers. H. of B., iii. 325, claims that 'Tuesday, 2 November' was fifteen days after Thomas's flight from Northampton, which had also been on a Tuesday. In fact, 2 November was a Monday; and Herbert's reckoning of time, like most of the mileages he gives, was well out.

58. *Mats*. no. 156 (Aug. 1165) to Alexander, p. 289; H. of B., iii. 312, 318–19; Gervase, *Chron.*, p. 189.

59. The rank of the Gilbertines Robert de Cave and Scaiman is never stated and modern opinion has been divided: canons (Hutton, *Thomas Becket*, p. 40), lay-brethren (Knowles, *TB*, pp. 99–100). The latter is by far the more likely.

60. For Canterbury's disputed title to Sandwich, N. Brooks, *The Early History of the Church of Canterbury*, pp. 292–4. For the dangerous crossing, *Mats*. no. 221 (p. 469). For Oye, Michelin map 51, plis 2–3. Arnulf, *Letters*, no. 42, p. 72. For GFol's view that Thomas was in no danger and that there was no pursuit, *Letters*, no. 170 (pp. 238–40).

7 Thomas on the defensive, November 1164–April 1166

General

For papal politics, see Reuter, 'Papal Schism'. For Anglo-French relations, see K. Norgate, *England under the Angevin Kings* (1887), i, ch. 8–11; ii, 1, 2, 4; A. L. Poole, *Domesday Book to Magna Carta*, ch. 10 (1951); F. Barlow, *The Feudal Kingdom of England*, ch. 9 (1955, 1972); W. L. Warren, *Henry II* (1973). L. Halphen, 'Les Entrevues des rois Louis VII et Henri II durant l'exil de Thomas Becket en France', *Mélanges Charles Bémont* (Paris, 1913).

1. The best account of the events between the landing in Flanders and Thomas's entry into Pontigny Abbey is given by H. of B., iii. 324ff., who was the only biographer certainly involved in the events. A.I. iv. 55–64, who may have served Thomas at this time, and Guernes, vv. 2081ff., add some information. W. fS., iii. 70ff., and R. of C., p. 390 (Benet, pp. 619b–621b), write from the standpoint of the royal court. Cf. also J. of S., ii. 313; E.G., ii. 400–4; A.II, iv. 106–9; W. of C., i. 42–6; A. of T., ii. 335–45; *Thómas Saga* i. 247–313. Fullest list of royal ambassadors in Guernes, vv. 2161ff.; the bishops confirmed by W. fS., iii. 70 and H. of B., iii. 323. A. of T., ii. 336, adds, probably mistakenly, Arnulf of Lisieux.
2. H. of B., iii. 330. A.I, iv. 57, thought that Thomas's servants brought a large part of the archiepiscopal furnishings to Clairmarais.
3. *Mats.* no. 140; cf. H. of B., iii. 525–6.
4. Scaiman mentioned by A.I, iv. 57 only. The others witness three documents probably issued by Thomas at St Bertin's, although the date 1162–4 is possible: J. H. Round, *Calendar of Documents preserved in France* (1899), nos. 1337–8, cf. 1327ff.; Thomas, *Acta*, nos. 26, 39–40. For Silvester, Arnulf, *Letters*, p. xiii and n., *Mats.* nos. 269, 304. Richard of Salisbury, *capellanus*, who, after a sojourn at Orleans and a visit to the pope, perhaps at Christmas 1165 (*Mats.* no. 135), had rejoined the archbishop by Christmas 1170 (see p. 233), is to be distinguished from the master of the same name, an undoubted kinsman of John of Salisbury and a pupil of Gerard la Pucelle, who died in 1168 (see p. 131). Neither seems to have been normally in the archbishop's household in exile, and both must be distinguished from John's brother, Richard *Peccator*, his companion until 1170 at Rheims.
5. For Milo, cf. J. of S., *Letters*, nos. 108, 142. W. fS. imagines that Thomas was again travelling in great state and had a retinue of forty horsemen; H. of B. lends some support.
6. Guernes, vv. 2291–320; and see p. 107.
7. H. of B., iii. 237. Cf. *Mats.* no. 537 (p. 18). W. fS., iii. 74.
8. See also *Mats.* no. 74; Diceto, *Ymagines*, p. 316. For the warm greetings, W. fS., iii. 74; Benet, p. 619b. A. of T., ii. 337, 341, however, says that both H. of B. and then Thomas were greeted coldly by the cardinals. H. of B. may have presented *Mats.* no. 74 to the pope. There is a short hostile account in *Draco Normannicus*, pp. 741–2: Thomas told the pope lies. For the clerks' reluctance, A.I, iv. 61, who explains their refusal by their fear of the king. For the condemnation of the customs: condemnation of the 'usurpations', W. of C., i. 46; total condemnation, E.G., ii. 404; Guernes, v. 2390; A.I. iv. 64; nine clauses condemned, 7 tolerable, H. of

B., iii. 342–3; cf. *Thómas Saga* i. 303. In 1166 at Vézelay Thomas condemned eight clauses: see p. 147. Thomas's complaint of April 1170: *Mats.* no. 664 (p. 285).

9. The starting-point seems to be A.II's statement, iv. 109, that Alexander granted Thomas an indulgence for any sin committed while entering the archbishopric and in his subsequent fall from grace, and confirmed him in his office. J. of S., *Letters*, nos. 225 (Oct. 1167), 288 (Feb. 1169), claims that Thomas confessed his fault of swearing to the Constitutions and accepted penance from the pope. For Ralf Niger, *De Re Militari*, III. 15, see ch. 3, n. 3.

10. For the text, used later by Alexander to Thomas, *Mats.* no. 491 (p. 564), and Peter Lombard's Great Gloss on it, Smalley, *Becket Conflict*, p. 158.

11. *Mats.* no. 60. John had entrusted Guichard with a secret mission to the pope re the archbishop of York's legation and the abbot of St Augustine's profession. For the abbey, R.H. Bautier in Foreville, *TB* (Sédières), p. 41. For Guichard and Lyons, Reuter, 'Papal Schism', pp. 191ff. He was consecrated archbishop by Alexander on 8 August 1165 at Montpellier, but did not obtain his see until 11 November 1167: see also *Mats.* no. 105; J. of S., *Letters*, nos. 144, 173 *ad fin.*, 236. For Thomas's view of his absolution, see especially his letters in 1166 to the bishops and clergy of England, *Mats.* nos. 121–3.

12. J. of S., *Letters*, no. 228; E.G., ii. 404; W. of C., i. 46; W. fS., iii. 76, 78; Guernes, vv. 2556ff.; A.I, iv. 64; A. of T., ii. 344ff.; H. of B., iii. 357ff.; *Thómas Saga* i. 313ff. A.II, iv. 109, thought that Alexander sent Thomas to Pontigny so that he could atone for his sins there. For the *mansiunculae* (Gen. 6: 14), H. of B., iii. 373, cf. 366, 379, and *Mats.* no. 221 (pp. 468, 474).

13. Fullest account of Henry's measures in W. fS., iii. 75–6; cf. also J. of S., ii. 313–14; E.G., ii. 404–5; A.II, iv. 108; W. of C., i. 46–7; Guernes, vv. 2566–640; A.I, iv. 64–5; H. of B., iii. 358–75. Royal writ to bishops, *Mats.* no. 77, to sheriffs, no. 78; cf. also 87. Thomas's views in 1170, no. 723 (p. 401).

14. For Ranulf and his family, see ch. 6, n. 55. W. of C., i. 120; B. of P., ii. 10; *Thómas Saga* i. 321. For the farm, *PR 11 Hen. II* (1164–5), p. 108, and in subsequent rolls until *19 Hen. II*, p. 90. For Ranulf's acquittance, *PR 18 Hen. II*, p. 140. The irregular figure for the farm makes it likely that some individual items, perhaps the temporalities of the proscribed clerks, had been added. For the monastic estates, Gervase, *Chron.*, i. 197, and pp. 175–6. For the changes in the liturgy, W. fS., iii. 83–4.

15. J. of S., *Letters*, nos. 152, 159–60; *Mats.* nos. 132, 167.

16. *Mats.* no. 116. For the sureties and their debts, see ch. 6, n. 49. For William of Eynesford's recovery of the sum, *Domesday Monachorum*, p. 110.

17. See also *Mats.* nos. 88, 235, 264; 254; J. of S., *Letters*, no. 152; *PR 11 Hen. II* and subsequent vols. Cf. *PR 5 John*, p. 103.

18. W. fS., iii. 78–81; 59.

19. Most detail in W. fS., iii. 75–6. Alexander's letter of thanks, *Mats.* no. 133. For the nephews, see ch. 1, n. 7. For Thomas's attitude, H. of B., iii. 370; cf. *Mats.* no. 74 *ad fin.*

20. For the dispersed clerks, W. fS., iii. 78; J. of S., *Letters*, no. 179; for France, *Mats.* no. 136, Sicily, no. 595. For Gerard, Philip and Ralf, J. of S., *Letters*, nos. 158, 179, *Mats.* nos. 86, 146. For Richard *clericus*, J. of S., *Letters*, no. 142; for Richard *capellanus*, *Mats.* no. 135. For Ernulf, nos. 163, 233.

21. Most information in H. of B., iii. 362ff.; cf. E.G., ii. 412–14; Guernes, vv.

3626–30; A.I, iv. 64–5; R. of C., p. 390 (Benet, pp 621b–622b). Fullest account of the papal garment in A. of T., ii. 345–6 (making the necessary change in the last line of p. 345 of *adunisse* to *adimisse*). See further p. 239. For the pope's suggestion (Montpellier, 6 Aug.), *Mats.* no. 104. For the dispensation, H. of B., iii. 358; cf. 376, where the archbishop temporarily, as a special penance, ate the conventual food. For his eating of meat, also *Mats.* no. 96. Gervase, *Chron.*, p. 199. See also pp. 233, 239.

22. *Mats.* no. 221 (pp. 468, 474); H. of B., iii. 376–9; J. of S., *Letters*, no. 150. Smalley, *Becket Conflict*, p. 82.

23. H. of B., iii. 379, 523–4; W. fS., iii. 77; J. of S., *Letters*, nos. 144, 150, 167 (p. 99).

24. For sympathizers in the royal court, H. of B., iii. 412.

25. *Catalogus*, H. of B., iii. 523–31; J. of S., *Letters*, no. 228.

26. See pp. 120 and 171. For the deaths, J. of S., *Letters*, nos. 176, 277 (p. 594). For Master Richard, see also nos. 142, 161.

27. For Gilbert, *Mats.* nos. 47–8; J. of S., *Letters*, nos. 216–18, cf. 215; Arnulf, *Letters*, nos. 86–7. For Hubert, *Mats.* no. 308. For Henry (of Houghton), *Mats.* nos. 29–33, cf. 36; J. of S., *Letters*, no. 136 (p. 8); see also p. 181. For Hervey, *Mats.* nos. 47–8, 62, 96; J. of S., *Letters*, no. 176. For John the Cantor/Planeta, *Mats.* nos. 285, 359, cf. 348, 635; see p. 77; W. fS., iii. 59, 131. He is also probably W. of C.'s John of Canterbury, i. 115. A Roger chancellor witnesses with other clerks Thomas, *Acta*, no. 26.

28. For Alexander, J. of S., *Letters*, nos. 173, 228; *Mats.* nos. 359, cf. 348; 635; W. fS., iii. 131; *Mats.* no. 735. For Gunter, Luke 19; *Mats.* nos. 47–8, 735; 273 *ad fin.*

29. *Mats.* no. 739.

30. I have greatly profited from a discussion with Dr Anne Duggan on the authorship of Thomas's letters; but the views expressed here are not necessarily hers. Herbert, Lombard and John of Salisbury claimed authorship of some. My feeling is that H. of B. had a hand in a good many. But Alexander and John (if he was John Planeta) also had the necessary skills and so may some of the other clerks and chaplains. Roland and Ariald were presumably letter writers. A letter which must have been dictated (if in French) by the archbishop is *Mats.* no. 612: see p. 192.

31. For Brown, see p. 159. For William de Capes, Guernes, vv. 2046ff., 2596–601, 3626–35; Urry, *Canterbury*, p. 183. For Richard, *Mats.* no. 508 (p. 604), and see p. 185. For the replacement of losses, H. of B., iii. 415–16.

32. For the schism, see p. 60. For its history after 1159, Reuter, 'Papal Schism'.

33. Cf. J. of S. on Louis in January 1165, *Letters*, no. 144, and on the fallibility of both in July 1166, no. 175 (p. 164). Barlow, *William Rufus*, pp. 397–8.

34. J. of S., *Letters*, nos. 138–9, 143, 149–51, 177, 181–6; cf. my review in *J.E.H.*, xxxii (1981), 89–91.

35. *Mats.* nos. 75–6, cf. 134, 137, 139, 275; J. of S., *Letters*, no. 152, for the king of Scots; Arnulf, *Letters*, no. 41. *Mats.* no. 251, to Reimund, c.d. of St Mary in Via Lata, would seem to be of this time.

36. *Mats.* no. 156.

37. For Gisors, W. fS., iii. 98. Eyton, p. 78. For the attitudes of Henry, the empress and the archbishop of Rouen, *Mats.* nos. 275–6. For Würzburg, *Mats.* nos. 213, 82–4, 91; J. of S., *Letters*, no. 177 (pp. 182–4); Torigni, *Chron.*, p. 224; Diceto, *Ymag-*

ines, p. 318. Eyton, pp. 77–9; Reuter, 'Papal Schism', pp. 124ff., 252–4. For Henry's repudiation of his ambassadors, *Mats*. nos. 101, 108. For Ralf Niger's letter, M. Preiss, *Die politische Tätigheit und Stellung der Cisterzienser im Schisma von 1159–1177* (Berlin, 1934), p. 261. For Thomas's trip to Bourges, A. of T., ii. 347; J. of S., *Letters*, no. 323 (p. 796). For John of St-Satur, J. Châtillon, 'Thomas Becket et les Victorins', Foreville, *TB* (Sédières), pp. 89–90.

38. *Mats*. nos. 80, 94; 81, 93. Cf. also Alexander to Robert of Hereford, no. 141.

39. GFol, *Letters*, nos. 155–6; *Mats*. nos. 106, 157 and probably 255 are from this time. Nos. 107, 111 and probably 109, which also concern GFol and Peter's Pence, come from later years.

40. *Mats*. nos. 156; 102, cf. 96; 103–4; 131–2.

41. *Mats*. no. 95, cf. 171. The former is dated by Robertson, following Jaffé, 'Clermont, June', and, by Duggan, ?8 June 1165, although the reason is not obvious.

42. R. L. Poole, 'The early correspondence of John of Salisbury', *Proceedings of the British Academy*, xi (1924–5), 5–6; Barlow, *William Rufus*, p. 54; T. Reuter, 'Zur Anerkennung Papst Innocenz' II: eine neue Quelle', *Deutsches Archiv*, xxxix (1983), p. 398, n. 14.

43. For Bangor, *Mats*. nos. 117–28, cf. also 129–30. For Sempringham, nos. 148–9; R. Foreville, 'La Crise de l'ordre de Sempringham au XII^c siècle: nouvelle approche du dossier des frères laïs', *Anglo-Norman Studies*, ed. R. A. Brown, vi (1984), 44–6. For Pentney, GFol, *Letters*, pp. 210–14; *Mats*. nos. 725–6; Foreville, *ER*, pp. 206–9; Thomas, *Acta*, no. 30. For the deanery of Salisbury, J. of S., *Letters*, pp. xxxi–xxxiii and n., nos. 168, 176, 213.

44. *Councils and Synods*, no. 162; *SSC*, pp. 161ff. GFol, *Letters*, nos. 157–8 and nn.; Diceto, *Ymagines*, p. 318. Thomas's letter, *Mats*. no. 603 (misplaced by Robertson).

45. W. fS., iii. 98–101; J. of S., *Letters*, nos. 161, 164, 167, 181. Eyton, pp. 92–3; Foreville, *ER*, pp. 169–70.

8 Thomas on the attack, April 1166–May 1167

1. For Thomas's decision to attack, H. of B., iii. 380–3, 387–91; for the mission to Rome (winter 1165–6), 396–7. As usual Herbert does not name the nuncios. Hervey of London had not returned by the end of July, J. of S., *Letters*, no. 176 (p. 176, cf. 164) and seems to have died at Rome or on the way back. For the package of letters obtained, see pp. 145–6.

2. *Mats*. no. 699.

3. J. of S., *Letters*, no. 161.

4. *Mats*. nos. 184; 152–4; 188, cf. 195 (p. 387). H. of B., iii. 383–5. But Thomas's letters to Henry are difficult to place in order of mounting severity. For Cercamp, Michelin map 51, pli 13. Urban died on 31 August 1166: *Gallia Christiana*, x. 1338. Henry's protest, *Mats*. no. 188, cf. 195 (p. 387).

5. H. of B., iii. 385–6. Primacy, *Mats*. no. 170; for the verbal confirmation at Sens, no. 315 (p. 215). Privilege of crowning, no. 169. Style, C. R. Cheney, 'On the acts of Theobald and Thomas, archbishops of Canterbury', *Journ. of the Soc. of Archivists*, vi. (1981), p. 477. *Councils and Synods*, no. 147. For the rivalry with York, Foreville, *ER*, pp. 263ff.

6. Papal legation (2 May 1165), W. Holtzmann, *Papsturkunden in England*, ii (1935), no. 121. The notification to the English clergy, *Mats*. no. 173, is, however, dated 24 April. For the grant of a legation dated Anagni 9 October, no. 172, see Foreville, *ER*, p. 315, n. 4, where dated 1170. *Councils and Synods*, no. 149.

7. *Mats*. nos. 164–5; J. of S., *Letters*, no. 174 (p. 150), cf. no. 275 (p. 580) of May 1168. *Mats*. nos. 178 (3 May), 166; 182 (16 May).

8. Cheney, 'On the acts', pp. 468ff., especially 478ff. H. of B., iii. 387ff.

9. J. of S., *Letters*, no. 176 (p. 176), 168 (p. 110); H. of B., iii. 392; Letters, nos. 22–3.

10. J. of S., *Letters*, no. 168 (pp. 110–16). Eyton, pp. 93–5. For Bernard and Vézelay, Torigni, *Chron.*, p. 152; Arnulf, *Letters*, p. xxv. E. Willems, 'Cîteaux et la Seconde Croisade', *Revue d'hist. ecclés.*, xlix (1954) 126.

11. Thomas once met Guichard, archbishop of Lyons, about 22 July in the nunnery of Crisenon, on the Yonne 23 km. south of Auxerre, to try to settle a quarrel between the abbot of Vézelay and the count of Nevers: *Hist. Vizeliacensis* in Migne *PL*, cxciv, col. 1672. H. of B., iii. 392–6. He dates the Vézelay sentences the patronal feast of St Mary Magdalene (22 July) and the annual fair. But it seems that his memory failed him. Thomas may have considered further measures on that day: see p. 151. For accounts of the proceedings at Vézelay, see below, n. 14.

12. *Mats*. no. 250 (p. 59). For counsels of moderation, cf. nos. 209, 219 (p. 454), 221 (pp. 461–4); J. of S., *Letters*, nos. 168 (pp. 112, 114), 176 (p. 176); H. of B., iii. 383. For the pope's view, *Mats*. no. 701 (p. 364). J. of S., *Letters*, no. 174 (p. 148), thought that Thomas had informed the pope that Henry was *ipso facto* excommunicate.

13. J. of S., *Letters*, no. 171 (p. 126).

14. *Mats*. nos. 195–6, 201, 198, 203, 239, 297, cf. 183. J. of S., *Letters*, no. 174. *Mats*. no. 239 is the follow-up letter to GFol. Thomas's letter to the pope (195) was said to have been lost at Viterbo, when the messenger was captured. It was obtained by Henry at Christmas, but John of Poitiers believed that the royal agents got it from the papal chancery: no. 283 (p. 148). Diceto, *Ymagines*, p. 318. *Councils and Synods*, no. 161. Papal confirmation, *Mats*. no. 197. For the return of the mission, H. of B., iii. 408–9.

15. *Mats*. nos. 199–200, cf. 209 (p. 421). Principal earlier documents re John of Oxford, nos. 180 (18 May), 193 (8 June), 197; J. of S. *Letters*, no. 174 (p. 148); R. of C., p. 392 (*Thómas Saga* i. 358). For the case of William of Salisbury, *Mats*. nos. 88, 219–20, 235, 246, 248; J. of S., *Letters*, no. 174 (pp. 148, 152); GFol, *Letters*, nos. 169, 171; W. fS., iii. 78; Thomas, *Acta*, no. 30.

16. J. of S., *Letters*, nos. 168 (p. 114), 171 (pp. 124–6), 173 (p. 134), 174 (p. 148), 192 (p. 266); GFol, *Letters*, nos. 166–7. For J. of S. on these, *Letters*, no. 175. For the Council of London and bishops who, he claimed, played no part, W. of C., i. 56. Gervase, *Chron.*, p. 200. Eyton, p. 95. Jocelin's appeal, *Mats*. nos. 206–7, cf. papal letter dated 27 May (1167) (by Robertson 1166), no. 187; J. of S., *Letters*, no. 171 (p. 124); *Mats*. no. 241. For GFol's nuncios, Nicholas and Ric. d'Amari, Thomas, *Acta*, no. 30.

17. GFol, *Letters*, no. 168; *Mats*. no. 297 (July–Aug.). For Northampton, *Mats*. no. 209, *ad fin*. See Brooke, J. of S., *Letters*, p. xxxviii.

18. *Mats*. no. 209; J. of S., *Letters*, no. 179. For those disturbed, see pp. 159–60.

19. H. of B., iii. 396–7. *Mats*. no. 253, *ad fin.*; J. of S., *Letters*, no. 181 (p. 200).

20. J. of S., *Letters*, nos. 173, 174 (pp. 148, 150–2), 175 (pp. 156, 160); *Mats*. nos.

219–20, 237–8. Geoffrey appealed against the summons to 25 March 1167: *Mats.* no. 254. For Robert of Melun's views and behaviour, Smalley, *Becket Conflict*, pp. 51ff.

21. *Mats.* nos. 221–4. Cf. Thomas, *Acta*, no. 30.

22. *Mats.* no. 223 (pp. 510–11).

23. GFol, *Letters*, no. 170. For an essay on this, Morey and Brooke, pp. 166ff.

24. J. of S., *Letters*, no. 187; cf. also 225, to Peter the Scribe.

25. T. Reuter, 'Das Edikt Friedrich Barbarossas gegen die Zisterzienser', *Mitteilungen des Instituts für österreichische Geschichtsforschung*, lxxxiv (1976), pp. 333–6; *Mats.* nos. 246, 242–3; H. of B., iii. 397ff.; cf. J. of S., ii. 314; E.G., ii. 414–15; W. fS., iii. 83–4; Guernes, vv. 3676ff.; A.I, iv. 65; *Thómas Saga* i. 368–74.

26. For William, see Brooke, J. of S., *Letters*, no. 272, n. 28. For Sens and Ste-Colombe, Michelin map 97, pli 42. Now a *maison de repos*, little of the Benedictine monastery remains above ground. The architect of the cathedral, William of Sens, was to rebuild Canterbury cathedral after the fire of 1174.

27. *Gallia Christiana*, xii. 150: *HF*, xii. 288.

28. Approximate date only in Gervase, *Chron.*, p. 202. For the dream, W. of C., i. 51–2; H. of B., iii. 405–6. For his life at Sens, E.G., ii. 417–19; cf. Guernes, vv. 3891ff.; J. of S., *Letters*, no. 305 (p. 728). H. of B., iii. 460–1, refers incidentally to their attendance at Nocturns.

29. Guernes, vv. 3916–40. The poet describes Thomas's shirt and breeches of hair. Benet, vv. 1115–16. For Brown, his 'valet', Guernes, v. 3978.

30. Papal confirmation of the Vézelay sentences, a remarkably short document, *Mats.* no. 197. Ralf of Diss, *Mats.* no. 211. J. of S. seems to have remained friendly with Richard, whom he hoped might reconcile him to the king: *Letters*, nos. 177, 181; see also 180 and especially 182 on the problems of social intercourse at the royal court. For Henry's behaviour, *Mats.* no. 253, 'a friend' to Thomas. This friend was certainly at the very centre of the royal court and knew not only what went on in the king's privy council but also his future movements and plans. In view of what happened to Walter (see p. 161), he would seem to be a strong candidate. See also p. 163 and J. of S., *Letters*, nos. 161, 168 (p. 114), 180, 189.

31. *Mats.* no. 253; W. fS., iii. 85; *Mats.* no. 254 (p. 77).

32. *Mats.* nos. 254 (p. 77), 253; Arnulf, *Letters*, p. xlv.

33. *Mats.* nos. 253, 256, 285, 292; J. of S., *Letters*, no. 196; W. fS., iii. 85; for Roger's later adventures, 86–7.

34. J. of S., *Letters*, nos. 161 (p. 78), 180, 189; *Mats.* nos. 253–4; W. fS., iii. 82.

35. J. of S., *Letters*, nos. 188, 190–1, 201; *Mats.* no. 272.

36. *Mats.* nos. 246–9; H. of B., iii. 408. John the C. also went to Rome, *Mats.* no. 285.

37. *Mats.* nos. 283, 285, 292; J. of S., *Letters*, nos. 174 (p. 148), 214 (p. 354), 219 (p. 372), 234 (p. 428), 241 (p. 466). Boso, *Vita Alexandri*, ii. 393, states that the Council of Tours (1163) was held in the church of St Maurice; but this may be a mistake for St Martin. It does not seem that the cathedral, which is now dedicated to St Gatien, or any other ancient basilica in the city was ever dedicated to St Maurice.

38. *Mats.* nos. 257, 273.

39. *Mats.* nos. 258–9, 274, 272. Diceto, *Ymagines*, pp. 318–19.

40. *Mats.* no. 307, cf. 324 (22 Aug.), 331 (after 19 Nov.), 497 (Mar. 1169). J. of S., *Letters*, no. 219.

41. J. of S., *Letters*, nos. 216–18. Dated ? March by Brooke, but possibly a little earlier.

42. *Mats.* nos. 283 (pp. 147–8), 307. There is no letter written by Peter de Chastres, archbishop of Bourges, in the collections. For J. of S.'s acquisition of *Mats.* no. 213 and of at least one other letter, *Letters*, nos. 174 (p. 146), 177 (pp. 182, 184).

43. J. of S., *Letters*, nos. 197–200, 212, 214–15; *Mats.* nos. 269, 283, 285–8, 290–4. For resentment among the exiles against John of Oxford in April 1170, nos. 664 (pp. 286–7), 665 (p. 290).

9 The path of truth and justice, 1167–1169

1. *Pontificum Romanorum . . . Vitae*, ed. J. M. Watterich (Leipzig 1862, reprinted 1966), ii. 377; martyrdom and canonization, pp. 418ff. For Boso, Barlow, *EC*, p. 266 and n.

2. *Mats.* nos. 306–7, cf. 324 (22 Aug.); J. of S., *Letters*, no. 231 (p. 418). Accounts of this mission are in W. of C., i. 64–71; W. fS., iii. 95–6; H. of B., iii. 408–13. Gilbert Foliot travelled by the same route in reverse in the winter of 1169–70.

3. *Mats.* nos. 309, 311–13; J. of S., *Letters*, nos. 227–9; *Mats.* nos. 314–15 (all to be dated July–Aug.). Cf. GFol, *Letters*, nos. 181–2 (the bishop's appeal to the pope in November).

4. J. of S., *Letters*, nos. 221–5; *Mats.* no. 324. Eyton, p. 107. According to *Draco Normannicus*, p. 676, Thomas was with Louis at the conference at Gisors.

5. *Mats.* nos. 322 (a moderate letter to the pope), 329–30; 355–6 (all to be dated Sept.–Oct.). For the meeting, H. of B., iii. 409; Gervase, *Chron.*, pp. 203–4.

6. Report of the legates to Alexander, *Mats.* no. 342; archiepiscopal reports, J. of S., *Letters*, nos. 230–1, 237; *Mats.* no. 331.

7. For the places, Michelin map 97, pli 15; see also map in Barlow, *William Rufus*, p. 377. According to W. fS., iii. 95, the conference was at Les Planches. There are several places with this name in Normandy, but none now, it seems, in this area. For the clerks. see pp. 131–2.

8. H. of B., iii. 412.

9. GFol, *Letters*, nos. 180–2; J. of S., *Letters*, nos, 236, 241; *Mats.* nos. 342–3; J. of S., *Letters*, no. 238; *Mats.* no. 359. H. of B., iii. 412–13, says that the appeals were made at Le Mans; cf. Eyton, pp. 111–12. For the farewells at Argentan, *Mats.* no. 339 (p. 273).

10. *Mats.* nos. 355–7, 353, 359; 362–3; cf. GFol, *Letters*, no. 181; J. of S., *Letters*, nos. 237–8, 241.

11. *Mats.* nos. 348, 352, 359; J. of S., *Letters*, nos. 232–3, 236–41.

12. *Mats.* no. 397.

13. J. of S., *Letters*, no. 274.

14. H. of B., iii. 413–17.

15. *Mats.* nos. 348, 359; J. of S., *Letters*, no. 272.

16. J. of S., *Letters*, nos. 242–8; *Mats.* no. 412.

17. J. of S., *Letters*, nos. 272–4. For Roger, nos. 238, 281; *Mats.* nos. 403, 401. For Gerard, *Mats.* nos. 420–2, 419; J. of S., *Letters*, 275, 277. For Lombard, *Mats.* nos. 642 (wrongly dated there 1170 and by Duggan Feb.–Mar. 1168), 406; J. of S., *Letters*, nos. 279, 286.

18. *Mats.* no. 642 (see n. 17); J. of S., *Letters*, nos. 246, 249–66, 282–4. W. of C., i. 327.

19. W. fS., iii. 101–2; J. of S., *Letters*, nos. 279–80. For the place, Michelin map 60, pli 15. For Thomas at Orleans, *Mats.* no. 617, at Fleury, W. fS., iii. 59.

20. *Mats.* nos. 395–6, 400, 406, 414; J. of S., *Letters*, nos. 275, 272, 276, 278, 280. For Thomas's mission, *Mats.* nos. 413, 415. There was also the letter to Christ Church, see p. 176.

21. *Mats.* nos. 642 (see n. 17), 643 (wrongly dated there 1170 and by Duggan June–July 1169); J. of S., *Letters*, nos. 279–80. For the 'licence to sin', see also *Mats.* no. 440. Letters of protest, *Mats.* nos. 435–46; 448. H. of B., iii. 415.

22. *Mats.* no. 446. H. of B., iii. 415. See also p. 247.

23. *Mats.* no. 693.

24. *Mats.* nos. 404, 423–4; 460; 448. No. 460 is to be dated 1168 rather than 1169 because of the mention of a possible meeting and because the vacancy at Ely (May 1169) is omitted. Cf. J. of S., *Letters*, nos. 274, 280. Bernard *de Corilo* in *Mats.* nos. 423, 451, A. of T., ii. 351; de Grandmont in 461, 471; *de Corileto*, H. of B., iii. 439; *de la Coldre*, Guernes, v. 4077; *del Coldrei*, v. 4147. In 1171 he styled himself *Petrus Bernardi*, ex-general-prior of Grandmont, *Mats.* nos. 744, 746, cf. 747, and was styled by the general-prior as *corrector* of Vincennes (Seine), no. 747. See also Brooke's note, J. of S., *Letters*, p. 648. For Engelbert, ibid., nos. 183 and n., 206–7, 304 (p. 722). For Val-St-Pierre (Aisne), Michelin map 53, pli 16. It is 10 km. SE of Vervins, just south of the river Brune.

25. *Mats.* nos. 451, 746 (cf. 745, 747); J. of S., *Letters*, no. 288; E.G., ii. 416; A.II, iv. 113; W. of C., i. 73–5; W. fS., iii. 96–7; Guernes, vv. 4071–190; A. of T., ii. 347–51; H. of B., iii. 418–40; Gervase, *Chron.*, pp. 207–11. For the place, Michelin map 60, pli 15.

26. Barlow, *William Rufus*, pp. 343–4.

27. H. of B., iii. 426ff.

28. A. of T., ii. 349–50.

29. *Mats.* nos, 451–2, 462–3, 476; J. of S., *Letters*, nos. 287–8.

30. Reports of this colloquy in *Mats.* nos. 465–71, cf. 458–9, 496 (pp. 575–6); J. of S., *Letters*, nos. 286–8. Walberg's note to Guernes, v. 3815 (p. 276, cf. 278–9). For the place, Michelin map 97, pli 8.

31. *Mats.* nos. 453–4; J. of S., *Letters*, nos. 285–6, 288; W. of C., i. 75; Guernes, vv. 4196–215. J. of S., *Letters*, no. 287.

32. *Mats.* nos. 476; 491; 496 (p. 576), 497 (p. 581), 537; Anon. II, iv. 114–18.

33. For the location at Clairvaux, see 'discussion A.H.Bredero' in Foreville, *TB* (Sédières), pp. 86–7. Notifications and lists of the sentenced, *Mats.* nos. 479–80, 488–90, 494–8, 507; appeals, GFol, *Letters*, nos. 198–200; *Mats.* nos. 478, 518; J. of S., *Letters*, no. 289. All parties accepted that the bishops had not been cited on this occasion, yet in Gilbert's letter to Jocelin in March (no. 199) he says that it is reported that the two of them have again been cited to attend Thomas in France under threat of excommunication. Presumably the rumour was false or the citations could not be served.

34. *Mats.* nos. 488, 494, 496–7, 499–500 (the last two dated too early by Duggan), 507, 538, 550.

35. See his revealing letter to Roger of Worcester, *Mats.* no. 496.

36. *Mats.* nos. 508, 551.

37. *Mats.* nos. 497–8, 538, 540–6; J. of S., *Letters*, no. 289; *Mats.* no. 531. C. R. Cheney, *Journ. of the Soc. of Archivists*, vi (1981), 474, doubts the authenticity of the unique address to 531, 'archbishop of Canterbury, primate of all England and legate of the apostolic see'.

38. *Mats.* nos. 506, 515, 538; J. of S., *Letters*, no. 290.

39. GFol, *Letters*, nos. 198–202; *Mats.* nos. 508, 518–21; 478–80, 488; 508, 510; 553 (not to be dated 1168, as Duggan); cf. J. of S., *Letters*, no. 248; W. fS., iii. 87–92. Gilbert also planned a council in London for 7 June, no. 204. For the metropolitan claim for London, Morey and Brooke, pp. 151ff., Barlow, *EC*, pp. 35–6. For appeals *ad cautelam*, which Gilbert popularized, Morey and Brooke, pp. 162ff. *Mats.* nos. 538, 454–6, 547, 551–3; 'Causa' in *Mats.* iv. 213–43; cf. A.II, iv. 114–18; *Mats.* no. 537.

40. GFol, *Letters*, nos. 200–4; *Mats.* nos. 505, 510, 538; letters testimonial, nos. 514, 518–28; cf. GFol, *Letters*, no. 205; Arnulf, *Letters*, no. 54a. Letters on behalf of Thomas against GFol, *Mats.* nos. 547–8, 652–4. For Master David, Z. N. Brooke, 'Master David of London and the part he played in the Becket Crisis', *Essays in History presented to R. L. Poole* (1927), pp. 227–45.

41. GFol, *Letters*, nos. 206–8; *Mats.* nos. 515, 530; J. of S., *Letters*, nos. 289–90. The apparent recipient of 290, Hugh de Gant (presumably Ghent), is neither identified nor even indexed in the editions. Papal letters, *Mats.* nos. 491, 493.

42. J. of S., *Letters*, nos. 289–90. *Mats.* nos. 561, cf. 570–2. For the events of the mission, *Mats.* nos. 563 (nuncios' report); 564, cf. 565–8 (Henry's report); 560 (a friend to Thomas). W. of C., i. 72–6; A.II, iv. 119; W. fS., iii. 97–8, 102; Guernes, vv. 4216–57; H. of B., iii. 440–58, where he concentrates on the meeting at Montmartre. Bur-le-Roi, the scene of the meeting on 1 September, is located by T. Stapleton (according to Eyton, p. 189n.) in the parish of Noron (-la-Poterie), on the outskirts of the Bois du Vernay, which is some 10km. SSW of Bayeux. It does not seem to be shown on modern maps, nor is it easily identified on the ground. It is now undulating enclosed fields, mostly pasture. Cf. Michelin map 54, pli 14.

43. *Mats.* nos. 604, 607, cf. 560, 568.

44. According to W. fS., iii. 111, Henry exclaimed at Fréteval in 1170, 'I will kiss his mouth (*os*), hands and feet a hundred times'. In 1164, according to Benet, p. 619b, the pope kissed Thomas on the lips as well as on the eyes and the face.

45. For Geoffrey of Auxerre, A. H. Bredero in Foreville, *TB* (Sédières), pp. 55ff. GFol, *Letters*, no. 210.

46. *Mats.* nos. 579, cf. 570–2.

47. *Mats.* nos. 582–9.

48. *Mats.* nos. 578–80; 560; 565–7; 582–9. J. of S., ii. 315; W. of C., i. 76.

49. *Mats.* nos. 599–600; *Councils and Synods*, i. 926ff. *Mats.* nos. 598, 636, 610 (pp. 175–6); J. of S., *Letters*, no. 296; A.II, iv. 118–19; W. fS., iii. 102; A.I, iv. 65–6. M. D. Knowles, A. J. Duggan, C. N. L. Brooke, 'Henry II's Supplement to the Constitutions of Clarendon', *EHR* lxxxvii (1972), 757, 763. The approximate day and month of the drafting of the Royal Constitutions is fixed by references to the feasts of St Denis (9 Oct.) and St Martin (11 Nov.) and by the equation of the term of three months with 13 Jan. As it is certain that Henry imposed some such measures in 1169, there is no reason to doubt that the extant texts substantially reproduce them, although there may be some contamination with earlier (? 1166) royal security ordinances. Cf. Brooke in GFol, *Letters*, p. l, n. 10. For the punishment of suppliers of money, W. fS., iii. 106.

50. *Mats.* nos. 579–81. For Geoffrey Ridel and Otford, *Mats.* no. 631.

51. *Mats.* nos. 554, 612.

52. *Mats.* nos. 606, 620; 605–7, 609–11; 623, 626; W. of C., i. 75–6; W. fS., iii. 97–8; Guernes, vv. 4216–57; H. of B., iii. 444–58.

53. *Mats.* nos. 601–2, 604.

54. W. fS., iii. 97–8; H. of B., iii. 445–6. *Draco Normannicus* ends, p. 756, with negotiations between the two kings and Thomas at 'Poissy'.

55. *Mats.* nos. 610, 626; W. of C., i. 75; the figure also appears in Guernes, v. 4536; cf. p. 125.

56. *Mats.* no. 626; W. of C., i. 75; Guernes, vv. 4256–7.

57. W. fS., iii. 98; H. of B., iii. 445.

58. *Mats.* no. 653 (pp. 266–7); cf. W. fS., iii. 111; *Draco Normannicus*, p. 757.

59. *Mats.* nos. 573–8, 608, 610 (p. 175); cf. J. of S., *Letters*, no. 295; A. II, iv. 114–18.

60. *Mats.* nos. 610 (pp. 175–8), 612.

61. Eyton, p. 131. *Mats.* no. 610 (pp. 175–6), 636, 650; W. fS., iii. 102.

62. *Mats.* no. 669. For the main headings of this *forma pacis*, nos. 626, 644.

10 The road to glory, 1170

1. *Mats.* nos. 655, 696. The identity of Master Walter, presumably a papal clerk, is uncertain. He is not Walter de Lisle, who was in England at the time.

2. Cf. *Mats.* no. 668.

3. J. of S., *Letters*, nos. 297–8; *Mats.* nos. 537 (pp. 19–23), there wrongly dated 1169, 646; 637–9. No. 638 is addressed to Geoffrey of Auxerre – not bishop of, as there, nor bishop of Autun, as in Duggan. We are still concerned with the ex-abbot of Clairvaux. The activities of the papal commissioners are poorly described in the *Vitae*: cf. H. of B., iii. 462–4.

4. *Mats.* no. 626. See p. 196.

5. *Mats.* nos. 622, 662–3, 674; 627, 656, 658–67, 655; GFol, *Letters*, no. 211; Diceto, *Ymagines*, pp. 338, 351; Brooke, GFol, *Letters*, p. 271.

6. For William's legation, cf. *Mats.* nos. 570 (late Aug. 1169), 654 (? March 1170). Papal letters, *Mats.* nos. 623–5, 635.

7. *Mats.* nos. 629–30, 634; 631, 633.

8. *Mats.* nos. 654, cf. 646, 652–3; 639; 669; W. of C., i. 77; Torigni, *Chron.*, p. 244.

9. W. fS., iii. 107. The Emperor Frederick had had his son, Henry (VI), crowned king of the Romans at Aachen on 15 August 1169.

10. See p. 68.

11. *Mats.* no. 628.

12. J. of S., *Letters*, no. 301; *Mats.* no. 654 (pp. 271–2).

13. *Mats.* no. 644; cf. J. of S., *Letters*, no. 299.

14. *Mats.* nos. 666; 648–51, 670; J. of S., *Letters*, no. 300; *Mats.* no. 676. For Henry and Roger of Worcester, W. fS., iii. 103. The royal clerk, who was in the best position to know, states that the prohibition was proffered to York and London on the day before the ceremony. But they may have declined to accept it.

15. *Mats.* nos. 673, 676; 685 (p. 338); A.II, iv. 120–1; W. of C., i. 81.

16. Thomas impetrated papal letters of censure, *Mats.* nos. 700–1, dated 16 September, on York and the eight English and Welsh bishops for taking part in the coronation. Torigni, *Chron.*, p. 245, supports the attendance of the six English bishops; W. of C., i. 82, supports Rochester. For the exculpation of Exeter, see p. 218. For Evreux's attendance, *Mats.* no. 730. For the regularity of the coronation service, ibid. and 732; Arnulf, *Letters*, no. 59. For expenditure on the coronation, *PR 16 Hen. II*, pp. 15–16 (London), 126 (Winchester).

17. *Mats.* no. 675; J. of S., *Letters*, no. 301 (the crucial *si pax non fuerit* in line 3 is misplaced in the translation); *Mats.* nos. 678–83.

18. *Mats.* nos. 698–701. See p. 228. Foreville, *ER*, p. 314, suggests that the ordinand qualified his oath to observe the liberties of the church with *salvo honore regni mei*, a proviso which reappeared at Fréteval.

19. The meeting-place is described exactly by H. of B., *Mats.* no. 685 (p. 339): see Michelin map 64, pli 7. For Henry and Worcester, W. fS., iii. 104–6.

20. *Mats.* nos. 684–5; the former links in content and style with the latter, which was undoubtedly written by Herbert, although Foreville, *ER*, p. 308, n. 5, attributes it to J. of S.; H. of B., iii. 463–7; W. fS., iii. 107–12. Cf. *Mats.* nos. 688, 691–5; J. of S., ii. 315; E.G., ii. 422; A.II, iv. 119–21; W. of C., i. 83–4; Guernes, vv. 4266–440; A.I, iv. 67–8.

21. *Mats.* no. 684 (p. 327), 685 (pp. 339–40); W. fS., iii. 111; Guernes, vv. 4427–30. H. of B., iii. 466, perhaps with reference to W. fS., denies that at the conference the kiss was either requested or offered – no mention was made of it at all.

22. Guernes, vv. 4351–5.

23. See p. 68.

24. Sanders, *Baronies*, pp. 40, 10. Thomas had been a canon of Lincoln and had had some territorial interest in the Bedford area. But he can hardly have been so out of touch with politics even in 1170 as to think that Hugh would have been an acceptable *rector regis et regni*.

25. W. of C., i. 129; *Mats.* no. 736.

26. *Mats.* no. 686, is the bare text, shorn of protocol, of the peace granted by Henry. It concludes with the proviso, 'saving the honour of my kingdom', a limitation of doubtful relevance and purpose.

27. See pp. 140–2.

28. Guernes, vv. 4439–40.

29. *Mats.* no. 628, cf. 692.

30. *Mats.* nos. 691–5, 705.

31. H. of B., iii. 467.

32. J. of S., *Letters*, no. 302; W. fS., iii. 112–13. Brooke dates this copy of the royal writ, addressed to Bartholomew of Exeter and preserved by J. of S. because of its special interest to him, mid-October, but allows, p. 711 n., that July is a possibility.

33. *Mats.* no. 685 (*ad fin.*); H. of B., iii. 467–8; Howden, *Benedict*, pp. 6–7, and for his dates see next note. J. Châtillon, 'Thomas Becket et les Victorins', Foreville, *TB* (Sédières), pp. 95–6.

34. The accounts of these meetings in W. fS., iii. 115–16, Guernes, vv. 4441–525 and H. of B., iii. 468–71 tend to complement and confirm each other. A.I, iv. 67, puts the Mass mistakenly at Fréteval in July. The exact chronology, however, is uncertain. Howden, *Benedict*, p. 8, *Chronica*, ii. 10, is the only one to provide dates: Henry meets Theobald at La Ferté-Bernard about 6 July, meets Louis at Vendôme about 22 July, falls ill about 10 August, goes to Rocamadour about 29 September, and meets William, archbishop of Sens, and Theobald, who have Thomas with them, at Amboise about the feast of St Denis (9 Oct.), on Monday 4 Id. Oct. (12 Oct.). It should be noticed that Vendôme replaces Fréteval and that the meeting at Amboise seems to be Fréteval in disguise; also that all the dates are qualified by *circa*, although the last is also given an alternative very precise indication. There is good reason to think that Howden advanced the date of Rocamadour and Amboise by at least a fortnight. A royal writ addressed to the young king in England, *Sciatis quod Thomas*, issued at Chinon (*Mats.* no. DCLXC = 690), would seem not only from its contents to have been issued after Amboise but also to have been the one delivered to the young Henry on 5 October (an unimpeachable date). The alternatives to moving Amboise (and Rocamadour) back so as to fit, are either to imagine that the writ was issued *en route* for Rocamadour (which does not suit H. of B.'s story or the contents of the writ) or to postulate that Thomas's messengers delivered another, lost, writ to England on 5 October. The story is simplified by changing Howden's dates. Diceto, *Ymagines*, p. 339, puts the writ after Amboise; Gervase, *Chron.*, p. 221, who mentions no meeting after 'Traitors' Meadow' (Fréteval), says that Thomas sent his agents to England with this writ and they arrived in October. Duggan dates this Chinon writ August–September (p. 267) and mid-October (pp. 234, 283). I would date it *c.* 30 September.

35. J. of S., *Letters*, no. 303. If Howden's chronology is abandoned, the letter can be dated a little earlier. Thomas lodged at Chaumont, 'where the king took him back into favour', with the Lady Emeline, who seems to have given up her own bed to him: W. of C., miracles, VI. 42.

36. *Mats.* no. 717 (715 in text). To be dated 5–15 (not post-10, as in Duggan) October.

37. For the weather, which remained very warm until Martinmas (11 Nov.), Lambert of Waterlos, *Annales Cameracenses, MGH SS*, xvi. 554. *Mats.* no. 718.

38. *Mats.* nos. 698–701, 696 (text corrected Foreville, *ER*, p. 315n.). No. 707 (Cardinal Humbald to Thomas), as it is concerned only with the coronation, seems also to be in this series.

39. *Mats.* nos. 695, 716.

40. W. fS., iii. 113; H. of B., iii. 471.

41. J. of S., *Letters*, no. 304; Guernes, vv. 4540, 4551–5; cf. A.II, iv. 121; W. of C., i. 83; W. fS., iii. 112–13. Thomas was almost certainly at Paris on 4 September (see p. 214). It is not known whether he went there again.

42. Eyton, pp. 148–9; W. fS., iii. 116; Guernes, vv. 4596–625. H. of B. omits all mention of Rouen. For Thomas's indebtedness at death, W. of C., miracles, IV. 15.

43. For the date, Thomas to Alexander, *Mats.* no. 723 (p. 402); cf. J. of S., *Letters*, no. 304; Guernes, vv. 4556–60.

44. A.II, iv. 120; above, pp. 184–5, 195–6, 201, 212; *Mats.* no. 711.

45. J. of S., *Letters*, no. 304; W. of C., i. 85, 102; Guernes, vv. 4586–95; *Mats.* no. 723.

46. *PR 16 Hen. II*, p. 161, *17 Hen. II*, p. 142.

47. Cf. also *Mats.* no. 723 (p. 402); A.II, iv. 127.

48. *Mats.* nos. 172 (see ch. 8, n. 6), 709–12, 714–15; 703–6, 708.

49. *Mats.* no. 689, more likely to be dated 8–13 October than Duggan's August–September.

50. Above, pp. 44, 58 and nn. A story in a St Bertin chronicle, *Mats.* iv. 262, that Philip, count of Flanders, conducted him through his county and that Thomas dedicated a chapel for him at Male, his castle near Bruges, seems most unlikely, as Bruges is at least 130 km. from Wissant. Even while waiting at the port, Thomas is unlikely to have travelled so far. For the *bibliotheca*, W. of C., i. 86–7. For the archbishop's library, Smalley, *Becket Conflict*, pp. 135–7.

51. A.II, iv. 123, 125–6, who represents London opinion, makes much of this issue.

52. W. of C., i. 87–8; A.II, iv. 123–4; Guernes, vv. 4681–700 (very detailed); A.I, iv. 68, for the name of the messenger; H. of B., iii. 471–2; W. fS., iii. 116–18; J. of S., *Letters*, nos. 299 and n., 303; Gervase, *Chron.*, p. 222.

53. H. of B., iii. 472–6.

54. So W. fS., iii. 118. H. of B., iii. 476, gives the vaguer date, the second or third day after the feast of St Andrew (30 Nov.) in Advent (Advent Sunday was 29 Nov. in 1170), although a few pages later (484) he imagines it was 29 November. This early date is supported by W. of C., i. 99 (dawn, first day of Advent). Gervase, *Chron.*, p. 222, has him land on 30 November and reach Canterbury on 1 December. Diceto, *Ymagines*, p. 339, dates the crossing 1 December. The most likely order of events (cf. Thomas's own account, *Mats.* no. 723) is: 28 November, Robert the Sacrist arrested; 29 November, letters sent; Monday, 30 November (St Andrew's day), news of delivery received, Thomas and party embark; Tuesday, 1 December, landing at Sandwich.

11 The end of the road

General

At this point W. of C. becomes an eye-witness and contributes a rather long-winded account of Thomas's last days. Some of the *Vita* written by B. of P., another Christ Church monk, is also available. W. fS. rejoins the archbishop before Christmas and remains particularly interested in London. H. of B. stays in the archbishop's company until 27 December. The problem of the 'synoptic' narratives of the martyr-dom was considered by E. A. Abbott, *St Thomas of Canterbury* (2 vols., 1898). But he took no account of the literary relationship and lacked an adequate background of historical knowledge. For maps of Canterbury, Urry, *Canterbury*, and N. Brooks, *The Early History of the Church of Canterbury* (1984), p. 18.

1. Thomas's report to the pope, *Mats.* no. 723 (pp. 403–4); J. of S.'s report to Rheims, *Letters*, no. 304 (pp. 718–20); A.II, iv. 124; W. of C., i. 99–102; W. fS., iii. 118–19; H. of B., iii. 477–8; cf. A.I, iv. 68.

2. J. of S. and H. of B. agree that the party went to Canterbury on 'the next day', against W. of C. who makes them go straight on from Sandwich. A source of confusion is the likelihood that the sea-crossing was overnight. The next day of J. of S. and H. of B. could be the day following the embarkation. All agree, however, that the interview with the royal officials at Canterbury took place on the day after the landing. For the events, *Mats.* no. 723 (p. 404); W. of C., i. 102; W. fS., iii. 119–20; H. of B., iii. 478–80. For the gilded pinnacles, Margaret Gibson, *Lanfranc of Bec*, p. 163. For the 'angel steeple' and cockerel weather-vanes, E. Gilbert, 'The first Norman cathedral at Canterbury', *Arch. Cant.*, lxxxviii (1973), 34–5.

3. *Mats.* no. 723 (pp. 405–6); J. of S., *Letters*, no. 304 (pp. 720–2); W. of C., i. 102–5; W. fS., iii. 120; H. of B., iii. 480. For David and Thomas, Z. N. Brooke, in *Essays . . . presented to R. L. Poole* (1927), pp. 239–40.

4. A. II, iv. 123–5, 127–8; cf. Gal. 6: 3; Acts 19: 36.

5. W. fS., iii. 120; J. of S., *Letters*, no. 304 (p. 722); E.G., ii. 426–7; A.I, iv. 68; *Mats.* nos. 725–8, and see p. 139. *Mats.* no. 723.

6. W. of C., i. 105–12; W. fS., iii. 121–2; Benet, p. 625b, vv. 673ff.; H. of B., iii. 481–2. For the young king's court at this time, J. H. Round, 'A glimpse of the young King's court (1170)', *Feudal England* (1895), pp. 503ff.

7. *Mats.* no. 723 *ad fin.*; J. of S., *Letters*, no. 304 (p. 722); A. II, iv. 126; W. of C., i. 112–14; W. fS., iii. 122–4; H. of B., iii. 482–3; Matthew Paris, *Historia Minor*, ed. F. Madden (Rolls ser., i, 1866), p. 358. Benet, p. 625b (? following R. of C.), makes Thomas set off for London on the third day (?5 Dec.). Diceto, *Ymagines*, p. 342, dates the interview at Southwark 15 Kal. Jan., i.e. 18 December. It would be about this time that Thomas returned there from Harrow. For the wine, see also B. of P., ii. 7; W. of C., i. 129–30.

8. W. of C., i. 114; W. fS., iii. 124; H. of B., iii. 482–3; *Chronica Monasterii S. Albani*, ed. H. T. Riley (Rolls ser., i, 1867), pp. 184–8; Matthew Paris, *Historia Minor*, i. 359–61, *Chronica Majora*, ed. H. R. Luard (Rolls ser., ii, 1874), pp. 278–9. In the three inter-dependent St Albans accounts (Benet is uninformative) it is believed that the young king was at Woodstock. Diceto, *Ymagines*, p. 342, thought likewise. The king could have travelled from Woodstock to Fordingbridge. For the archiepiscopal deaneries of the Immediate Jurisdiction, I. J. Churchill, *Canterbury Administration* (1933), pp. 62ff., list of churches, 63n. For Charlwood in Surrey, W. fS., iii. 82, 130, where erroneously identified by the editor with Throwley near Faversham in Kent. For Abbot Simon, who was an admirer of J. of S., cf. R. Thomson, in *World of J. of S.*, pp. 287–90, 296–9.

9. W. of C., i. 114–19; W. fS., iii. 124–6.

10. W. of C., i. 114–15.

11. W. fS., iii. 124–5, 131. E.G., ii. 428; B. of P., miracles, ii. 164–5, 168–9, 171; Guernes, v. 4939; W. of C., i. 119–21.

12. E.G., ii. 428; W. fS., iii. 126, 151; H. of B., iii. 483–4. B. of P., ii. 128, and Guernes, v. 5751, followed by A.I, iv. 78, call Robert de Broc 'usher of the king's chamber'. He was certainly a clerk. Cf. ch. 6, n. 55.

13. E.G., ii. 428; W. of C., i. 120; W. fS., iii. 130–1; H. of B., iii. 484–6. For Thomas's reference to St Ælfheah, see also E.G., ii. 434, Guernes, vv. 5432–5. For the ritual of excommunication, Guernes, vv. 4966–70; Diceto, *Ymagines*, p. 342.

14. E.G., ii. 428–9; W. of C., i. 105, 121; W. fS., iii. 127–8; Guernes, vv. 5042ff.; H. of B., iii. 481. *Mats.* nos. 729–30, 732; Arnulf, *Letters*, nos. 59, 54b, 60; 57. For Saltwood church, see also Saltman, *Theobald*, charter, no. 297.

15. E.G., ii. 429; W. of C., i. 121–3; W. fS., iii. 127–9; Guernes, vv. 5046ff.; H. of B., iii. 487.

16. A.II, iv. 128; W. of C., i. 123–4, 128; Guernes, vv. 5106ff. For the conspirators, Walberg, Guernes, pp. 295–8; *Tracy: DNB*, lvii. 142; Sanders, *Baronies*, pp. 20, 85–6; Lord Sudeley, *Becket's murderer, William de Tracy*, in *Family History*, xiii, no. 97, n.s. no. 73 (1983); *fitzUrse*: J. Collinson, *History and Antiquities of Somerset* (1791), iii. 487; *DNB*, xix. 218; Sanders, pp. 22–3; *VCH, Som.* v (1985), 151–2; *Morville*: D. & S. Lysons, *Magna Britannia, Cumberland*, pp. 5, 49, 120, 127, 134; *DNB*, xxxix. 168; Sanders, pp. 23–4, 50n., 57, 59; *le Bret*: Dugdale, *Monasticon* (1661), ii. 271; Collinson, *Somerset*, iii. 543–4, 594. See further, B. of P., ii. 9; W. of C., i. 133; 129, cf. 132; W. fS., iii. 142; and pp. 58, 106; Benet, v. 931. Cf. Green, *op. cit.*, p. 147.

17. W. of C., i. 126; W. fS., iii. 129; Guernes, vv. 5106–10.

18. W. of C., i. 127; W. fS., iii. 129–30, 139; Guernes, vv. 5146–55; H. of B., iii. 488. Cf. William Rufus's similar journey from Rouen in 1086: Barlow, *William Rufus*, pp. 53–4.

19. E.G., ii. 430; W. of C., i. 127; W. fS., iii. 131–2, 136; Guernes, vv. 5150–1; Gervase, *Chron.*, p. 224.

20. J. of S., *Letters*, no. 305, *Mats.* ii. 316ff.; W. fS., iii. 132ff.; B. of P., ii. 1ff.; W. of C., i. 129ff.; E.G., ii. 430ff. Cf. A.II, iv. 128; Guernes, vv. 5161ff.; A.I, iv. 70ff.; H. of B., iii. 488ff.

21. Guernes, vv. 5776–810, cf. 581–5. The top fur pelisse, although distinguished by name from the other two (*pliçuns*), may be a repetition caused by a digression. J. of S., *Letters*, no. 305 (p. 734); E.G., ii. 442; B. of P., ii. 17; W. fS., iii. 147–9; H. of B., iii. 521, cf. 193. Gen. 37: 23; cf. 4 Kings (2 Sam.) 13: 17–18. For the 'cowl without a hood' see also p. 128.

22. For the discipline, Guernes, v. 5821. For the dinner, Gerald, 'De Thoma Cantuariensi', in *Anglia Sacra*, ed. H. Wharton (1691), ii. 423. The timing of the events between the fixed span of dawn (about 8) and sun-set (about 4) is fixed roughly by the expected time of dinner (2) and vespers (4). Anon. I, iv. 70, puts the arrival of the barons at Canterbury at None (about 2); and their introduction into the chamber is timed as about the tenth hour (about 2.40) by W. fS., iii. 132, and about the eleventh hour (about 3.20) by B. of P., ii. 1. There is no great problem in all this.

23. Until the survey of 1983 Lanfranc's great hall was believed to be on the same site as Hubert Walter's, built about 1200. It is now known to have been some 65 yards to the south of it. See the report and plan in *Medieval Archaeology*, 27 (1983), 186–7, T. Tatton Brown, 'Three great Benedictine houses in Kent', *Archaeologia Cantiana*, c (1984), pp. 173–5, fig. 2, and the report by N. Hammond in *The Times*, 29 August 1983. For the older views, Urry, *Canterbury*, pp. 104, 201–2, 213–14. For the de Porta family, ibid., p. 88.

24. Guernes, vv. 5186ff., shows a particular interest in the seneschal or steward. Thomas's first agents to Kent in October had served mandates on William of Eynsford and William fitzNeal, whom they had found uncooperative: *Mats.* no. 717, *ad init.*, see p. 215.

25. The securing of the gatehouse and of the porch to the hall are described only by W. fS., iii. 136; and, although his account could have been clearer (there may be textual corruptions), it can be rearranged to make good sense. Since Arthur P. Stanley in 1853 it has usually been held that William fitzNeal and Simon de Criol were stationed on the inner (yard) side of the street gate. But W. fS. states unequivocally that they were put *infra atrium aulae* (within the porch to the hall), where Reginald fitzUrse (*in ipso proaulo*), separate from his comrades, armed himself. What the writer meant by *atrium* (porch) and *aula* (hall) is clear from his subsequent narrative. He also distinguished clearly, and necessarily, between the porch's outer door (*janua*) and inner door (*ostium*). This correction to the received interpretation makes, of course, better military sense. A further difficulty is W. fS.'s statement that Reginald took an axe from carpenters repairing some stairs. But although this looks like a confusion with Robert de Broc's later action, it may be that, owing to the dilapidation of the palace during the exile, a lot of repairs were going on. Reginald is said to have had an axe in his left hand when he entered the cathedral church.

26. E.G., ii. 433; W. of C., i. 130; B. of P., ii. 9–10; W. fS., iii. 136–7; Guernes, vv. 5396–440; A.I, iv. 74–5; H. of B., iii. 491.

27. E.G., ii. 434–5; W. of C., i. 131–2; B. of P., ii. 10–11, who says that the door into the cloister was opened by the cellarers; W. fS., iii. 138; Guernes, vv. 5441–65; A.I, iv. 75; H. of B., iii. 491; *Thómas Saga* i. 534. It used to be thought that Thomas and his pursuers entered the north-west corner of the cloisters and went round the north and east sides. With the relocation of the hall (see n.23), it is likely that all used the south cloister passage. For Henry of Auxerre, W. fS., *loc. cit.*

28. Cf. E.G., ii. 434; J. of S., *Letters*, no. 305 (p. 726).

29. For the killing, J. of S., *Letters*, no. 305 (pp. 730–2); E.G., ii. 435–9; W. of C., i. 132–5; B. of P., ii. 11–14; W. fS., iii. 138–42; A.II, iv. 129–31; Guernes, vv. 5466–640; A.I, iv. 76–7; H. of B., iii. 491–509.

30. For William of Norwich's verses, Barlow, *English Church*, p. 244. In W. fS., iii. 154, the correct text is to be found in the notes. Gervase, *Chron.*, pp. 231–2, explains how, according to different systems of reckoning, the martyrdom was dated either 1170 or 1171.

31. J. of S., *Letters*, no. 305 (pp. 732–4); E.G., ii. 439; A.II, iv. 132; W. of C., i. 135; B. of P., ii. 14–15; W. fS., iii. 144; Guernes, vv. 5641–5, 5656–80; A.I, iv. 77–8; Howden, *Benedict*, i. 13.

32. Miracle of the monk William, W. of C., miracles, I. 148; E.G., ii. 439–40; A.II, iv. 135–9; B. of P., ii. 14; W. fS., iii. 148.

33. B. of P., ii. 15–16; W. fS., iii. 141, 146–7; Guernes, vv. 5743–7; A.I, iv. 78; H. of B., iii. 519–20. It is possible that either the prior of Dover or the abbot of Boxley, both of whom had arrived at Canterbury on the very day of the murder and had seen the corpse, is the anonymous reporter of the event to the pope, *Mats.* no. 737.

34. J. of S., *Letters*, no. 305 (p. 734); E.G., ii. 441; B. of P., ii. 16; W. fS., iii. 148; Guernes, vv. 5749–75; A.I, iv. 78; H. of B., iii. 521.

35. For the fate of the cloak, see p. 266. Also Benedict took to Peterborough, among other relics, Thomas's shirt (*camisia*) and surplice (*superpellicium*), Robert of Swapham, *Coenobii Burgensis Historia*, in J. Sparke, *Hist. Anglicanae Scriptores Varii* (1723), p. 101.

36. J. of S., *Letters*, no. 305 (pp. 734–6); E.G., ii. 441–2; B. of P., ii. 16–17, 21; W. fS., iii. 148–9; Guernes, vv. 5776ff.; A.I, iv. 78–9; H. of B., iii. 521–2. For the tomb, cf. W. Urry, 'The resting places of St Thomas', Foreville, *TB* (Sédières), pp. 195–6.

12 From death unto life

General

Councils and Synods, pp. 940ff. Foreville, *ER*, iv.

1. W. fS., iii. 149; *Mats*. no. 738; cf. B. of P., ii. 29–30; *Bosonis Vita Alexandri*, in *Pontificum Romanorum Vitae*, ed. J.M. Watterich (Leipzig 1862, 1966), ii. 418. J. of S., *Letters*, no. 305.

2. *Mats*. no. 735.

3. *Mats*. nos. 740 (p. 443); 744–7.

4. See p. 234; *Mats*. nos. 751–2, 756; Arnulf, *Letters*, nos. 73–4. There would seem to have been two Master Henrys – of Northampton and Pinchun – one in each of the main divisions, but it is not always easy to sort them out.

5. *Mats*. nos. 734–6; 750 (p. 473), where Gunter is, very oddly, called 'of Flanders'.

6. For the papal letters, see p. 222; *Mats*. nos. 740 (p. 442), 741 (p. 444); cf. Howden, *Benedict*, i. 16. For the council, nos. 740–2; for the English legation, also nos. 750–1. The interdict was lifted presumably after the Concordat of Avranches in May 1172.

7. *Mats*. nos. 740, 743.

8. *Mats*. nos. 738–9; H. of B., iii. 540–1. An anonymous correspondent, perhaps Richard of Dover or Walter of Boxley, who had reached Canterbury on the very day of the murder and had seen the body, informed the pope that it was wrong to believe that the king had ordered the killings: no. 737. Cf. C. Duggan on nos. 739, 742 in Foreville, *TB* (Sédières), pp. 192–3.

9. The events at Frascati were reported by the royal clerks to Henry on 25–7 March (*Mats*. no. 750) and by a nuncio to Richard of Ilchester in mid-April (no. 751). It would seem that both were written by the same hand, possibly Richard Barre. For other accounts, nos. 752, 754, 756; *Bosonis Vita Alexandri* (ed. Watterich), ii. 418–19; papal letters, nos. 753–5. For the significance of the personal interdiction on Henry, Foreville, *ER*, p. 325n. Master David was rewarded by the king with a grant in Artington (*Ertedun*), south of Guildford, in the royal manor of Godalming (Surrey), which he sold to Ranulf de Broc, who held nearby Catteshill: *Book of Fees*, p. 67; Round, *Serjeants*, p. 102.

10. The legates seem to have returned as raggedly as they had travelled out. An anonymous writer, probably Master Hugh or Master David, reported to Gilbert Foliot, *Mats*. no. 756, that their legates, having bribed the Roman Senate with £20, had passed by safely and had reached Bologna by 9 May. The bishop of Worcester and Reginald fitzJocelin, however, had not dared trust the Romans. And the dean of Evreux had gone off to Sicily to visit the king and relatives. He enlisted the support of the royal family for Jocelin of Salisbury: see p. 259.

11. *E.H.D.* ii. 828. *Mats*. no. 750, *ad fin*.

12. Gerald of Wales. 'De Thoma Cantuariensi', *De vitis sex episcoporum coaetaneorum*, in *Anglia Sacra*, ed. H. Wharton (1691), ii. 424–5; Howden, *Benedict*, i. 13, *Chronica*, ii. 17; Diceto, i. 346; Lansdowne Anonymous, iv. 161–6; W. of C., miracles, II. 37. Robert was dining with another friend, Stephen of *Huerveltuna* (unfortunately unlocated). For Henry's inability to arrest the murderers, see the versions of the 'Compromise of Avranches' in Howden, *Benedict*, i. 32–3, *Chronica*, ii. 35–6; Gervase, *Chron.*, p. 238.

13. For the murderers, see pp. 235–6 and ch. 11, n.16. The fullest, but not necessarily most trustworthy account of their later history is in Lansdowne Anonymous, iv. 150, 160–4. See also H. of B., to legates, *Mats.* no. 769 (after 13 Dec. 1171), iii. 512, 535–8; pope to Exeter, no. 780; *Thómas Saga* (? following R. of C.), ii. 38–40; Howden, *Benedict*, i. 13–14, *Chronica*, ii. 17; Diceto, *Ymagines*, p. 346; Newburgh, *Historia*, i. 163–4; Romuald of Salerno, *Annales*, ed. W.Arndt, in Pertz, *Mon. Germ. Hist.*, Script., xix. 439; *Landboc ... de Winchelcumba*, ed. D.Royce (Exeter, 1892), i. 190; Stanley, *Memorials*, p. 224, for the Cosenza charter; Round, *Calendar of Docs.*, no. 538; Dugdale, *Monasticon* (1661), ii. 271; G.E.C., *Complete Peerage*, xi, app. D; Sanders, *Baronies*, pp. 20n., 22–3.

14. For the custody, see p. 221. For the de Brocs, see ch. 6, n.53; Eyton, pp. 198, 281; Foreville, *TB* (Sédières), pp. 168, 186; see pp. 264, 267.

15. Gilbert Foliot's case, *Mats.* nos. 752–3, 767, cf. 757; GFol, *Letters*, nos. 217–18; Diceto, *Ymagines*, pp. 347, 351. Roger of York's case, Arnulf, *Letters*, no. 75; *Mats.* nos. 763–6, 769; J. of S., *Letters*, no. 306. Jocelin of Salisbury's case, *Mats.* no. 768. *Sarum Charters and Documents*, ed. W.Rich Jones and W.D.Macray (Rolls ser., 1891), pp. 35–6. Cf. also Foreville, *ER*, p. 333.

16. *Mats.* nos. 769–70, 798 (= 801); J. of S., *Letters*, no. 307; *Mats.* no. 798 and see p. 96; Diceto, *Ymagines*, p. 354. F.Liverani, *Spicilegium* (Florence, 1863), p. 546.

17. Their dealings with Henry and the English and Norman churches are well recorded. The cardinals' official record and reports (although not to the pope) are *Mats.* nos. 772, 774–5; other reports, nos. 771, 773; A.II, iv. 143; H. of B., iii. 543; Lansdowne Anonymous, iv. 166ff.; Howden, *Benedict*, i. 24ff., *Chronica*, ii. 28ff. (in both versions the legates are called Vivian and Gratian); Diceto, *Ymagines*, pp. 347ff.; Gervase, *Chron.*, pp. 234ff. Best text of the 'Compromise of Avranches', *Councils and Synods*, pp. 942ff. For the legation, Foreville, *ER*, pp. 333ff.

18. C.Johnson, 'The reconciliation of Henry II with the papacy: a missing document', *E.H.R.* lii (1937), 465; Foreville, *ER*, pp. 341ff.

19. *Mats.* no. 773.

20. See pp. 13–15. Guernes, vv. 6038–40. Urry, *Canterbury*, p. 182. The original chirographs of the presentations to the two Johns are in Canterbury Cathedral, City and Diocesan Record Office, Ch. ant., H. 89, L. 4. Miss Anne Oakley kindly provided me with xerox copies.

21. For Richard of Dover, Diceto, *Ymagines*, pp. 368ff. For W. fS., Mary Cheney, as in Introduction. For J. of S., Brooke, *J. of S., Letters*, ii, pp. xlvi–xlvii. For Henry of Houghton, B. of P., ii. 161–4. For H. of B., *Mats.* nos. 769–70, 798 (= 801), cf. 778; iii. 156, 531–3, 553; Smalley, *Becket Conflict*, pp. 70ff. For Benedict and Richard of Ely, Robert of Swapham, *Coenobii Burgensis Historia*, p. 102.

22. For Alexander, W. of C., miracles, VI. 152. For William of Capes, *Epistolae Cantuarienses*, ed. W.Stubbs (Rolls ser., 1865), ii. 313; Urry, *Canterbury*, p. 183.

23. For the *Brokeis*, B. of P., ii. 119–20; miracles, III. 17. Papal and legatine permission for the reconciliation, *Mats.* nos. 787–8. Accounts, Lansdowne Anonymous, iv. 169; E.G., ii. 443; Diceto, *Ymagines*, p. 349; Gervase, *Chron.*, pp. 229, 236.

24. J. of S., *Letters*, no. 305 (pp. 736–8); *Mats.* no. 749; St Augustine, Letter no. 89 and Sermon no. 275, 1: Migne *PL*, xxxiii. 310, xxxviii. 1254; H. of B., iii. 156. Cf. J. Armitage Robinson, *Gilbert Crispin abbot of Westminster*, p. 92. GFol in 1166 had used the text from St Augustine against Thomas; see p. 155.

25. Matt. 10: 8; 11: 5.Cf. *Vita Ædwardi Regis*, ed. Barlow, p. 81; B. of P., ii. 26.

W. of C., miracles, IV. 15, III. 33, 48, where St Denis hands a man on to St Thomas; cf. Gervase, *Chron.*, p. 230. For a more generalized account of the miracles, A.II, iv. 140–3.

26. B. of P., ii. 35, 43, 51; W. fS., iii. 151.

27. B. of P., ii. 42–3, 54; 1 Kings 17: 16; B. of P., ii. 55.

28. B. of P., miracles, I. 11–12, 22–4.

29. B. of P., miracles, I. 17–21. Hollingbourne, an exempt parish in the deanery of Sutton, although more distant from Canterbury than the others, is also a possibility.

30. B. of P., miracles, II. 1–3, 5; Urry, *Canterbury*, pp. 162–3.

31. B. of P., miracles, I. 8–10, 13–16; II. 26; II. 14; 23–4. It is possible that an obscure letter of H. of B. to the pope, *Mats.* no. 798 (*recte* 801), mentioning the hunter Robert now setting his nets to catch relics of his dead father, refers to this attempted snatch.

32. B. of P., miracles, II. 29, cf. 31; 18–21; 20–2; III. 22–5; W. of C., miracles, III. 54; VI. 62; H. of B., iii. 551–2. W. fS., iii. 150, says that he has seen inscribed on many phials the verse, 'Fertur in ampullis aqua Thomae sanguine mixta.' For the reinforced tomb, with illustrations, see Urry in Foreville, *TB* (Sédières), pp. 196–7, 198–9, 202, 244.

33. For the conversion of sceptics, cf. B. of P., miracles, II, 43–4, 51; W. of C., I. 9, 12–13. For William's appointment as guardian, see prologue to the miracles.

34. W. of C., miracles, IV. 9–10; A.II, iv. 143. E. W. Kemp, 'Pope Alexander III and the canonization of saints', *Trans. R. Hist. Soc.*, 4th ser., 27 (1945), 13–28, *Canonization and Authority in the Western Church* (1948), 86–9.

35. H. of B.'s justification, *Mats.* no. 779. Papal letters, nos. 783–6. *Bosonis Vita Alexandri* (ed. Watterich), ii. 420. C. Duggan in Foreville, *TB* (Sédières), p. 79. For the Jubilee, R. Foreville, *Le Jubilé de St Thomas Becket du XIIIᵉ au XVᵉ siècle (1220–1470): étude et documents* (Paris, 1958), pp. 3ff. For the later history of the cult, A. Duggan, 'The cult of St Thomas Becket in the thirteenth century', in *St Thomas Cantilupe Bishop of Hereford*, ed. M. Jancey (Hereford, 1982), pp. 21–44.

36. For Henry Junior's pilgrimage, Lansdowne Anonymous, iv. 178; M. Bouquet, *Recueil des Historiens ... de la France*, xvi. 644; *Councils and Synods*, p. 958, n. 2. For the senior king's, E.G., ii. 445–7; W. of C., miracles, VI. 93; Guernes, vv. 5916ff.; H. of B., iii. 544ff.; Howden, *Benedict*, i. 72, *Chronica*, ii, 61–2; Diceto, *Ymagines*, p. 383; Gervase, *Chron.*, pp. 248–50.

37. H. of B., iii. 547–51, cf. 541–2, and see p. 255.

38. B. of P., ii. 23–6; cf. W. fS., iii. 153. For Odo, Lansdowne Anonymous, iv. 176ff. Odo said uncomplimentary things about Thomas, because he had not been a monk, later during the negotiations over the election, p. 184. M. A. Harris, 'Alan of Tewkesbury and his letters', *Studia Monastica* (Abadia de Montserrat, Barcelona), xviii (1976), pp. 80–92, 310, 343. Robert of Swapham, *Coenobii Burgensis Historia*, p. 101. Cf. J. C. Robertson, 'Becket Memoranda', *Arch. Cantiana*, x (1876), 10–11.

39. 'De Principis Instructione', ed. G. F. Warner, in *Giraldi Cambrensis Opera* (Rolls ser., 1891), viii. 170. E. M. Hallam (-Smith), 'Henry II as a founder of monasteries', *J.E.H.* xxviii (1977), 113.

40. For the episcopal elections, especially *Mats.* nos. 782, 789–93; Lansdowne Anonymous, iv. 176ff.; Diceto, *Ymagines*, pp. 353ff.; Gervase, *Chron.*, pp. 239ff. Vacant abbacies were dealt with in 1175: Diceto, p. 401. Cf. also Brooke, GFol, *Letters*, pp. 291–3.

41. For free elections, *Mats.* no. 790, cf. Gervase, *Chron.*, p. 242. For the concordat, H. Mayr-Harting, 'Henry II and the Papacy', *J.E.H.* xvi (1965), 48–9; *Councils and Synods*, pp. 993ff.; Foreville, *ER*, pp. 431ff.

42. *Decretal.*, II. i. 3; V. xl. 27. R. Génestal, *Le Privilegium Fori en France* (1924), i. 14ff.; R. M. Fraher, 'The Becket dispute and two decretist traditions: the Bolognese masters revisited and some new Anglo-Norman texts', *Journ. of Med. Hist.*, iv (1978), 347. For general developments in the English church, C. R. Cheney, *From Becket to Langton* (1956).

43. *Mats.* no. 795, cf. 796.

INDEX

Persons are usually indexed under their first name.
Most places in France are identified on Michelin Cartes A 1/200,000 by no. and pli.

Abbreviations:

abp	archbishop	card.	cardinal	e.	earl
abt	abbot	ccl	council	k.	king
archd.	archdeacon	ch.	church	M.	Michelin map
bp	bishop	ct	count	mr	master
bpric	bishopric	ctess	countess	pr.	prior